HOLLYWOOD DIVAS
The Good, the Bad, and the Fabulous

JAMES ROBERT PARISH

Chicago   ty
Mil

The McGraw·Hill Companies

Library of Congress Cataloging-in-Publication Data

Parish, James Robert.
  Hollywood divas : the good, the bad, and the fabulous / James Robert Parish.
    p.   cm.
  Includes bibliographical references and index.
  ISBN 0-07-140819-3 (alk. paper)
    1. Motion picture actors and actresses—United States—Biography.
  2. Actresses—United States—Biography.   I. Title.

  PN1998.2 .P367   2002
  791.43′028′092273—dc21   2002073643
  [B]

1 2 3 4 5 6 7 8 9 0   AGM/AGM   1 0 9 8 7 6 5 4 3 2

ISBN 0-07-140819-3

Cover photographs, clockwise from top left: Sharon Stone, AFP/Corbis; Bette Davis, Bettmann/Corbis; Jennifer Lopez, Reuters NewMedia Inc./Corbis; Elizabeth Taylor, Douglas Kirkland/Corbis; Diana Ross, Douglas Kirkland/Corbis; Madonna, The Kobal Collection/DeLaurentis/Propaganda/Boy Toy; Joan Crawford, Bettmann/Corbis; Whitney Houston, Neal Preston/Corbis
Cover illustration: movie reel © Paul Eekhoff/Masterlife
Interior design by Nick Panos

McGraw-Hill books are available at special quantity discounts to use as premiums and sales promotions, or for use in corporate training programs. For more information, please write to the Director of Special Sales, Professional Publishing, McGraw-Hill, Two Penn Plaza, New York, NY 10121-2298. Or contact your local bookstore.

This book is printed on acid-free paper.

To the late Alan G. Barbour (1933–2002) and Jean Barbour
who cheerfully hosted the Friday Night Film Group
resulting in entertaining movie watching and new friendships

CONTENTS

ACKNOWLEDGMENTS

With appreciation to the following for their kind assistance: Academy of Motion Picture Arts and Sciences—Margaret Herrick Library; Billy Rose Theater Collection of the New York Public Library at Lincoln Center; Michael Gene Ankerich; John Cocchi; Ernest Cunningham; Eleanor K. Dugan; Echo Book Shop; JC Archives; Jane Klain (Museum of Television and Radio—New York); Alvin H. Marill; Doug McClelland; Jim Meyer; Robert W. Nott; Albert L. Ortega (Albert L. Ortega Photos); Michael R. Pitts; Barry Rivadue; Brenda Scott Royce; Arleen Schwartz; André Soares; David Stenn; Allan Taylor (editorial consultant and copy editor); Vincent Terrace.

Special thanks to my literary agent, Stuart Bernstein, and to my editor, Matthew Carnicelli.

INTRODUCTION

In Hollywood, there's an old sexist saying: "If a man is aggressive, he's dedicated; if a woman is assertive, she's a b****." This chauvinistic belief is still entrenched in the entertainment industry, even nowadays when there are far more women in positions of power and sexist attitudes toward ambitious, successful females are slowly diminishing. But sometimes the actress's actions are so over the top that they move from acceptable assertiveness to outlandish behavior, deeds that are excessive whether initiated by an egocentric woman or man. This belligerence is one of the "crimes" often associated with some of the divas profiled in this book.

What is a diva? In bygone eras, a diva was considered a goddess in her sphere of activity—often in the world of opera, classical music, or dance. Such a female artist might also be called a prima donna. In those days, such descriptors had no particular negative connotations. Over the course of the twentieth century, however, when a woman of fame (usually in the performing arts) was called a diva (or prima donna), it increasingly connoted that she was demanding, temperamental, and self-centered. The term was frequently applied to established performers who had the reputation of being extremely difficult (for example, Joan Crawford, Bette Davis, Jeanette MacDonald, and Lana Turner) or those who were wildly self-indulgent (such as Judy Gar-

land, Jean Harlow, Mae West, and Lupe Velez). In more recent times, the expression *diva* has frequently been used by the media to label pop singers/actresses (from Liza Minnelli and Madonna to Britney Spears, Jennifer Lopez, and Mariah Carey) who suddenly have the world at their pretty feet and frequently indulge their wildest whims in front of, or away from, the spotlight. Chronicling such extreme, often mind-boggling behavior is part of the agenda in *Hollywood Divas*.

In the past, when a diva was doing what she did best (that is, throwing her power around; flaunting her wealth; playing bedroom games; and generally leading an exuberant, wild life), such negative events were downplayed by the woman's studio or TV network. As such, these excesses often became known to the public at large only years later when someone wrote a tell-all book. Or sometimes examples of unbridled behavior by a diva seemed, at the time, to be isolated events not to be taken "too" seriously. However, by reexamining the actress's *full* life—both on and off camera—a different picture emerges, one in which there is a pattern of repeated—sometimes absorbing, sometimes repellant—behavior that would certainly not win the subject any humanitarian awards. Then, too, the extreme activities of these overly pampered, frequently high-strung celebrities are all the more dramatic when we contrast their shenanigans with the far stricter standards demanded of ordinary mortals. Regardless of how we judge their high (or low) jinks, the peccadilloes, abuses, and often garishly lavish living of these women make fascinating reading and allow us to contemplate the price of fame for such celebrities. It is for these reasons that this book was written.

In *Hollywood Divas* I have chronicled the lives of some of the most intriguing, colorful women of twentieth and twenty-first century American show business. I selected a representative sampling of fascinating luminaries who were at their peak of Tinseltown fame and power in different decades from 1910 through today. (To keep the volume to a reasonable length, some equally marvelous candidates—such as Mary Pickford, Constance Bennett, Ruth Chatterton, Jennifer Jones, Esther Williams, Kim Novak, Farrah Fawcett, Debra Winger, Sean Young, and Anne Heche—had to be put aside for, perhaps, another volume.) The notables presented herein encompass an array of women stars whose lifestyles have been full of intriguing excesses—ranging from conspicuous consumption to destructive behavior (frequently in which the subject was her own worst enemy and victim).

Sometimes, as with silent screen vamp Theda Bara, their primary vice was excessive joie de vivre, living exotically and in luxury far beyond what the average person could even contemplate. Others, such as Gloria Swanson, flaunted the conventions of their time with affairs, abortions, and the grand belief that as queen bees they could do exactly as they wished. But even Swanson's sexual escapades paled in comparison to the bedroom antics of the screen's Clara Bow or Louise Brooks.

As talkies took over Hollywood in the late 1920s, the film colony had a colorful set of major players. They included the bisexual antics of voracious Tallulah Bankhead and hedonistic Kay Francis, as well as that moody iconoclast Greta Garbo. One of the latter's biggest rivals, Marlene Dietrich, dabbled with lesbian liaisons while simultaneously embarking on an impressive number of affairs with famous men around the world. A star like Loretta Young could appear completely virtuous on screen, but off camera she drove several of her leading men (for example, Spencer Tracy and Clark Gable) into a frenzy. The result of her affair with Gable led to her having a child out of wedlock that, months later, she adopted as her own. That was the Hollywood of the thirties.

In fact, the 1930s were the heyday of Hollywood movie queens who considered their home studios as regal domains. They could demand almost anything of their studio bosses or coworkers and expect to have their exacting orders followed explicitly. This might mean a choice of screen roles and casts, or the royal right to have their director or leading man pay obeisance to them in bed. Such was the power of Bette Davis at Warner Bros., Joan Crawford and Norma Shearer at Metro-Goldwyn-Mayer, and Mae West at Paramount.

By the 1940s, the divas were frequently of a new breed. Sometimes they were drawn to substance abuse (like Judy Garland, Betty Hutton, or Veronica Lake) or to the pleasures of excessive seductions (like Ava Gardner,

Paulette Goddard, Rita Hayworth, Susan Hayward, and Lana Turner). As detailed in *Hollywood Divas*, their overwhelming addictions often shaped and/or ruined their careers and private lives. A few, such as the very genteel Greer Garson or highly tempestuous Maria Montez, were throwbacks to the old guard. They expected to be treated regally on the set; away from the studio lot, they demanded that their world revolve precisely around them.

In the 1950s, the years of voluptuous Marilyn Monroe and Jayne Mansfield, such personalities were both the aggressors and victims of their sex siren images, and their oversized, high-drama lives ended in tragedy. Also in that decade—the Eisenhower years—one saw the emergence of such shapely show business personalities as Elizabeth Taylor, Grace Kelly, Joan Collins, Natalie Wood, Shelley Winters, and Zsa Zsa Gabor. These femme fatales used their physical assets, wits, and charm to be playgirls of the Western world and damn the expense to anyone.

By the 1970s, Hollywood was pampering such contrasting personalities as Liza Minnelli, Diana Ross, Cybill Shepherd, and Barbra Streisand, allowing them—as long as their popularity was at a commercial peak—to enjoy their own established life rules, which often included mixing material splendor with stunning hauteur. In the late 1980s, the big screen's Meg Ryan, Sharon Stone, and Demi Moore paralleled TV's Roseanne as each made her presence felt during a rapid rise to privileged status. Sometimes, as with the frequently crude, rancorous, and unpredictable Roseanne, this bred an imitator (such as Brett Butler). Like Roseanne, Butler had moved from the world of stand-up comedy to TV sitcom fame. Such quick and gigantic success on the small screen made the celebrity extremely tough to deal with in many flabbergasting ways.

The last decade of the twentieth century (and first years of the twenty-first) saw a fresh breed of Hollywood divas demanding special attention from their (adoring) public. Whether from the world of TV (like Shannen Doherty), films (like Jennifer Lopez), or pop music (like Mariah Carey, Janet Jackson, and Britney Spears), these were youngish women who suddenly found themselves with often bewildering riches, celebrityhood, and the tantalizing ability to indulge themselves however they pleased.

This then is the wild world of *Hollywood Divas*, filled with exciting, highly dramatic, and self-focused personalities who consider(ed) the world their personal stage and playground. These colorful women have *never* lived life by short measures. Their extravagant lifestyles—sometimes enviable, other times pitiable, and oftentimes bewildering—are fascinating life illustrations of what fame can do.

Jean Arthur

[Gladys Georgianna Greene]

OCTOBER 17, 1900–JUNE 19, 1991

Many notable Hollywood actresses (like Greta Garbo, Tallulah Bankhead, and Bette Davis) boasted distinctive voices. Another such star was Arthur, she of the smoky timbre and a great flair for comedy.

Unlike many of her Tinseltown peers, Jean has frequently been neglected by film historians, movie buffs, and biographers. Even during her professional heyday she was extremely shy, private, and insecure off camera and loathed giving interviews. As such, reports about her during her lifetime were relatively minimal. Then, too, on and off the sound stages, she remained largely secluded in her private, eccentric world in which only a few people were admitted. Even some of these intimates felt they'd never gotten to know the real Jean Arthur. (For example, during the location shoot on her final movie, 1953's *Shane*, she much preferred spending her off-camera time visiting a litter of pigs being used in the Western.)

Offscreen Jean was noted for her aloof manner, which stemmed from her lack of self-confidence and performance jitters, as well as her fear of sharing events in her private life with others. (Even after becoming an established star she was prone to throwing up in her dressing suite before she nervously appeared on the set for the day's shoot.) The results of her emotional peculiarities often led Arthur to drop out of creative ventures to which she had already committed, to act autocratically with cast and crew, and to give an icy reception to reporters who tried to interact with her. Her rationale was "When I have something to say, I'll say it, but when I haven't, then I won't talk for publication."

If Arthur felt slighted, she would fly into a tirade. When she got a strange notion into her head, it was hard to shake it loose. (For example, she was one of the four finalists for the coveted role of Scarlett O'Hara in the 1939 epic, *Gone with the Wind*. Rather than wear a costume that was to be used in the film, she demanded to wear one of her own choice and was troublesome on the set that day. She lost the role.) Then there was her bitter working relationship with Harry Cohn, the Columbia Pictures chieftain; she went on suspension at

1

Gary Cooper and Jean Arthur in *Mr. Deeds Goes to Town* (1936). (Courtesy of JC Archives)

least three times during her decade with the studio. While Jean was not the only star to take umbrage with the crude mogul, she was his only major contractee to run shouting with glee through the movie lot when her studio contract finally ended. Nevertheless, such unique behavior was only the tip of the iceberg with Jean.

Although she listed her birth year variously as 1905 or 1908, she was actually born Gladys Georgianna Greene in Plattsburgh, New York, in 1900. She was the fourth and final child of Hubert Greene, an itinerant photographer and painter, and his wife Hannah (Nelson) Greene. Because her three siblings (all boys) were several years older than she, the girl developed an inferiority complex from being bossed around by the four men in her life. As the family moved so frequently, it was hard for her to make friends and she withdrew into herself. Adding to her complex nature, she also developed a protective superiority complex, convinced that a special person lurked inside her. During childhood Gladys became fascinated with acting, but it was a profession on which her straight-laced parents frowned. So she kept her creative ambitions largely to herself. In 1909, Hubert Greene walked out on his family but returned the next year. This pattern continued over the years while the pragmatic Hannah ran a boardinghouse in Portland, Maine, to support her clan.

By 1915, Gladys and her parents—her brothers were now on their own—were residing in New York City, where Mr. Greene worked for a photography studio. But that job did not last long and the father departed yet again. As a result, Gladys quit high school in her junior year to work as a stenographer. About 1920, the five-foot, three-inch young woman with striking features and bobbed blond hair began a side career as a model. In mid-1923, she was screen-tested by Fox Films and signed to a studio contract. She and her mother moved to Los Angeles. (It was at this time that she became known as Jean Arthur, supposedly derived from two of her heroes: Joan of Arc and King Arthur.)

The studio cast her in the lead of *The Temple of Venus* (1923), but the untrained performer panicked and was replaced in the silent photoplay. The nightmare of this embarrassing start to her movie career marked her for life. After a few more months with Fox (who put her into supporting roles), she was let go. She then worked for independent film companies and made several Westerns in which her love of horseback riding proved useful. Occasionally she was in a contemporary tale, such

as *The Cowboy Cop* (1926). A few years later, the major studios took fresh interest in her. She signed with Paramount Pictures, making her bow in *Warming Up* (1928). That year Arthur found romance with carefree photographer Julian Ancker, but the latter, a Jew, was anathema to Arthur's mother, an ardent Christian Scientist. The couple eloped, but the marriage was annulled after one day. One version has it that the idealistic couple split when they realized they could not support themselves on their own. Another account insists that Jean had overlooked a term in her contract that forbade her to marry without Paramount's consent (which they did not give). Ancker quickly disappeared from Jean's life; he later died of sunstroke while out fishing.

In 1929's *The Canary Murder Case*, Arthur made her talking film debut and was described as strange by the fan magazines because she labeled herself "a negative personality," one who preferred to read a book than attend a party, and so forth. The publications judged her an odd bird (by Hollywood standards). By 1931, Paramount let Arthur's option expire. Refusing to give up on acting, the spunky performer relocated to New York and found stage work (including 1932's *The Man Who Reclaimed His Head*). While in Manhattan she wed Frank Ross Jr., a singer–turned–actor, four years her junior, with whom she had worked at Paramount. By 1934, she was back in California working under a five-year contract with Columbia Pictures.

Arthur rose from the studio ranks in the John Ford–directed *The Whole Town's Talking* (1935). Frank Capra, Columbia's prized contract director, later acknowledged that he knew of Jean's growing reputation as being somewhat "cuckoo" but that he still chose her to join Gary Cooper in *Mr. Deeds Goes to Town* (1936). The hit picture made her a bona fide star, leading to such successful vehicles as *The Plainsman* (1936), *You Can't Take It with You* (1938), *Mr. Smith Goes to Washington* (1939), and *The More the Merrier* (1943, for which she was Oscar-nominated). By then, her uncooperative image was frozen with the movie press, as a result of which her fans rarely got to read about the "real" Jean Arthur. So strained was the situation between Jean and the media that Columbia Pictures concocted a special article by John Wayne (Jean's costar in 1943's *The Lady Takes a Chance*) for *Screenland* magazine. Titled "Jean Arthur As I Know Her," the piece carried the legend: "She's the most criticized star in all Hollywood: Yet a man who knows her well comes to her defense so convincingly that there may be a decided change of opinion about Jean Arthur. Read what John Wayne says and then see what YOU think." Nonetheless, the ghostwritten article was promotional pap.

Arthur's Columbia pact ended with *The Impatient Years* (1945) and she focused on stage work. She signed to star in the Broadway comedy *Born Yesterday* (1946), but during tryouts she went into an emotional funk/panic and left the cast. Judy Holliday took over the role and became a hit, as did the play. Frank Capra asked Jean to join Jimmy Stewart in *It's a Wonderful Life* (1946), but she declined and Donna Reed inherited the part. (She likewise turned down 1947's *The Voice of the Turtle* at Warner Bros.) Instead, at age forty-six, Arthur chose to take courses at Stephens College in Columbia, Missouri. However, she left after some weeks when she agreed to make the Paramount movie *A Foreign Affair* (1948) with Marlene Dietrich (also making a comeback) and John Lund. Dietrich emerged as the hit of this black comedy. For years, Jean blamed Wilder for slanting the production in Marlene's favor. She eventually forgave him but never lost her anger at Dietrich.

By 1949, Arthur was undergoing psychoanalysis, and she divorced Frank Ross who was now a film producer. They had not gotten along for years and he was already engaged to wed actress Joan Caulfield. (Over the years, there was gossip that Arthur may have been a lesbian, rumors fueled by her longtime rapport with singer/actress Mary Martin and by a fictionalization of their special friendship in a 1966 novel.) In 1953, Jean was lured back to the screen for *Shane*, her big-screen finale. In 1966, physically fit and looking younger than her age thanks to plastic surgery, she starred in a short-lived TV sitcom, *The Jean Arthur Show*.

Her last decades were spent mostly in seclusion in upstate California. Occasionally she attempted a new play project, but, as with *First Monday in October* (1975), she usually left the show during the pre-Broadway tryout. Arthur died from a heart attack in mid-1991 at the age of ninety. At her request, her body was cremated and her ashes scattered at sea. In her last years, whenever the media sought to interview the reclusive star, her response was always, "No! I'd rather slit my throat."

Lucille Ball

[Lucille Désirée Ball]

AUGUST 6, 1911–APRIL 26, 1989

Years after her death, she remains a pop culture icon, universally beloved by young and old. Her great acclaim—and hallowed memory—does *not* rely on the many feature films she made during Hollywood's Golden Age nor on the Broadway musical (1960's *Wildcat*) in which she starred. Rather, her legendary status rests on her classic 1950s TV series *I Love Lucy* (and to a lesser extent on her follow-up sitcoms). That is the Lucy everyone remembers—the well-meaning but scatterbrained redhead who was a magnet for trouble of all sorts. Watching heroine Lucy Ricardo survive a wild pratfall, react to a daunting situation, or contort her expressive face in bemusement is always joyous to behold—regardless of how often one has seen the footage. This is the comedic genius that everyone recalls so fondly. But was that the *real* person, the one who remained a TV superstar for decades?

A television network employee who worked with the legend described her thus: "If she doesn't know you, she's cold as ice. Naturally, you feel *you* know her, and you *love* her, as a result of the *Lucy* shows. But it's a shock to realize she's not the childlike Lucy character she plays. She's diamond-hard, extremely bright, and extremely cautious with people."

Fellow comedienne Phyllis Diller, who had mingled with all types in her many years in show business, once evaluated the multitalented Lucy as follows: "Lucille Ball was a control freak. Had to be in charge of everything. Never saw a woman who took her comedy so seriously." Actress Edie Adams, the widow of comedian Ernie Kovacs, who had performed on camera with Ball in 1960 and then again in 1968, found that the passing years had made Lucy more "driven." She also noted, "I never understood why Lucille was so concerned about her looks. She was still a very attractive woman, but she wore so much makeup . . . and was constantly sucking her cheeks in to try to look like an ingénue. Lucille's voice had gone from soprano to bass. The only thing I can imagine that would do that to a voice is a little bit too much scotch."

Then there was Desi Arnaz, wed to Lucy for twenty years and her *I Love Lucy* costar. "Lucy isn't a redhead for no reason. She has a big comic talent, but she also has a big, not very funny *temper*. Not a temperament but a temper. Her tongue is a lethal weapon. She can be very cruel when she wants to be." Ball aptly illustrated Arnaz's point when, on one tense domestic occasion, the riled actress screamed at her spouse: "You bastard! You cheat! You drunken bum! I got enough on you to hang you. By the time I get through with you you'll be as broke as when you got here [that is, to the United States from Cuba]." Being fair to Lucy, Desi was a renowned ladies' man, and, when exasperated, she minced no words in inventorying the downsides of her errant husband: "Desi is a loser. A gambler, an alcoholic, a skirt-chaser . . . a financially smart man but self-destructive."

This is the less-revered side of the very human, very demanding Lucille Ball who once (co)ruled a TV empire with iron fists.

She was born Lucille Désirée Ball in 1911 in Celoron, a small town adjacent to Jamestown in upstate New York. She was the firstborn of Henry and Désirée (Hunt) Ball. In 1915, Henry died of typhoid fever. Three years later the mother remarried, but that union ended in divorce. As a result, for much of Lucy's childhood, she and brother Fred considered their loving but stern (and sometimes eccentric) grandfather, Fred Hunt, to be their father figure. As she grew up, Lucy determined that somehow she would become a show-business performer.

In September 1926, ambitious Lucy moved to New York City. She studied acting at the Robert Milton–John Murray Anderson School, where one of her classmates was Bette Davis. Ball proved inept in her studies and failed more than once when auditioning (or even when

cast) in a Broadway musical. Discouraged but determined, she refused to abandon her career goal. In the late 1920s, she became seriously ill (some accounts list the ailment as severe fatigue and malnutrition; another rendition had her the victim of an auto accident; yet another suggested the possibility that she may have had an abortion that went bad or even given birth to a child).

Regardless of the cause of her ill health, Lucy returned to her family in upstate New York to recuperate. By 1930, the statuesque (five feet, six inches) Ball was back in New York, where she worked as a Hattie Carnegie Agency model. One of Lucy's print ads came to the attention of movie producer Samuel Goldwyn, who brought her to Hollywood to be one of his on-screen Goldwyn (chorus) girls. As such, she helped to decorate the scenery in the Eddie Cantor musical *Roman Scandals* (1933). A year later, Lucy was toiling at Columbia Pictures while supporting her relatives (mother, brother, grandfather, and cousin), who had joined her in Hollywood. Three months after signing with Columbia, she left the lot (for lack of opportunities) and moved over to RKO Pictures, where she remained for the next seven years.

At RKO, Ball had on-the-job training. During her apprentice period, she was a workhorse on the sound stages, playing supporting roles in big productions such as *Stage Door* (1937) and *Having Wonderful Time* (1938), and handling leads in such modest fare as *The Affairs of Annabelle* (1938). Before long she was the studio's "Queen of the B Pictures." Throughout this period, Lucy found time to date, including a relationship with director Alexander Hall. However, it was not Hall with whom she fell wildly in love. While making the musical *Too Many Girls* (1940), she began a heated romance with her colead, Desiderio Alberto Arnaz y De Acha III—known to Broadway and New York club audiences as Desi Arnaz. The conga-thumping Cuban heartthrob was six years her junior. On November 11, 1940, the couple eloped to Greenwich, Connecticut.

When Lucy departed RKO in 1942, she was making a relatively modest $1,500 weekly. She transferred to glittery MGM, where the studio remolded her image to big-screen glamorous. Part of the dramatic transformation was changing her subdued hair color to bright red, which made her an attention-getter. She was best showcased at the studio in two 1943 musicals: *DuBarry Was a Lady* and *Best Foot Forward*. However, it soon became clear that MGM had more interest in promoting far younger studio sexpots Lana Turner and Ava Gardner than in building Ball's career. During this stressful period, in 1944, Lucy became fed up with Desi's unfaithfulness and filed for divorce. However, before the decree became final, the couple rekindled their marriage.

In 1946, MGM dropped Lucy's contract and she freelanced. The next year she bravely tried other media. She toured in the stage play *Dream Girl*, proving her acting range. More successful was her 1947 radio series *My Favorite Husband*. The domestic comedy became very popular on the airwaves.

By the new decade, there didn't seem much hope for Lucy and Desi's decaying marriage. Each partner was extremely career-minded,

Lucille Ball in a glamorous mood from the 1940s.
(Courtesy of Echo Book Shop)

and the hard-playing Arnaz couldn't control his wandering eye. Yet the couple gave their relationship one more try. So they could work and spend time together, they put together a pilot for a TV sitcom. When it was filmed in March 1951, Lucy was already pregnant with their child Lucie Désirée (born that July). *I Love Lucy* debuted on October 15, 1951, and the comedy series, costarring Vivian Vance and William Frawley, quickly became a major success. In mid-January 1953, Ball gave birth to

By the time of *The Lucy Show* (1962–68), veteran TV star Ball was increasingly dictatorial on the studio set. Sometimes she was brutal to guest stars, even to such legendary figures as Joan Crawford, who appeared on the teleseries in February 1968. Joan was rehearsing a Charleston number for the episode. A displeased Ball stalked over to Crawford and growled, "You got into the movies as a Charleston dancer and you can't dance! I can't believe it. . . . We'll try this one more time and if it doesn't work, it's out!" She then ordered the Oscar winner, "Come on, let's do it again." Still dissatisfied, Lucy snarled, "This number is out!" A shattered Crawford retreated to her dressing room, where she collapsed on the floor in tears.

Desi Arnaz Jr., an event paralleled on the hit teleseries with the birth of Little Ricky. By the end of the fifties, *I Love Lucy* had played itself out; more important, so had its stars' marriage. They divorced in May 1960, a decision made tougher by the fact that the couple co-owned Desilu Productions whose assets included the RKO lot where Ball had once toiled.

While starring on Broadway in *Wildcat* in 1960, Lucy met comedian Gary Morton. The following November, Ball and the six-year-younger Morton wed. Addicted to remaining in the limelight, Ball returned to TV with *The Lucy Show* (1962–68) and *Here's Lucy* (1968–74). By now, the show-business veteran had hardened into a tough taskmistress who brooked no dissent in her domain. Everyone had to kowtow to Madame Boss or else—and that included famous guest stars such as Jack Benny. Some on-scene observers credit Ball's micromanagement and her cheapness on the set as primary factors in her new series not reaching the caliber of *I Love Lucy*.

In 1974, Lucy made her final movie, the musical *Mame*, which was a disaster on nearly every level. Thereafter, the aging star took the route of many other veteran talents. She made the circuit of talk shows and game programs and participated in many award specials. By the mid-1980s, Lucy's health was poor, but she refused to retire. She played a pitiable bag lady in the TV movie, *Stone Pillow* (1985). Never acknowledging her glory days were long over, the compulsive and very demanding actress returned to the rigors of a weekly TV series. Her new offering, *Life with Lucy*, was a sad showcase for the star who insisted on acting like a character several decades her junior. After only a few months, the show was pulled from the network schedule. The humiliation of this public defeat devastated Ball.

In May 1988, Lucy, a longtime, heavy smoker, suffered a stroke. She rallied from that setback and appeared on the March 1989 Academy Awards telecast. Some days later she had a heart attack but delayed being taken to Cedars-Sinai Medical Center until she had put on her makeup. She survived the subsequent open-heart surgery, but days later the seventy-seven-year-old died of a massive heart attack. Per her request, there was no funeral service before she was buried at Forest Lawn Memorial Park in Hollywood Hills.

Lucy was once asked what drove her so fiercely in her lengthy career. The husky-voiced actress replied, "I have to work or I am nothing."

Tallulah Bankhead

[Tallulah Brockman Bankhead]

January 31, 1902–December 12, 1968

She belonged to that rarified group of celebrities (like Garbo and later Madonna) who were known to the public by a single name. Tallulah was immediately identifiable by her deep, throaty voice and her mane of long, dark hair. If the expression *bigger than life* wasn't coined for Bankhead, who stood five feet, two-and-a-half inches, it certainly described this irrepressible personality who was a performer for over half a century. A few years after she entered show business, Tallulah gained tremendous acclaim in the 1920s on the London stage. Word of her allure abroad preceded her 1931 return to America, where she remained a controversial celebrity for decades to come.

Tallulah once described a diva as "an actress who brings the public into a theater or opera house—in droves, darling—by sheer force of her unique and individual self." She did just that, whether or not the play or she was dramatically sound. Often, in midlife, she would down several drinks before dashing on stage. However, inebriation never made her performance less appealing to the always fascinated public.

Opinionated, outspoken, and pampered, the indomitable Bankhead, who defied all of life's conventions, claimed to have three dislikes: "I hate to go to bed, I hate to get up, and I hate to be alone." As such, when she wasn't hosting a sparkling, celebrity-filled gathering, she was a dedicated partygoer. Tallulah could always be counted on to stir up the fun. She might strip naked and do cartwheels or break into song, although she couldn't really sing. Being a passionate exhibitionist, she thought nothing of inviting a guest into the bathroom while she peed so that their train of conversation wouldn't be broken. In the boudoir, the lusty star didn't much care if her bed partner was male or female. She was quite open about her bisexuality. (At a fashionable wedding, she commented loudly to a friend about the bride and groom, "I've had both of them, darling—and neither of them is any good.") On another occasion, she told an interviewer, "I've tried several varieties of sex. The conventional position makes me claustrophobic, and all the others give me either a stiff neck or lockjaw." Tallulah was also well known for her drug addictions over the years. On this topic, she quipped, "Daddy always warned me about men and alcohol, but he never said a thing about women and cocaine!"

Indubitably, self-involved Bankhead could be a trial to others both on and off the stage. It was difficult to keep up with this high-energy woman who had a fondness for unusual household pets such as lions and monkeys. In the long run, however, what made this

Tallulah Bankhead in *A Royal Scandal* (1945).
(Courtesy of JC Archives)

remained too distraught to supervise his children's needs, so Tallulah and the year-older Eugenia were soon sent to relatives in Montgomery and Jasper, respectively. (Their father was eventually persuaded to enter politics and would serve in Congress for many years, as did his father, John Bankhead, a member of the U.S. Senate.) As a youngster, Tallulah suffered from bronchial ailments, which caused her voice to deepen so distinctively. She attended several boarding and convent schools in the South and New York, and found time to study piano and violin.

At age fifteen, self-willed, impetuous Tallulah decided to become an actress and entered her photo in a movie magazine contest. The prize was a chance to appear in the silent film, *Thirty a Week* (1918). Mr. Bankhead allowed his daughter to go to New York to accept the role and try show business. She lived at the Algonquin Hotel and became a fringe member of the intelligentsia set there. Her mentor and good friend in this period and later was the older Estelle Winwood, a British-born actress. Tallulah began running with a fashionable British set, one of whom was Napier Arlington, the third Arlington baron. Bankhead fell in love with the bisexual nobleman but he refused to commit to marriage. Meanwhile, besides appearing in *The Wishful Girl* (1918) and a few other silent movies shot on the East Coast, the fledgling actress was on Broadway in such plays as *Squab Farm* (1918) and *The Exciters* (1922).

In late 1922, Bankhead visited a fortune-teller and was advised that her future "lay across the water." Early the next year the per-

exhausting whirlwind (whose dictum of life was "Press on!") so palatable to others was her engaging self-mockery. (For example, referencing her spicy reputation, she said, "I'm as pure as the driven slush.")

She was born in Huntsville, Alabama, in 1902, the second daughter of William Brockman Bankhead, an attorney, and his wife Adeline Eugenia Sledge, a popular Virginia beauty. Mrs. Bankhead died a few days after Tallulah's birth. The grieving, heavy-drinking father

former sailed for England. Ostensibly her aim was to make good on the British stage, but she really wanted to reunite with Arlington. After her London debut in *The Dancers* (1923) and over the next eight years, she headlined in more than fifteen West End shows. Although she became the darling of British society and was beloved by her shop-girl fans, Arlington still would not wed the cool beauty. Signing a contract with Paramount Pictures, the ever-restless Bankhead returned to the United States in early 1931.

Her first three American talkies (including 1931's *Tarnished Lady*) were filmed in New York. They were claptrap, but the money was good and the work relatively easy. She traveled to Hollywood to make her next three. There, her hard-partying lifestyle upset Paramount executives, as she behaved recklessly on and off the set with the likes of Gary Cooper (with whom she made 1932's *The Devil and the Deep*) and Marlene Dietrich. When Paramount did not renew her contract, Tallulah

went to MGM for 1932's *Faithless*, and studio head Louis B. Mayer grew apoplectic at her wild, bisexual ways. When he chastised the zesty hedonist, the unflappable Bankhead stopped him cold when she threatened to publicize her recent romances with several Metro luminaries (both male and female). After telling the mogul to f*** off, which ruined any chance of a long-term pact with the ritzy studio, she blithely returned to New York.

Back on Broadway, Bankhead starred in such vehicles as *Forsaking All Others* (1933), *Dark Victory* (1934), and *Reflected Glory* (1936), many of which were adapted into films, but *not* starring Tallulah. With her Southern background, Tallulah tested for *Gone with the Wind* (1939), but her uncontrolled lifestyle and age militated against her getting to play Scarlett O'Hara. Returning to theater work in the East, she met John Emery, a rising actor who bore a striking resemblance to John Barrymore (on whom Bankhead had once had a huge crush). "He's mad as a hatter, but then so am

The legendary Tallulah was a master madcap, famed for her wicked wit and uninhibited behavior. Typically, whenever exhibitionist Bankhead had a call of nature, she never thought of closing the bathroom door to shield herself from others. Once, Tallulah was hosting Eleanor Roosevelt, the widow of President Franklin Delano Roosevelt, for afternoon tea. Needing the powder room, Bankhead hurried off to use the facilities. Fearful of missing any words of wisdom, she left the door open. Later, Tallulah insisted of the former first lady, "I'm sure she didn't even notice. She pees herself, you know."

A great conversationalist, it was tough to best the unconventional Bankhead in discourse. Discussing her psychosomatic habit of developing the same symptoms when she heard of a friend's illness, her listener inquired, "What happens when you hear about a rape, Tallulah?" She instantly replied, "I masturbate, darling."

I," she said of her new lover but gave marriage a whirl in August 1937. A few months later, the husband-wife team costarred on Broadway in *Antony and Cleopatra*. He got better notices than she, and, by the time the show folded after just five performances, the marriage was doomed. Thereafter, the couple drank, fought, cheated on one another, and had constant separations and reconciliations. They finally divorced in June 1941 but remained on good terms. She never remarried and claimed, later in life, not to regret never becoming a parent. "I'm not childless," said the woman who'd had several abortions in her younger years. "I am child-free."

Her greatest stage triumph was headlining in *The Little Foxes* (1939). In 1942, she had another Broadway triumph with *The Skin of Our Teeth*. She returned to Hollywood to star successfully in Alfred Hitchcock's screen thriller *Lifeboat* (1944). Later, she revived Noël Coward's *Private Lives* on Broadway (1948) and on an extended tour. In 1950, Tallulah turned to radio where she was mistress of ceremonies on a weekly network variety program (*The Big Show*), which lasted into 1952. Next, she hosted a TV series (*All-Star Revue*) for a season (1952–53). During this productive period, her ghostwritten autobiography, *Tallulah* (1952), became a sensational bestseller.

By the 1960s, Tallulah had given up Windows, her country house in Bedford, New York, in Westchester County, and had relocated to an East Side townhouse in Manhattan. Her career was winding down due to ill health brought on by excessive hard living. But as always, the star found amusement even in her diminished looks. (When a stranger stopped her on a New York City street to inquire, "Are you Tallulah Bankhead?" she replied, "What's left of her.") As had happened throughout her career, Bankhead had little cash flow ("I'm worse than broke, darling, I'm shattered") and needed to keep working. She toured in stock (*Here Today* and *Glad Tidings*) and made her final Broadway appearance in Tennessee Williams's short-lasting *The Milk Train Doesn't Stop Here Anymore* (1964). Her last movie was the British-shot campy horror entry *Die! Die! My Darling!* (1965). In 1967 she was asked to play the Black Widow character on the *Batman* TV series. One of her "caddies" (her term for the young gay men who served as her gofers/companions over the years) urged her to take the television offer. "It will be a camp," he insisted. To which she replied, "Don't tell me about 'camp.' I invented it!"

Having long suffered from emphysema, she contracted the flu in late 1968, and it later turned into pneumonia. As she lay dying in December 1968, her last discernible words were "Codeine . . . bourbon."

Throughout her career, the spirited Bankhead was devoted to stage acting. Her greatest sadness was that her theater work would not be remembered over the years. Although she considered films a lesser medium, she lost some choice roles, especially to Bette Davis, who starred on screen in parts Tallulah had done on stage: *Jezebel* (1938), *Dark Victory* (1939), and *The Little Foxes* (1941). The final straw occurred when Davis triumphed in *All About Eve* (1950), doing a Tallulah-like characterization. Furious that she had lost the chance to play herself on the screen, Bankhead was convinced that her rival was spreading unflattering stories about her within the film industry. Tallulah carped, "And after all the nice things I've said about that hag. When I get hold of her I'll tear out every hair of her mustache!"

Looking back on her indulgent, colorful past, Bankhead once said, "The only thing I regret about my past is the length of it. If I had to live my life again, I'd make the same mistakes, only sooner."

Theda Bara

[Theodosia D. Goodman]
July 29, 1885–April 7, 1955

Between 1910 and 1920, there arose a new kind of screen character: the vamp, a predatory woman who blithely brings about the ruin of her male victims. (The name derived from Rudyard Kipling's 1897 poem "The Vampire," which told of a foolish man beguiled into disaster by a voracious villainess.) During the World War I era, the vamp—with all the exaggerated traits and overacting associated with this early period of filmmaking—became an exceedingly popular type in the silent cinema.

One of the earliest examples of this daring screen vixen was exotic Theda Bara. She was an actress said to have been born in Egypt in the shadow of the Sphinx and to be the reincarnation of a long-ago rapacious siren. In actuality, she was a Jewish girl from the Midwest. On the strength of her vamp portrayals, she rose to global superstardom in the second decade of the twentieth century. Before long, this fabricated celebrity began to believe the outrageous studio-generated publicity that surrounded her mystique, bringing about her downfall.

She was born in 1885 in Cincinnati, Ohio, the first of three children of Bernard Goodman, a Polish immigrant, and his wife, the Swiss-born Pauline. The ambitious Mr. Goodman became a partner in a Cincinnati tailoring/clothing establishment, and the family moved to the suburbs. An exceedingly shy child, dark-haired, plump Theodosia fantasized about becoming an actress in grand stage roles. After graduating from high school in 1903, she enrolled at the University of Cincinnati where she spent the next two years.

In 1905, the twenty-year-old moved to New York City, determined to become an actress. For professional purposes, she chose a new surname (de Coppet), adapted from her mother's middle name. She performed in stock companies and at a Jewish theater on Manhattan's Second Avenue. Later, billed as Theodosia de Coppet, she was on Broadway and in touring shows.

In 1914, Theodosia—now nearing thirty—was already matronly in face and figure. Anxious for new income, she accepted an extra's role in *The Stain*, a silent photoplay being shot by Pathé in Long Island. The picture's director, Frank Powell, was impressed by the movie newcomer's brief appearance in a crowd scene and vowed to employ her on-screen again soon.

Meanwhile, in late 1914, William Fox, the head of the New York–based Fox Film Corporation, bought the film rights to *A Fool There Was*. The 1909 melodrama had been inspired by Kipling's 1897 poem. Finding an actress to play the key role of the morally reckless vamp proved difficult. Many established performers rejected the part as too unsavory; others were vetoed by Fox and his recently hired director, Frank Powell, as inappropriate. Finally, the latter suggested Theodosia for the assignment, and she was offered the part if she signed a five-year contract at a starting salary of $100 a week. She brazenly insisted on $150 weekly, a counterdemand that was grudgingly accepted. It was the start of the battle of wills between the actress and the studio.

As *A Fool There Was* completed production, William Fox hired two ex-newspapermen to promote the picture. Needing a publicity angle to lure moviegoers, they let their imaginations run wild and devised an outrageous promotion. To test its impact, the publicists organized a press conference at a Chicago hotel where the movie's exotic star—now called Theda Bara—was to be introduced. (Her new moniker derived from a contraction of her first name and her grandfather's family name of Baranger.) The duo concocted a crazy tale that Theda, an Arab (which spelled backward is Bara) born in Egypt, had performed successfully on the French stage and was a reincarnation of an alluring femme fatale from centuries earlier.

The press "debut" was held in a darkened hotel suite filled with pungent incense and Asian statuary, as well as scattered skulls and stuffed snakes. Draped in a provocative outfit and wearing many veils, Bara greeted the intrigued press from her chaise lounge. As an added twist, it was arranged that after the conference ended a chosen female reporter would remain behind to be the "accidental" witness to the actress whipping off her veils and heavy coat and rushing to open the windows for gasps of fresh air. The journalist duly reported this "exposé" in her newspaper coverage, which added fuel to the excitement being generated by the other reporters on Bara's bizarre press meeting.

The gambit worked exceedingly well, and *A Fool There Was* became a big hit. Fox immediately rushed Bara into her next project. However, fearing that fame might go to her head (as it did), the studio insisted that she be treated as just another regular player on the studio lot in Fort Lee, New Jersey. Bara made one movie after another—eight in 1915, including *Carmen*. With her income assured, Theda moved her family into a spacious, fashionable Manhattan apartment from which she imperiously reigned.

One of the terms of Bara's studio contract demanded that she perpetuate the studio-engineered myths by never appearing in public without wearing veils or her trademark white makeup. It was stipulated she was not to marry during the contract's term and that she should do whatever else was deemed necessary to keep her special image intact. She went along with the gambits, which, for a time, amused her and did so much to ensure her popularity at the box office. Before long, however, her giddy success went to her head. For the time being—while her pictures kept making so much money—the studio indulged her.

By now the raven-haired personality, with her ample figure and prominent profile, was very well known to her fascinated public. (At the time, it was estimated that 182 million people a year saw her pictures.) One day, while strolling in Manhattan, Bara stopped to chat with a little boy who had momentarily escaped his mother's supervision. When the parent caught up with her offspring, she was aghast to see him in the presence of this shocking celebrity. As the account goes, the hysterical mother screamed for the police to save her child from the clutches of this villainous creature. Such was Theda's fame!

Before too long, Bara became bored with her confining screen image and demanded to stretch her artistic abilities on-screen. She insisted she was too talented just to play her stock vamp. As such, one of her 1916 film entries showcased her as the heroine in *Romeo and Juliet*, but the studio nevertheless made sure that her role was more vampish than tragic. Then it was back to tried-and-true assignments (such as *The Vixen*). Concerned by Theda's increasingly erratic demands, William Fox hired Virginia Pearson and other similar-type actresses to play vamps at Fox Films, hoping to humble Theda. However, for the time being, moviegoers remained loyal to Bara.

Theda Bara as Cleopatra (1917).
(Courtesy of JC Archives)

The in-demand Bara renegotiated her contract to an enormous $4,000 weekly, and it was announced she would next star in *Cleopatra* (1917). The lavish, million-dollar epic was to be shot in Los Angeles, so Theda and her family took up permanent residence on the West Coast. The picture boasted elaborate sets and costumes, and the star enjoyed another big-screen success.

By 1919, the regal Theda, increasingly weary of her celluloid stock-in-trade, insisted she play the young Irish heroine in *Kathleen Mavoureen*. She also demanded a new director, and British-born Charles J. Brabin was given the assignment. Unfortunately, *Kathleen Mavoureen* was a major flop. Not only did movie patrons refuse to accept the matronly looking Theda (now a mature thirty-four years old) as a young lass, but many Irish people in the United States were incensed that a Jewess was playing the lead role and boycotted the picture. The movie's failure was the beginning of the end for difficult Bara, who never arrived at the studio in her chauffeur-driven limousine until noon, left the set early, and remained temperamental in front of the camera.

After two more unremarkable movies in 1919, Theda left Fox Films. To save face, she insisted she was fleeing to Europe for a much-needed vacation. (However, industry insiders knew that Theda's tenure ended because of her prima donna habits.) After an unsatisfactory Broadway return in 1920, she married film director Brabin in the summer of 1921. The couple took up residence in a lavish Beverly Hills mansion. Bara made an unsuccessful bid to reclaim her movie throne, but times had changed—it was now the Roaring Twenties and the age of the chic, young flapper. Her screen career ended with a disappointing 1926 two-reel comedy in which she satirized her former celluloid alter ego. Eventually, the humbled actress resigned herself to being merely a Beverly Hills matron who gave fashionable dinner parties. Sadly, when she died of stomach cancer in 1955, she was already long forgotten by the studio (which had become Twentieth Century-Fox) she had helped to build and by her once fascinated, loyal public.

Drew Barrymore

[Drew Blythe Barrymore]
FEBRUARY 22, 1975–

"First I thought it was my [last] name that made me famous, and I resented it," said Barrymore. "Then I thought it was being pretty, and I resented that for a while. Now I don't care about why, just so people keep noticing me." There need be *no* worry on that score. As the latest generation of the renowned Barrymore tribe—once Broadway's royal family of acting greats—Drew has been in the limelight all her life. Sometimes, it was her binges of substance abuse and wild behavior, rather than her acting talent, that brought her into the spotlight. In this, she was also living up to her heritage. For just as many of her illustrious ancestors had been thespians, so the Barrymore curse of alcoholism had afflicted several of Drew's relatives. For a time in her teens, the talented young actress pursued her forebears' fondness for drink (and drugs), ending up in rehab on more than one occasion. She seemed destined to self-destruct in the Barrymore tradition.

She was born in 1975 in Culver City, California, the only offspring of John Drew Barrymore (also known as John Barrymore Jr.), a failed actor and drunk, and Ildiko Jaid Mako, a would-be actress/waitress. Her father was the second child of the illustrious John Barrymore (the Great Profile), a celebrated stage and film star whose massive drinking problem led to his death in 1942. John Jr.'s beautiful mother was silent screen leading lady Dolores Costello, who had made some sound features before retiring from pictures in 1943. Reckless and rebellious, John Jr. had made his film debut in 1950 and, for a few years, the handsome young actor appeared to be on the brink of movie stardom. But he turned to drink and erratic behavior, ruining his career and dissipating his looks. By the time he met Ildiko Jaid in the early 1970s, he had been married twice and his life was in ruins. However, Jaid (as she frequently was called) was enthralled with this offspring of the famed Barrymores. She had gone to the West Coast from Pennsylvania, hoping to build a film acting/modeling career.

When she met John Jr. at the Troubadour rock club, she was a waitress there, struggling to get an acting break. The couple soon married but separated before Drew's birth.

Jaid usually waitressed in the evenings so that her days would be free to make the round of casting agents. Her cherubic infant was left with a series of baby-sitters. Because the youngster was so cute and amiable, family friends suggested that she should be in commercials. However, Drew's mother, concerned with her own unresolved career future, didn't want her daughter entering the difficult field. It was only when an acquaintance submitted a photo of Drew to an agent that the youngest Barrymore was taken to audition for a dog-food commercial. She got the assignment. A year later, the little tyke made her TV debut in the telefeature *Suddenly Love* (1978)—playing a boy. In 1980, the occasional model had a small role in the feature *Altered States*. By now, as she made clear to her mother, she really liked acting. During this period, John Jr. occasionally appeared on the domestic scene, often drunk and usually violent. Typically, he would explode into a rage and become physically abusive to his wife and young daughter.

Drew's leap into major fame occurred when Steven Spielberg cast her in his sci-fi fable, *E.T.: The Extra-Terrestrial* (1982). Having no

*A*s an adorable child star, Drew got a jump on living the fast life. Having experimented with other drugs, she then "discovered cocaine, and it was like standing on top of a mountain and yelling, 'Eureka! I found it!' . . . Coke allowed me to soar above my depression and sadness, above all my problems. What I couldn't see is that it eventually makes you go crazy."

father figure, Barrymore latched on to Spielberg as a substitute dad; she regarded the cast and crew as her family unit and was saddened when filming ended. With Drew's $75,000 salary, Jaid quit her waitressing job. She now divided her time between pushing her own ambitions and managing her daughter's burgeoning career. When *E.T.* was released, its enormous success made Drew a nationally known figure. At age seven, the child hosted an episode of TV's *Saturday Night Live*. But her public appearances did not stop there. Accompanied by her publicity-conscious mother, she was frequently seen on the party circuit, attending premieres, festivities, and clubs, just as an adult performer would do to make industry contacts. For the young celebrity, such sophisticated evening activities did not seem abnormal but a pleasant way to reaffirm that she was wanted (in contrast to school, where she felt so estranged from her normal classmates). For Jaid, chaperoning her famous daughter was a mixed blessing. Part of her delighted in Drew's fame; part of her was envious that her offspring was succeeding in the very field where she could not make inroads. Occasionally, Drew's dad, a virtual recluse now, made contact with his daughter, usually to demand money.

In 1984, Drew starred in *Firestarter* (1984) as an adolescent with the psychic ability to start fires. She was even more impressive in the same year's *Irreconcilable Differences*, in which a precocious youngster sues to "divorce" her neglectful parents. The preadolescent Barrymore related well to that role. Meanwhile, Drew continued to feel alienated

A young Drew Barrymore in the early 1980s.
(Courtesy of Echo Book Shop)

from her classmates and still reveled in being part of the nighttime (mostly on weekends) social scene where "I belonged. If for no other reason than I was Drew Barrymore."

By the time she was nine, precocious Drew was secretly smoking cigarettes. Soon she was drinking, and by the time she was thirteen, she'd sampled cocaine and other drugs. After a while, she made little effort to hide her activities from her bewildered mother. She and Jaid fought constantly, with the rebellious young actress refusing to accept any boundaries. During one of Drew's tantrums, the out-of-control girl demanded that her mother leave their home. As the battle of wills raged, Drew grew more hysterical.

This time, Jaid took charge of the situation. She took her daughter to a substance abuse center in the San Fernando Valley. Barrymore responded to treatment at the Van Nuys facility, but after only twelve days she left for New York City to fulfill a commitment to make the movie *Far from Home* (1989). A few months thereafter, while still on the East Coast, Drew fell off the wagon and reverted to using cocaine. She and a girlfriend took one of Jaid's credit cards and booked a flight to Hawaii. When they stopped over in Los Angeles, two detectives whom Jaid had hired corralled Barrymore, and she was escorted back to the rehab facility. She remained there for three months, being discharged on December 21, 1988.

To counter the lurid tabloid accounts of her emotional/drug crash, the actress told her story to *People* magazine and then joined with reporter Todd Gold to write her autobiography (1990's *Little Girl Lost*). On the surface, everything seemed rosy for the rehabilitated performer. However, in March 1989, she began smoking pot again. She reached a crisis point on July 4, 1989, when she cut her wrist with a knife. The supermarket publications asserted that the popular young actress had tried to commit suicide. Contrariwise, Drew insisted it was a dramatic cry for help and returned to the ASAP Family Treatment Center in Van Nuys for another three months of treatment.

By her early teens, a now-plump Drew had reached an awkward stage for child performers: too old to play cute youngsters and too young to portray young adults. Also, the publicity about her substance abuse had damaged her career. Said Barrymore, "People wouldn't touch me; they just thought I was some loser drug addict." In this period of struggle, she broke away from her controlling mother, took her own apartment, waitressed for a time, and tried to put her life in order. Her big break came with the lead role in the low-budget *Poison Ivy* (1992). In that entry, the five-foot, four-inch blond displayed solid acting skills and revealed that she was growing into an attractive, sexy young woman. Her comeback was confirmed when she played the wayward teen in *Guncrazy* (1992). During 1992 and 1993, the teenaged actress had a live-in relationship with actor Jamie Walters, six years her senior.

While her career was rebuilding, Drew remained unpredictable as a person. For example, in March 1994, she had the impulse early one morning to wed Jeremy Thomas, a thirty-one-year-old Hollywood bartender she'd known for merely a few weeks. They quickly hired a psychic priest to conduct the ceremony. The impromptu union lasted less than a month, and the couple divorced. She was humiliated by the nonsensical experience, which she claimed had taught her a few life lessons, and she moved on.

In 1995, Barrymore further enhanced her rising screen reputation with *Boys on the Side* and *Mad Love*. Off camera she still had the urge to shock. She did a nude layout for *Playboy* magazine, confirming to herself and the world that she'd become a strikingly pretty adult. Then the irrepressible actress was a guest on David Letterman's late-night TV talk show that spring. On a whim, she jumped up on the host's desk and, with her back to the camera/audience, did a sexy dance and flashed her breasts at the nonplussed Letterman. It was her birthday present to him.

Drew was credited later with much foresight and savvy for taking a cameo role (rather than a lead) in the teen slasher film entry *Scream* (1996). As she anticipated, audiences were surprised when her character was murdered early in the picture. The hype concerning her part in this box-office bonanza helped to make her even more marketable within the film industry. Having already taken control of her personal life, she now did the same professionally—she formed her own production company (Flower Films) to create movie vehicles for herself. Sometimes, as with *The Wedding Singer* (1998), she badgered a celebrity (Adam Sandler) into doing a joint vehicle. At age twenty-three, she starred in (and executive produced) *Ever After* (1998), a new telling of the Cinderella fable. Besides being one of the trio of female leads, she was also a producer of 2000's big-screen version of the old TV series, *Charlie's Angels*. (It was a blockbuster hit, leading to 2003's *Charlie's Angels 2*.)

If Drew had (re)built her reputation as a talented, reliable movie star, there was still a zany, nonconformist side to this young veteran. This cropped up in her love life, which was filled with contrasting types (and included a few rumored same-sex liaisons earlier in her career). For a time in the 1990s, Barrymore was involved with Eric Erlandson, the guitarist with Courtney Love's band, Hole. From 1997 to 1998, she had a relationship with actor Luke Wilson, her leading man from *Home Fries* (1998). Her next attachment was to Canadian-born comedian Tom Green. Outrageous on and off camera, he was an offbeat presence whether in his bizarre variety/comedy TV series or in such lowbrow features as *Freddy Got Fingered* (2001). Despite not being conventionally handsome and having an unconventional personality, he struck a romantic cord with Drew. They became a couple. She remained loyal while he endured a health crisis (testicular cancer), and in July 2001, she and the five-year-older comedian wed. For a time there was great media speculation about whether the duo had actually married, a fact they kept deliberately clouded. However, there was no guesswork when the pair split up in December 2001 and divorced. By mid-2002 she was dating Fabrizio Moretti, the drummer for the rock band the Strokes.

In less than three decades, Drew Barrymore has packed a great deal of living into her drama-filled life. Unlike most of her forebears, not only has she exhibited an inner resiliency that salvaged her career from free fall, but she has confronted enough of her personal demons to convert herself into a much-appreciated individual. Her two-prong comeback was a remarkable exception in the annals of Hollywood. Perhaps most engaging about Barrymore is that, despite her professional pedigree and her own acting acumen, she learned early on never to take her art too seriously. As she said, "If I ever start talking to you about my 'craft,' my 'instrument,' you have permission to shoot me point-blank."

Ethel Barrymore

[Ethel Mae Blythe]

AUGUST 15, 1879–JUNE 18, 1959

Today she is known to some as the great-aunt of movie star Drew Barrymore. However, in her era, Ethel was glittering theatrical royalty. She was descended from a long line of well-known actors, a dynasty that reached its peak with her and her two brothers, the year-older Lionel and the three-year-younger John. They were a triumvirate of leading American stage notables in the early twentieth century. While all three made movies at different points in their lengthy careers, Ethel was not an enthusiast of the newer medium until late in life, when films offered her the income and audience exposure that the stage no longer afforded.

She was in her prime in the 1900s. In her twenties at that time, the five-foot, seven-inch actress had become the rage in America, famed for her regal bearing, her patrician profile, her distinctive low voice, and her large, expressive eyes. Shop girls copied her hairstyle and imitated her aristocratic strut. She had many male admirers, including young British politician Winston Churchill, who became entranced with Ethel during her British stage tour in the late 1890s. England's future prime minister was so fascinated with her that he proposed marriage. However, as she had done before and would do later with other suitors in America, she rejected the offer. For Ethel, her devotion to the theater was her principal interest in life.

As the queen of the stage—who even had a Broadway theater named after her—Ethel took her growing fame seriously. In fact, she became so accustomed to being the center of attention and applause in front of the footlights that she soon took it as her rightful due when away from the stage as well. Always of a reticent nature, which made her seem aloof, she became increasingly haughty and imperious as her successes mounted. She didn't suffer fools easily, whether they were members of her theater company or fellow guests at a social function. To be the victim of one of her legendary withering looks was a fate few wished to repeat.

Besides great vanity, Ethel also suffered from another family trait—a love of imbibing. Not only did she acquire the habit, in the 1920s, of drinking a good deal late in the evening (hoping it would counteract her insomnia), but she began to drink during the workday as well. She insisted that it would not affect her imperial highness's performance. But it did, and in many of her stage and vaudeville tours, especially in the 1930s, embarrassed and shocked audiences witnessed the inebriated great lady of the theater stumbling through eccentric performances.

She was born Ethel Mae Blythe in 1879 in Philadelphia, the second child of Maurice Barrymore (real name, Herbert Blythe) and Georgiana Drew. Both parents were theater folk; he was a matinee idol, and she was both a constantly working trouper (a comedienne) and the sister of the noted stage talent John Drew Jr. While still a tyke, Ethel had a commanding presence, and her two siblings did her bidding, even joining her in performing *Camille* and other play(let)s for which they charged neighbors a penny per ticket. Although Ethel had a love of piano playing, it was inevitable—and she accepted it as an imperial responsibility— that she go on the stage. Thus, after being educated at a convent school in Philadelphia until 1894, she joined *The Rivals*, a production in which her grandmother (Mrs. John Drew) was touring in Canada. Ethel reached Broadway in *That Imprudent Young Couple* (1895), written by her uncle, and her London bow was in *Secret Service* (1897). Back in America, her reputation was made when she starred on Broadway in *Captain Jinks of the Horse Marines* (1901).

Ethel enjoyed several Broadway successes, including *Alice Sit-by-the-Fire* (1905) and *Lady Frederick* (1908), many of which she took on tour across America. In March 1909, the nearly thirty-year-old actress finally wed. The groom was Wall Street stockbroker Russell Griswold Colt, three years her junior and son of the president of the United States Rubber Company. They had three children (born

The stately Ethel Barrymore in the early 1950s.
(Courtesy of JC Archives)

in 1909, 1912, and 1913). Over the years, the incompatible couple (he was a confirmed playboy and financially irresponsible toward his family) separated and reunited many times. Finally, in 1923, Ethel had enough and divorced Colt. Being Roman Catholic, she chose never to remarry (although she allowed herself the pleasure of a few dalliances).

Queenly Ethel had been shocked when brother Lionel had sunk to working in (lowly) vaudeville in 1910 to earn income, but she was aghast when he made his debut in the disreputable—by stage performers' standards—medium of film later that year. (A few years later, brother John also tried filmmaking.) However, by 1912, Ethel had to face reality. Now the breadwinner of her growing family with an overhead that included the upkeep for their spacious home in Mamaroneck, New York, she required a constant cash flow. She'd been unhappy with the play scripts being sent her and was in a financial bind. She threw caution to the wind by making a vaudeville tour and, two years later, turned to the detested film business to replenish her bank account. For $10,000, the thirty-five-year-old star made her debut in *The Nightingale* (1914). Although still unimpressed with moviemaking but encumbered by financial difficulties, she signed a multipicture pact with Metro Pictures at a reported $40,000 per film. Between *The Final Judgement* (1915) and *The Divorcee* (1919), Ethel made several silent films for that studio.

By 1932, the fifty-three-year-old Ethel was in another of her recurrent financial dilemmas. Thus, she gave in to the blandishments of MGM, which wanted to unite the three Barrymores (both Lionel and John were already established stars of the talkies). There was much publicity about the venerated Ethel making her sound movie debut. While she insisted for the record that she was breaking her own ban on making pictures so that she could spend time with her siblings on the West Coast, she thought the movies might offer a new professional lease on life for her.

However, during the making of *Rasputin and the Empress* (1932), she was a royal pain to the studio. On camera she was the Russian czarina; on the set she argued with the director about how her performance should be interpreted and was aloof toward both crew and supporting cast. During the shoot, an old rivalry flared up with her brothers and she upstaged them at every turn, particularly using the gambit of not raising her eyes to meet theirs in joint scenes. When the expensively mounted feature was finally released, it was not the major hit everyone had anticipated, and it was Lionel (as the mad monk Rasputin) who earned the best notices. As for trouble-provoking Ethel, MGM's chieftain, Louis B. Mayer, refused to renew her option for two more pictures. To disguise her humiliation, the star pretended it was she who (still) detested Hollywood, declaring, "The whole place is a glaring, gaudy, nightmarish set, built up in the desert." She fled back to the East Coast.

By 1940, Ethel, who had mostly overcome her drinking problem, had celebrated forty-five years in the theater and was starring in *The Corn Is Green*. It proved to be her last big stage hit. Still having money problems because she was continuously self-indulgent and careless in monitoring her funds, she returned to pictures. The film-industry moguls greeted her enthusiastically, counting on her presence to bring prestige to their studios. Playing Cary Grant's mother in *None but the Lonely Heart* (1944), she won a Best Supporting Actress Oscar for her efforts. Taking advantage of the career momentum, she made more movies, first under a pact with producer David O. Selznick and then with MGM. She was Oscar-nominated for *The Spiral Staircase* (1946), *The Paradine Case* (1947), and *Pinky* (1949).

Despite (or because of) her great success in films, sixty-something Ethel continued her haughty, uncooperative approach on movie sets. She was perturbed when directors tried to tell her what to do on camera, and she was as aloof, insulting, and mercurial with her costars as she was to her real-life offspring (none of whom succeeded in show business and counted on their mother's financial support). Even Katharine Hepburn, also part of the MGM acting family at the time, who idolized Miss Barrymore, later said of the icon, "Ethel in Hollywood made appallingly accurate observations and simply didn't know the meaning of caution."

Ethel celebrated her seventy-fifth birthday on the set of *Young at Heart* (1954), a Doris Day–Frank Sinatra picture. (Brother Lionel died that same year; John had passed away in 1942.) Thereafter, she wrote a benign memoir (*Memories*, 1955) and hostessed a short-lived TV anthology series (*The Ethel Barrymore Theater*). After making *Johnny Trouble* (1957), Ethel was forced to retire from show business because of poor health.

Suffering from a heart condition and advanced arthritic rheumatism, her last several months were spent bedridden in her relatively modest Beverly Hills home. On June 18, 1959, Ethel who was a great boxing and baseball enthusiast, listened to a doubleheader ball game on the radio. Afterward, she turned to friends who had congregated in her bedroom and said, "Is everybody happy? I want everybody to be happy, because I'm happy." With that wish voiced to her subjects, she drifted into unconsciousness and died.

Kim Basinger

[Kim Basinger]
DECEMBER 8, 1953–

What's a movie star to do when she has an irresistible itch to shop? Perhaps buy Braselton, Georgia, a 1,728-acre town with a population of five hundred. Regarding her wild shopping spree in 1989, Basinger explained, "I never intended to buy a whole town, but sometimes you start out shopping and wind up investing. It's nice when you can mix the two." But one mustn't assume this made the five-foot, seven-inch statuesque blond an airhead. Because, as Kim self-evaluated, "I'm a highly, highly, highly creative human being." Granted, she later went on to win a Best Supporting Actress Oscar for *L.A. Confidential* (1997). However, in the period of her impetuous real estate purchase, she was better known for her offbeat relationship with the artist then known as Prince, her prima donna behavior on film sets, and the golden locks on her pretty head. Regarding the latter two attributes, one of the weary crew on the trouble-plagued *The Marrying Man* (1991) advised temperamental Kim, "You can have diva behavior, but you've got to back it up with more than *hair*."

Another time Kim observed, "You have to be a little unreal to be in this business," which some aspects of Basinger are. For example, she suffers from agoraphobia, which is doubly unfortunate, as she chose to become a performer (and previously a model) who must deal constantly with crowds as part of her professional life. The actress also has a penchant for placing her foot in her mouth by becoming overly explicit in media interviews. This once led her father to send his famous daughter a package containing a tennis ball, adhesive tape, and the following suggestion: "When you give an interview and the feeling of being outrageous is present, please place this ball in your mouth and then tape your mouth shut. If you are still able to say 'oral sex' after doing this, then you are hopeless."

She was born in 1953 in Athens, Georgia, the third of five children of Donald Basinger, a loan company manager, and Ann Cordell, a former model. Her father had been a big-band musician in Chicago before his World War II military service, while her mother had been a talented swimmer who had performed in water ballets with movie star Esther Williams. As a child, Kim was so abnormally shy that it was thought she might be autistic. Part of her problem was an emotional reaction to her parents' incessant bickering and her father's constant criticism. By high school she had partially outgrown her shyness, and, to further the process, she forced herself to audition for the cheerleading squad. She was accepted into the pep group. By age sixteen, the blue-eyed beauty was entering beauty contests. This led to her (and her mother) doing a print ad for Breck shampoo and to Kim being spotted by Eileen Ford, who operates a celebrated modeling agency in New York City.

Ford offered Kim a modeling contract, but Basinger declined. Instead, she enrolled at the University of Georgia. Before the end of her first year, she had left college and moved to

Kim Basinger in the 1980s.
(Courtesy of Echo Book Shop)

New York to be a fashion model. From the start, she disliked the work, but it was a way to leave home, make a name for herself, and hopefully transition into a movie career. Before long Kim was earning $1,000 a day but still disliked her career. Never one to care about money management (she often came across uncashed checks she'd stashed away in a drawer), she also had little regard for money itself or how she spent it. For example, in one of her many moves within Manhattan, she bought a floor in a Greenwich Village apartment building and lost a good deal of money in the process. But, said the actress, "It didn't matter because I could make it so easily." Bored with her profession, she argued constantly with Ford regarding assignments (including a refusal to take bookings in Europe). She was much happier attending acting classes or strumming her guitar in Village cafés. Sometimes, she sang at club gigs using the name Chelsea.

In 1976, Basinger left modeling and New York to move to Los Angeles, accompanied by her then-boyfriend, model Dale Robinette. As they embarked on their cross-country car trip, she had Dale stop the car on the Brooklyn Bridge so that she could toss her modeling portfolio into the river. Once on the West Coast, her good looks soon got her small acting assignments on different TV shows. By early 1977, she was costarring in a police drama series, *Dog and Cat*, but it only lasted a few months. By the time of the TV movie *Katie: Portrait of a Centerfold* (1978), Kim had the lead role.

She made her theatrical movie debut in *Hard Country* (1981), a low-budget feature starring Jan-Michael Vincent. During the shoot, she met makeup artist Ron Britton, fifteen years her senior. Already star conscious, Kim demanded that her new boyfriend change his surname (which he did for a few weeks) and quit his profession (which he did recurrently) so that she would not be perceived as being involved with someone beneath her class in the industry. The couple wed in October 1980 with Ron becoming her de facto business manager. In 1983, she was in the James Bond action entry *Never Say Never Again* and received positive notices for her "golden-eagle elegance." She received even more attention that February for her striking *Playboy* magazine layout.

While Basinger despised playing a sexual slave in *9½ Weeks* (1986), the critically lambasted picture proved a sizeable moneymaker and won her industry attention. Wanting to play comedy, she happily accepted lead roles in such films as *My Stepmother Is an Alien* (1988). In the past, Kim had been rumored to continue relationships with her leading men off the soundstage, but during the making of *Batman* (1989), she became involved with her producer, Jon Peters. It was the final straw for her faltering marriage to Britton, and they divorced in December 1988. She paid him $8,000 monthly alimony and made the mortgage payments on their San Fernando Valley home where he continued to reside.

There had been talk that once she was single again, Kim would wed her Australian personal fitness trainer, but that relationship fizzled. Instead, she bonded with singer/musician Prince who had written songs for *Batman*. The singer was five years her junior and five inches shorter than she. Kim moved to Minneapolis to be with Prince and joined him in a rock music video, "Scandalous Sex Suite." During her midwestern sojourn, she recorded an album ("Now people will be able to see what I can do") but later, unhappy with the results, vetoed releasing it. She was to have starred on screen with Prince, but their sudden breakup led to Ingrid Chavez replacing her in his *Graffiti Bridge* (1990).

For a former model, Kim failed to display much fashion sense, at least according to fashion designer Mr. Blackwell. He rated her one of the worst-dressed women of 1989 ("This parading peep show should be banished to the back cave"). But Basinger didn't care. Her career was going well. She was soon costarring for $2.5 million in a film comedy (1991's *The Marrying Man*) and, during production, began an intense affair with costar Alec Baldwin. From the start, they seemed to bring out the worst in each other. Their demands, tardiness on the set, temper tantrums, and arguments with the film's producers and Disney Studio were so over-the-top that they became the talk of the town. (Later, a national magazine published a full account of the gory details on the *Marrying Man* set.) Basinger and Baldwin's attitudes and actions on the picture led one movie staffer to insist, "Honest to God, if I were destitute and living on the street with no food and somebody offered me $1 million to work with Kim and Alec, I'd pass." When released, *The Marrying Man* was a commercial and artistic bust.

In the early 1990s, Kim made an occasional movie (for example, 1993's *Wayne's World 2*), but her life was now engulfed in litigation that originated when she reneged on an alleged oral contract to star in the picture *Boxing Helena* (1993). The case went to trial and Basinger ended with a $9 million (later reduced) judgment against her. She declared bankruptcy, which included bailing out of her involvement with her investment group to modernize/commercialize Braselton, Georgia. Baldwin stuck by her through the ordeal—even helping out financially—and the couple married in August 1993. Returning to work, she costarred with Alec in the heist yarn *The Getaway* (1994). In October of 1995, she gave birth to their child, Ireland Eliesse. When Alec brought Kim and the baby home from the hospital, he got into a scuffle with paparazzi camped out in front of their house. This led to another court case for the Baldwins.

After winning her Oscar for 1997's *L.A. Confidential*, Kim did not make another movie until 2000's *I Dreamed of Africa*, followed by such pictures as *People I Know* and *8 Mile* (both 2002) and *Aurora Island* (2003). Meanwhile, her stormy marriage to Baldwin had crumpled. He wanted to live on the East Coast and enter politics, she wished to remain in Los Angeles and, because of her agoraphobia, shuddered at the thought of becoming a politician's wife. She filed for a divorce in January 2001, which became final in February 2002. But the tabloids reported that Kim was so intimidated by her belligerent ex-spouse—who supposedly wanted to be back in her life beyond just visits with Ireland—that she hired a bodyguard to protect her from him.

Having belatedly received recognition within the film industry, Kim is still enthralled with the movie business—at least parts of it: "I truly love this business between action and cut, but there's a certain energy out there that wants to bring down somebody who's on their way up. . . . There's an element of 'let's find something on somebody so we can bring them down.' It's not about the truth. It's about seeing people squirm." But when one presents such a wide target over the years, what's the poor media to do?

Clara Bow

[Clara Gordon Bow]

July 29, 1905–September 27, 1965

Seldom has one personality so symbolized a decade as Bow did the Roaring Twenties. She shot to fame during the heyday of the silent cinema, where her youth, beauty, and uninhibited vivacity mesmerized moviegoers and made her a top star. Off camera, this archetypal flapper *appeared* to lead a wonderfully madcap existence. Her unbridled behavior titillated the public. Many fans wished they might share in her fun-filled, often-risqué times as she zoomed along in her Kissel convertible (painted to match her dyed fiery red hair). To much of the public, Hollywood's "It Girl" seemed to have everything: money, fame, power, and a major movie studio dancing to her every whim.

In reality, Clara was one of life's perpetual victims, who had endured a horrendous childhood. Later, in Hollywood, the poorly educated, emotionally precarious Bow was exploited by her studio bosses and frequently by her entourage of leeching relatives, acquaintances, and lovers. She was unprepared to exercise the power of her fame and, in her desperation to find happiness, she often made unwise choices. Caught up in bewildering

celebrityhood, tangled love alliances, and increasingly reckless behavior, she became more uncertain and negative about her acting career. Clara's fears about her professional future were soon accentuated by the trauma of adapting to talkie movies. By the early 1930s, the Great Depression had changed America's mood and created new screen types (for example, the brassy, self-sufficient dame). Amid scandal and a subsequent short-lived comeback, Clara's film career vanished. The former jazz baby became a relic from a bygone era, leaving her perplexed at how her life had gone so wrong.

She was born in a Brooklyn tenement apartment in 1905, the offspring of Robert Bow, a sometime busboy in slum restaurants, and his wife Sarah (Gordon) Bow. Sarah, who suffered from epilepsy, emotional problems, and depression about her difficult life, had seen her first two babies—both girls—die shortly after birth. She had expected—even hoped—the same would happen to this latest, unwanted child. During Sarah's pregnancy with Clara, her irresponsible, heavy-drinking husband deserted her, returning only when he learned the newborn had survived unexpectedly.

In the next few years, Robert dropped in and out of his family's life, leaving the ill-equipped Sarah to raise their child. Sometimes Sarah turned to prostitution to keep food on the table, as they moved from one slum apartment to another. As Clara matured, she fastened on moviegoing as an escape from her blighted childhood. She dreamed of becoming a film actress one day, hoping to find security in that magic world. But the youngster feared

Katherine De Mille (left) and Clara Bow (right) on the set of *Love Among the Millionaires* (1930).
(Courtesy of JC Archives)

sharing this dream with her mother because Mrs. Bow believed movies were the devil's work and something Clara must avoid at all costs. As the girl grew older, her father sometimes reappeared in her life and, during one of these periodic stays, began to sexually molest her. Because she was so desperate for her father's love, she excused his abuse (as she would his later financial demands), telling herself that she must remain loyal to him.

In 1921, Clara wheedled a dollar from her father to enter a movie magazine contest and won a screen test in New York City. It led to her movie debut that year in *Beyond the Rain-*

bow, although most of her scenes from this silent photoplay ended on the cutting room floor. When Mrs. Bow learned of Clara's moviemaking perfidy, it triggered a mad reaction. One night, the sixteen-year-old girl awakened to find her mother standing over her with a butcher knife, screaming, "You'd be better off dead than an actress!" Although Clara escaped her mother's wrath, she claimed later that she could never again sleep through a full night.

By 1923, Clara had made more movies and been offered a Hollywood film contract. (Earlier in the year, her mother, suffering from untreated epilepsy and mental illness, had died just prior to her recommitment to a mental asylum.) At Preferred Pictures in California, her employer, B. P. Schulberg, charmed the unsophisticated Clara and exploited her financially in the coming years. She made several films before she really caught on with moviegoers as the high-spirited flapper in *The Plastic Age* (1925). Within two years, Schulberg became a top executive at Paramount Pictures and he took his prized moneymaker with him. *It* (1927) turned Bow into a major box-office star, a status reinforced by the same year's World War I epic *Wings*.

Shortly after Clara first went to Hollywood, she had a live-in lover, agent Arthur Jacobson, whom she'd known on the East Coast. A while later, Bow allowed her shiftless father to move to Los Angeles, and the jealous man succeeded in breaking up the couple. During the making of *Mantrap* (1926), the actress fell in love with director Victor Fleming, which complicated her ongoing romance with actor Gilbert Roland. Bow's colead in *Children of Divorce* (1927) was lanky Gary Cooper with whom she had a passionate romance. All these relationships fizzled, but she was most sorry about losing Fleming. In 1927, gossip arose over Clara's supposed carousing with the entire University of Southern California football squad. It was more lurid fantasy than reality, although she did hostess wild get-togethers with gridiron heroes at her Garden of Allah apartment hideaway, where she could escape her intrusive father who lived at her modest Bedford Drive home.

The undisciplined Clara was a full-time problem for Paramount Pictures. She tested the studio's patience with her bouts of gambling, her raucous treks to Mexico, and her other unrestrained activities. However, not only was she a great breadwinner for the studio, but the hugely popular actress was also receiving a comparatively low salary given her enormous worth to Paramount. Thus, for the time being, the film company ran interference with the media whenever Hollywood's prettiest playgirl indulged in her latest indiscretion.

In February 1928, when Clara underwent an appendectomy at a Los Angeles hospital, the surgery made national headlines. One of the interns at the facility was handsome William Earl Pearson. Bow became intrigued with the twenty-seven-year-old despite learning that he had a wife back in Texas. It led to a romance, even after the fledgling doctor's spouse threatened to sue Bow for alienation of affection. Paramount stepped in and paid off the angered woman. The crafty executives did not dip into their own coffers but instead used $56,000 taken from Clara's bonus-per-movie fund, which had been kept from Bow as a wedge to curtail her indiscreet behavior.

Bow made her talkie debut in 1929's *The Wild Party*, and, despite her Brooklyn twang, critics and filmgoers alike accepted her speaking voice. Still very popular, Clara did not have the business sense to demand a higher salary from the studio or to invest her weekly income of $5,000 wisely. During this period, Clara had a brief affair with her *Wild Party* costar, Fredric March, but that was nothing compared to her entanglement with popular song-and-dance man Harry Richman. He was in Hollywood making *Puttin' on the Ritz* (1930) and romanced Bow largely in hopes of trading on her fame and adding to his reputation as the supreme ladies' man. As Harry anticipated, the Bow-Richman on-again, off-again romance made great headlines. Meanwhile, Paramount held its collective breath hoping Bow's shenanigans, with and without Harry, would not further mar her already declining box-office standing. (By now, her future at the studio was problematic. Due to ongoing fears about performing in sound films, she'd lost much of her enthusiasm for picturemaking. She also still fantasized about giving up the business for marriage and a family.)

The beginning of the end of Clara's career occurred in January 1931, when she charged Daisy DeVoe, her former secretary (who'd previously been a studio hairdresser) with thirty-seven counts of grand theft. Gutsy Daisy went on the offensive by letting details leak out about the movie star's wild ways. By the time the high-publicity trial ended, DeVoe had been given a relatively short sentence and would serve only a year in prison. On the other hand, Clara's reputation with the public had been virtually destroyed.

In the past, the overworked and very hard-playing Clara had suffered from physical exhaustion. Now the trauma of the DeVoe fracas led Bow to suffer a nervous breakdown. On physician's orders, she recuperated at a sanatorium. Thereafter Paramount and Bow agreed to end her contract. Instead of following through on job offers from other studios who still had faith in her bankability, Clara eloped to Las Vegas in December 1931 with cowboy actor Rex Bell. The newlyweds moved to his ranch in Searchlight, Nevada. Later, having dropped some of the weight she gained during retirement, she returned to make *Call Her Savage* (1932) and *Hoopla* (1933). She then quit the movies for good. The Bells had two sons (born in 1934 and 1938). The marriage was troubled by her emotional problems and his strong interest in politics (which went against her need to lead a private life). The couple mostly lived apart, especially after he was elected lieutenant

The movies' vivacious It Girl had a golden rule in life: "Never lie to a man unless you absolutely know you can get away with it." This came in handy, because in the 1920s "I went everywhere and did everything." Her many sexual flings included coplayers Gary Cooper, John Gilbert, Bela Lugosi (the star of 1931's *Dracula*), Fredric March, and Gilbert Roland, as well as directors Victor Fleming and A. Edward Sutherland. One of her more serious liaisons was with hard-living Broadway/club performer Harry Richman, a man famed for his sexual prowess/endurance. Pretty Clara once gave her boyfriend a picture of herself inscribed, "To My Gorgeous Lover, Harry. I'll trade all my It for your That."

governor of Nevada in 1954 and again in 1958. He died of a heart attack in mid-1962 while campaigning for the Nevada governorship.

Clara's last years were spent in seclusion in Culver City, California, where she lived modestly, attended by a nurse/companion. In September 1965, while watching an old movie on TV, she died at her bungalow. The former star was buried at Forest Lawn Memorial Park in Glendale, California, in a vault adjacent to her husband's.

Bow had once planned to write a tell-all autobiography but later changed her mind. She reasoned it would upset her sons and their families. Explained Clara with typical understatement, "There are many things in my life that might possibly cause them embarrassment."

Louise Brooks

[Mary Louise Brooks]
November 14, 1906–August 8, 1985

To be artistic, intellectual, avant-garde, and uninhibited are wonderful assets for any performer. On the other hand, if the entertainer exhibits self-destructive behavior in the guise of impracticality and a lack of diplomacy, that individual's life can easily turn from heaven to hell. Such was the case with Brooks who, in the 1920s, was considered by many movie reviewers to be the most vibrant of Hollywood's screen flappers. Many decades later, several worldly movie critics judged that the five-foot, two-inch actress, who usually wore her shiny black hair in a bob, perhaps possessed the cinema's most sensual image ever!

Mary Louise Brooks was born in 1906 in Cherryvale, Kansas, the second of four children of Leonard Peter Brooks, an attorney, and his much younger wife, Myra Rude. Her mother, the eldest child of a large family, had no real enthusiasm for raising another brood. Thus she generally left them to their own devices as she pursued her own interest in music. From an early age, Mary Louise was drawn to dancing, and she made her artistic debut at four by performing in a church-given production of *Tom Thumb's Wedding*. When she was twelve, the family relocated, first to Independence and then to Wichita, Kansas. In a more sophisticated environment, the teenager expanded her dancing repertoire as she performed for local groups. At age fourteen, boy-crazy Mary Louise became sexually involved with an established businessman in town.

With her love for dance, Brooks attended performances by visiting troupes whenever possible. On one such occasion, in November 1921, she saw the Denishawn dance company perform. She was intrigued by its cofounder, Ted Shawn, and went backstage after the show. He mentioned the company's training school in New York and suggested she apply. With her mother's blessing and her father providing the tuition, she and a chaperone (who quickly proved ineffective at supervising her wild charge) embarked for Manhattan in July 1922.

Louise Brooks—as she now called herself—became a dedicated member of Denishawn's arduous training program. She toured the United States with one of the school's performance companies from 1922 through 1924. Despite the creativity of her dance life, Louise felt artistically restricted, hating the regimentation demanded of the troupe; it made her petulant and rebellious. She took out her excess energy by being promiscuous with tour crew members and men she met on the road. Eventually there was a showdown. Ruth St. Dennis fired Louise at the end of the 1923–24 season. It upset Brooks that her rejection had been based on the quality of her personal life. However, Louise, who had something of a persecution complex, convinced herself that the firing was an example of the world's mistreatment of her.

Determined not to return to Kansas, the seventeen-year-old found employment in the chorus line of *George White's Scandals* in mid-1924. With her dancing pedigree and uppity ways, Brooks was not a favorite with her peers, and her defiant attitude caused her difficulties with White. However, as one of the producer's famous showgirls, her social life increased. Before long, the too-playful Louise was asked by the management of the Algonquin Hotel where she stayed to find other living quarters. By the end of 1924, Brooks was overwhelmed by her hectic lifestyle. Without giving White notice, she quit the *Scandals* and sailed to England with a friend. By February 1925, Louise was back in New York as a cast member of the Florenz Ziegfeld–produced musical, *Louis the 14th*. A few months later, rather than fire the disruptive, frequently tardy Brooks, Ziegfeld switched her to his summer

edition of the *Follies*. There she became friendly with another chorus member, Peggy Fears, who was rumored to be bisexual.

In the summer of 1925, Louise had a two-month affair with screen comedy king Charlie Chaplin, who was in New York on business and vacation. Later in the year, the restless Brooks, anxious to expand beyond the monotony of her *Follies* chores, made her film debut. She played a gun moll in the silent photoplay, *The Streets of Forgotten Men* (1925), shot at Paramount's Long Island studio. It led to a five-year studio contract, which Brooks accepted "just for the money" rather than any great desire to be in pictures. Meanwhile, she caused a sensation when she brought action against a theatrical photographer and prevented him from exhibiting draped nude shots of her. She thought the pictures' circulation might ruin her chances for marriage.

Louise's fourth Paramount picture shot on the East Coast was *It's the Old Army Game* (1926). During production, she was courted by the picture's director, A. Edward Sutherland. Eleven years her senior, the British-born filmmaker had ended his marriage to silent film actress Marjorie Daw in 1925. He and Brooksie (as friends called her) wed in July 1926. Although she liked Sutherland well enough, she was still deeply in love with actor William (Buster) Collier Jr., with whom she had worked in *Just Another Blonde* (1926). But Buster was too close to his mother and had already returned to the West Coast. Brooks and Sutherland had a two-day honeymoon before he rushed back to California to start a new film. She stayed in New York to make—

on loan to Fox—*Love 'Em and Leave 'Em* (1926).

The picture, including Brooks's performance, was well reviewed. However, it was her last picture shot on the East Coast, as she went to Los Angeles to be with her husband and to work at Paramount's Hollywood facility.

Louise made five features in 1927, including *Rolled Stockings*, which solidified her screen image as the carefree, emancipated flapper. Off camera, her marriage was mostly in name only. She and Sutherland were hardly ever in the same city at the same time, and, when apart, each had grown increasingly accustomed to finding pleasures with new companions. Buster Collier was still part of Brooks's life, as was well-to-do laundry king George Preston Marshall, whom she had met a few years earlier on the East Coast. William Wellman directed Louise in *Beggars of Life* (1928), and her playing of the girl-dressed-as-a-boy on the lam was one of her most dimensional roles. In June of that year, Brooks divorced Sutherland, citing "extreme cruelty" in her legal action.

While making *The Canary Murder Case* in 1928, Louise was summoned to the studio's executive offices. Now making $750 weekly, her contract provided a raise to $1,000 weekly if her option was taken up. By now, as Hollywood transitioned from silents to talkies, the film companies were being very stringent about plant overhead, unsure of what the future might bring. Her friend, executive Walter Wanger, was no longer at Paramount and instead she met with B. P. Schulberg. He casually informed her she could remain at the studio for the same $750 weekly. On impulse, she

Louise Brooks in *Pandora's Box* (1929).
(Courtesy of JC Archives)

said no thanks and departed the studio once her *Canary* chores were finished.

Thereafter, accompanied by her lover, George Marshall, Louise sailed for Europe. En route, Florenz Ziegfeld cabled her to offer her the lead in a pending Broadway production. Marshall intercepted the telegram and sent back a reply: "You couldn't offer me enough money to do it." Unaware of her companion's meddling, Brooks went on to Germany to make a silent *Pandora's Box* (1929) for G. W.

Pabst. This was followed by another silent (*Diary of a Lost Girl*) the same year for the same director. Both were highly innovative and highly erotic, but they were badly censored/edited when finally released in the States. Then, too, American moviegoers only wanted to see talkies.

On a return visit to America, Louise was contacted by Paramount who asked—then begged—her to come back to Hollywood to shoot sound sequences that would make *The Canary Murder Case* (1929) more viable to filmgoers. Indifferent to her future, she refused their final, generous offer of $10,000 to do the scenes. (Paramount finally used a stand-in for the needed footage.) Brooks's latest rejection of Hollywood ruined her reputation with the major studios. Through contacts, however, she grabbed an occasional assignment (such as 1931's *God's Gift to Women*).

Broke and disheartened, Louise fell back on a new marriage to resolve her problems. She wed wealthy Chicago playboy Deering Davis in October 1933. For a brief spell, they formed a society dance act, but their relationship quickly fell apart and they divorced in February 1938. Brooks joined another dance act in New York City; one of her lovers during this period was William Paley, the rising media industry magnate. By now, a few studios had made offers for Louise to return to pictures, but the deals never materialized.

In 1936, a projected comeback project with G. W. Pabst fell through, and Louise, already in Hollywood, accepted a comedown role in a pedestrian Buck Jones Western, *Empty Saddles*. Her final movie was another sagebrush tale—1938's *Overland Stage Raiders*, starring John Wayne. At age thirty-two, her movie career was gone.

In the 1940s, Louise had infrequent jobs on radio but finally abandoned show business altogether. Late in the decade, she was a sales clerk in New York City. By the end of the forties, she was a recluse. Her dismal life did a turnabout when, in the mid-1950s, critics and movie buffs rediscovered her from the screening of several of her old pictures in the United States and abroad. By 1956, she had relocated to Rochester, New York, at the prompting of a curator (James Card) for the George Eastman House film collection. It led to her studying movies, and she began writing for film journals. In the sixties, her working relationship with Card fell apart, and she broke from him as she did from her newly found faith in Catholicism. More bleak years passed for astute but embittered Louise in upstate New York. In 1982, *Lulu in Hollywood*—her well-crafted book of reminiscences and observations on old Tinseltown—was published. In August 1985, she died of a heart attack in Rochester, New York. At the time, she was, as in so many of her last years, alone and broke.

Later on, actor and photographer Roddy McDowall, who'd known Brooks in her writing years, would say of the tragic muse, "She was on some personal vendetta against herself. . . . It was part of that volatile, pyrotechnical personality—when she was young she must have been like a whirling dervish. . . . She had no respect for herself as an actress. . . . She was so difficult because she couldn't accept the full measure of the regard people had for her."

Brett Butler

[Brett Anderson]

JANUARY 30, 1958–

In past decades, when comediennes such as Lucille Ball or Carol Burnett first headlined their own TV series, they had already been well trained under the old movie studio system or by working in theater or smaller TV jobs. They already knew how to work with production teams and handle the cumulative stress that would come from starring in a weekly TV show. On the other hand, recent prime-time TV female comedy stars (for example, Paula Poundstone, Ellen DeGeneres, Roseanne) have largely emerged from the world of stand-up comedy. That brutal training ground is a hotbed of cutthroat competition. In addition, these funsters constantly have to struggle to survive the exhausting years of one-night gigs on the road. Such tough work experience teaches the stand-up comedienne to be very self-sufficient and self-confident, and to work as a one-person entertainment entity who shares the spotlight with no one. In this rugged club arena, being highly individualistic in personality and comedy routines is a keynote to success. Thus, such laughmakers are hardly prepared to work as part of an ensemble with the cast and crew of a weekly TV program. Being thrust suddenly into a high-profile situation in which the comedienne must adjust to great fame *and* to being part of the show's team can lead to disaster on the TV studio set. Such was the case with Brett Butler, the queen

bee of the TV sitcom *Grace Under Fire* (1993–98).

Brett was born in 1958 in Montgomery, Alabama, the first of three daughters of Robert Decatur Anderson Jr., a public relations executive, and his wife, Carol Jean Parker. The parents had an abusive relationship, which ended when Brett was four. For a while, Carol and her three children stayed with Carol's parents in Marietta, Georgia. Later, Carol and her parents had an argument over her unsettled lifestyle, and she relocated with her girls to Miami, Florida, where she worked for a physician. Short of cash, they lived a precarious existence. Later, Carol met Bob Butler and they married. Her parents paid for a house in Marietta for the newlyweds so that the family of five could move back to Georgia. Butler, a traveling salesman, adopted Carol's offspring. The Butlers had two children together, but their marriage fell apart in 1971. Suddenly thirteen-year-old Brett found herself caring for her four siblings, while her depressed mother often slept away the day. To relieve the stress of the situation, Brett began watching comedians perform stand-up on TV. She came to appreciate the magical power comics had to make audiences laugh and forget their troubles for a time.

In 1974, Carol, who still suffered from recurring bouts of depression, entered a suburban Atlanta hospital to deal with her problems. Brett felt abandoned and angry. Rather than live with relatives as her sisters did, she struck out on her own. She quit school and worked as a waitress. She found refuge in a menu of sex, alcohol, and marijuana. Eventually, she completed high school at night and enrolled at Southern Technical Institute, a branch of the University of Georgia, but her stay there wasn't long. She went back to waitressing and her assorted addictive behaviors. In 1978, twenty-year-old Brett met (at a pool hall) and later married Charles "Mike" Wilson who was three years her senior. According to Butler, their relationship turned violent, and once, during an argument, he fired a shot at her. He turned around and left, and the couple separated. A few weeks later, on May 31, an inebriated Butler had a close call with death. Her car spun out of control, went off the road, slammed into a mailbox, and then plowed into adjacent trees. She was rushed to an Atlanta hospital where she was treated. She was also arrested for drunk driving and taken to jail. Released on her own recognizance, the first-time offender was later ordered by the court to pay a $250 fine and to attend traffic school.

By 1982, Carol Butler was living in Houston, Texas, and Brett joined her there. That spring, on a Monday open-mike night at a local comedy club, Brett debuted as a stand-up comic. It fulfilled a dream she had nurtured for some time, and, having done it, she liked the experience. She began appearing regularly at comedy venues in Houston. However, outspoken Butler, whose favorite comedy targets were her father and ex-husband, was too forward-thinking and indecorous (with her sex jokes) for conservative Houstonians. It prompted Brett to relocate back to Atlanta in 1984. There she found club audiences more accepting of her liberal point of view and her barrage of comical observations about tacky life in the

Brett Butler speaking out at the People's Choice Awards in 1994.
(Photo by Albert L. Ortega)

South. The next year she moved to New York City, determined to break into the big time. She did stand-up comedy, often working for $10 an appearance. To ease the pain of the struggle, she turned to drinking again. By 1986, her hard work paid off and she was headling at Manhattan comedy clubs. Her dream of appearing on *The Tonight Show Starring Johnny Carson* came true on May 14, 1987. She was well received and asked back again. Gleeful over her breakthrough, she and boyfriend Ken Zeiger, a twenty-five-year-old law student, wed that August.

Brett's comedic prowess came to the attention of country singer Dolly Parton. The latter was hosting a new variety show on ABC in the fall of 1987. Butler was hired to write for the program and went to Los Angeles. The program barely lasted a season and Brett, who hated the experience, vowed never to live in Tinseltown again. Back on the comedy club circuit, she freshened up her professional look by changing from brunette to blond and adopting a more contemporary wardrobe. One thing hadn't changed for the five-foot, seven-inch talent—she was still using drugs and drink.

By 1992, an exhausted Brett was thinking of quitting the business. Then she had a lucky break. A New York club owner was asked by the casting director of the Carsey-Werner Company (which produced *Roseanne* and other TV comedies) if he could suggest a female stand-up comic for a new blue-collar sitcom they were prepping. Brett was mentioned. She flew to Los Angeles to audition and soon was hired to star on *Grace Under Fire*. The role was of a feisty divorcée struggling to raise her three children on her own while working at an oil refinery.

Everything should have been wonderful for Butler (and her lawyer husband), with her upcoming national showcase and her greatly improved finances. However, almost from the start, there was dissension on the set. Butler and executive producer Chuck Lorre clashed over their creative differences. She felt that, since she was the star of the show, she should be treated as such. In interviews and on the set, she displayed a lack of humility that was not appreciated by her fellow workers.

The sitcom debuted on September 29, 1993, and within a few weeks was ranked a solid hit. That was enough for Brett to demand more control over "her" show. She also wanted more money. With the series already so popular, she got her way, including a salary raise to $50,000 per segment (which later escalated to nearly $200,000 per segment). But the situation on the set did not improve. During script readings and rehearsals, the Hollywood newcomer was temperamental and often cussed out her coworkers (especially the scriptwriters, who were the most frequent targets of her viciousness). Meanwhile, on the home front, she and her husband had personality clashes and separated. But as far as the public was concerned, everything was going perfectly for Butler and her hit series, which often ranked in the top five. In May 1994, she received a People's Choice Award for her work on *Grace Under Fire*.

Season number two (1994–95) saw the arrival of a new executive producer. Again, Brett and he conflicted. She was guilty of more outbursts on the set, where her anger might flare at anyone. Butler was on a power trip, but no one in charge was willing to disturb the successful show. During this time, the high-profile star underwent breast implant surgery and, being an exhibitionist, felt the need to show

The TV sitcom *Grace Under Fire* (1993–98) survived enough seasons for its stand-up comedy star to become a holy terror on the set. Like Roseanne, Butler was notorious for being abrasive with her writing staff. She was frequently displeased with their efforts. At one production summit meeting, she suggested, "Why don't you write your next script on Kleenex? That way when you hand it in, we'll have some use for it!"

one and all her new additions. By now, her bad behavior on the *Grace Under Fire* set was the buzz of the industry. However, nothing changed on the show except that Brett was made a coexecutive producer of the series in April 1995. It was hoped this gesture would please Butler, but she remained edgy and dissatisfied.

In 1995, Brett and her husband reconciled and moved into a big home in the Hollywood Hills. She wrote her autobiography, *Knee Deep in Paradise*. That summer she hurt her back and was prescribed painkillers. She didn't stop taking them. The third season began and things continued to deteriorate. Sometimes she ordered the script changed on a daily basis. At a Friday night taping in early January 1996, Butler for some reason lifted up her skirt in front of twelve-year-old Jon Paul Steuer, who played her son on the show. He was embarrassed and asked her to stop. She didn't. That April, the boy quit the series and had to be replaced.

By the fourth season (1996–97), Brett was even more out of control, often becoming, in the view of others on the series, incoherent. That October, friends and family conducted an intervention, but she refused to enter a substance abuse facility. She tried outpatient treat-

ment but soon quit. By the spring of 1997, *Grace Under Fire* had dropped from its once-high ratings to number sixty-one on the charts. The series continued, management determined to reach at least one hundred episodes, which is considered the minimum number of segments needed to make a lucrative syndication deal.

In the summer of 1997, the sitcom taped three episodes for its upcoming fifth season, but after that the increasingly confused Butler could not go on. She entered a substance abuse center in Malibu. However, when she returned to the show that December, her problems and addictions were still very much with her. One Friday night in early 1998 during the *Grace* taping in front of a studio audience, Brett flew into a rage. She shouted expletives at Tom Straw, the fifth and latest executive producer hired for the troubled show. As Butler argued with him, she flung a half-full can of soda at him. A few days later after another taping, Carsey-Werner announced it was suspending production so that the star could deal with her personal problems. The show's last episode— its 112th—aired on February 17, 1998.

Later in 1998, Butler entered a rehab facility and began attending twelve-step meetings. The next spring, she and husband Ken Zeiger divorced. In 2000, it was announced that Butler and ABC (which had aired *Grace Under Fire*) were working on a pilot for a new TV series, but the show did not materialize. To keep busy—and to regain industry standing—Brett began performing on the comedy club circuit again. It was almost like starting all over.

As Butler acknowledged to the media a few years ago, "I lost a lot and I created a great deal of wreckage and I don't have anyone to blame but myself."

Mariah Carey

[**Mariah Carey**]

MARCH 27, 1970–

"If you see me as just the princess, then you misunderstand who I am and what I have been through," insists the five-foot, nine-inch Carey, with her glorious multioctave voice that moves seamlessly from serious ballads to hip-hop flavored dance pop. Who is the real Carey? For one thing, she is a person who fulfilled her life's dream by becoming a professional songster. ("There's never been anything else in my life that inspired me at all. It's crazy, but I've always loved music and I've always known this was what I wanted to do. I can't remember a time when I didn't want to be a singer.") Since the release of her first album (*Mariah Carey*) in 1990, she has won many industry awards, made millions of dollars from album sales, gained tremendous fame, and enjoyed a pampered life full of material splendor. However, she has also suffered from the strains of her high-pressure career, and those around her have often felt the brunt of her growing stress.

In the highly competitive music business, a performer must maintain high public visibility. However, the emotionally sensitive Mariah has admitted in the past, "It's hard to be someone that people talk about and write about, you know? They don't know me." She proved to be a vulnerable person who, despite great professional success, remained racked by insecurities: "I always felt like the rug could be pulled out from under me at any time. And coming from a racially mixed background, I always felt like I didn't really fit in anywhere." She also had to deal with ongoing rumors that her career was jump-started because of her special relationship with the head of a major record label. It made her extremely defensive: "People all of a sudden just see me and hear me having hit records and it seems to have come out of the blue. But really I have been working toward this my whole life, and this is what I say when people say I haven't paid my dues." Unfortunately, along the way, others had to pay her dues as well.

She was born in 1970 in Huntington, Long Island, New York, the third child of Alfred Carey, an aeronautics engineer, and Patricia Hickey, an opera singer and voice coach. Her father was of African American and Venezuelan descent, while her mother was the offspring of Irish immigrants and had grown up in the Midwest. The interracial marriage caused the newlyweds great problems—not only with her bigoted family but with intolerant neighbors as the couple moved from one predominantly white Long Island town to another. When Mariah (named after the song "They Call the Wind Mariah" from the musical *Paint Your Wagon*) was two, her parents separated and, the next year, divorced. After the split, Mariah and her brother Morgan stayed with their mother while sister Alison lived with her dad. Life became a financial struggle for Mrs. Carey, who expanded her work as a vocal coach to sustain her household. Sometimes the trio had to bunk down at friends' apartments.

Despite the distractions of work, Mrs. Carey found time to give precocious young Mariah music lessons. The girl also learned to appreciate gospel music from rare visits to her paternal grandmother. When Mariah was six, the first-grader made her music debut singing "Honey Bun" in a high school production of *South Pacific*. During her childhood, she suffered from racial discrimination and felt like an outcast among her peers. This situation was exacerbated by her refusal to call herself either black or white, insisting instead that she was "black, Venezuelan, and Irish."

When Mariah was ten, her mother had saved enough money so that the family could set up permanent headquarters in Huntington Bay on Long Island. Glad to be settled into a more stable environment, the youngster still suffered from living in a neighborhood where everyone had more and better material possessions than she did. At age fourteen, the future star worked after school singing on

Mariah Carey meeting the media.
(Photo by Albert L. Ortega)

demo records at Long Island recording studios. When she entered high school, she was already writing songs and telling friends that she was going to be a professional singer. With this goal in mind, she grew bored with many of her classes, especially math. She frequently cut school to do something music related or because she'd been up too late the night before, writing songs or out listening to music at parties or clubs. Discouraged teachers called Carey "the Mirage" because she was seemingly never there. Her writing partner at the time was young Ben Margulies.

Days after graduating from Harborfields High School in spring 1987, Carey moved to Manhattan. She shared a seedy apartment with two other girls and supported herself through odd jobs. Most of her time was devoted to making the rounds of record companies, trying to get someone to listen to her demos. Through a musician friend, she met R&B singer Brenda K. Starr, who hired Mariah as one of her backup singers for live shows. One Friday evening in November 1988, Starr took Carey with her to a music business party. There the eighteen-year-old met Tommy Mottola, the head of CBS Columbia Records. She gave him a demo tape, which the powerful executive thrust into his pocket. As the legend goes, while being driven home from the gathering in his limousine, he listened to Carey's cassette. Mottola was so impressed that he returned to the party looking for Mariah. She had already gone, but he made contact with her the following Monday. Weeks later, Carey signed a recording contract with CBS Columbia.

During much of 1989, Mariah recorded an album, using many of the songs she and Ben Margulies had written in recent years. During this period, her relationship with the almost twenty-year-older Mottola developed roman-

tically. Since he was still married, the growing bond was kept low-key. By the end of June 1990, her first disc, *Mariah Carey*, had debuted at number eighty on the music charts. Before long she had two number-one hits (including "Love Takes Time") and, in February 1991, won two Grammy Awards. By that August, her second album (*Emotions*) had debuted high on the charts, and her career was in high gear. Already coworkers from her road-to-fame were dropping by the wayside, including Margulies who had a contractual dispute with the rising diva.

In 1993, rich and famous Carey married the now-divorced Tommy Mottola at St. Thomas Episcopal Church in New York City. Cost was no obstacle for the lavish event. She wore a $25,000 wedding gown and $1,000 designer shoes. Among the three hundred celebrity guests were Barbra Streisand, Billy Joel, and Gloria Estefan. Following a honeymoon in Hawaii, the couple settled into dual residences: a plush Upper West Side Manhattan apartment in New York City and a spectacular $10 million home (on a sixty-acre estate) in Bedford in upstate New York. Mariah embarked on her first major U.S. tour, debuting in Miami in November 1993. She was obviously nervous during the live concert, and many of the local critics were unkind in their reviews. Angry at the slights, Carey lashed out at everyone. When the prima donna calmed down, she agreed that it would be more productive to channel her anger into relaxing more during her upcoming performances. It worked, but it still did not make life easy for those around the rags-to-riches princess.

By 1996, industry veteran Carey had released six albums and was used to fighting for the things she wanted. Her disintegrating marriage was no longer one of them. She was tired of her husband's Svengali-like control over her career and disheartened by the lack of mutuality in their interests. When she began asserting her independence, he became even more controlling. (A very public outburst between the couple occurred after the Grammys in 1995 where she did not win even one trophy.) In December 1996, Carey moved out of her Bedford, New York, home. (Their official separation was announced in May 1997 and she received her divorce in March 1998.)

Now a freewheeling single woman, she created a new sexy image for herself. She dated (first very quietly, then openly) New York Yankees shortstop Derek Jeter. That came to an end, and, by late 1998, she was involved with Latin singing star Luis Miguel. While her love life seemed harmonious, her attitude toward professional rivals was not. For example, she was with friends at a New York club in May 1999 when she spotted the arrival of Samantha Cole, a rising pop diva. An annoyed Carey reportedly chucked ice cubes across the room at her rival. When that didn't work, she supposedly asked club bouncers—without success—to remove Cole from the establishment.

Rainbow (1999) was Carey's last album for the Columbia label. Thereafter, she signed a $117 million, five-year contract with Virgin Records. Her debut album *Glitter* (2001) was tied into her first starring role in a feature film, the semiautobiographical *Glitter* due out the same year. Meanwhile, her life began unravel-

ing. Her high-profile relationship with Luis Miguel ended. In May 2001, while filming the movie *Wisegirls* (2002), she threw a hissy fit at costar Mira Sorvino, ending with Carey reportedly throwing a saltshaker at Oscar-winner Sorvino. During July, Mariah acted strangely in public appearances (including a bizarre outing on MTV's *Total Request Live* that left host Carson Daly stunned). In addition, the obviously distressed singing star sent rambling E-mail messages to fans on her website. Then, in late July, Mariah entered Silver Hill Sanitarium in New Canaan, Connecticut, to deal with "an emotional and physical breakdown."

Months later, seemingly recovered from her emotional problems, she faced the relatively poor response to her *Glitter* album. Mariah now became fixated on a perceived rivalry with hot Latina singing/acting star Jennifer Lopez, which led to public temper tantrums. Caving in to these self-induced pressures, Carey suffered a relapse and entered UCLA Medical Center. Thereafter, things did not improve. The movie *Glitter* finally opened in September 2001 and bombed. By early 2002, Virgin Records, unhappy with the weak performance of the *Glitter* album, negotiated a buyout of Carey's contract for $28 million. It was a public humiliation for the image-conscious singer. Adding to her woes, in July 2002 she had to cope with the death of her seventy-two-year-old father, who died of cancer at his home in Huntington Station, New York.

On the upside, Carey who once had to survive with one pair of worn-out sneakers, now had a glamorous Manhattan penthouse with a huge built-in closet to hold the many, many racks of shoes she owned. She began to recover from her 2001 career setbacks with her performance of "The Star-Spangled Banner" at the Super Bowl in February 2002. Her fit physical appearance at the event was the result of hard training at the Enchantment Health Spa in Sedona, Arizona. She contracted to make a new picture, *Sweet Science*, about an unknown female prizefighter who is guided by a resolute boxing manager. More important, in May 2002, she signed a three-album deal with Universal's Island Def Jam Music Group; the deal was worth more than $20 million and provided her with her own record label. Carey said she was happy to be "going to wherever the creative energy takes me." With her multifaceted career in high gear again, the question remains: Will this friendly alignment of moon and stars produce a new, kinder Mariah Carey?

Cher

[Cherilyn Sarkisian LaPiere]
MAY 20, 1946–

She is self-indulgent to the extreme, outrageous to a fault, opinionated beyond question, and sometimes foolish in career and life choices. On the other hand, Cher is an engaging talent who has successfully altered her musical style several times over the decades, has given memorable acting performances, and has long been a charismatic presence. Few women in the limelight have gotten away with

as much as this entertainer (and some people have never forgiven her for that). With her lanky five-foot, eight-inch frame, she has often worn the tackiest costumes possible to chic occasions (such as the Academy Awards) and still made a wild fashion statement with her daring ensembles.

She has been fearless in becoming a poster girl for tattoos, and she is as addicted as Joan Rivers to plastic surgery overhauls. In repeatedly changing her anatomy and overall look, she says defiantly, "It's my body and if I want to do it like Michael Jackson, I will. . . . If I wanna put my t*** on my back, they're *mine*!" On other topics, she has been equally blunt: "If I'd wanted to do drugs, I'd have done them. I just don't *like* them. They're stupid." (She also doesn't smoke and only drinks in moderation.) Having discarded two husbands, several musician lovers, and assorted boy toys, flippant Cher jokes about her colorful romantic life: "People thought I was sleeping with the entire Mormon Tabernacle Choir. They believe what they want to believe."

It is impossible to discuss Cher without mentioning the late Sonny Bono. He discovered, promoted, and teamed with her in recordings, movies, TV, and club engagements. They were married for over eleven years and had one child (Chastity) together. They symbolized the hippie/psychedelic era of the 1960s and 1970s. By the time they divorced in 1975, they were sharing their own love/hate relationship with the public. As their individual careers vacillated in subsequent years, their responses to each other also fluctuated. At one point, the former Mrs. Bono said of her ex,

Two Las Vegas headliners: Cher and veteran funnyman George Burns.

"We have absolutely nothing in common. I think he's a bit of a sad character." Later, after his death in a skiing accident in 1998, her attitude changed: "Sonny wanted recognition and he worked damn hard to get it. You may not have agreed with him, but I admired the length of his journey."

For his part, Sonny hated the fact that the strange young woman with so much innate talent grew up and no longer accepted being controlled by him. When she broke free of his Svengali-like control, it started an ongoing rivalry. Admitted Bono, "If I hadn't gotten into politics and won, I could never have held my head up after Cher became a movie star with an Oscar and everything." Like other battling duos, neither could ever shake the other's shadow. Their often unspoken need for each other was perhaps best said in their most famous duet, "I Got You Babe."

Cher was born in El Centro, California, in 1946, the daughter of George Sarkisian, a truck driver, and his very young wife, Jackie Jean Crouch. He was of Armenian descent; she was part Cherokee Native American. George, who led a checkered life, was rarely around, and he and Jackie eventually divorced (although they would wed and divorce twice more over the years). With her next spouse, Jackie had another daughter (Georganne). The mother tried to become an actress, billing herself as Georgia Holt but was more successful in the matrimonial field. As she wed and unwed, the family relocated from place to place (including New York City, Texas, and Bel-Air, California). It was Jackie's fifth husband, Gilbert LaPiere, who adopted both Cherilyn and Georganne. By age sixteen, Cherilyn—who suffered from undiagnosed dyslexia—dropped out of school. She also moved out of her mom's home and roomed with a girlfriend in Hollywood.

In November 1962, bohemian Cherilyn met Sonny Bono at a Hollywood coffee shop. Born Salvatore Philip Bono in Detroit, Michigan, he was eleven years her senior, was separated from his first wife, and had a small daughter. Determined to make it in the recording industry, the struggling songwriter/singer/promoter was then working for Phil Spector of Gold Star Studios in Hollywood. Before long, Cher and her two-inch-shorter boyfriend were living together. In 1964, Cher recorded a song for Spector's record label. Sonny, who had become her determined mentor and strict controller, insisted the pliable talent use an alias (Bonnie Jo Mason) for the record. Still later, Sonny and Cher (now billed as Caesar and Cleo) recorded singles together. In October 1964, they wed in Tijuana, Mexico, with a more "official" wedding in December 1965. (Some sources insist they did not legally marry until 1969, just before their child was born.)

By 1965, the odd duo had a hit with "I Got You Babe" (written by Bono). It was the first of several record successes and brought them a large income. They moved to an enormous mansion in Holmby Hills, adjacent to Beverly Hills. By the next year, their popularity had waned sharply. Hoping to bolster their fast-evaporating career and assets, Sonny mort-gaged everything they had to finance the vanity picture *Chastity* (1969). The arty road picture was a dud, and they were now considered has-beens.

Refusing to give up, Bono booked their act into small clubs around the country, which eventually led to better venues and to new TV exposure. This, in turn, brought them *The Sonny and Cher Comedy Hour* in summer 1971. The weekly TV show caught the public's fancy, and the pair were soon on top again. They recorded together and Cher did her own albums (for example, 1971's *Gypsys, Tramps & Thieves*) as well. By now, Cher was fed up with being under Sonny's thumb and increasingly asserted herself. The couple privately led separate existences and each dated other people. One of her boyfriends was powerful record producer David Geffen. In early 1974, Sonny filed for legal separation, and, a few days later, they recorded the last episode of their TV series. Cher grew vocal on her own:

Once she left her show-business partner/husband Sonny Bono, Cher blossomed as an individual. To symbolize her newfound freedom, she had a butterfly tattooed on her buttock. Part of her blooming thereafter involved handsome boyfriends, often years younger than she. The roster included actors Tom Cruise and Val Kilmer, musician Richie Sambora, and film executive Joshua Donen. One of her more famous boy toys—who really captured the public's fancy—was Rob Camilletti. He was eighteen years her junior and once worked as a bartender and bagel maker. Show-business lore has it that when Cher first spotted the handsome blue-collar worker from Queens she quipped, "Have him washed and brought to my tent!" Later she admitted, "He just kind of rocked my socks. . . . I've never felt a physical impact like that, except maybe when my children were born." On the other hand, she acknowledged one of her early thoughts about him was that "he was probably not a good thing to waste my time on." Nevertheless, free-spirited, impulsive Cher didn't heed her gut instincts, and their passionate attachment in the late 1980s was tabloid fodder for years.

"Now I have to break out. And Sonny's not willing to make the transition with me." An angered, humiliated Bono sued his former mate for contractual default. Suddenly, Cher had to grow up and take an interest in her financial rights.

In show business, nothing is forever. After both Sonny and Cher flopped in individual variety series, they reunited in February 1976 for a joint offering. They couldn't recapture the past (and the public couldn't forgive them for that). She'd wed rock musician Gregg Allman in mid-1975 and was now pregnant with his child (Elijah Blue, born in July 1976). The revived *Sonny and Cher Show* expired in mid-1977. The next year, the mismatched Cher and Allman divorced.

Thanks to the shove David Geffen had given her recording career, Cher continued to be an industry presence. Pushing limits, one of her album covers featured her nude and in chains. When not making music videos and albums, appearing in Las Vegas, or doing glitzy TV specials, she dated musician Gene Simmons of the rock group KISS. The thirty-something Cher flaunted her image as America's most emancipated celebrity. It pleased some, flabbergasted others, and fueled her detractors. Happy to be grabbing headlines, Cher seemingly didn't give a damn what anyone thought.

After appearing on the New York stage in *Come Back to the 5 & Dime, Jimmy Dean, Jimmy Dean* (1982), she performed in the film version as well. This led to *Silkwood* (1983), for which she was Oscar-nominated, playing the lesbian friend of Meryl Streep. Two years later, she was seen as the biker mother in *Mask*. While making the drama, she fought with director Peter Bogdanovich, which gave her a diva reputation in Hollywood. In 1987, she starred in the comedy *Moonstruck* and won an Oscar. Finally, she'd broken away from her Sonny and Cher image.

Of her many younger lovers, the one who most caught the media's fancy was Rob Camilletti, a one-time bartender/bagel maker who was nearly twenty years her junior. Once again, Cher boldly challenged convention, which yet again divided the public's feelings about her. Her long-awaited new film, *Mermaids* (1990), had many production problems and proved a commercial disappointment; her movie career seemed to fall apart. The star lost a good deal of credibility by doing a hair products infomercial; many thought she was now a pop-culture joke. On the other hand, in her sold-out Las Vegas act, on concert tours, and on her albums, the entertainer held her own as musical styles changed and the competition grew younger.

For part of the 1990s, she was out of professional commission due to chronic fatigue syndrome. She still, however, had the strength to undergo more cosmetic surgery, have her front teeth capped, find new young boyfriends, and add more tattoos to her shapely body. When her daughter Chastity came out as a lesbian in the mid-1990s, Cher acknowledged that in her younger years she'd tried same-sex situations herself, but they were not to her liking.

When Sonny Bono died in 1998, naysayers criticized Cher for switching from a critical ex-wife to a fond ex-lover giving a teary eulogy at his funeral and then hosting a one-hour TV tribute that year to their work together. She reaffirmed her music industry standing with her 1998 album *Believe*, wrote a book of casual vignettes about her life (1998's *The First Time*), made a good impression in her supporting role in 1999's *Tea with Mussolini*, and commuted between her London apartment and her U.S. abodes. In the new millennium, she projected a strong presence with her album *Living Proof* (2001). The new-era Cher sported a blond wig and embarked on a mid-2002 concert tour across America, which she insisted would be her "final" one.

Occasionally letting down her guard, Cher has acknowledged having concerns about coping with growing old(er). "Some years," she admits, "I'm the coolest thing that ever happened, and the next year everyone's so over me." Remaining a blazing iconoclast, she insists, "I answer to two people: myself and my God." As for her unconventional romantic life, she says, "A girl can wait for the right man to come along, but . . . that still doesn't mean she can't have a wonderful time with all the wrong ones."

Joan Collins

[Joan Henrietta Collins]
MAY 23, 1933–

As a novice screen performer in early 1950s England, she portrayed sulky delinquents and prostitutes. In the 1980s, five-foot, six-inch Joan Collins gained a new generation of fans as the ultra-glamorous, devilishly vengeful Alexis Carrington Colby on the popular American TV drama *Dynasty* (1981–89). In between these career "milestones," she starred in a pair of soft-core sexploitation features based on books by her novelist sister, Jackie. In both movies (the second of which was titled *The Bitch* [1979]), she played Fontaine Khaled, the nymphomaniac wife of the owner of a trendy disco who revealed not only her evil side but much of her shapely anatomy. Is it any wonder that Joan's longtime addiction to portraying on-camera vixens blurred the public's conception of the "real" Joan Collins?

Joan once acknowledged her career choice: "The compartment that's easy to put me in is: free-thinking, sexy broad with a dirty mouth, who pretty much does what she wants." But she insisted, "There's more to me than that." So why has she played heartless wenches for so many years? For one thing, "it's easy to play a bitch." For another, it provides the income, popularity, and power to live on her own terms. Her exciting lifestyle has included many steamy romances and five marriages—the most recent one (2002) to a suitor half her age. Her choices have paid for Joan's glamorous standard of living, encompassing such goals as (1) not giving in to the ravages of time and (2) not being bested by her younger sister, the wealthy author of many bestselling, steamy novels. (The latter's literary fame apparently prompted Joan to write not only two memoirs and a beauty tips book but several novels full of passionate romance as well.)

While there were career reversals and personal tragedies in her life (enough to have overwhelmed a less hard-edged person), she always knew that great material rewards lay ahead for a determined professional who was not only pretty but enterprising. Maintaining her celebrityhood required constant tenacity, byproducts of which were self-centered behavior on and off the set and, of course, aggression toward those who stood in her way.

She was born in London, England, in 1933. She was the oldest of three children (besides sister Jackie, there was brother Bill). Her parents were Joseph William Collins, a vaudeville booking agent, and Elsa Bessant, a homemaker who was overprotective of her children. As a youngster, Joan claims to have been introverted. But she was not too shy to observe her father's colorful clients when they came by the house, and it inspired her interest in show business. Addicted to moviegoing, she sometimes went to three different shows a day and dreamed of becoming a movie star. During her years at the Francis Holland School in London, the budding actress made her professional stage debut in a West End presentation of *A Doll's House*. Within two years, she had quit school to study at the Royal Academy of Dramatic Art. Her father was against his daughter entering the tough show-business world but said he'd provide for her financially for two years. If that failed, she must try something more practical, such as secretarial training, and Joan agreed.

To supplement the allowance from home, Joan modeled. One such assignment brought her to the attention of the Rank Organization, a major British film company, which put her under contract. She made her movie debut with a bit part in *Lady Godiva Rides Again* (1951). She had much larger roles in such pictures as *Turn the Key Softly* (1953). In 1952, she wed actor Maxwell Reed, who was fourteen years her senior. The marriage was a troubled one: He drank constantly, was explosively jealous, and was physically abusive toward his bride. The unhappy union ended (although their divorce wasn't final until 1956) when Joan went to Italy to play sinister Queen Nellifer in the Hollywood-produced *Land of the Pharaohs* (1955). This costume epic brought Collins to the attention of film mogul Darryl F. Zanuck, who signed her to a seven-year contract at Twentieth Century-Fox. During the making of her first Hollywood film, *The Virgin Queen* (1955), she came into direct conflict with the film's star, Bette Davis, who felt threatened by Collins's youth and beauty and resented the Britisher for being given too much screen time. Self-confident and competitive, Joan was soon waging a miniwar against studio executives who cast her in what she termed "wallpaper parts—the pretty girl who sort of stands there. . ." Tired of her sexpot typecasting (as in 1957's *Island in the Sun*), she announced, "I'd rather not work in something that's not rewarding, something I find distasteful." Her rebellion was met with a studio suspension, which ended when she agreed to make two additional films for the studio.

With so much free time in Hollywood, the sultry British girl was much noticed on the Hollywood social scene. Her string of high-profile escorts included actor Sydney Chaplin;

such wealthy playboys as Arthur Loew Jr. and Nicky Hilton; and Rafael Trujillo, the offspring of a Latin American dictator. During this period, the media described hedonistic Joan as "the British bombshell" and "the streamlined vamp." One of Collins's relationships—with actor Warren Beatty—turned serious. Their romance included an engagement, a live-in situation, and an abortion. Thereafter, Beatty dated superstar Natalie Wood, while Natalie's ex-husband, actor Robert Wagner, became friendly with Joan for a time.

Joan ended her Twentieth Century-Fox deal with the dreadful, biblical mini-epic *Esther and the King* (1961). Back in London, she fell in love with actor/director/writer Anthony Newley, and they wed in 1963. During their seven-year hitch, she gave birth to their two children (Tara and Alexander [known as Sacha], had a fling with actor Ryan O'Neal, and occasionally acted on-screen. One of these ventures, *Can Hieronymus Merkin Ever Forget Mercy Humppe and Find True Happiness?* (1969), was conceived and directed by Newley, who also costarred. Collins claimed that while she had previously coped with her spouse's obsession with very young women, she realized from this autobiographical feature that he would never change. The couple angrily divorced in 1971.

Her third mate was record company executive Ron Kass. He shared the same natal day (March 30) as her past lovers Sydney Chaplin and Warren Beatty. Astrology-minded Collins considered this a good sign. The duo married in March 1972; their daughter, Katyana, was born that June. Based first in London and then

Joan Collins in *Tales That Witness Madness* (1973). (Courtesy of JC Archives)

in Los Angeles, Joan appeared infrequently in films, and those she made were typically tight-budgeted horror entries such as *Tales That Witness Madness* (1973) and *Empire of the Ants* (1977). By now Kass had become a film producer and helped her to get the lead in *The Stud* (1977) and its sequel, *The Bitch* (1979). The pictures once again made Joan a viable name in the entertainment world.

In 1980, Collins's eight-year-old daughter Katy suffered brain damage in an auto accident. To fund the huge medical bills and to

*A*t the peak of her fame as TV's most glamorous vixen on *Dynasty* (1981–89), Joan confided to *Playboy* magazine, "I enjoyed being an adulteress . . . taking a certain vengeance for the fact that my husband was not being faithful." She was referring to husband number two, British actor Anthony Newley. Her first spouse, Maxwell Reed, was also a Brit and an actor. They had a short and stormy union in the early 1950s, which climaxed one evening when enterprising Reed suggested she bed a portly Arab sheik who was offering £10,000 for one night of Joan's company. "Never!" shrieked Collins, who ran home to Mummy.

divert herself from her child's critical condition (which eventually improved), Joan accepted any work offers. One of these assignments proved to be *Dynasty*, and playing the alluring heavy in this prime-time TV soap drama made her a household name. Newly popular, she wrote her first autobiography, *Past Imperfect* (1983). The next year, she divorced Kass. However, in October 1985, fit and trim Joan wed younger Peter Holm, a Swedish pop singer–turned–businessman. This unlikely match burned out in less than two years, and after a vicious court battle in which he demanded a huge settlement and monthly alimony, Holm settled for a modest sum. Friends gifted Joan with a T-shirt that read "Holmless."

There had been sibling rivalry between the Collins sisters years before when Jackie had attempted an acting career. She had since abandoned that ambition for writing and become an enormous literary success. Joan encroached on her sibling's turf when she began writing her own potboilers, including *Prime Time* in 1988 and *Love & Desire & Hate* in 1990. In 1990, Joan signed a $4 million deal with a prestigious New York publisher to produce two novels. Writing at her

lavish London apartment and her villa in the south of France, she delivered *The Ruling Passion* and *Hell Hath No Fury*. The publisher claimed not to be impressed with the results and demanded the return of its $1.2 million advance. She refused and eventually emerged the winner in the ensuing, highly publicized court case. A victorious Collins proudly returned to writing and continued to pull in big publishing advances.

In recent years, besides acting in films, writing, and dating (particularly art dealer Robin Hurlstone), Collins continued to perform on stage. While touring in a U.S. production of *Love Letters*, she met Peruvian Percy Gibson, a theater manager, who was the same age (mid-thirties) as her son. Despite the objections of friends and the wonderment of the press about this offbeat coupling, headstrong Joan and the amenable Percy wed in February 2002 at a posh ceremony held at London's swank Claridge's Hotel. The couple honeymooned at the elite resort of Pangkor Laut, situated off the western coast of Malaysia. Professionally, Collins was signed to a six-month stint on the daytime TV soap *Guiding Light* to begin in fall 2002. The veteran actress was cast to play

Alexandra Spaulding, a wealthy woman with an extremely nasty disposition.

Over the decades, Collins—whose 2002 novel was called *Star Quality*—has proved herself to be the essence of the emancipated female, one who grabs whatever she wants from life. But even this queenly sensualist, who has spent a lot of time and money to make time stand still regarding her looks, admitted a few years ago that it was never too late to learn life's lessons. Asked by a reporter what she wished she'd known in her twenties, the actress replied, "Oh, everything. I was probably always too nice to men. It was hard to say no. You didn't want to be impolite." She also noted of her several trips to the altar, "I've never married a rich man. Everything I have comes from me. That's a good feeling."

Joan Crawford

[Lucille Fay LeSueur]

MARCH 23, 1904–MAY 10, 1977

No one is a more fervent crusader than a born-again convert. Crawford, who reinvented her life—shedding her tawdry past—when she began in silent movies in the mid-1920s, was a devout advocate of being a glamorous movie star and doing everything expected by her employers and the public. After gaining fame with *Our Dancing Daughters* (1928), she became a passionate believer in following every guideline helpful to being a long-term movie star. Not only did she excel at studio politics

to keep in the bosses' good graces, but she was a supreme self-promoter. She expended great effort, time, and money to be a constant subject of fan magazines and other media outlets.

Other stars of Hollywood's Golden Age may have thrilled at their fans' adulation, but for Joan it was the nectar of life and a sacred responsibility. Every piece of fan mail sent to Crawford was answered, whether by the star herself (she even wore a special outfit to tend to the chore) or by her hirelings. Joan lived and breathed being the supreme movie star that Metro-Goldwyn-Mayer had created. Her studio bosses, coworkers, and fans were the only family that was real to her. Anything that threatened her established way of life had to be extinguished.

As revealed in *Mommie Dearest* (1978), the exposé written by her adopted daughter Christina, Crawford was a heavy-duty control freak about her career, private lifestyle, and children. Her compulsive need to keep a strict rein on these domains led to her obsessiveness about orderliness, cleanliness, punctuality, courtesy, and respect. If she was cutthroat with studio rivals (especially her arch adversaries Norma Shearer at MGM and Bette Davis at Warner Bros.), she was equally competitive with her four adopted children who not only had to obey her completely but were never allowed to steal her limelight. (When Crawford's brood—especially her two older children—violated any of her stringent and often peculiar rules of life, heaven help them!) Most of her marriages were like her showplace homes: means of supplementing the illusion that she was a reigning movie queen who was

Joan Crawford in the 1940s. (Courtesy of JC Archives)

"humble" enough to be a good wife (and mother). The enormous strain of maintaining the all-encompassing movie star image—particularly as the studio system broke down in the 1950s and she got older—led Joan into increased alcoholism, assorted affairs, and bizarre behavior. Almost until the time she died, Crawford struggled to keep vestiges of her screen stardom, and, as had happened throughout her extraordinary career, anyone and anything that got in the way were obliterated.

She was born Lucille Fay in San Antonio, Texas, in 1904 (although some sources suggest 1905, 1906, or 1908) to Thomas LeSueur, a French-Canadian laborer, and Anna Bell Johnson, a Scandinavian-Irish homemaker. The couple had had an earlier child (Daisy) who died in infancy, and there was also a son named Hal. Early in Lucille's life, the shadowy Thomas vanished, and Anna Bell—a promiscuous individual—eventually married a man named Henry Cassin. The household moved to Lawton, Oklahoma, and Lucille (known as Billie) became Billie Cassin. Henry got into trouble with the law, and the Cassins relocated to Kansas City. Soon afterward, his wife left him. Billie had a helter-skelter childhood, transferred from school to school and living in one fleabag hotel room after another. By age eleven, she was at Rockingham Academy, overworked as a kitchen helper to pay her board and tuition at the private school. Bad as that existence was, it beat being with her domineering mother and oppressive brother.

By 1922, Billie was at Stephens College in Columbia, Missouri, where she worked her way through school but felt too inferior to remain for long. She returned to Kansas City, where she became a shop girl and then was hired as a chorine for a traveling show. When the production went bust, she moved on to Detroit. There her checkered story becomes even more vague. It was rumored that she was arrested on prostitution charges, but no record of such an offense has ever surfaced. Later she turned up in Chicago and became, among other things, a dancer in gangster-controlled speakeasies. (Gossip suggested that during these years of struggle, the teenager made pornographic films and did whatever she could to make the next move from the streets to the more legitimate world of show business.) Eventually, the still-chubby, five-foot, four-inch Billie emerged as a Broadway chorus girl, appearing in *The Passing Show of 1924* and earning $35 a week. She also married, but musician James Welton did not remain her spouse for too long, as she quickly outgrew him.

Ambitious and always networking, she engineered a screen test and was signed to a studio contract at Metro-Goldwyn (later Metro-Goldwyn-Mayer) in 1924. The sexually experienced newcomer quickly learned the value of being "cooperative" with randy studio executives. By 1925, she had been in several silent pictures and had a new professional name: Joan Crawford. Passing through her apprentice period with flying colors, her popularity soared by the late 1920s as she transformed herself into the screen's most vivacious flapper.

Appreciating the virtues of a solid industry pedigree, Joan allowed herself to fall in love with (and marry) handsome young actor Douglas Fairbanks Jr. He was the son of Tinseltown's unofficial ruler, Douglas Fairbanks Sr., and the stepson of its queen, Mary Pickford. Doug Jr. was not as ambitious as his career-fixated wife, and each found refuge in extracurricular romances. She took up with Clark Gable, her married coplayer from *Dance, Fools, Dance* (1931), and their affair continued on and off for years, even as each of them gained and shed new mates. Two years after divorcing Fairbanks Jr. in 1933, Joan wed the sophisticated Broadway actor Franchot Tone, then under MGM contract. Her grand intellectual pretensions were sparked by Franchot's cultured background. He soon felt humiliated to be Mr. Crawford and engaged in adulterous relationships. The couple divorced in 1939. As had become customary with Joan, each time she shed a husband, she fully redecorated her lavish home—which included changing every toilet seat in the house.

Horrified to be on a career downswing in 1938, Crawford redoubled her efforts at the studio, rebounding with such strong fare as *The Women* (1939), *Susan and God* (1940), and *A Woman's Face* (1941). Meanwhile, in 1940, Crawford finally became a mother by adoption. (She had claimed for years that she wanted children and insisted that during her marriages to Fairbanks Jr. and Tone that she had had several miscarriages. Rumors suggested that during her wild earlier years she had had more than one bad abortion, which made it difficult for her later to have babies.) The three-month-old infant, first called Joan Jr., was renamed Christina.

In mid-1942, Joan's eighteen-year association with MGM was terminated. During this depressing period, vulnerable Joan diverted herself by wedding a young actor named Phillip Terry. He was such a minor part of her life that their sporadic sexual get-togethers were just one of several items listed on the

*G*iven Christina Crawford's graphic revelations (such as child abuse, alcoholism, and obsessive compulsive behavior) about her movie star mother in her book *Mommie Dearest* (1978), Joan's own benign tome, *My Way of Life* (1971), a how-to of gracious living by her own rules, takes on a whole new dimension. Some of her suggestions included the following:

"A dress of the wrong shade can bring out sallowness, highlight blemishes, and add years to a woman's face. It will make her look hard."

"Closets should be completely emptied twice a year. Four times a year is better."

"It's a rare woman who has exactly the proportions she wants, even with exercise and diet. . . . Learn to camouflage the points you don't like."

"All the beauty products in the world can't disguise a disagreeable expression."

monthly schedule distributed to her household staff. The unproductive union officially ended in 1946, and she swiftly altered the name of their adopted son from Phillip Jr. to Christopher.

Crawford the survivor rebounded at Warner Bros., where she was hired as a threat to that studio's monarch, Bette Davis. However, it was nearly two years before Joan found the right starring vehicle. It was *Mildred Pierce* (1945) and she won an Academy Award for her efforts. Now at another career peak and earning $200,000 a picture, Joan adopted two more girls, Cynthia and Cathy, who she decreed were twins, even though they were born several weeks apart and did not particularly look alike. With typical shrewdness, Crawford remained at Warner Bros. through 1952's *This Woman Is Dangerous*, outlasting Davis, who left the lot in 1949. (In the scramble to retain her star status, Joan became increasingly predatory, vigilant that no one steal any of the attention in her celluloid vehicles.) In 1952, Joan earned her third and last Oscar nomination for *Sudden Fear*, a thriller made at RKO.

In May 1955, Crawford wed dynamic Pepsi-Cola president Alfred N. Steele and launched a new career for herself as a dynamic corporate goodwill ambassador. She thought Steele would be her mate for life, but he died in 1959 of a heart attack. (Some sources noted the financial and emotional strain he had endured coping with his forceful wife as the cause of his early demise.) With few movie roles available to an aging screen legend, Crawford devoted herself to being a highly visible Pepsi executive.

Joan made a striking comeback when she and Bette Davis teamed (and steamed at one another's attention-grabbing antics on the set) for *What Ever Happened to Baby Jane?* (1962). The horror yarn led to Crawford starring in such twisted shock schlock as *Strait-Jacket* (1964) and *Berserk!* (1967). By now heavy drinking had long been part of her New York City–based life, and she was alienated from her two older children.

The mid-1970s saw Crawford coping with a subdued lifestyle in Manhattan, having been pushed out of her Pepsi promotional post. Becoming a Christian Scientist, she gave up drinking. Increasingly, she refused to be seen in public, feeling that, despite plastic surgery and exercise, age had too greatly diminished her appearance. A good deal of her daily life was devoted to watching TV soap operas and bemoaning the fact that the film industry had seemingly forgotten her.

Her final weeks—and her death—were shrouded in silence and contradictory facts. Reportedly, she suffered from pancreatic cancer. Although her death was listed as from natural causes, rumors surfaced that perhaps, tired of suffering and knowing the end was coming, she had orchestrated her finale. Whatever the situation, her body was cremated and her ashes interred in an urn next to Alfred Steele's in the Ferncliffe Cemetery in Hartsdale, New York.

A few years before her death, Joan was quoted in the show-business trade paper *Variety* as saying, "I was born in front of a camera and really don't know anything else." It could easily have been her epitaph.

Dorothy Dandridge

[Dorothy Jean Dandridge]

NOVEMBER 9, 1922–SEPTEMBER 8, 1965

In March 2002, Halle Berry was the first African American actress to win a Best Actress Academy Award. In accepting her Oscar, the tearful Berry acknowledged that it had been Dorothy Dandridge who years ago had helped to break down the walls of racial inequity in Tinseltown and made Halle's victory possible. Halle was well-acquainted with the facts in Dandridge's obstacle-filled life because, in 1999, Berry had starred in the made-for-cable movie biography, *Introducing Dorothy Dandridge*.

Dandridge was a beautiful and talented actress, singer, and dancer. She had been the first African American woman to be nominated for an Academy Award for Best Actress (for her memorable performance in 1954's *Carmen Jones*). A veteran who began performing when she was a tot, Dorothy faced a lot of roadblocks in her troubled life. Many of them stemmed from racial injustice; others were due to people who took advantage of her vulnerability and desperation to succeed. By

the time she gained mainstream recognition in mid-1950s Hollywood, she prayed that her years of being held back professionally by ethnic prejudice were finally over. In her optimism, she lost perspective in the Tinseltown firmament of the times. Later, bitterly disillusioned by the still-powerful bigotry that stymied her show-business career, she became increasingly self-destructive and temperamental.

She was the second child of Cyril and Ruby (Baker) Dandridge, born in 1922 in Cleveland, Ohio. By then, Cyril—whose work résumé included being a clerk, a mechanic, and a draftsman—had left the household. (Years later, when she was famous, Dorothy would encounter her father during a Cleveland singing engagement and learn that she was one-quarter white.) She and her year-older sister Vivian were raised by their mother, an ambitious actress. When still extremely young, the siblings—known as the Wonderful Children—performed for local church and school groups. Soon Ruby (abetted by her close friend Geneva "Neva" Williams) had them touring, doing their song-and-dance act at African American venues in and around Ohio. By the early 1930s, the quartet was based in Los Angeles, where Ruby hoped she and her daughters could break into the movies. At school, the girls met young

John Howard, Etta Jones, Dorothy Dandridge, and Vivian Dandridge in *Easy to Take* (1936).
(Courtesy of JC Archives)

Etta Jones and she was added to the young-sters' act (which became known as the Dandridge Sisters). In the mid-1930s, the trio had bit parts in studio films such as the Marx Brothers' *A Day at the Races* (1937).

Since Ruby was busy with her career, strict disciplinarian Neva chaperoned the girls when they took their act on the road. There was no love lost between self-willed Dorothy and domineering (and often hostile) Neva. One evening when Dorothy returned to their rooms after an innocent date, an overly suspicious Neva accused her of having had sexual activity with her escort. Determined to find out if her charge was still a virgin, she yanked off the shy teenager's dress and probed inside the

appalled girl with her finger. The traumatizing situation left Dorothy frigid for years.

In the late 1930s, the Dandridge Sisters performed at the Cotton Club in New York City's Harlem. There Dorothy met ladies' man Harold Nicholas, who was part of the extremely popular Nicholas Brothers dance duo. The couple continued to date when they were both cast in the movie musical *Sun Valley Serenade* (1941). They wed in September 1942, and the next year their daughter, Harolyn Suzanne, was born. (Later it was discovered that the baby had brain damage, which left Dorothy guilt ridden.) Throughout this period, Dandridge won bits in movies, the only roles available for most black talent in that era.

By 1950, Dandridge had divorced the womanizing Nicholas. When not taking acting lessons, she was guided by musician Phil Moore (who also became a love interest) and now, in her late twenties, had emerged as a self-assured, sexy chanteuse. Still hoping for success in Hollywood, she accepted the unfulfilling role of an earthy jungle princess in *Tarzan's Peril* (1951). In *The Harlem Globetrotters*, released that same year, she played a basketball player's wife. Meanwhile, her singing career escalated, and she had successful engagements at chic East and West Coast clubs. Before long, she was earning $3,500 weekly from her nightclub work. More important for her, MGM hired Dandridge to play a Southern schoolteacher (opposite Harry Belafonte) in *Bright Road* (1953). The little drama was well reviewed but little seen in mainstream theaters because of its black cast.

When Dandridge sought to be considered for the title role in Twentieth Century-Fox's all-black musical *Carmen Jones*, autocratic director Otto Preminger insisted she was too refined to portray the earthy temptress. Refusing to give up, she visited his office one day wearing the wardrobe and hairdo she thought appropriate for the vixenish character and flaunting a Marilyn Monroe–style wiggle. Preminger was amazed by her new look and gave her the role. Her joy turned to fear as she became overwhelmed with insecurity about her breakthrough role, and, at one point, she almost backed out of the project. The situation became even more stressful when the married filmmaker embarked on a "secret" affair with her, and she had to adapt to their very different on-set and off-set relationships. Also spoiling her joy was the fact that Preminger chose to dub her singing, using opera student Marilyn Horne to provide Dandridge's voice for the complex score.

When *Carmen Jones* was released in 1954, both the film and Dorothy were a big hit. Although she lost the Best Actress Oscar to Grace Kelly (*The Country Girl*), Dandridge was sure that more good screen roles lay ahead under her Twentieth Century-Fox contract. Next, studio mogul Darryl F. Zanuck assigned her to *The King and I* (1956), in which she was to play the secondary role of the Burmese Tuptim who was forced into a loveless marriage with the monarch. She refused the subordinate part and earned the studio chieftain's ire. Dorothy, however, did agree to make *Island in the Sun* (1957), a film touted for its interracial passion, but Zanuck feared pushing the boundaries with audiences too far and cut back on Dandridge's romantic interaction with her on-camera white lover. Again, she made her displeasure known, which in turn was held against her. Off camera the actress sued and won a lawsuit against *Confidential* magazine, which had detailed her supposedly scandalous sex life.

By the time of *Porgy and Bess* (1959), Dorothy's affair with Preminger was over, and he made life miserable for her on the set of the movie musical; she was difficult with him as well. Adding to her problems were the complaints of African American groups who felt the film's stereotyped characters and tawdry settings would reflect badly on their race. Some talents—like Harry Belafonte—had refused to appear in the picture for these reasons, leaving Dandridge ambivalent for seemingly choosing her career over the cause of racial equality. In the end, *Porgy and Bess* was not well received by critics or the public. Meanwhile, Dandridge had other woes. Against the advice of relatives and friends, she'd married Jack Denison, a white Beverly Hills restaurant owner, in June 1959. On their wedding night, she discovered two of the real reasons he had married her: His establishment was in trouble, and he needed her financial help as well as her singing to bring in customers.

In the early 1960s, Dorothy—now forty but looking much younger—saw her movie career stall because there were still few viable leading roles available for black women. Her costly union to Denison ended with their 1962 divorce. Overwhelmed by escalating frustrations, she turned increasingly to alcohol and sleeping pills. For financial reasons, she was forced to transfer her mentally disabled daughter from a private hospital to a state facility. The situation reinforced her old guilt about Harolyn's misfortunes, and Dandridge became more problematic to those around her. In April 1963, she had to declare bankruptcy, which let the public know how badly her life had fallen apart.

Thanks to her one-time manager, Earl Mills, the star put her life back together. She undertook singing engagements, including performing as Julie in a summer stock engagement of *Show Boat* with Kathryn Grayson in the female lead. In fall 1965, Dandridge was to appear at Basin Street East in New York City and had been offered two new movie projects in Mexico. On September 7, she packed for her Los Angeles–to–New York flight. The next morning she phoned Mills to reschedule a hospital appointment (to treat her ankle, which she had injured and which was still hurting). When Earl reached her West Hollywood home, she didn't answer when he rang the bell. He returned a few hours later, and, because there was still no response, he broke into the apartment. He found her lying dead on the bathroom floor, nude except for a scarf wrapped around her head. After a preliminary report listed the cause of death as an embolism, the coroner's office ruled that the victim had overdosed on Tofranil (an antidepressant that a physician had prescribed for her). However, because of her career upturn at the time of her passing, a team of psychiatrists would not conclusively state that she had committed suicide. (In the 1940s, Dorothy had overdosed on sleeping pills on several occasions.)

Had Dorothy burst upon the entertainment scene in the twenty-first century, there is no doubt that this talented but troubled artist would have found the road to success much easier for herself and those within her orbit.

Bette Davis

[Ruth Elizabeth Davis]
APRIL 5, 1908–OCTOBER 6, 1989

According to Davis, "Acting should be bigger than life. Scripts should be bigger than life. It should all be bigger than life." That was cer-

Bette Davis in *Hush . . . Hush, Sweet Charlotte* (1964). (Courtesy of JC Archives)

tainly true of Bette during Hollywood's Golden Age. She was the most vivid acting force on-screen and the industry's most defiant tyrant off camera. Her legendary fights with her film bosses were all the more extraordinary because in that pre-feminism era—and particularly under the studio system—such things were rarely done so blatantly. But Bette believed the old adage that "God helps those who help themselves," and her Yankee stock made her a tenacious fighter. As a result, during much of her lengthy Warner Bros. tenure

in the 1930s and 1940s, she was queen of the roost and not so facetiously referred to as the "Fifth Warner Brother." As such, she took on all comers, especially actresses Miriam Hopkins and Joan Crawford, who dared to step on her sacred turf at the Burbank film lot.

In the 1950s and thereafter, aging Bette was still searching for meaty acting roles. She vowed, "I will not retire while I've still got my legs and my makeup box." She also could have added that there was nothing like a good feud to keep the juices going. This was exemplified by her battle of words with Susan Hayward on *Where Love Has Gone* (1964), with Faye Dunaway on the TV movie *The Disappearance of Aimee* (1976), and her tirades against aged Lillian Gish when they costarred in *The Whales of August* (1987).

One dispute Davis hadn't counted on was her contretemps with daughter B.D., the product of Bette's third marriage. Davis, who had shed crocodile tears when Christina Crawford tore into her late mother (Joan Crawford) in *Mommie Dearest* (1978), was convinced that such a tome would never be written about her. Then came B.D.'s *My Mother's Keeper* in 1985, presenting a devastating portrait of the egocentric star and her purported acts of selfishness and cruelty to those caught in the upheaval of her volcanic life. When questioned by the surprised media, author B.D. insisted, "I did not write my book to get even," but it certainly seemed that way. Davis, elderly and in bad health, was confounded by the public betrayal. Retorted the aghast icon, "She lived off me, and I lent her husband money to start his own business, and they have both conspired against me. . . . I, who was not the best mother in the world, but in *no* way abusive . . . and I always tried my best!"

She was born in 1908 in Lowell, Massachusetts, the first of two daughters of Harlow Morrell Davis, a future patent lawyer, and Ruth (Ruthie) Favor, a portrait photographer. The ill-matched parents separated when Ruth Elizabeth was seven; three years later, the couple divorced. By her freshman year in high school, the teenager had decided to become an actress. After work in a stock company, she

moved to New York City where she studied drama at the Robert Milton–John Murray Anderson School. (Lucille Ball was a fellow student there.) In the fall of 1928, Bette Davis (as she was now known professionally) joined a stock company in Rochester, New York. Prodded by her pushy, ever-present mother, Bette took on Miriam Hopkins, a seasoned leading lady from Broadway. One night, Hopkins, an expert at scene-stealing herself, accused Davis of stepping on her precious lines. "The b**** doesn't know her place!" Miriam complained to director George Cukor. Before long, Bette had packed up her belongings and left in defeat.

Resilient Bette debuted on Broadway in *Broken Dishes* (1929). The next year she made a screen test for Hollywood film producer Samuel Goldwyn, but he was not impressed by the five-foot, three-inch Davis, with her pop eyes and boyish figure. Nevertheless, she was hired by Universal Pictures where she spent an unproductive year (1931) in unmemorable films. Her luck turned when she went to Warner Bros. for *The Man Who Played God* (1932). Now under contract, the brothers Warner tossed her into one picture after another with little regard for her career growth. (In frustration, she often vented her rage at her leading men, whether socking Charles Farrell or verbally assaulting cocky James Cagney whenever he tried to steal the scene from her.)

When Bette learned that RKO was making *Of Human Bondage* (1934), she fought hard to play the nasty waitress, Mildred. The unsympathetic part earned Davis the first of an eventual eleven Oscar nominations. She won her first Academy Award the following year for *Dangerous* (1935), during the making of which she developed a crush on her handsome leading man, Franchot Tone. The problem—or the enticement—was that this MGM star was the personal property of Metro's Joan Crawford. When the latter heard that Bette was hot for Tone, Joan insisted, "That coarse little thing doesn't stand a chance with Franchot." To ensure the fact, Crawford kept her conquest on a short leash by marrying him in October 1935. But the lines between Bette and Joan were drawn for future rematches.

In rebellion Davis walked out on Warner Bros. in 1936, sailing to England to make films there. But the studio filed an injunction and a subsequent lawsuit decreed Davis had to honor her Hollywood studio contract, which ran until 1942. She returned to the home lot for *Marked Woman* (1937) and all was forgiven—temporarily. By the next year, Bette, the star of *The Sisters* and *Jezebel* (for which she won her second Oscar) was Warner Bros.'s top actress. Then along came her old nemesis, Miriam Hopkins, who was hired to join Davis in *The Old Maid*. By now, Miriam had assorted grudges against Davis, ranging from concerns that Bette might be romancing Hopkins's husband—director Anatole Litvak—to the fact that Bette had starred in *Jezebel*, a role Hopkins had performed on Broadway. Using syrupy sweet charm and mock innocence, Miriam goaded Davis throughout production, but their mutual tension worked to improve their on-screen interaction.

The divine Bette could be malicious in her appraisal of other actresses. She once referenced Marilyn Monroe as "the original good time that was had by all." About another famous entertainer, Davis dissed, "Before I ever worked with Faye Dunaway, I admired her cheekbones. After all, she was a fashion model, wasn't she? Now I can only admire her cheek. And she acts like a fashion model!"

Many of Bette's coplayers returned the favor:

"That face! Have you ever seen such a tragic face? Poor woman. How she must be suffering! I don't think it's right to judge a person like that. We must bear and forbear."
—Lillian Gish, Bette's colead in 1987's *The Whales of August*

"I was never so scared in my life. And I was in the war!"
—John Mills, on acting with Davis in 1985's *Murder with Mirrors*

"I have always believed in the Christian ethic, to forgive and forget. I looked forward to working with Bette again. I had no idea of the extent of her hate and that she planned to destroy me."
—Joan Crawford, regarding 1964's *Hush . . . Hush, Sweet Charlotte*

Meanwhile, in late 1938, Bette bid farewell to her first husband, bandleader Oscar Harmon Nelson Jr., whom she'd married in 1932. The divorce was a result of several factors. She was the family's breadwinner; he stayed home most of the time. He—along with Ruthie Davis—had persuaded Bette to have an abortion in the mid-1930s rather than endanger her career. Now disillusioned with her marriage, Davis played the field, including a fling with ace playboy Howard Hughes. Then there was her grand passion for her *Jezebel* director, William Wyler. She did not pursue marriage with him, which she later regretted, but instead found comfort with frequent costar George Brent.

By the time *The Letter* (1940) and *The Little Foxes* (1941)—both directed by Wyler, who had since married—were released, Davis was ensconced as "First Lady of the Screen." As of December 1941, she had another title, that of wife to a New England innkeeper, Arthur Farnsworth. He was incapable of breaking out of her shadow, and she soon found pleasure in the arms of married director Vincent Sherman, who guided her through *Old Acquaintance* (1943). Shortly after that tearjerker—in which Davis once again battled Miriam Hopkins—was released, Farnsworth died of an aneurysm, the result of an earlier blow to the head. Davis later acknowledged to intimates that she was convinced the fatal injury had occurred months before when Arthur had tried to stop her leaving Los Angeles for Mexico, where she planned to have an assignation with Sherman (who, as it turned out, didn't show). Davis had shoved her argumentative spouse to get him to leave the train, which was departing. As the train gathered speed, he fell off and hit his head on the station platform.

In the mid-1940s, Warner Bros. hedged its bets with hot-tempered Bette by adding ex-MGM star Joan Crawford to the studio payroll. Studio head Jack L. Warner was fed up with Davis's tantrums on the sets, her costly demands, and her failure to keep to rigid shooting schedules. Ironically, Bette turned down the title role in *Mildred Pierce* (1945), which resurrected Joan's career and earned her an Oscar. By 1949's *Beyond the Forest*, Davis was history at Warner Bros, while her adversary remained with the film company through 1952. It was in that year that Davis, who had enjoyed her own comeback with *All About Eve* (1950) at Twentieth Century-Fox, made *The Star*. The script was a biting indictment of a Crawford-type movie star and Bette relished playing the role to the hilt.

Davis had wed artist William Grant Sherry in November 1945 and their daughter, Barbara Davis (B.D.), was born in May 1947. By July 1950, Bette had shed husband number three, having embarked on an affair with her *All About Eve* leading man, Gary Merrill. Bette and Gary wed twenty-five days after her divorce. The newlyweds adopted two children: Margot (who proved to be retarded and was eventually institutionalized) in 1951 and Michael in 1952. Before long the bloom was off the rose, and the battling, heavy-drinking Merrills were waging war on each other. In July 1960, the sadistic union finally ended.

By the early 1960s, heavy-smoking, hard-drinking Davis was at a career impasse. Then

Crawford suggested a costarring vehicle, *What Ever Happened to Baby Jane?* (1962) for them. Davis was desperate enough to accept the deal. She insisted upon playing the more deranged sister, while Crawford was cast as the wheelchair-ridden sibling. During production, Joan had her revenge on scene-stealing Bette by putting heavy weights in her dress, so that Davis wrenched her back in a sequence in which she had to carry her mortal enemy. Two years later, Bette had her payback. During their reunion horror film (*Hush . . . Hush, Sweet Charlotte*), Joan was hospitalized due to supposed illness but more a case of panic at making another picture with her enemy. Davis rejoiced in helping to push Crawford off the project and having Bette's pal, Olivia de Havilland, assume Joan's role.

Snarling her way into the 1980s, Davis had triumphantly outlived Crawford (who died in 1977) and was still reveling in putting down other on-screen annoyances (such as Miriam Hopkins and Faye Dunaway) at every opportunity. Bette survived both a mastectomy in 1983 and several subsequent strokes. Looking like heaven's wrath, she still would not retire. On the made-for-TV whodunit, *Murder with Mirrors* (1985), Bette's vituperation pushed the elder Helen Hayes to the limits of patience. But that was nothing compared to the viciousness that ailing Davis dished out to the even older and much-venerated silent screen star Lillian Gish on 1987's *The Whales of August*. Snapped Bette to the press, "[She] ought to know about close-ups. Jesus, she was around when they invented them!"

That, however, was not the finale of the divine Miss Davis. She signed to make *The Wicked Stepmother*, a low-caliber entry in which she was cast as a witch. Troublesome Bette quit the plagued project after a week in May 1988. She announced that she was upset by how poorly she'd been photographed in the movie. Therefore, she explained, "For the good of my future in films I had no choice but to withdraw." (Later, the picture was pieced together with new scenes shot with Barbara Carrera taking over a variation of Bette's role, and the embarrassing result made its way into scant release in 1989.)

At age eighty-one, Davis finally succumbed to her long battle with cancer and died in October 1989 at the American Hospital in Neuilly, France. She was buried at Forest Lawn Memorial Park in Hollywood Hills, California, where her burial site overlooks the Burbank movie studio she once ruled so strenuously.

Dolores Del Rio

[Lolita Dolores Martinez Asúnsolo y López Negrete]

AUGUST 3, 1905–APRIL 11, 1983

There are many intriguing aspects to the astonishing film career of Del Rio, the Mexican-born actress who was known as "The Most Beautiful Woman in the World." First of all, the exquisiteness of this 115-pound, five-foot, three-and-a-half-inch star—she of the lustrous black hair and luminous brown eyes—was not exaggerated. Not only was she gorgeous as a young woman, but she presented a striking figure even as a septuagenarian. Second, she had an extremely long span in pictures. Her debut was in the 1925 Hollywood silent feature *Joanna*; her final picture was the international coproduction *The Children of Sanchez* (1978). Most important, she was the first Latin-born actress to become a Hollywood film star and was *not* confined to playing mostly Hispanic stereotypes, as were such later imported talents as Lupe Velez and Katy Jurado. In her Tinseltown years, Dolores portrayed characters of assorted nationalities ranging from French to Russian to British to Polynesian to American.

Over the decades, Del Rio was frequently asked to describe the secrets of her seemingly eternal beauty. She explained that her daily regimen included sensible exercise, a simple diet, no smoking or drinking, and *plenty* of bed rest. To that checklist Dolores might have added being pampered extravagantly—which the star was by her succession of husbands and lovers and by her movie studio employers.

She was born in 1905 in Durango, Mexico, the only offspring of Jesus Asúnsolo, an important bank president and large landowner, and his wife, Antonia López Negrete. She was four when the family fled their home to escape a raid by Pancho Villa and his pillaging troops. After seeing his wife and daughter safely to Mexico City, Jesus relocated temporarily to the United States (but later returned to his homeland). Lolita was educated at the French con-

Dolores Del Rio and Joel McCrea in *Bird of Paradise* (1932).
(Courtesy of JC Archives)

vent of Saint Joseph. Part of her education included the study of Spanish dancing and singing. Later, after returning home from a European trip with her parents, the gorgeous teenager came to the attention of Jaime Martinez Del Rio. Descended from one of Mexico's oldest Castilian families, he was a lawyer and eighteen years older than fifteen-year-old Lolita. The two wed in 1920. After a luxurious two-year European honeymoon, the couple established themselves at a ranch in northern

Mexico that had been in his family for over three hundred years.

Within a few years, Lolita had tired of her privileged but too placid lifestyle. Jaime had an interest in playwriting and, with her encouragement, contemplated moving to Paris where he could mingle with the city's creative set and write. Fate, however, intervened. Hollywood filmmaker Edwin Carewe was honeymooning in Mexico City with his bride, Mary Akin, an actress. Through mutual friends in the diplomatic corps, the Carewes met Lolita and Jaime. The forty-year-old director was so entranced by Lolita's beauty that he proposed she come to Hollywood to make pictures. While he saw that the young lady was intrigued by his suggestion, he made a point of telling Jaime that Hollywood offered great opportunities for a man of Del Rio's background and intelligence. The would-be playwright was interested and soon traveled to Los Angeles to explore the situation. A week later, an enthusiastic Jaime cabled Lolita to come north. Ignoring the protests of her traditionalist parents and friends, the determined young woman went to Hollywood where a second cousin, Ramon Novarro, was already established as a leading man in the cinema.

While Jaime sought scriptwriting opportunities in pictures, Carewe placed Lolita under personal contract. Using the professional name of Dolores Del Rio, she played a vamp in her screen debut, the silent photoplay *Joanna* (1925), made at First National. By her third film, *Pals First* (1926), she had the leading female role. Fox Films borrowed her to play the spitfire French girl Charmaine in *What Price Glory?* (1926). The boisterous comedy and Dolores were a big hit. The much-in-demand actress was showcased by her mentor Carewe in *Resurrection* (1927) and *Ramona* (1928).

It was no secret in the film colony that Edwin Carewe loved Dolores. Speculation ran high that once his pending divorce from Mary Akin was finalized, he would wed his protégée. There was, however, the matter of Dolores's husband. He had yet to make a breakthrough in writing. Just to have something to do, he accepted the position of script clerk on her screen projects. Deeply embarrassed by his inability to make headway professionally or to retain his wife's love, the humiliated man broke away from the Hollywood scene. He went to New York, where he collaborated on a play (*From Hell Came a Lady*) that failed to reach Broadway (although it was eventually made into a 1929 Fox film). Too mortified to return to Los Angeles, the fledgling playwright fled to Europe. In 1928, career-obsessed Dolores filed for divorce from the man who had become an encumbrance to her in her role as a movie star.

Once abroad, the desperate Jaime accepted work with the American Play Company in Germany. Later in 1928, Dolores received word that he was in a Berlin sanatorium. He had reportedly contracted blood poisoning following a minor operation and was now in critical condition. The movie actress sent her spouse a cablegram: "Wish I were with you because I love you. God bless you. I love you." He was said to have been clutching her message in his hand when he died. With no need to further pursue her divorce petition, the widow Del Rio continued her film career, including making the Carewe-directed *Evangeline* (1929).

Evangeline was a box-office success. Its profitability led United Artists, who had released the picture, to offer Dolores a mighty $9,000-a-week contract. The movie colony was taken aback when she accepted the lucrative offer because of her past relationship with Carewe (she had stopped seeing him by that time). Carewe sued Del Rio for violating their contract and the case was settled out of court. Meanwhile, *The Bad One* (1930), her first all-talking picture was released and Dolores's career in talkies was assured.

Del Rio was part of the A-list at Tinseltown parties. At one such swank gathering, Dolores met Cedric Gibbons. The thirty-seven-year-old, Irish-born Gibbons was the supervising art director at MGM. A bachelor, most of his staff assumed that he was homosexual. Thus there was great surprise when a few weeks after meeting, Dolores and Cedric announced their engagement and then wed in August 1930. (Meanwhile, Carewe remarried his ex-wife. His career lost its momentum after Dolores's defection and, in 1940, he committed suicide.)

Several weeks after returning from their honeymoon to Los Angeles, where Gibbons owned two homes (one in Santa Monica Canyon, the other near the MGM facility), Dolores fell ill. The official diagnosis was pyelitis (an inflammation of the renal pelvis), but in actuality she'd had a nervous breakdown. What part Gibbons's lifestyle played in her emotional collapse remains speculation.

Because of her ailment, Dolores's agreement with United Artists was dissolved. When she was well enough to work again, she signed on at RKO, where she made such entries as *Bird of Paradise* (1932) and *Flying Down to Rio* (1933). When that studio did not renew her option, she moved over to Warner Bros., making *Wonder Bar* (1934), *Madame Du Barry* (1934), and other lesser entries. Later in the decade, she transferred to Twentieth Century-Fox, but her assignments there were relatively minor fare.

During the thirties, Dolores jumped from one studio to another, while she and her husband remained at the hub of the industry's social life. What no one could appreciate was the couple's unique living arrangement. In their main house, she had a luxuriant, sunny bedroom on the first floor where she slept alone. Gibbons, on the other hand, had a small and unremarkable room beneath hers. The only link between the two rooms was a stepladder that could be dropped down from Del Rio's room once the trapdoor in the floor of her room was opened. Friends who toured the house noted that in Gibbons's chamber there was a long stick leaning against a wall. It was assumed that he used it to rap on the floor of Dolores's room when he wished to be admitted.

The unconventional couple separated in 1940 and divorced the following year. By then, she'd begun a romance with Hollywood's latest golden boy, Orson Welles. He was ten years younger than the still-radiant Dolores. Welles gave her the starring role in *Journey into Fear* (1942), but the espionage thriller failed to rekindle her movie career. In addition, Orson had become entranced with rising young star Rita Hayworth and dropped Dolores to pursue that relationship. A miffed Del Rio returned to Mexico to become part of that country's film industry.

Back in her homeland, Dolores starred in *Flor Silvestre* (1943), which established her as a major star in Mexican cinema. As such, she headlined many features over the next two decades. Occasionally, she made a Hollywood-produced feature such as 1947's *The Fugitive* and 1960's *Flaming Star*. (Several potential Tinseltown projects that had been earmarked for her during this period fell through because she had been blacklisted for her sympathies to leftist political causes in the 1930s.) In November 1959, Del Rio wed American stage/film producer Lewis A. Riley, who produced her stage vehicles in Mexico City. The couple pursued an extravagant lifestyle, alternating between a home in a chic suburb of Mexico City and their residence in upscale Newport Beach, south of Los Angeles. In her senior years, Dolores became deeply involved in charity work, in particular, founding the Estancia Infantil, a day-care center for children of Mexican performers. She died of liver failure in Newport Beach in 1983.

In later years, Dolores chose to recall only selective events in her exotic life, insisting, "I have a bad memory for bad memories." However, on the subject of her creed for success, she expounded fully: "Discipline will help you not to have heartaches and run away when things go bad, and it will keep you from getting drunk when something goes wrong and you think you can't pull yourself together. There are ten thousand disappointments facing anyone who goes into this business, and discipline will give you the guts to get through them, to not let them destroy you, and to help you endure." One can only surmise what some of her husbands and lovers would have thought of her creed.

Marlene Dietrich

[Maria Magdalena Dietrich]
NOVEMBER 27, 1901–MAY 6, 1992

In *A Foreign Affair* (1948), she sang "Illusion" and that word symbolized a key ingredient of Dietrich's mystique over many decades. For example, while she registered as a Teutonic exotic in her movies, in real life she preferred the posture of hausfrau who cleaned, cooked, and sewed. The five-foot, five-inch celebrity was blessed with shapely legs, and, once she lost the pudginess of her teen years, her face thinned sufficiently to showcase an intriguing bone structure.

With expert makeup and lighting, Marlene appeared luminous on screen, an achievement that required increasing visual tricks as the years passed. When she performed a trademark song (for example, "Falling in Love Again" or "See What the Boys in the Back Room Will Have"), there was actually no melodious voice to captivate the listener.

Rather it was her dramatic talk-singing that made her limited vocal range and styling seem so captivating.

She built her Hollywood persona in the 1930s as an international film celebrity, one who—if her publicity were to be believed—lived a glamorous, thrilling life in which she basked in fans' adulation. However, as she insisted in her 1987 memoir, *Marlene*, "I was always indifferent to the glitter of fame. I found it troublesome, crippling, and dangerous. I detested it. . . . Admiration from unknown persons leaves me cold. The fame that can completely alter the personality of a human being has no power over me."

Marlene's many ambiguities extended to her sexual preferences. She had affairs with several film stars (including Gary Cooper, John Gilbert, Jimmy Stewart, John Wayne, and Jean Gabin). She also found time for liaisons with singer Eddie Fisher, politicians Joseph P. Kennedy and his son John, and an American army commander (during World War II). Then there were her lesbian encounters, which included brief flings with fellow Paramount stars Kay Francis and Tallulah Bankhead in the early 1930s and an intense amour with socialite/author Mercedes de Acosta in the same decade. (Earlier, back in Germany, Marlene had had close relationships with several different women with whom she worked on stage and in film, one of whom may have been Greta Garbo.)

With so many contrasting facets of her outer and inner self to control, it is little wonder that Dietrich, the supreme narcissist and determined living legend, had little time or much regard for those around her. This sphere included studio bosses; costars; lovers; a compliant husband who led a separate life from Marlene; and the couple's only child, Maria. The latter, herself a busy stage and TV performer in the 1940s and 1950s, has devoted a lot of energy to writing about and being interviewed concerning her famous mother. Maria best summed up the bleak, often sterile relationship they shared with the line "Don't have an actress for a mother."

Dietrich was born in 1901 in Schöneberg, Germany, a Berlin suburb. Maria was the second daughter of Prussian police officer Louis Erich Otto Dietrich and his wife, Wilhelmina Elisabeth Josephine Felsing. Her father died when she was nine, and Wilhelmina later wed Edouard von Losch, a German army officer. Her mother was a strict disciplinarian and that influence marked the future actress for life. Long intrigued with motion pictures, Maria dreamed of becoming some type of performer. As a teenager, she studied the violin but that

When filmmaker Josef von Sternberg was asked if he intended to wed Dietrich, his protégée and lover, the director of *The Blue Angel* (1930) and *Shanghai Express* (1932) admitted, "I'd as soon share a telephone booth with a frightened cobra."

Marlene Dietrich, the sultry star of *Seven Sinners* (1940). (Courtesy of JC Archives)

ended due to a wrist injury. Meanwhile, she had her first affair (with her much-older music instructor). By 1921, Maria was both studying acting in Berlin and winning minor assignments in stage dramas and revues. Now using the name Marlene Dietrich, she made the round of film studios, eventually winning parts in movies such as *Die Tragödie der Liebe* (*Love Tragedy*, in 1923).

Marlene's entry into filmmaking had been eased by Rudolf Sieber, an assistant director, who had become enamored of the vivacious, plump, young actress. The couple married in May 1924. The next January, their only daughter, Maria, was born. Undaunted by the conventions of marriage or motherhood, Dietrich continued to indulge her active social life, which included relationships with both men and women. She became part of the city's young intelligentsia, mingling with future film director Billy Wilder (who would guide her in 1948's *A Foreign Affair*) and author Erich Maria Remarque (with whom she had an off-and-on affair over the years, eventually losing him to actress Paulette Goddard).

Hollywood film director Josef von Sternberg came to Berlin to make *Der Blaue Engel* (*The Blue Angel*, 1930) and cast Marlene as the dissolute cabaret singer who destroys a besotted middle-aged professor (played by Emil Jannings). The evening the picture premiered in Germany to great acclaim, Marlene departed Berlin to follow von Sternberg to Hollywood, where a Paramount studio contract awaited her. Dietrich left her husband and child behind in Germany as she blazed through *Morocco* (1930) in Tinseltown and had an affair with her leading man, Gary Cooper. Later, von Sternberg's wife became so incensed by the complex relationship between her husband and the German actress that she sued Dietrich for alienation of affection. Meanwhile, Marlene and von Sternberg made other features together such as the popular *Shanghai Express* (1932) and *The Devil Is a Woman* (1935), their last together and a box-office flop. During these years, Dietrich perfected being the "star" on movie sets, growing more temperamental and more demanding of her perks and in her choice of vehicles, casts, and crews. Between films, she maintained an exhausting schedule of overlapping extracurricular romances that only a methodical and calculating star of her caliber could have endured. By now, Maria—her official age reduced by a few years to make Dietrich seem younger—was living with her mother in Los Angeles, although their paths crossed only infrequently. Dietrich's spouse, Rudi, was in Paris with Russian dancer Tamara Matul. (Rudi and Tamara remained together until her death in 1968. He would die in California in 1976 on a chicken farm that Dietrich bought for him.)

After 1936's *Desire* (which reunited Marlene with Gary Cooper) and the sterile *Angel* (1937), the new Paramount regime felt it could do nicely without high-maintenance Dietrich. To everyone's surprise but her own, Dietrich made a stunning comeback in Universal's *Destry Rides Again* (1939), in which she kidded her past image as a sexy siren. A trio of her early 1940s features (such as 1942's *The Spoilers*) teamed Marlene with her new lover, John Wayne. To keep him happy, she spent some of their free time together on hunting and fishing trips in the wilderness, although such outdoor diversions were not really her thing.

In the 1930s, Dietrich had refused Adolf Hitler's offer for her to return to Germany to make movies extolling the Third Reich. To emphasize her allegiance to the West, she became an American citizen in 1938. During World War II, she was a tireless volunteer at the Hollywood Canteen, went on war bond–selling tours, and performed overseas for the troops (often in dangerous front-line zones). Less publicized during her extensive USO tours were her romances, including intermittent ones with Allied officers. Occasionally, she reconnected with French film star Jean Gabin, who was serving with the Free French Army. (Dietrich and Gabin had had a passionate connection in late 1930s France and later when he was in Hollywood. After the war, they made one picture together—1946's *Martin Roumagnac*—but their "great love" failed to last.)

In her mid-forties, Dietrich adjusted her glamorous image to suit post–World War II Hollywood. Playing a conniving gypsy, she teamed with Ray Milland in *Golden Earrings* (1947), but she and the past Oscar-winning star feuded for much of the production. By now Marlene's daughter, Maria, had wed for a second time and the couple had their first child in 1948. Dietrich used the situation to promote herself as the "World's Most Glamorous Grandmother."

The 1950s found Marlene starring in a radio series (*Café Istanbul*), making records and occasional movies (1952's *Rancho Notorious*), and having a variety of romantic connections that included actor Yul Brynner and swinging Rat Pack leader Frank Sinatra. Professionally, she launched herself as a cabaret chanteuse, which led to tours around the world. Craftily creating the mirage of youth on stage, she intrigued audiences well into the 1970s. Then age caught up with her, causing a hardening of the arteries (which made it difficult for her to stand for long periods), and she began to lose her hearing. After suffering a series of accidents on stage, she finally retired her act.

Ensconced in her Paris apartment, she made a brief return to filmmaking—receiving a $250,000 salary for two days' work—in *Just a Gigolo* (1979).

Determined to protect her legend, she became increasingly reclusive in her Paris digs, communicating mostly by phone with friends around the world. Often lonely and frequently drunk, she struggled through her final years, dying in May 1992. At her request, she was buried in Schöneberg, Germany, at the Friedenau Cemetery beside her mother's grave.

With Dietrich's passing, the world lost a twentieth-century legend. She was a complex, self-absorbed screen goddess who whirled through the tapestry of an amazing life—one filled with the famous from the creative arts and politics. However, in her glittery journey around the globe and through the decades, she usually paused only long enough to appreciate her own image in the mirror.

Shannen Doherty

[Shannen Maria Doherty]
APRIL 12, 1971–

Like Cybill Shepherd, another native of Memphis, Tennessee, Doherty gained a reputation early in her show-business career for being outspoken, headstrong, and self-centered. While Shannen was building her fame in the early 1990s on TV's *Beverly Hills, 90210*, she also became known for being hard-edged in interviews, for annoying coworkers by some-times showing up late to the set, and for being fearlessly confrontational with her employers. Away from the soundstage, Doherty added to her young diva résumé by partying hard on the Tinseltown club circuit and by repeatedly exhibiting reckless behavior (which sometimes got her into legal scrapes). All of this made it easy to understand why the media soon pigeonholed her as a holy terror. With such a bad girl reputation, she was an easy target for TV comics who lampooned her surly ways; she even became the subject of an "I Hate Brenda" newsletter (and later a book) put out to mock her TV alter ego, Brenda Walsh, and the actress herself.

Unsurprisingly, Shannen had a different perception of herself and her strange life choices. For example, in 1994, she and producer Aaron Spelling came to a greatly publicized parting of the ways and she departed *Beverly Hills, 90210*. According to the much-misunderstood Doherty, "Let me start by saying it wasn't like I walked out one day and said, 'I quit.' It was a very long process of quitting the show. Aaron got as fed up with me as I was with the show, and I think it was because the notoriety was too much. People were hating the character and I couldn't take the abuse that came with that. People couldn't separate me from her and I got sick of people assuming that I was as naughty and bad as Brenda was. It was all very hurtful." The actress insisted, "I don't think anybody allowed me to grow up. They didn't look at it objectively and say, 'You know what, this girl got on the show [*Beverly Hills, 90210*] when she was eighteen and a half years old. My God, let's cut her a break. Of course, she's going to go out there and trouble may come her way because of who she is.' Instead it was like this fleet of piranhas attacking me and putting me out there for a feeding frenzy." Thus, in Shannen's special world, it was the press who unfairly gave her a bad rap.

Born in Memphis in 1971, she was the second child (there was already a boy named Sean) of Tom and Rosa Doherty. She was brought up in a conservative Southern Baptist household and an overall environment where men were the dominant sex. This chauvinistic way of life angered the youngster: "I saw how women were treated and I wasn't going to be treated like that."

When she was six, the Doherty clan moved to Southern California, where Tom had acquired a trucking firm. The family settled into an ocean-view home in Palos Verdes, a pleasant upscale Los Angeles neighborhood. A few years later, Tom's business fell apart and money became tight.

While her father was transitioning to a new occupation (he later became a mortgage consultant), Shannen began her own career. She went along with Sean when he auditioned for a community center play. She found herself cast as Sneezy, one of the dwarfs in a production of *Snow White and the Seven Dwarfs*. This led to her doing commercials and, in late 1981, a guest role on the TV series *Father Murphy*. Actor/producer Michael Landon spotted her and cast her as Jenny Wilder on the last season (1982–83) of his popular *Little House on the Prairie* series.

By the time *Little House* ended, twelve-year-old Doherty was attending a Baptist

A smiling Shannen Doherty.
(Photo by Albert L. Ortega)

school and was not pleased by the "repressed" atmosphere there. Going against school policy, she organized a school dance. The unhappy principal summoned the teenager to his office. Said Doherty, "He had his Bible out there on his desk and told me how God would punish me. I flipped through his Bible and found references to people dancing and rejoicing. I said to him, 'It clearly shows they danced and rejoiced. Just what the f*** is wrong with you?' " Since her family was once again financially stable, independent-minded Shannen was transferred to a private school. From 1986 to 1988, she played one of Deidre Hall's children in the teleseries *Our House*. In 1989, she had a role in the movie *Heathers*, playing a bitch.

In 1989, eighteen-year-old Doherty upset her parents by leaving home to move in with a thirty-one-year-old boyfriend. During this time she experimented with drinking and drugs and was out clubbing almost nightly. The bad scene came to an end six months into the relationship, when her boyfriend slapped her. She turned on her heel and returned home. (Later, she bought her own place.)

It was Aaron Spelling's actress daughter, Tori, who had seen Doherty on *Our House* and recommended the young woman to her father for a key role in *Beverly Hills, 90210*. When the TV series debuted in October 1990, Shannen and Tori were both key players in the ensemble cast. Before long, five-foot, four-inch Doherty became known on the set as someone who marched to her own beat. For example, if she had evening plans, she'd walk up to those in charge and insist it was time to quit for the day. In addition, friction developed between Shannen and some of her female costars.

Meanwhile, she was briefly engaged to Dean Factor (of the Max Factor makeup family) in 1990. They had a volatile relationship, which ended the next year. (Dean later petitioned the courts for a restraining order against his ex-fiancée, claiming she had tried to run him over with her car. He also alleged other unfriendly actions: She threatened him with a loaded gun; she threw a log through a window of his home

in order to break in; and according to the complainant, she mentioned her desire to "hire a few guys to beat me up and sodomize me on the front lawn.") Also in 1991, Doherty, who had problems with checks that didn't clear, became involved with real estate developer Chris Foufas. Although they exchanged engagement rings, they separated in 1992.

That same year club-loving Shannen was a guest on Dennis Miller's cable TV talk show. On camera, she undiplomatically asked the then-novice host whether his twitching eyebrow might indicate he was nervous. (The displeased host retaliated by making her the butt of jokes on later installments of the program.) At the Emmy Awards later in 1992, Doherty was scheduled to be a presenter, but she dropped out of the proceedings the day before the show. She claimed her manager had yanked her from the festivities because the event was not going to showcase her as promised. The angered producer of the event labeled the actress a "colossal pain in the a**."

May 1993 found Shannen in Dallas, Texas, out on the town with Judd Nelson (a former Brat Packer); she was drinking "heavily" and, according to the restaurant's manager, she "puked at her table." After she and Nelson parted, Doherty rebounded by marrying Ashley Hamilton in September 1993. She had known the four-year-younger Ashley (son of actor George Hamilton) for only a few weeks. Their unstable union terminated in April 1994 when she decided their marriage was "stupid."

Also in 1994, Shannen made her high-profile exit from *90210* and could be seen in the movie *Blindfolded: Acts of Obsession*, in which she appeared nude. As if embarrassed by her on-screen nakedness, she claimed that the producers had used a body double for at least half the revealing shots. However, it was Shannen who had been featured revealingly in *Playboy* in both 1993 and 1994. In the latter year, Doherty began a relationship with actor/director Rob Weiss. It lasted four years before they called it quits. For a change, the breakup was friendly.

Doherty had a colead in the 1995 cable movie, *Jailbreakers*, but she almost wasn't part of the proceedings; filmmaker William Friedkin was highly upset when she failed to appear for the initial day of filming and almost canned her. In August 1996, a belligerent Doherty had another encounter of the unpleasant kind. She got into a confrontation with a fellow diner at a Los Angeles restaurant. Unsatisfied with the resolution, a steamed Shannen followed the man out to the parking lot where she broke a beer bottle against his car window as he attempted to drive away. The charge was dropped to a misdemeanor for vandalism, thanks to a plea bargain. Pleading no contest when she appeared in Beverly Hills Municipal Court, she paid a $2,500 fine and undertook required anger-management counseling.

To the industry's surprise, producer Aaron Spelling asked Shannen to be one of the three female leads in a new TV series, *Charmed*, in which she played a witch. The show debuted in fall 1998 and everything appeared to be harmonious. However, by the start of its third season, there was gossip that Doherty and one of her costars, Alyssa Milano, were no longer on good terms. The discord was allegedly over the show's focus and promotion favoring Milano. The frosty soundstage atmosphere led to Shannen leaving the hit show midway through its 2000–2001 season after the producers (including Spelling) sided with Alyssa. But Doherty had her revenge; she owned a small percentage of the program. Said Shannen gleefully, "They get to go to work every single day, and in the long run, I'll collect the money. It's great."

Doherty, the queen of the tabloids, was back in the news in December 2000. She was stopped by the California Highway Patrol for erratic driving. She vetoed a sobriety test and was arrested and given a nonconsensual blood alcohol test. It registered 0.13 percent, putting her over the legal limit. After ten hours in a holding cell, the actress—who claimed to suffer from claustrophobia—became very upset before she was finally released on her own recognizance. The case came before the court in mid-2001, and Shannen was ordered to pay a $1,500 fine, do twenty days (later reduced to five days) in a work-release program, serve three years' probation, and give lectures to teenagers on the dangers of drunk driving. After a few months of giving talks at Mothers Against Drunk Drivers meetings, the judge reduced her work-release program sentence from twenty to five days.

In 2001, Shannen had dated Julian McMahon, a *Charmed* cast member. But later that year, she met Rick Salomon, a film producer, at a Sunset Strip club. In short order, she moved into his Beverly Hills home. On January 27, 2002, Shannen (thirty) and Salomon (thirty-three) married in Las Vegas.

Six months later, however, the marriage took a sour turn when Salomon temporarily moved out of the couple's home. He claimed he could no longer deal with her excessive jealousy and rages over his supposed infidelities.

Not long ago, Shannen said, "I want to do work that is fulfilling and challenging. If I read something that I find a little scary because I'm not sure I can pull it off, that means I have to do it." It sounds like the same philosophy that the troubled actress has used in her private life.

Patty Duke

[Anna Marie Duke]
December 14, 1946–

Sometimes child stars (like Shirley Temple and Gary Coleman) who continue in show business into adulthood find they cannot recapture their past fame. Others (such as Elizabeth Taylor and Rick Schroeder) are fortunate enough to enjoy equal or greater success in their grown-up years. In either case, it requires a great emotional effort on the part of the ex–child celebrity to cope constructively with adulthood. Few have had a more traumatic or publicized period of adjustment than Patty Duke.

At age thirteen, she was the youngest Broadway performer ever to have her name placed above the title on a theater marquee. A few years later, the famous teenager won a Best Supporting Actress Academy Award for recreating her powerful stage role of young

Patty Duke in *Billie* (1965).
(Courtesy of JC Archives)

Helen Keller in *The Miracle Worker* (1962). Next, she was starring—in dual roles—in the hit TV sitcom *The Patty Duke Show* (1963–66). Unfortunately, by then she'd gained a reputation with coworkers as "The Little S***," a foul-mouthed, rampaging tyrant encased within a petite five-foot-tall body. Later, when Patty had leading roles in movies (for example, 1967's *Valley of the Dolls*), her horrendous mood swings upset the casts and crews.

Many thought her erratic behavior was caused by escalating substance abuse. Stuck with a reputation of being "difficult," many work opportunities became unobtainable. If that wasn't bad enough, she'd also been labeled an unpredictable kook. For example, she chased after the younger Desi Arnaz Jr., married a near-total stranger on a sudden impulse in 1970, and ended the hasty union thirteen days later. In 1971, she gave birth to a baby, and in later annulment proceedings stated that her husband wasn't the child's father. As a result, much of Hollywood and the public regarded Patty as just another spoiled-rotten ex–kid star barreling along on a self-destructive path. What no one—not even Patty—knew at the time was that she was suffering from severe manic depression.

She was born Anna Marie Duke in New York City in 1946, the third child and second daughter of John Patrick Duke, a cab driver, and his wife, Frances McMahon. By the time Anna was seven, her alcoholic father had left the family for good (he died when she was a young teenager), and her mother was working as a restaurant cashier. Anna attended the Sacred Hearts of Jesus and Mary School near the Dukes' modest Manhattan apartment.

In the early 1950s, Anna's brother Raymond joined the Madison Square Boys' Club and participated in some of their plays. He came to the attention of John and Ethel Ross, who managed child actors. They took Raymond on as a client and began booking him for TV roles. When Anna was eight, her brother introduced her to the Rosses. They decided not only to represent the budding actress but also to remold her. They coached her in acting, worked to rid her of a pronounced New York accent, and revamped her hairstyle and clothing. By 1956, she was performing in small roles on live TV in Manhattan.

In their reshaping of the youngster—and to distance her further from her family—the Rosses one day told the girl, "Anna Marie is dead. You're Patty now." The unilateral decision so upset the newly named Patty Duke that she developed a morbid fear of death. Before long the couple decided that Patty should live with them in their Manhattan apartment in the West Seventies. The pliant Mrs. Duke agreed, thinking she was helping her daughter gain a better life. However, Patty was traumatized by the move. She was convinced that her mother had abandoned her because she'd been a bad child.

At the Rosses, Patty did not have her own room, sleeping on a sofa in the hall instead. Her mentors introduced the youngster to their lifestyle, which included taking pep pills and injections and, later, drinking alcohol. Further down the line, she suffered from attempted sexual molestation by each of her strict instructors. (Duke repressed these traumas for years.) During this period, Duke usually only saw her mother when she came to clean the Rosses' apartment, which was part of the deal for their training of Patty.

Besides acting on television and in an occasional film shot in New York, Duke became a contestant on TV's $64,000 Challenge in 1958. She won $32,000, which went into her income accounts that the Rosses controlled and used largely for themselves. The next year, Patty was summoned to appear before a New York grand jury that was investigating rigged TV quiz shows. Upon direction from the Rosses, Duke lied about not being prepped as to the winning answers. Later, she perjured herself with a U.S. Congressional Committee on the same topic. She subsequently recanted and told the committee the truth but was not punished.

In preparation for an audition for a forthcoming Broadway play that had a demanding role for a young actress, the Rosses tutored Patty for several months in playing a blind and deaf girl. Thus, she was well equipped to shine at her audition for *The Miracle Worker*. From its October 1959 opening until five weeks before it closed in July 1961—with only a few brief vacations in between—Patty played the exhausting and very physical role of the young, handicapped Helen Keller. During the lengthy run, Duke's costar Anne Bancroft left the production. Patty was so upset at losing her beloved substitute mother that she reacted by being aggressive and negative toward Bancroft's replacement, Suzanne Pleshette.

While starring on TV's *The Patty Duke Show*, the actress appeared as her well-rehearsed, sweetness-and-light self in interviews with the media. In actuality, she was deeply upset. She had a growing resentment against the Rosses, who had not only cast off her real name and mother but had also manipulated her income to their own financial advantage. In rebellion, Patty wed thirty-two-year-old TV director Harry Falk Jr. in November 1965. She severed her ties to the Rosses but nevertheless felt guilty about doing so. (John Ross died in 1970; Ethel, in 1978.)

By the time *The Patty Duke Show* left the air in 1966, the young star was an emotional and physical mess. She suffered from anorexia, was extremely depressed, and attempted suicide in 1967. She announced on a TV talk show that she was retiring from show business to build an ark in the desert. Nonetheless, she signed to make *Valley of the Dolls*. She hoped her screen role as an addicted singer/actress would give her a new, more mature image. While the trashy movie didn't, her activities on and off the set did. As her marriage and life were falling apart, she was hospitalized a few times for emotional distress. After she and Falk divorced in 1969, she dated Desi Arnaz Jr. The media hyped the fact that she was a twenty-three-year-old divorcée and he was a seventeen-year-old kid. The boy's mother, Lucille Ball, made it clear publicly that she disapproved of the love match.

At the Emmy Awards on June 7, 1970, Patty won a trophy for her fine work in the telefeature *My Sweet Charlie*. Accepting the prize on national TV, she delivered a rambling, incoherent speech. The media linked her irrational behavior to substance abuse. (Years later, Duke explained that, because of the pressures in her life then, she was having an emotional breakdown during the ceremony.) Three weeks later, the unstable actress married twenty-five-year-old rock 'n' roll promoter Mike Tell, whom she hardly knew. By July, she had announced she was pregnant and that she and Tell were breaking up. What she refused to reveal at the time was that her baby was the result of an affair with married actor John Astin. As she was Catholic, an abortion was not an option. During this anxious period, she underwent psychiatric therapy.

In August 1972, Patty and the now-divorced Astin (who had three sons by his first marriage) wed. They worked together frequently on TV and in stage tours. On the surface, Duke, who became the mother of Mackenzie Astin in May 1973, seemed to have recovered from her troubled past. In actuality, however, she was still struggling with great emotional tensions, aggravated by the pressures of her and John working constantly to support their family. Throughout this stressful decade, Patty appeared frequently in TV movies and miniseries—she won Emmys for 1976's *Captains and the Kings* and 1979's *The Miracle Worker* (playing Annie Sullivan in this remake)—and only occasionally in a theatrical feature (such as 1978's *The Swarm*).

Finally, in 1982, Patty Duke was diagnosed as manic depressive and given treatment (which included doses of lithium). She regained her life, a blessing, which she wrote about later in 1992's *A Brilliant Madness: Living with Manic-Depressive Illness*. Nevertheless, her marriage to Astin was over. They divorced in 1985, the same year in which she was elected president of the Screen Actors Guild. While filming the made-for-TV movie *A Time to Triumph* (1986) at Fort Benning, Georgia, she met Staff Sergeant Michael Pearce. They wed in March 1986. Later, he left the military and became her business partner. Eventually, the couple relocated to Coeur d'Alene, Idaho, and, in 1989, they adopted a baby whom they named Kevin. During and since the 1990s, Patty has continued to be extremely active in TV, her work ranging from telefeatures (1993's *No Child of Mine*, 1997's *A Christmas Memory*, 2002's *Little John*) to a series (1995's *Amazing Grace*). In June 2002, Duke appeared in a Los Angeles stage production of the musical *Follies*.

In 1987, Duke coauthored her bestselling autobiography (*Call Me Anna*). She pulled no punches about her abusive childhood or the years of manic rage, uncontrollable spending sprees, and turbulent relationships. At the end of her harrowing memoir, she wrote, "I've survived. I've beaten my own bad system and on some days, on most days, that feels like a miracle."

Faye Dunaway

[Dorothy Faye Dunaway]
JANUARY 14, 1941–

"The fact is," Dunaway once noted, "a man can be difficult and people applaud him . . . a woman can try to get it right and she's a pain in the ass." Perhaps Faye's remark was prompted by a statement made by Roman Polanski, her *Chinatown* (1974) director: "She was a gigantic pain in the ass. She demonstrated certifiable proof of insanity." On another occasion, the Oscar-winning Dunaway further discussed her industry reputation: "I'm not difficult. Never difficult. I'm talented. I am demanding. I give my best. I expect the same from others. I'm deeply serious about my work." Some heartily disagreed

The driven Oscar winner, long noted for doing things Faye's way, has her own theory about living life: "They say that quality time is better than quantity time, but I don't agree. I think quantity is a lot better. . . . I get a lot done. I know how to work very fast. I do three or four things at once, which actually I enjoy doing. I like being very busy. I think that's the definition of stardom, really. It's energy. It really is."

on the merits of that statement, including two-time Oscar-winner Bette Davis, who costarred with Dunaway in the 1976 telefeature *The Disappearance of Aimee*. Said the legendary Bette: "Faye Dunaway is the most unprofessional actress I ever worked with, and that includes Miriam Hopkins, even!" These were strong words from Davis, who despised Hopkins even more than she did "that bitch" Joan Crawford. Another woman who worked on that infamous 1970s TV movie about Sister Aimee McPherson was hairdresser Peggy Shannon. She reported that Dunaway was "the biggest disaster in my years in the business. . . . I had to run like hell because she was going to belt me."

The five-foot, seven-inch cyclone known as Faye Dunaway, however, felt she had righteousness as her ally. The rarely modest actress explained, "When I'm working well, I like to think I'm doing God's work."

She was born Dorothy Faye Dunaway in 1941 in the small town of Bascom, Florida, located on the state's panhandle. Dorothy was the older of two children (her brother was named Mac) of John MacDowell Dunaway, a farmer, and Grace April Smith, a homemaker. During World War II, John served in the army. He remained in the military when he returned

to the States after the armistice. His family moved with him as he was restationed from one military post to another, including sojourns in Texas, Arkansas, Utah, and Germany. Dorothy was a high school sophomore when her parents divorced. She and Mac moved with their mother (who later remarried) to Tallahassee, Florida. Although money was tight, Grace scraped together enough for her daughter to have dance, piano, and voice lessons. Even as a child, Dorothy had a driving ambition to succeed and to be, as her mother recalled, "the best and the biggest" at whatever she chose to do.

After a year on scholarship at Florida State University, Dunaway matriculated at the University of Florida to be close to her boyfriend, a gridiron player. As part of the campus drama group, she played the title role in *Medea*. The green-eyed blond also entered local beauty pageants. In fall 1960, she transferred to Boston University's School of Fine and Applied Arts, having broken off with her suitor. To help pay her way through school, Dorothy worked as a waitress. In her senior year at Boston University, she performed the lead in *The Crucible*. That drama's director, Lloyd Richards, was so impressed with her acting talents that he referred her to the creative heads of the Lincoln Center Repertory Theater. When she was accepted into the Manhattan group, she rejected a Fulbright scholarship to London's Royal Academy of Dramatic Arts. Meanwhile, she was also cast to play the lead character's daughter in the ongoing Broadway show *A Man for All Seasons*. As a result, the ambitious newcomer—now called Faye Dunaway—was performing on the New York stage just a few weeks after her mid-1962 graduation from BU.

From July 1962 until the following June, Faye played on Broadway in the evenings and studied acting with the theater company during the day. (During this period, she had a brief love affair with controversial stand-up comedian Lenny Bruce.) Her first featured role with the repertory group was in the comedy *But for Whom Charlie* in March 1964. At the end of that year, the group's leadership changed, and, a few months later, Dunaway was among those let go. A few weeks thereafter, she was cast in the off-Broadway production of the drama *Hogan's Goat*. It opened in November 1965 and Faye earned excellent notices.

Her *Hogan's Goat* performance led to her being hired for her first movie, the heist yarn *The Happening* (1967). Although few moviegoers saw Dunaway in this box-office misfire, she already had a multipicture deal with veteran filmmaker Otto Preminger. He cast her in *Hurry Sundown* (1967), a trashy Southern melodrama starring Jane Fonda and Michael Caine. On location in the broiling Louisiana heat, she and the autocratic director differed about the interpretation of her earthy, farm girl character. Tempers flared, with Dunaway

Faye Dunaway on the Hollywood scene.
(Photo by Albert L. Ortega)

refusing to yield to the director's point of view because, "Once I've been crossed, I'm not very conciliatory." This led her to announce that she would not make any of the five remaining pictures required by her contract. Otto said fine. The two completed Faye's remaining scenes in icy politeness. Thereafter, Dunaway assumed she was through with dictatorial Otto. However, he later changed his mind, and Dunaway eventually had to buy her way out of the pact. The much-publicized case put Hollywood on notice that Faye was *not* to be taken lightly.

After Jane Fonda and others had turned down costarring with Warren Beatty in *Bonnie and Clyde* (1967), Dunaway was hired. To play the Depression-era gun moll, she dropped thirty pounds. During production, she not only insisted on doing her own stunts, but also demanded that she—*not* the film's professional crew—apply her makeup. The concessions were made. When this remarkable gangster picture was released, her performance stood out. She was Oscar-nominated and her asking fee per picture leaped tenfold to about $300,000. Being in demand, however, doesn't mean a (new) star can smell a good project. Her next film, *The Extraordinary Seaman* (1968), flopped, as did the Italian-made *A Place for Lovers* (1969). The latter at least allowed her to pursue her romance with costar Marcello Mastroianni. On the plus side, she had a glamorous role in the hit caper yarn *The Thomas Crown Affair* (1968). However, chauvinistic Steve McQueen and his aggressive leading lady remained extremely wary of each other throughout production.

Before her romance with Mastroianni, Faye had been engaged to fashion photographer–turned–moviemaker Jerry Schaltzberg. After her Italian sojourn ended, Dunaway still agreed to star in Jerry's *Puzzle of a Downfall Child* (1971) as a neurotic fashion model who undergoes a nervous breakdown. The reaction to this arty entry was mixed at best. By 1974, thirty-something Dunaway needed a hit. She had it with her Oscar-nominated role in the film noir *Chinatown*. But during the high-profile production, she and diminutive director Roman Polanski battled constantly and publicly.

Having proved off camera and on that she was convincing as a tough dame, she grabbed the role of steel-hearted, driven Diane Christensen, the TV network vice president of programming in *Network* (1976). She finally won her Oscar and had unknowingly reached her career peak. Meanwhile, in August 1974, she wed rock singer Peter Wolf of the J. Geils Band. However, the match ended in 1977 after she encountered British photographer Terrence O'Neill. Their romance progressed; they married secretly; and their child, Liam, was born in 1980.

Originally, Anne Bancroft was to star in *Mommie Dearest* (1981), the screen adaptation of Christina Crawford's tell-all book about her movie star mother, Joan. Bancroft backed out, and Dunaway took over. The tragedy and horror delineated in Christina's vengeful text became overdone melodrama on screen, reducing the intended biographical exposé to farce. Faye attacked her characterization with ferocity, which in the context of the unsubtle production, caused her to emerge as high camp in what one publication called the "comedy hit of the season." So trashed was the film and Faye's over-the-top performance that her career went into a free fall.

Dunaway spent much of the early 1980s in England with O'Neill and Liam. The couple formed a production company, but it did nothing to bolster her faltering career. By 1987, Faye and her son were back in Los Angeles and her marriage to O'Neill was over. Now in her mid-forties, Faye found the movie pickings lean. Occasionally she shone—as in 1987's *Barfly* and in the 1993 police detective TV movie *Columbo: It's All in the Game* (1993)—but more often she just added character lead presence to fluff such as *Dunston Checks In* (1996). Meanwhile, her efforts at TV sitcom failed when she teamed with Robert Urich for *It Had to Be You*, which lasted on air for only a month in fall 1993.

During this time, she went up against Britain's Andrew Lloyd Webber, the creator of the musical *Sunset Boulevard*. In 1994, it was announced that Faye would take over on July 12 for Glenn Close as the star of the Los Angeles production of the hit show. In June, however, Webber announced that he had let Dunaway go ("She could not satisfactorily sing the part," the composer insisted) and was closing the show there. In August, Faye, who had told the media that Webber's action was "yet another capricious act by a capricious man," sued him for $6 million. She claimed breach of contract, defamation, and fraud. The battle of wills raged until January 1995, when an out-of-court settlement was reached with victorious Dunaway receiving hefty compensation for her distress.

Still keeping professionally active (2001's *The Calling*, 2002's *The Rules of Attraction*, and 2003's *El Padrino*), the passing years have softened Dunaway's hard edges, if not her thirst to keep her star shining. Once, when asked what makes a star, she shot back, "Everything! Charisma—what I used to call in drama school, the shine. Internal, emotional, physical energy—it goes beyond the body and you can't control it."

Jane Fonda

[Jane Seymour Fonda]

DECEMBER 21, 1937–

Over several decades in the limelight she has been a chameleon, shedding one public image for another. Whatever her posture at any given time—and her viewpoint often changed drastically over the years—she has always been a vociferous crusader, determined to convert everyone within hearing range and brooking no opposition in the process. Sometimes her causes (such as fitness) were endorsed by the masses and made her a tremendously wealthy woman. On other occasions, her agenda (for example, feminism) created less enthusiasm in some quarters. In contrast, her strong views in the 1970s against America's participation in the Vietnam War drew a tremendous negative reaction from both zealous right-wingers and patriots across America. Some members of the U.S. Congress wanted her censured; other hotheads insisted "Hanoi Jane" should be branded a traitor, tried, and shot.

The fervor of Jane's activism was equally intense whenever she supported the beliefs of her then-current husband (whether French filmmaker Roger Vadim, extreme left-wing Democratic politician Tom Hayden, or media mogul Ted Turner). Each time she divorced one of these completely different men, she moved on to a *new* Jane and a new cause. Such turnabouts left many observers wondering whether Fonda was more stimulated by the act of proselytizing than by a deep belief in the message she presented. This theory gained credence when she told a British publication in April 1980, "Today I'd be a dyed blonde, a numb and dumb pill-popping star, if I hadn't taken up a cause. I could very well be dead like Marilyn [Monroe]. Not through drugs but dead just the same."

She was born in New York City in 1937, the first child of film and stage star Henry Fonda and his second wife, Frances Seymour Brokaw, an East Coast socialite and widow of George Brokaw, a New York congressman and playboy. (Jane's brother Peter, who also became an actor, was born in 1940; there were also two half-sisters—Frances, the Brokaws' daughter, and Amy, whom Henry adopted with his third wife, Susan Blanchard.) Because of her ancestral relationship—on her mother's side—to Lady Jane Seymour, the third wife of England's King Henry VIII, the future actress was nicknamed "Lady Jane" as a child. As her dad

Rod Taylor, Jane Fonda, and Robert Culp in *Sunday in New York* (1963). (Courtesy of JC Archives)

moved back and forth between New York and Los Angeles for acting assignments, the girl had a bicoastal childhood, attending assorted private schools. When Jane was thirteen, her emotionally disturbed mother, who had been put in a private sanatorium, committed suicide. It wasn't until a year later that Jane learned from a movie magazine that Frances had not died of a heart attack (as Jane had been told) but had slashed her throat. These traumatizing events left a mark on Jane for life.

In 1955, Jane made her stage debut in a small role in *The Country Girl*, presented in Henry's hometown of Omaha, Nebraska. During the summer of 1956, following her freshman year at Vassar, she apprenticed at the Cape Playhouse in Dennis, Massachusetts. More concerned with her enthusiastic partying than studying, the aimless rich girl left Vassar after her sophomore year. She spent a few months in Paris, ostensibly to study the arts, but instead majored in the jet-setting lifestyle. An annoyed Henry insisted she return to the United States. Bored by a clerical job in Manhattan at the *Paris Review*, the dilettante enrolled at the Actors Studio. To pay for her acting lessons, the five-foot, seven-inch Jane became a fashion model. In class, she met actor/instructor Andreas Voutsinas. Jane was enthralled by the dominating Voutsinas, but her usually undemonstrative father disliked the man intensely, calling him "an evil molder of Jane's personality."

One of Henry Fonda's good friends was producer/director Joshua Logan, who placed Jane under personal contract. He cast her as the rape victim in the short-lived Broadway drama *There Was a Little Girl* (1959) and then directed Jane in her film debut, the comedy *Tall Story* (1960). Despite these and other projects, Jane defiantly remained under Voutsinas's control. That changed, however, after he directed her in *The Fun Couple* (1962), an instant flop on Broadway. She decided she must become a star and to do so she must be free of Andreas.

Between Broadway ventures, Jane made more movies. In *Period of Adjustment* (1962), she showed a flair for comedy. Wanting freedom to expand herself, she relocated to France where she made *Joy House* (1963) and had a fling with Alain Delon, her handsome leading man. The French media was enthusiastic about Fonda and labeled her "La BB Americaine," referring to France's reigning cinema sexpot, Brigitte Bardot. The latter's intrigued husband, Roger Vadim, directed Jane in the movie *Circle of Love* (1964). Vadim then divorced Brigitte, and he and Jane wed in Las Vegas in August 1965. Their daughter, Vanessa, was born three years later. Between projects with Vadim, Jane flew to Hollywood to make the popular Western spoof *Cat Ballou* (1965) and such other entries as *Barefoot in the Park* (1967) with Robert Redford.

Back when Jane made her first screen test, studio mogul Jack L. Warner had warned her,

"You'll never become a movie star if you're flat-chested." But with padding, careful costuming, and creative camera angles, Jane proved him wrong in the Vadim-directed *Barbarella* (1968), a bizarre science-fiction spoof. The movie exploited her sexuality, and her delayed anger over that fact soured her marriage to Vadim. Back in the States, she had a highly dramatic role in *They Shoot Horses, Don't They?* (1969), for which she received the first of seven Oscar nominations. However, she won an Academy Award playing the nervous prostitute in *Klute* (1971), a thriller costarring Donald Sutherland (who was Jane's friend and lover during this period).

In the early 1970s, the previously apolitical Jane became extremely militant about her politics. She was especially vehement about her anti–Vietnam War stance and her support of the Black Panther and Native American movements. This put her at odds with her conservative father, made her an archenemy to President Richard Nixon and his followers, and got her into legal trouble. Under constant government surveillance, she was arrested at the airport in Cleveland, Ohio, in November 1970, on suspicion of illegal importation of drugs (which proved to be vitamins) from Canada. Later released, she reveled in her new-found celebrity and "martyrdom."

Fonda took her image to a whole new level when, on an invitation from the North Vietnamese, she visited that country. While there she did broadcasts on Radio Hanoi, advocating that the U.S. military stop bombing North Vietnam. Back in America, she was blacklisted by the major studios, who feared her negative public image had ruined her box-office appeal. Meanwhile, she had fallen in love with California politician Tom Hayden, joining his anti-war and anti-Nixon campaigns. Pregnant with his child, she divorced Vadim in early 1973, married Hayden a few days later, and in July of that year gave birth to their son, Troy. Because the Haydens' funds were at a low ebb, they resided very frugally in Venice, California—a lifestyle Jane found invigorating for a time—and she worked industriously on Tom's bid for the U.S. Senate. That race failed and the Haydens increasingly turned their efforts to environmental causes.

Jane made peace with Hollywood and had a box-office success with *Fun with Dick and Jane* (1976), followed by her Oscar-nominated role in *Julia* (1977). Wanting more control over her pictures, she formed the IPC production company and won her second Oscar for *Coming Home* (1978). After another strong message film, *The China Syndrome* (1979), she costarred with her father in *On Golden Pond* (1981). Orchestrating the situation, she used the project to reach a personal accord with the dying Henry.

During this period, Jane, who had overcome many years of bulimia, turned her addiction to fitness into a business venture (and another crusade). She opened her first workout studio in Beverly Hills in 1979. Its success led to branches in other cities, a hugely best-selling workout book in 1981, several audio and video workout tapes, and a line of exercise clothing. As America's chic fitness guru, Fonda gained tremendous visibility. Meanwhile, in her sporadic acting career, by the

time of the poorly received *Old Gringo* (1989) and *Stanley & Iris* (1990), Jane was over fifty and movie offers were scarce. Also finished was her marriage to Hayden; they filed for divorce in 1989 and it became final in 1990.

Yet another Jane—one further enhanced by plastic surgery to keep that youthful look—emerged in the 1990s and demanded a fresh forum. She was now the trophy wife of a corporate mogul. Fonda had begun dating one-year-older Ted Turner, the media entrepreneur (worth about $1.6 billion), in late 1989. The couple wed on her fifty-fourth birthday at his Avalon Plantation estate in Florida. Pronounced the new Jane, "I firmly believe that we're at the perfect age to start over. There's so much that Ted and I can do to help make this a better planet for all of us. We're fortunate to have the tools."

But after a decade of being an adjunct to the Turner empire and keeping busy with civic duties (founding the Georgia campaign for Adolescent Pregnancy Prevention, donating $12.5 million to the Harvard Graduate School of Education for a study dealing with the role that gender plays in education, and so on), Jane and Ted divorced in May 2001. Said Fonda, "Now it's time to move on, and I wish him well." Later that year, she was ensconced at her New Mexico ranch, writing her memoirs. After appearing in the documentary *Searching for Debra Winger* (2002), Fonda allowed that she was considering the possibility of a film comeback. The latest Jane, who has rediscovered Christianity, pointed out she is now in the third act of her life, and as for being alone, "it is fascinating to me how good I feel about it."

Kay Francis

[Katherine Edwina Gibbs]

JANUARY 13, 1899–AUGUST 26, 1968

During Hollywood's Golden Age, she was one of Hollywood's top leading ladies. Acclaimed for her ability to showcase ultrachic wardrobes, the five-foot, nine-inch star was noted for her ravishing, dark looks (which included sad eyes and a famous widow's peak). Her laugh was lilting and many found her lisp (she had difficulty pronouncing the letter *r* properly) charming. In the early 1930s, Warner Bros. stole her away from Paramount Pictures, and for several years, she was their studio queen—established as one of Hollywood's highest-paid leading ladies, enjoying a charmed life, indulging her every whim.

Then, in 1938, Francis's screen career fell apart. The downfall was dramatically rapid, and even worse, her home lot made no bones about humiliating her within the industry and to her shocked fans. It was studio head Jack L. Warner's crude revenge on the high-priced, often temperamental player he no longer needed (Bette Davis became tops at Warner Bros.). The mogul hoped Kay would cancel the remainder of her lucrative contract out of sheer embarrassment. Francis, however, who had been cavalier about many aspects of her movie career, was *never* mindless of money. She gritted her teeth and worked her way through shoddy budget features. Even the press, whom she had frequently ignored or treated badly during her diva heyday, commented strongly about the cruel and childish treatment given this major screen name. In the entire history of American films it was one of the meanest put-downs ever carried out against a luminary.

Despite efforts to claim 1906 or 1910 as her birth year, she was born Katherine Edwina Gibbs in 1899 on Friday the 13th in Oklahoma City, Oklahoma. She was the only child of Joseph Sprague Gibbs (a former businessman–turned–hotel manager) and Katherine Clinton Franks, an actress. The family moved around the country a good deal because her father, an irresponsible heavy drinker, kept losing his job. By the time little Katherine was about four, mother and daughter had returned to the East Coast where the elder Katherine worked in theater. Contrary to later studio-manufactured publicity, which concocted a privileged childhood and education for Kay, the future movie star had, as one family friend observed, a very "third-rate" upbringing. She did spend one year at the Cathedral School of St. Mary in Garden City, Long Island, where she made her stage debut. Later, she attended secretarial school and began an assortment of jobs that included helping to arrange debutante parties in New York City. She married her first husband, playboy James Dwight Francis, in December 1922. By the time the ill-fated union ended in 1924, she'd had an abortion and suffered his physical abuse. (It was the first of her several unwise marriages, all of which ended in divorce.) She retained her married name, eventually shortening it to Kay Francis.

From her parents, Kay had inherited a thirst for drinking (which often led her to boisterousness and nastiness) and a love of partying. She moved in and out of relationships, leading a madcap life made possible by her beauty, fun-loving ways, and knack for networking among the sophisticated social set. One contact led to her being hired—because of her physical resemblance—as understudy to Katharine Cornell in the Broadway play, *The Green Hat* (1925). She would claim offhandedly that it was her casual attitude toward stage work that led to lucky breaks in gaining more theater assignments (such as 1927's *Venus*). Walter Huston, her costar from Broadway's *Elmer the Great* (1928), was hired by Paramount Pictures to star in *Gentlemen of the Press* (1929), to be shot at their Long Island studio. He suggested Kay for the part of a villainess. This screen debut earned her a studio contract and she was assigned to be a vamp in the Marx Brothers' *The Cocoanuts* (1929). Next, Paramount relocated the raven-haired actress to Hollywood for *Dangerous Curves* (1929), starring Clara Bow.

Stereotyped as a screen vamp, Francis made *Behind the Make-Up* (1930), the first of her many pictures with dapper William Powell. In January 1931, frolicking Kay wed dialogue director Kenneth McKenna, another marital mismatch that ended only months later, although the divorce was not finalized until 1934. En route, she'd had a fling with Paramount's French import, Maurice Chevalier. (It was also rumored that while at Paramount, the most cosmopolitan of all the Hollywood studios, Kay had had a brief affair with Marlene Dietrich and, possibly, one with Tallulah Bankhead.) On the social scene, Francis was

Kay Francis, the Queen of Warner Bros., in the mid-1930s. (Courtesy of JC Archives)

part of the smart, gay set that included Lilyan Tashman, her costar in *Girls About Town* (1931). Unlike other rising stars, Kay, who could be temperamental on the set, was firmly focused on money and fun and had little patience for fighting the studio for better roles or taking the time to cultivate the press.

Warner Bros., looking to bolster its star roster, secretly negotiated with Kay, William Powell, and Ruth Chatterton to abandon Paramount and come to its Burbank facility. The trio were wooed by high salary offers and multiple perks. With her improved income, Francis now rented a far more impressive home, but her only companion was her African American maid. (Kay's mother was scarcely part of her daughter's life, and on the rare occasion when she came to visit, she was kept under wraps and never allowed to visit her daughter at the studio.)

On-screen, Kay was again paired with William Powell, most notably in the romantic tearjerker *One Way Passage* (1932). That same year, she found herself loaned to Paramount for the sophisticated *Trouble in Paradise*. Instead of appreciating the opportunity to work with the great Ernst Lubitsch, she pouted because the production interfered with a planned vacation abroad. On *The Keyhole* (1933), she was teamed with George Brent, ironically then wed to her greatest studio rival, Ruth Chatterton. Francis moved from picture to picture—making five releases in 1934, including the musical *Wonder Bar*—coiffed and garbed as only a major star should be and expecting to be waited on hand and foot. Refusing to take her acting seriously, she didn't complain very much when some of her key scenes were cut to showcase a colead. Her bank account, her good times, and the satisfaction of her latest whims were the most important things. Or so it seemed.

Even a pampered leading lady can eventually tire of being primarily a clotheshorse in glossy women's pictures. She noticed how fellow contractees like Bette Davis were fighting tooth and nail for better parts. If they did, so should Kay. She demanded a highly dramatic role, a vehicle that would display her *real* acting abilities. Kay insisted on starring in a screen biography, a genre in which Warner Bros. excelled. They eventually gave her *The White Angel* (1936), the story of nursing great Florence Nightingale. The production proved uninspiring, with Francis miscast and looking unappealing in her Victorian nurse's garb. The studio and critics put the blame on Kay for the movie's failure, and it was the start of her professional decline. Off camera, Francis was involved romantically (and not very discreetly) with studio scripter Delmer Daves, and the differences in their work status made the relationship a no-no at Warner Bros. (There were also rumors of the highly sexual star having indiscreet flings with studio starlets, which further upset the studio brass, as did her romance with a German baron suspected of being a Nazi spy.)

Warner Bros. had previously promised to star Francis in the screen adaptation (1937) of Broadway's *Tovarich*, and when they gave this plum role to Claudette Colbert, an incensed Kay took the studio to court, demanding to be released from her contract. Because she had formerly alienated the press, they were generally unsympathetic to her legitimate gripe. After closed-door negotiations, she dropped her legal action and determined to stick it out at Warners to the bitter end. She was going to collect her $5,250 weekly salary "even if they put me in a bathing suit and have me walk up and down Hollywood Boulevard!" As a result, she suffered through six slapdash B pictures (such as 1938's *My Bill*) that destroyed her once-glamorous image as a major player. By the time Francis departed the studio in 1939, Bette Davis was the undisputed queen bee of the lot.

Thereafter, Kay worked freelance. Her projects ranged from playing the other woman in Cary Grant's *In Name Only* (1939) to supporting Rosalind Russell in *The Feminine Touch* (1941). She ended her Hollywood years coproducing and starring in low-budget junk (including 1945's *Allotment Wives*) at poverty-row Monogram Pictures. Francis returned to Broadway to take over the colead in *State of the Union* in 1946, toured in summer stock, and guest-starred on a few TV anthology drama shows in the early 1950s. By 1952, she had retired from show business. Still bitter about the ill treatment she'd received from Warner Bros., she lived in New York City, where her heavy drinking alienated many of her friends. Lonely, sad, but rich, she died of cancer in 1968. The bulk of her $1 million estate was left to the Seeing Eye Dog Foundation because "A dog has kindliness in his heart and dignity in his demeanor, the finest qualities anyone can have."

Once, years after her heyday, Kay encountered her former Warner Bros. rival, Bette Davis. When Bette asked why Francis had tolerated such abuse from Jack L. Warner, Kay responded, "I didn't give a damn. I wanted the money." Davis commented, "I didn't. I wanted the career."

Zsa Zsa Gabor

[Sari Gabor]

FEBRUARY 6, 1917–

Zsa Zsa once said, "Getting married is just the first step toward getting divorced." The glamorous Hungarian spoke from a great deal of experience, having shed several mates over the decades. When someone inquired exactly how many husbands she had had, Gabor parried, "You mean apart from my own?" Actually Zsa Zsa had a total of eight (plus one union that was declared invalid), which, when added to those of her sisters (Magda and Eva) and mother (Jolie) brought the total number of spouses for the Gabor girls to more than twenty!

If Eva was the best actress of the Gabor siblings, Zsa Zsa was the most colorful. She took the art of self-promotion and narcissism to an outrageous but generally entertaining level. She created an engaging persona for herself as a gold-digging femme fatale ("I am a marvelous housekeeper. Every time I leave a man I keep his house"). Her interest in jewels, furs, and ostentatious living was matched only by her overwhelming self-absorption ("As a woman, you have to choose between your fanny or your face. I chose my face"). What also made the witty Zsa Zsa so compelling were her exaggerated accent (punctuated constantly by drawn-out "darlings") and her rapid-fire delivery that buried the logic of her onslaught of verbiage.

She was born in Budapest, Hungary, in 1917 (although she later claimed her natal year to be as late as 1930). Sari was the second of three daughters of Vilmos and Jolie (Tilleman) Gabor and was soon nicknamed Zsa Zsa by her socially ambitious parents. Her father owned a jewelry establishment, and her mother had a porcelain and crystal store. Social-climbing Jolie, who had wanted to be an actress, was convinced that her three girls would become "rich, famous, and married to kings." As such, she ensured that their preparation for greatness included learning the piano, dancing, fencing, and several languages. When Zsa Zsa was thirteen, she attended a swank finishing school in Lausanne, Switzerland, as her older sister Magda had done. During the summer vacation of her second year there, she entered a Miss Hungary beauty pageant but missed winning because she'd lied about her age. Later, she studied at the Academy of Music and Dramatic Arts in Vienna, where she came to the attention of tenor Richard Tauber. He advised her to audition for an operetta (*Der Singende Traum*) for which he had provided the music and in which he planned to star. She won the soubrette's part and made her stage debut in Vienna in August 1934. About this time, the teenager had her first affair—with long-established German composer Willi Schmidt-Kentner.

Once back in Budapest, the restless young woman tired quickly of her father's strict supervision. To escape the discipline, she married the much-older Burhan Belge, the press director of the Turkish foreign ministry. She—along with her dog, Mishka—accompanied the Turk to Ankara. As a diplomat's wife, she came into the limelight (and claimed to have become close to President Kemal Ataturk). Zsa Zsa gained further publicity when she visited London in 1939 for sister Eva's first marriage.

By now, wherever she went, Zsa Zsa attracted media attention.

By 1941, Gabor ended her marriage and went to visit Eva, who was starting a film career in Hollywood. When Zsa Zsa encountered the (again) much-older Conrad Hilton, a hotel magnate, she told Eva, "*This* man I could marry." The couple wed in 1942 and established their life together in Bel-Air, the upper-crust Los Angeles suburb. It was not a happy union for either party and the couple finally divorced in 1946, although Zsa Zsa was then pregnant. Their daughter, Francesca, was born in 1947. From round two of her marital exploits, Gabor learned, "I have never hated a man enough to give his diamonds back."

While still wed to Hilton, Zsa Zsa had taken a strong liking to movie actor George Sanders from seeing his films. When she finally met the urbane, arrogant actor with the distinctive British accent, he immediately nicknamed her Cokiline (which translates to "little

As glittery and eye-catching as her beloved jewelry collection, Gabor made a spectacular career of her many marriages and self-promotion of her celebrityhood. But despite her high profile and many recorded words of "wisdom" on a multitude of topics, the Hungarian-born Zsa Zsa has claimed to be terribly misunderstood. Points of character she clarified in her second autobiography, *One Lifetime Is Not Enough* (1991) included:

"I would sacrifice every single diamond I own . . . for the life of one of my animals."

"I love and respect America and . . . I would give up everything for the good of my adopted country."

"I'm not a spoiled movie star, but a hardworking actress. . . ."

Vivacious Zsa Zsa Gabor in the 1970s.
(Courtesy of Echo Book Shop)

cookie"). They wed in April 1949, but she soon discovered the huge gulf that existed between her cynical, dour mate and her exuberant self. Sanders was frequently away on location making movies, leaving his bored bride to fill her days as best she could. Sometimes George's actor brother Tom Conway was her escort for an evening out on the town. On occasion, she consoled ex-husband Hilton's son Nicky, who was having problems in his marriage to Elizabeth Taylor. On a visit to New York City in 1952, Zsa Zsa encountered Dominican diplomat/playboy Porfiro Rubirosa, which began a long on-again, off-again courtship that spanned the United States and Europe; all the while she was still officially wed to the emotionally distant Sanders. The Rubirosa affair eventually expired. Meanwhile, Zsa Zsa and George divorced in 1954. (Later, Gabor insisted the primary problem between her and George had been that they were both in love with the same person—him! Years later, Sanders briefly wed Zsa Zsa's older sister, Magda. In 1972, he committed suicide. Zsa Zsa always said he was *one* of the true loves of her life.)

It was during those endless hours of having nothing to do while wed to Sanders that Zsa Zsa had fed her thirst for public attention by appearing on a TV quiz show (*Bachelor's Haven*). She proved to be so delightfully charming, witty, and electrifying that her appearance opened up a nearly full-time career for her as a favored guest on television talk shows and variety programs. Now her appetite was whetted for greater show-business challenges. If Eva could have a stage and film career of sorts, so could Zsa Zsa. The five-foot, three-inch blond made appearances in such movies as *Lovely to Look At* (1952) and *Lili* (1953). She registered strongly in *Moulin Rouge* (1952) as the beautiful model who poses for the famous French artist Toulouse-Lautrec (played by José Ferrer). Later came a starring role in the espionage spoof *The Girl in the Kremlin* (1957), a part in the camp favorite *Queen of Outer Space* (1958), and several movie cameos (such as 1958's *Touch of Evil* and 1967's *Jack of Diamonds*). She even starred on the Broadway stage, taking over the lead in *40 Carats* in 1970. However, the best forum for Gabor remained in front of the TV cameras (including a long stint on the *Hollywood Squares* quiz show).

If Zsa Zsa never had a hit TV series like Eva's *Green Acres* (1965–71), she continued to generate worldwide headlines through her multiple marriages, romances, television guest appearances, and knack for delivering bons mots (for example, "To a smart girl, men are no problem. They're the answer"). By 1986, she was wed to Prince Frederick von Anhalt, Duke of Saxony. During this union, Gabor had one of her most infamous run-ins with the law. In June 1989, she was stopped by a Beverly Hills policeman for driving with expired registration tags on her Rolls-Royce. The two got into an argument, she supposedly swore at him, slapped him in the face, and threatened to "call the [Ronald] Reagans." In response, he handcuffed her and took the raging "darling" to jail. The smack heard round the world led to extensive media coverage of her trial on charges of two driving violations (the second one was for allegedly altering vital statistics on her driver's license) and battery. During her fifteen days in court, Zsa Zsa modeled an array of fashions on her ample figure, made sketches during the proceedings to entertain herself, and engaged in occasional dramatics such as storming out of the courtroom. Outside she commented to the media about the unfairness of it all ("I think people are really biased when you are famous"). Her consort, Prince Frederick, didn't help matters by insisting, "The rich and famous should be judged differently. This city couldn't live with the little people's tax money." Gabor was sentenced to three days in jail, 120 hours of community service, and a $12,350 fine. Later, in 1993, Zsa Zsa and her husband lost a $3.3 million suit filed against them for having made negative remarks about actress Elke Sommer in a German publication. The costly judgment led Zsa Zsa to declare bankruptcy.

By the mid-1990s, time seemed to have finally caught up with the roving Gabors. Eva died in 1995, and both Magda and Jolie passed away in 1997. After that, outspoken, bejeweled, clever Zsa Zsa went into semiseclusion. Nevertheless, by then she'd cinched her title as one of the twentieth century's most fascinating divas.

Greta Garbo

[Greta Lovisa Gustafsson]
SEPTEMBER 18, 1905–APRIL 15, 1990

In a stunning moment during the finale of *Queen Christina* (1933), Garbo's seventeenth-century Swedish queen is shown aboard a vessel sailing the high seas to Spain. Purportedly she is contemplating the recent death of her lover and her self-imposed exile. While shooting this climactic sequence, director Rouben Mamoulian urged the great actress to clear her mind—make it a total blank. In that way, he explained, every moviegoer will form his or her own interpretation of what the tragic heroine is really thinking. The resulting footage is one of the most famous visuals in Hollywood history.

Similarly, in real life—then and even now, years after her death—people have devoted much time and effort trying to figure out the enigmatic Garbo. Their goal is to find the actual woman beneath the layers of myths. What made Garbo a mystery from the start for Americans was the difficulty of relating to her Scandinavian background and point of view. Add to this the fact that she was a bisexual—some say lesbian—at a time when such revelations could have destroyed her movie career. It made her more ambiguous and reticent than normal on the rare occasions when she talked to the press over the years and made her activities and choice of companions a puzzle.

Early in Garbo's Hollywood career in the 1920s, MGM executives decided they would save much potential grief if Greta, who had not yet fully mastered the English language or American ways, was kept away from prying journalists as much as possible. Building on a posture of glamorous aloofness, the studio promoted its import as the sex siren who "wants to be alone." Garbo, always of two minds about being a movie queen (she loved the income it offered but disliked the lack of privacy it demanded), went along with the ruse.

Perhaps it is just as well that this mystique was allowed to build into an established style because Garbo's conversations (as recalled by others) and correspondence proved to be commonplace rather than ethereal. Symptomatic were her decades of New York living following the collapse of her movie career in the early

1940s. Much of her time in Manhattan was filled with mundane activities like grocery shopping or watching television. In relationships, the very earthly celebrity could be impetuous and self-absorbed. When she felt her privacy or comfort was compromised in any way, her immediate reaction was to remove the interfering individual(s) from her increasingly limited lifestyle. Then too, strains of both narcissism and jealousy appeared in the woman so many placed on a lofty pedestal. Thus, the real Greta Garbo was not what the public envisioned the legendary love goddess to be like. In actuality, the pragmatic, often indecisive, and poorly educated Garbo had large feet of clay.

Born in Stockholm, Sweden, in 1905, she was the third child of Karl Alfred Gustafsson, an unskilled laborer who worked for the city's sanitation department, and his wife, Anna Lovisa Karlsson. When Greta was thirteen, her father—who had been often unemployed— became quite ill. She left school to take care of him while her mother worked, and he died within a year. Her first paying job was soaping men's faces in a barbershop. Later, she was employed at the PUB department store. There, in 1921, the still-plump, five-foot, seven-inch teenager made her film debut, appearing in an advertising short subject. Eventually this led to her auditioning for and obtaining a scholarship to the Royal Stockholm Theater School. Later, director Mauritz Stiller, a Russian Jewish émigré prominent in Swedish cinema, cast Greta Garbo (her new screen name) as the ingénue in his silent film *The Atonement of Gosta Berling* (1924). The next year she appeared in

G. W. Pabst's *The Street of Sorrow*. At this time, MGM chieftain Louis B. Mayer was searching for new talent. He wanted Mauritz Stiller to come to Hollywood to direct features. The latter would accept only if Greta was also part of the deal. Mayer, who thought Greta—with her chubbiness and crooked teeth—unlikely movie material, reluctantly hired her at a relatively modest salary. Stiller and Garbo sailed for New York.

Once on the studio payroll, Greta was made to diet and have her teeth fixed. She was cast as a Spanish peasant in the silent photoplay *The Torrent* (1926). Audiences reacted positively to her as an exotic vamp. After a similar seductive role in *The Temptress* (1926), she was matched with John Gilbert in *Flesh and the Devil* (1927). The couple caught the public's fancy, especially when the studio bolstered the illusion with a campaign about the stars' off-camera romance. Sources differ as to how much Greta truly cared for John or how much this caring was designed to advance her career and/or disguise her interest in female partners. What is clear is that once the "great" romance was in high gear, impetuous, hard-living Gilbert asked the elusive Garbo on several occasions to become his third wife. Out of indolence, indecision, or wisdom, each time she failed to keep their wedding date. By then, hotheaded John felt his masculinity was at stake. He impulsively rushed off to Las Vegas to wed actress Ina Claire in May 1929, a union that proved to be short-lived. As for the Swedish sphinx, she calmly focused on her career, which now paid her a lofty $5,000 weekly and provided many perks. (When she

The elusive Greta Garbo in the early 1930s.
(Courtesy of JC Archives)

didn't get her way with her employers, she would announce, "I think I go back to Sweden." The ruse was always successful.)

It was not until 1930 that Garbo made her sound film debut because the studio worried that her still-thick Scandinavian accent might ruin her box-office appeal. However, she was well showcased in *Anna Christie* (1930). Thereafter, she was rushed into such glossy claptrap as *Susan Lennox: Her Fall and Rise* (1931) with Clark Gable and the elegantly slick, all-star *Grand Hotel* (1932). In *Queen Christina* (1933), her costar was former lover John

Gilbert. By then, the fast-fading matinee idol was divorced from Ina Claire and married to the young actress Virginia Bruce.

Off camera, Greta avoided the usual Tinseltown social life, which received high-level media coverage. Instead, she socialized with a sophisticated group of lesbians and mingled with a Continental set that understood alternate lifestyles. Garbo's best friend was the intriguing Mercedes de Acosta, with whom the star had an on-again, off-again affair (as did Greta's great movie rival, Marlene Dietrich). Other intimates in the Swede's crowd were Eastern European–born Salka Viertel, a screenwriter and adviser, and Garbo's *Queen Christina* director—and sometime lover—Rouben Mamoulian. Always restless and disinterested in most material possessions, the free-spirited actress would reside in eleven different homes during her sixteen-year Hollywood stay.

By 1935, Greta had grown bored with the tedious process of filmmaking, disliked exposing her emotions in front of a film crew, and was weary of portraying a succession of tragic characters. However, no matter how troublesome it was for her to agree on and prepare for a new picture, her $250,000-per-film salary was too tempting to throw away. (On its part, MGM was tired of catering to this moody actress. However, her costly pictures still made money abroad and brought prestige to the studio.) Thus it was back to the soundstage, where Garbo shone in *Anna Karenina* (1935) and *Camille* (1936). She received her second Oscar bid for the latter (her first nomination had been for 1930's *Romance*). In 1937,

Garbo and famed musical conductor Leopold Stokowski caused great speculation when they vacationed together in Rapallo, Italy. However, the alliance soon ended.

As the world grew increasingly somber with the approach of World War II, MGM decided it was time to lighten and modernize Greta's gloomy on-screen alter ego. She was cast in *Ninotchka* (1939), and, to promote the sparkling comedy, the studio announced, "Garbo Laughs!" The movie succeeded, and she was Oscar-nominated for a third (and final) time. Next, she was assigned to *Two-Faced Woman* (1941). The trite sex farce awkwardly displayed her as a conventional heroine. Moviegoers were not enthralled with this demystified Garbo, and she and MGM parted company.

During World War II, Garbo kept a low profile. (Only years later was it revealed that during the 1940s, Greta had helped England by identifying key Nazi sympathizers in Stockholm, as well as providing introductions and carrying communications for British agents.) One of her escorts in the late 1930s and early 1940s had been dietitian/lecturer/writer Gaylord Hauser. He was a decade older than Greta and lived in Beverly Hills. In the mid-1940s, Garbo rekindled a relationship from the 1930s with British photographer/set designer/diarist Cecil Beaton. Several months older than Greta, he was a homosexual who felt his place in history demanded that he one day marry and have children. He became obsessed with Garbo, as she did, to a degree, with the aesthetic side of his personality. Each was selfish, ambivalent, and reticent with the other. Their tenuous rapport sparked and waned. (Later, the liaison collapsed after social-climber Beaton sacrificed their privacy by releasing private photos of her and then including embellished accounts of their times together as a part of his published diaries.)

In the early 1950s, occasional efforts to return to moviemaking fell apart, and Garbo felt too insecure about her aging looks to seriously entertain a return to the screen. Having become a naturalized American citizen in 1951, she divided her time among Switzerland, the French Riviera, and an apartment suite on New York's East Fifty-second Street. Living in the same building was her good friend/mentor George Schlee, a Russian-born financier/lawyer whom Garbo had first met in the 1940s. His wife was fashion designer Valentina. By the time Schlee died in 1964, the two women who had jealously shared the attention of George for years refused to speak to one another. When abroad, Greta hobnobbed with such jet setters as Aristotle Onassis and the Rothschilds.

In her last decades, a glum Garbo could occasionally be spotted stomping along Manhattan streets, seeking privacy beneath her sunglasses, large hat, and trench coat. Occasionally, she permitted a walking partner (such as film producer Raymond Daum who later authored 1991's *Walking with Garbo*) to join her on her strolls, but she always kept such associations within rigid limits. By the late 1980s, Garbo's kidneys had begun to fail and she abandoned her walks. In her final years, she was close to her few surviving relatives, especially her New Jersey–based niece (Gray Reisfield), the daughter of her late brother Sven

(who had emigrated to the United States years earlier). Greta died of pneumonia in April 1990. Her body was cremated, and the location of her ashes was kept a deliberate secret because her family feared unwanted publicity. Thus, in death as in life, the reluctant movie star remained inaccessible to her public. She died knowing that she had kept her great mystique intact and was a cult figure for the ages.

Ava Gardner

[Ava Lavinia Gardner]
DECEMBER 24, 1922–JANUARY 25, 1990

When MGM mogul Louis B. Mayer viewed her screen test in 1941, his snap judgment was "She can't talk. She can't act. She's terrific." The naturally pretty teenager from the South was quickly signed to a studio pact and, within a few years, emerged as one of moviedom's most awe-inspiringly beautiful leading ladies. On-screen, she developed tremendous presence and excelled at being a temptress, as seen in *The Killers* (1946); *The Snows of Kilimanjaro* (1952); and *Mogambo* (1953), for which she was Oscar-nominated. Off camera, she was moody, impulsive, hard-living, and increasingly self-destructive. Her beauty drew many men to sleep with her, but she invariably allowed the wrong ones to wed her. This woman who never felt fulfilled by life or career ran through men like she did the money from her movies, leaving them haunted. (Self-deprecating Gardner rarely took her screen accomplishments seriously, even when she was at the top of her game, as in 1954's *The Barefoot Contessa* or 1964's *The Night of the Iguana*.)

She was born in Grabtown, North Carolina, the seventh and final child of Jonas Bailey Gardner, a tobacco sharecropper, and his wife, Mary Elizabeth. Her impoverished childhood (when she often went barefoot) grew worse in 1932 when, as a result of the Depression, Mr. Gardner was thrown out of work. (He died two years later.) Her mother took Ava and her sister Myra to live with her in Smithfield where she ran a boardinghouse. (By then, Ava's other siblings were living on their own or with other relatives.) The trio moved frequently, depending on where Mary Elizabeth could find a boardinghouse to operate. After high school, Ava attended Atlantic Christian College, planning to become a secretary, but she had already grown quite cynical about life ("I didn't have any interests, and there was nothing I wanted to do").

Fate intervened in the summer of 1941, when Ava visited her eldest sister, Beatrice ("Bappie"), in New York City. Bappie's husband was a photographer, and he had Ava pose for a layout to be displayed in the Fifth Avenue shop where he was employed. An MGM gofer spotted the pictures in the store window and was so entranced by her beauty that he distributed them at the studio's New York office. This led to her audition for pictures. MGM signed the vibrant young woman with a thick Southern accent and no acting skills to a $50-a-week contract.

Five-foot, four-inch Ava had been at the Culver City lot for a week when, during a tour of the facility, she encountered Mickey Rooney. He was shorter than she, but he was a giant on the screen—the studio's biggest star. Blasé Ava was not all that impressed by

Ava Gardner posing for a 1950s' publicity shot.
(Courtesy of JC Archives)

his fame, but randy Rooney was enthralled and campaigned hard to win her interest. They began dating. He coached her for her first bit in a feature (1942's *We Were Dancing*). The couple wed in January 1942. MGM insisted on a publicity staff member accompanying them on their honeymoon to Carmel in upstate California. Ava quickly learned that Rooney was more interested in playing golf, gambling, and enjoying drinking sprees with his buddies than in building a good marriage. Full of ego if not ambition, Gardner quickly tired of being known as Mrs. Mickey Rooney. The battling couple divorced on May 21, 1943, the same day Ava's mother died of breast cancer.

At MGM, gorgeous Ava was cast in B pictures and slowly groomed for possible stardom. She dated an assortment of eligible and married men, including actors Peter Lawford and Robert Walker from the lot. These excursions were foreplay to her liaison with bashful billionaire Howard Hughes. He was eccentric and fickle with her as he'd been with countless other Hollywood actresses he had dated over the years. Because she came across as self-absorbed and diffident, his interest in her increased. Her unfaithfulness made him jealous, which led to huge arguments and sometimes brawls. They broke up repeatedly, but he couldn't get her out of his system. During one of their separations, she met famed bandleader Artie Shaw, who had four prior marriages (including one to MGM's Lana Turner) to his credit. The mismatched couple wed in October 1945; he spent much of the honeymoon trying to improve her mind. In customary fashion, Artie was soon berating her in public for

her limited educational background. The incompatible duo divorced in October 1946. By now she was threatening to quit acting and earn a degree at the University of California in Los Angeles. The studio convinced her to abandon that notion.

On the acting front, a friendship with screenwriter Philip Yordan led to Ava playing opposite George Raft in United Artists' crime drama *Whistle Stop* (1946). Her work in that film prompted another loanout the same year for a film noir (*The Killers*) at Universal. The picture and she garnered good reviews. Finally, MGM awoke to Gardner's screen potential and began grooming her as a rival to their resident screen sexpot, Lana Turner. The studio cast Ava as the second female lead in *The Hucksters* (1947), the first of her several features with Clark Gable. By now, Gardner was again seeing Hughes but finally gave up on his demanding ways. He tried to reopen the romance by offering her $250,000 in cash to make a movie for him. She told him to "lump it." (Eventually she did make 1951's *My Forbidden Past* for his RKO studio.)

The new man in Ava's reckless life was Universal's handsome contract player Howard Duff. Like so many others, he was bewitched by her beauty and the touching vulnerability beneath her outer toughness. But Duff knew he wasn't capable of lasting for too long with this complicated woman. Their final split occurred in 1949. By the end of the decade, hard-partying Gardner had had an abortion, a botched procedure that lessened the likelihood of her ever having children. This traumatic event left her more bitter about life, and she buried her pain in escalating bouts of drinking and carousing.

Since they were both on the MGM payroll in the 1940s, Ava had encountered crooner/actor Frank Sinatra many times over the years. However, they had instantly disliked one another. This smoldering hostility turned to passion in 1950. Married and the father of three, Frank was in a temporary career slump. This appealed to the mothering and dominating aspects of Gardner's personality and she became obsessed with him, as he did with her. Fearing a great scandal, Louis B. Mayer begged the two studio players to be discreet—or better yet, break up. Spurred on by her rebellious nature, Ava pointedly expanded her campaign to encourage Frank to divorce his wife and marry her. Cautious because of her box-office appeal, Mayer censured Ava but kept her on the payroll to make *Pandora and the Flying Dutchman* (1951). (Sinatra was let go by the studio.) While shooting the arty *Pandora* abroad, Gardner fell in love with Spain and developed a yen for bullfighters. This led to spats with the explosively jealous Sinatra. The couple patched up their quarrels sufficiently to wed five days after his November 2, 1951, divorce from wife Nancy.

As Ava left for Africa to make 1953's *Mogambo*, Frank's career was slowly starting to rebuild. To help the process, she arranged for him to test at Columbia Pictures for *From Here to Eternity* (1953), a picture he was desperate to make. The audition led to his being cast in the World War II drama. As he began to recapture the limelight, her tremendous possessiveness over her husband turned to scorn

and disinterest. (This led her to have an abortion to spite him.) Frank went on to win a Best Supporting Actor Academy Award for *Eternity*, while Ava made *Knights of the Round Table* and *The Barefoot Contessa* in 1954. Each of them had been having flings on the side, and they finally called it a day that year (although their divorce was not official until 1957). Eventually the former soul mates became good friends, with Sinatra coming to Gardner's financial and emotional rescue many times in later years.

After making MGM's *Bhowani Junction* (1956), Ava made Madrid her permanent home base, where her romances included Spanish matadors and Italian-born actor Walter Chiari. In the late 1950s, while playing at bullfighting at a friend's ranch in Spain, Gardner was thrown from her horse and struck in the cheek by her lance. Terrified that the accident had disfigured her permanently, she refused to believe doctors or friends that the facial injury had healed and that cosmetic surgery had made the scar all but invisible. At age thirty-six, she developed a phobia about being photographed and was convinced her career was doomed.

The dreadful *The Naked Maja* (1959), made on loanout, ended her MGM contract. Thereafter, she had occasional good roles (including 1959's *On the Beach* and 1964's *Seven Days in May*), but her years of heavy drinking and playing the field had taken a toll on her greatest asset—her beauty. Director John Huston, a longtime friend, cast her as Sarah in *The Bible* (1966), and her torrid romance with abusive costar George C. Scott made global headlines. Guest-starring roles or extended cameos in such entries as *Earthquake* (1974) and *City on Fire* (1979) did nothing to salvage her flagging career; it merely provided her with needed "loot." Her final work was in television, including the series *Knots Landing* in 1985 and the telefeature *Harem* in 1986.

By the mid-1970s, London had become Ava's residence. Her men of choice included the likes of Spanish financier Riccardo Sicre and young black singer Freddie Davies. She had said once, "I don't mind growing old. . . . If I have to go before my time, this is how I'll go—cigarette in one hand, glass of scotch in the other." However, by the late 1980s, she was plagued by ill health, including strokes. The once-vibrant Gardner became a recluse. In her last years, she worked on her autobiography (*Ava, My Story*, released in 1990). However, she died of bronchial pneumonia in January 1990, not living to see her memoir published. She was buried in North Carolina in the family plot.

Judy Garland

[Frances Ethel Gumm]
JUNE 10, 1922–JUNE 22, 1969

The trenchant TV movie *Life with Judy Garland: Me and My Shadows* (2001) conveyed the mere tip of the iceberg regarding this tragic songbird. While the telefeature suggested some of the peaks and valleys of the public and private Judy, her stormy existence was actually one long, out-of-control roller-coaster ride as she careened between triumphs and disasters.

When the legendary talent began writing (but never completed) her memoir in the 1960s, she enthused that "It's going to be one hell of a great, everlastingly great book, with humor, tears, fun, emotion and love." For once, Garland was understating the facts about her emotion-charged life. Actually, it played out like a grand opera, complete with a victimized singing heroine (herself), larger-than-life villains (her mother, studio bosses, and several of her ex-husbands), and the leading lady's daunting quest to achieve magical goals (her performances). What made the saga so pitiable was that so often the "enemies" Garland was combating were demons constructed out of her own great paranoia and self-destructive behavior.

Garland once said, "If I'm such a legend, then why am I so lonely?" It was not a rhetorical question, for Judy spent much of her life trying to fit into a world where she felt totally out of place. Her beloved, if flawed, father had died when she was thirteen. As such, she felt abandoned by the one person who had given her unconditional love. (Judy always had a love-hate relationship with her mother, a situation that was still unresolved when her parent died in 1953.)

In 1935, Judy had signed an MGM contract that brought her fully into a world where beauty was prized and the ordinary—as she viewed herself—was disdained. As she began comparing herself to more physically mature, more glamorous ingénues on the film lot, her self-esteem withered further. These young starlets, Judy berated herself, did *not* suffer her deficits: plumpness, shortness (she was only four feet, eleven-and-a-half inches tall), and a curvature of the spine that caused her to hunch slightly.

As for her studio bosses, personified by MGM's Louis B. Mayer, she regarded them as unloving, demanding substitute fathers, who treated the "little hunchback" with disdain because she defied them and was never sufficiently appreciative of their supposed benevolent control. Convinced she was an ugly duckling, unworthy, and used, Judy solidified a lifelong pattern. Whenever she felt overworked and unappreciated, she rebelled with a vengeance. She might overeat to show authority figures that only she controlled her weight; she might fail to show up on a film set, or if she did, she would be a reckless prima donna. With the later escape mechanisms of drugs and alcohol added, one can get a glimmer of Judy's grim world.

She was born Frances Ethel Gumm in 1922 in Grand Rapids, Minnesota, the third daughter of struggling Irish tenor Frank Avent Gumm and his wife, Ethel Marion Milne, a vaudeville house pianist. Her parents operated the local New Grand Theater. When Frances was two and a half, she entered show business by joining her parents on stage to perform "Jingle Bells." (The "spontaneous" event had been engineered by her mother.)

Hoping to get her offspring into movies and to get Frank away from the scandal of his rumored relationship with a young man, ambitious Ethel relocated her family to California. Initially they settled in Lancaster, seventy miles north of Los Angeles. There Judy's father operated a movie theater. After many tries, the three Gumm girls were signed by the Meglin Kiddies, a talent agency that specialized in child acts. Between 1929 and 1931, the trio appeared in movie shorts and toured with their singing act. While performing in Chicago in 1934, the girls appeared on the same vaudeville bill as headliner George Jessel. It was he who suggested the sisters adopt a new surname. (Supposedly, Jessel's inspiration was taken from the name of a friend, columnist Robert Garland.) Later, Frances picked "Judy" on her own, drawing on the title of a popular song.

While the Garland girls auditioned for several movie studios, it was Judy alone who was signed by MGM in 1935. With Mr. Gumm's death, Judy's $150 weekly salary supported her family. Unsure how to showcase the plump, teenaged talent, Mayer assigned her to a short subject (1936's *Every Sunday*) in which pretty, young Deanna Durbin was her colead. Unconvinced of Judy's future, the studio loaned her to Twentieth Century-Fox to appear in the musical *Pigskin Parade* (1936). Garland proved a vocal delight on camera. She was quickly put to work in MGM features.

Metro had wanted to borrow Shirley Temple from Twentieth Century-Fox to star in *The Wizard of Oz* (1939). When that did not happen, Garland was substituted as Dorothy and got to sing "Over the Rainbow," which became her signature tune. (She also won a special Academy Award for her pivotal performance.) Her screen success continued when she made *Babes in Arms* (1939), one of several pictures to pair her with Mickey Rooney.

A pensive Judy Garland in the 1940s. (Courtesy of Echo Book Shop)

In her early MGM years, Judy was somewhat compliant with her bosses, except when it came to dieting. Eating put her into a comfort zone. To curb her appetite, Judy was placed on a regimen of diet pills, which established her drug addiction, compounded by pills to put the hyper girl to sleep at night and then to get her up in the morning. By now, she had fixated on slightly older studio contractee Lana Turner as her point of comparison. Turner was shapely, sexy, and devil-may-care—everything Garland was not. Lana was playing adult roles, while Judy was frozen into playing lovelorn adolescents. The rivalry escalated when playboy bandleader Artie Shaw, whom Judy had dated, eloped to Las Vegas in February 1940 with Lana. Determined to have a man of her own and to show the studio that she was an adult and should be treated like one, Garland rushed into a marriage with composer David Rose, twelve years her senior, in July 1941. It was a mismatch from the start. The catalyst that ended their relationship occurred when Judy became pregnant. She was jubilant. However, the studio and her mother (whom Garland viewed as an MGM spy) pleaded with her to have an abortion. Rose went along with their reasoning, which devastated Judy (who did have the abortion). The couple soon separated, although Rose didn't make the breakup official until 1945.

Feeling betrayed by the key figures in her life, the continually nervous Judy became even moodier at the studio and more resistant to her star's regimen. Matters accelerated when she became involved with the older, married Joseph L. Mankiewicz, a writer/producer under MGM contract. It was he who urged Garland to undergo psychiatric therapy. While somewhat helpful, the sessions also intensified her me-against-the-world syndrome.

Initially, Garland resisted making the musical *Meet Me in St. Louis* (1944) because it meant playing another young unmarried woman. She clashed with director Vincente Minnelli, causing on-set problems and costly delays. In the end, though, the picture was a huge hit. A pleased Judy and Vincente wed in

As much as Garland craved the waves of love emanating from devoted fans at her concerts, she was far more addicted to her regimen of drugs (including Demerol, Dexamyl, Nembutal, Seconal, and Tuinal). When deprived of her daily fix, her body reacted adversely and she rebelled. One night in the mid-1950s, the beloved songbird was to perform at a Pacific Northwest venue. However, her well-meaning retinue had hidden her pills. An indignant Judy insisted no drugs, no performance. To cap her argument, she yelled, "And don't give me that 'show must go on' shit!" Insisting she was much too ill to perform, she had the management summon an ambulance. As she was carted out on a stretcher, the little martyr forced a smile or two at the sympathetic crowd of fans. "God bless," she murmured. "God bless." Unbeknownst to the well-wishers, Garland was clutching a tumbler of vodka under the hospital blanket.

June 1945 and their daughter, Liza, was born the following March.

Bad times again set in, despite the success of *The Harvey Girls* (1946). Suffering from postpartum depression, Judy was further upset at having been cajoled into signing a new MGM contract. (She had wanted to retire into motherhood with, perhaps, occasional free-lance moviemaking chores.) Making matters worse, Tyrone Power, with whom she'd had a past romance, had begun a grand amour with Lana Turner. Everything combined to make her extremely problematic during the making of *The Pirate* (1948). Back on diet pills, she was now overly thin, constantly jumpy, and per-petually paranoid (a situation intensified by her other drugs). She was convinced Minnelli (long known in Hollywood for his special interest in men) was favoring costar Gene Kelly (a past unrequited love of Judy's). With so many demons at work in her mind, she was off the set repeatedly and the picture dragged to its bitter finale. Studio executives looked even more unkindly on Garland's shenanigans when the expensive property did not do well at the box office.

At Judy's insistence, Charles Walters, not Minnelli, directed her and Fred Astaire in *Easter Parade* (1948). That project was a rela-tively peaceful one, and a relieved MGM announced that Garland would reteam with Astaire for *The Barkleys of Broadway* (1949). But Judy's increased instability caused her to be replaced in the project by Ginger Rogers. By the time of *Annie Get Your Gun* (1950), Judy was an emotional wreck. She was shipped off to Boston for a rest cure, while Para-mount's Betty Hutton took over the lead in *Annie*, which became a big hit.

MGM was now being increasingly con-trolled by cost-conscious Dore Schary, who pressured the still-ailing Garland into making *Summer Stock* (1950). Again she made life a costly hell during production. Now Judy hoped to take a breather, but MGM wanted her for *Royal Wedding* (1951). The distraught talent collapsed under the pressure, and Jane Powell took her place in the musical.

In June 1950, Garland felt adrift from her studio and her marriage. Unable to cope and seemingly without sympathy or love, she cut her throat with a piece of glass. The cry for help was not a success. MGM humiliated her by ending her contract and, in March 1951, she and Vincente divorced.

For a time thereafter she was rescued by strong-willed Michael Sidney Luft, who helped her to refocus her career on the concert stage. She made a tremendous comeback at London's Palladium and New York's Palace Theater. A grateful (and pregnant) Judy wed Luft in June 1952. Their daughter, Lorna, was born that November and their son, Joseph, in March 1955. It was also Sid who maneuvered the seemingly impossible—a comeback movie for his wife. The project was the expensive *A Star Is Born* (1954). But with so much resting on this costly musical, Judy caved under the pres-sure and reverted to her former bad habits. She was tardy, drank too much, and was on a heavy pill regimen to keep her ballooning weight under control. The lavish film earned Judy an Oscar nomination but reinforced her reputation as a hellion on the soundstage.

In subsequent years, Judy seesawed back and forth between highly successful and very sloppy concert engagements, all dependent on her degree of substance abuse and resultant emotional and physical exhaustion at the time. She had a triumph at Carnegie Hall in April 1961; was Oscar-nominated as Best Supporting Actress for *Judgment at Nuremberg* (1961); and made her last movie, *A Child Is Waiting*, in 1963. Her own weekly TV variety show was supposed to set her up financially for life. However, the series lasted but one season (1963–64), during which she was the victim of network vagaries, the enormous weekly work pressure, and her own tremendous insecurities. Thanks to a bad deal and her own ineptness with finances, she ended up nearly broke by the time the show was cancelled. In 1967, she was to be in *Valley of the Dolls*, but she had mixed feelings about the tawdry screen project and was replaced by Susan Hayward. The prior year, she had burned her professional bridges in the TV medium when she was a guest host on *The Hollywood Palace*. During the taping, she became convinced that she was losing her voice and locked herself in her dressing room. Pandemonium ensued until a worker crawled through a ceiling duct into the dressing room and opened the locked door from the inside. Judy eventually completed the shoot. However, after everyone else had left, she destroyed her expensively appointed dressing suite (letting the toilet and sink overflow, dumping cigarette butts between the keys of the piano, and using her lipstick to smear graffiti on paintings).

In the 1960s, Judy once called daughter Liza—by then embarked on her own show-business career—to invite her to Garland's latest wedding. Minnelli pleaded a heavy work schedule but said without thinking, "Don't worry, Mama, I'll come to the next one." In real life, it wasn't so funny. Judy and Luft ended their increasingly acrimonious relationship (which included a bitter custody battle over the children) in May 1965. That November, she wed young actor Mark Herron in Las Vegas. They went their separate ways after six conflict-filled months and were divorced in April 1967. Her fifth groom was discotheque manager Mickey Dean, also years younger than Judy. They married in London where, three months later in June 1969, Judy was found dead in her apartment, a victim of an (accidental) pill overdose.

In death, the incandescent talent was finally at peace, but she—as did so many others in her orbit—had paid a great price during her lifetime.

Greer Garson

[Eileen Evelyn Greer Garson]
SEPTEMBER 29, 1904–APRIL 6, 1996

During Hollywood's Golden Age, there was no one more ladylike (almost regal) on or off the American screen than Garson. Hollywood movie mogul Louis B. Mayer, a crude, self-made man and devoted Anglophile, imported redheaded Greer from the British stage in 1937. For a time she would become his favored royalty in the Metro-Goldwyn-Mayer domain. At his will, she ruled majestically on the Culver City lot in the 1940s, replacing sophisticated Norma Shearer as queen of the grand studio.

The piety and nobility of Greer's compassionate screen ladies were much appreciated by moviegoers during World War II. In the process, however, she became stereotyped, unable and/or unwilling to play roles of more modest goodness as tastes changed. During her charmed reign, many in Hollywood were unenthusiastic about this sometimes-haughty sovereign with the peaches-and-cream complexion. As for the press, they learned that meeting with Garson was not a casual occurrence but more along the lines of a royal audience. (This situation and Greer were lampooned in "The Interview" segment of MGM's 1946 musical potpourri, *Ziegfeld Follies*, in which a great lady of the screen—played by Judy Garland—deigns to converse with the press about her forthcoming movie.)

While she would later subtract eight years from her age and claim she'd been born in Ireland, Eileen Evelyn Greer Garson was really born into a modest household in London in 1904, the only child of George and Nancy (Greer) Garson. George was a commercial clerk in the import business. Two years after Eileen was born, he died during surgery. Nancy supported her frail baby by managing family properties. However, Eileen's health grew worse and the increasing costs for her medical needs put a strain on Mrs. Garson. One of the girl's ailments was chronic bronchitis, which required that she be confined to bed for six weeks each spring, autumn, and winter. Being homebound so much, she spent

a lot of time with adults, which speeded the youngster's emotional maturity. Despite her many illnesses, spunky Eileen boasted a lively imagination. Her interest in the stage developed early and she attended the University of London to be near the world of theater. After graduating, she supervised the research library for a London advertising firm. But her heart was in acting and she finally auditioned for the Birmingham Repertory Theatre, where she made her stage debut in 1932.

Eventually Greer Garson—as she was now known—progressed to London's West End. In September 1933, she wed Edward Sneldon, whom she had known for years. He was then a junior judge in the Indian civil service. After two weeks of marriage, Garson knew she had made a bad mistake. Sneldon returned to India, with Greer offering vague promises of joining him there later. In subsequent years, he would visit her in London, they would quarrel, and he would go back to India. (The messy domestic situation ended only when Greer negotiated a divorce in 1940.) More important to the dedicated actress was progressing her career. (Her motto was "Keep your horizons wide and your waistline slim.") In August 1937, she was in the melodrama *Old Music* on London's West End. MGM's Louis B. Mayer came to see the bright "young" actress he'd heard so much about from local MGM representatives. He was enthralled with the regal performer, whom her gaggle of loyal shop girl fans called the "Duchess of Garson." After a positive screen test, she accepted a seven-year contract. By the end of 1937, she and her mother were in Los Angeles.

Greer Garson and Louis Calhern in *Julius Caesar* (1953). (Courtesy of JC Archives)

Greer imagined she'd be put to work immediately, but such was *not* the case. Her majestic bearing, her unconventional facial features, her relative height (five feet, six inches), and that titian hair left producers perplexed about how to cast her. One studio bigwig suggested she might make a good villainess in an upcoming Marx Brothers picture. An irate Greer stormed into Louis B. Mayer's office and that was the end of that bizarre notion. A year passed and the dejected newcomer was preparing to return to London. At that juncture, she was offered a smallish role in *Goodbye, Mr. Chips* (1939), to be shot in England. She accepted the assignment. While the picture's

focus was on Robert Donat as the shy British schoolmaster, she made a memorable impression as his cheery wife who dies early in the proceedings. So strong was her performance as the uplifting, decent spouse, that she was Oscar-nominated (the first of seven times in her career).

Now a prestigious presence at MGM, Greer and her mother took up permanent residence in the film colony, creating a "proper" British home in their upscale digs, complete with a traditional British flower garden and afternoon tea. On camera, Garson was authentic in the period piece *Pride and Prejudice* (1940), with Laurence Olivier as her foil and love interest. In 1941's *When Ladies Meet*, she did battle on and off camera with predatory costar Joan Crawford, the latter fighting vainly to maintain her place in the MGM hierarchy. Also that year, Greer was teamed memorably with Canadian-born contract player Walter Pidgeon in the well-mounted *Blossoms in the Dust* (1941). She was noble—he was stolid; together they represented romanticized respectability.

MGM's Norma Shearer rejected the lead in *Mrs. Miniver* (1942), refusing to play the gallant mother of a young adult in wartime Great Britain. However, Garson was persuaded to accept the cast-off assignment, and she and the picture were an enormous hit. It won six Oscars, including a Best Actress prize for Greer. Her five-and-a-half minute acceptance speech at the Academy Awards ceremony was not as long as legend has it. However, to the weary attendees that evening, she seemed to be droning on forever. (One wag insisted, "Her speech was longer than her part.") Having been crowned, nothing was out of Queen Garson's reach at the studio. That included handsome, twenty-six-year-old Richard Ney, who had played her son in *Mrs. Miniver*. The unlikely duo fell in love and informed Mayer that they planned to marry. Greer acquiesced to studio concerns that the couple wait until after *Mrs. Miniver* was in general release. So it was not until July 1943 that Garson united with the thirteen-year-younger actor (who was then on leave from World War II military duty). Meanwhile, she continued her lofty cinema pairings with Walter Pidgeon in *Madame Curie* (1943) and *Mrs. Parkington* (1944).

By the time of *The Valley of Decision* (1945) with Gregory Peck, Greer was in a career rut. She used her clout to force the studio to cast her with popular Clark Gable, who was just back from wartime duty. The picture was *Adventure* (1945) and it was promoted with "Gable's Back and Garson's Got Him!" Unfortunately, it proved to be a stale love story in which she was miscast as the down-to-earth librarian chased by a sailor. Its failure started a downturn for the actress, a situation emphasized by Mayer having hired a younger English redhead (Deborah Kerr) to take some roles that once would have been Garson's.

In 1947, the year Greer and Ney divorced, she made the putrid *Desire Me*. Pretty, young Elizabeth Taylor was the key attraction of *Julia Misbehaves* (1948), despite Greer taking a much-publicized bubble bath on camera. *Scandal at Scourie* (1953) was Greer's ninth and final screen matching with Walter Pidgeon, and it did poorly at the box office. That same year, she had a cameo in MGM's *Julius Cae-*

sar, starring Marlon Brando. Old-guard Garson was not amused at working with the acclaimed method actor: "I do not enjoy actors who seek to commune with their armpits, so to speak."

Leaving MGM in 1954, Garson did occasional stage work (such as assuming the lead in *Auntie Mame* on Broadway in 1958), television (for example, 1963's *The Invincible Mr. Disraeli*), and a few movies (including *Sunrise at Campobello* in 1960, for which she received her final Oscar nomination, and *The Singing Nun* in 1965 back at MGM, in which she was the mother prioress). If she was no longer active show-business royalty, she had found a good substitute in private life. In 1949, she had married wealthy Texas rancher and sportsman Edward E. "Buddy" Fogelson, and they spent much of their time on an elaborate spread outside of Santa Fe. He died in 1987. She continued with philanthropic work until her health (heart problems) forced her to spend her last years in long-term care at a Dallas hospital. After her passing, one of the actress's longtime friends cited her special qualities as "her own stoicism and her own class."

Paulette Goddard

[**Marion Goddard Levy**]
JUNE 3, 1910–APRIL 23, 1990

Many Hollywood film stars (including Marion Davies and Joan Crawford) had their inauspicious beginnings as Broadway chorus girls, using their beauty, wit, and talent to attain success. However, few such performers were as dedicated to spectacular material wealth as Goddard. (When she died, she left a $30 million estate.) Her motto in life was "We have one tomorrow: ourselves."

Paulette's favorite expression was "Isn't that silly?" and she might have applied it to her lifelong, childish delight in receiving presents of any sort. However, being extremely practical, her favorite gifts in adulthood were receiving expensive jewelry, fine art, lavish furs, and cash. But there was another side to this five-foot, four-inch brunette with sparkling blue-green eyes, a distinctive, full-throated voice, and an appetite for fun. This gold-digging coquette—nicknamed the Bronze Butterfly—was especially astute in choosing (most of) her husbands because they could help her show-business career and/or provide material luxuries and because of their bright minds. Reviewing her matrimonial accomplishments late in life, Paulette decided, "The men I married, I chose because they were intellectuals—Charlie Chaplin, Burgess Meredith, and Erich Maria Remarque. They were my second, third, and fourth; I don't count my first husband—it wasn't memorable, and he was *not* an intellectual." What she casually ignored regarding spouse number one (Edgar James) was that when they divorced in 1929, he gave her a lofty $375,000 settlement.

Much remains ambiguous about her childhood. She was born in 1910 in either Great Neck, Long Island, or Whitestone Landing, Queens. Although her birth certificate listed her name as Marion Goddard Levy, she was later called Pauline, perhaps in honor of her paternal grandmother. Her father, Joseph Russell Levy, was Jewish and part owner of the family's cigar manufacturing operation in Salt Lake City, Utah. Her mother, Alta Mae Goddard, was Episcopalian and the daughter of a real estate investor who had suffered financial reverses. When Pauline was very young, her parents separated, and after a brief episode where he "kidnapped" her before she was stolen back by her mother, she did not deal with her father (who later spelled his surname LeVee or LeeVee) again until years later when he sued her for financial support.

During Pauline's childhood, Alta and her very precocious daughter hopscotched around the country, bent on improving their precarious situation. Pauline, a natural beauty who matured physically at an early age, began modeling. Thanks to Alta's brother Charles, who lived well on Long Island and mingled with the theatrical set, Pauline (and her mother) made many useful contacts. By carefully observing interactions at her uncle's house parties, the youngster absorbed a good deal about social graces.

In 1926, the teenaged Pauline was in Palm Beach, Florida, a chorus member of Florenz Ziegfeld's revue *Palm Beach Girl*. By now, the sixteen-year-old had dyed her hair blond and was calling herself Paulette Goddard. She'd also mastered the art of generating publicity about herself and bending the truth to fit the situation. The musical show, retitled *No Foolin'*, opened successfully on Broadway that year. By spring 1927, her latest theatrical venture had closed and she had met Edgar William

Charles Boyer and Paulette Goddard in *Hold Back the Dawn* (1941). (Courtesy of JC Archives)

James, a lumber magnate from North Carolina. He was twice her age and very rich. After a brief courtship, they wed in June 1927. Before long, the entrepreneur realized that he and his child bride had little in common. In 1929, the situation led Paulette (accompanied by Alta) to settle in Reno, Nevada, to file for divorce. With the settlement cash she received, she and Alta vacationed in Europe in 1930.

Ambitious Paulette had made her first foray into Hollywood in 1929. She earned a bit in a Laurel and Hardy short (*Berth Marks*) and was an extra in the Barbara Stanwyck feature *The Locked Door*. The pretty twenty-year-old and her mother returned to Tinseltown in late 1930 (after her divorce was finalized), and she obtained walk-on roles in such films as

City Streets (1931). In 1932, she became one of independent producer Samuel Goldwyn's chorus girls. When Goddard was not fighting with or being fired and rehired by the idiosyncratic Goldwyn, she appeared in such Eddie Cantor screen musicals as *The Kid from Spain* (1932) and *Roman Scandals* (1933).

More important for Paulette's future, she met film executive Henry Ginsberg, who signed the pretty miss to a contract at Hal Roach's comedy studio to appear in short subjects. Through Ginsberg she met Joseph Schenck, who ran the United Artists studio. The film mogul and Goddard, with her shapely figure and insouciance, became friendly. It was aboard Schenck's yacht in 1932 that she first came to know forty-three-year-old screen comedy king Charlie Chaplin. By then, Chaplin was divorced from his second child bride (Lita Grey). His last movie had been *City Lights* (1931), and he was fastidiously planning his next, which would require a new leading lady. Charlie almost immediately thought Paulette would be ideal to play the gamine in *Modern Times* (1936). By the end of the yacht party, Chaplin had advised Goddard on her financial investments, convinced her to return her hair to its natural chestnut brown, and told her they belonged together.

With Chaplin as her mentor and suitor, Paulette burst into the limelight and shrewdly manipulated the media with witticisms, half-truths, and lies about her colorful background and especially about her romantic status with Charlie. Everyone wondered if this couple who lived together in his mansion had perhaps already wed—and if so, when. The couple refused to say. Meanwhile, Chaplin set about teaching Goddard the finer points of acting and life. She proved to be an apt pupil, and when *Modern Times*—largely a silent movie—was finally released, Paulette's participation was well received.

By 1938, Chaplin was far from ready to make his next feature, so Goddard returned to the screen under special contract to producer David O. Selznick for *The Young in Heart*. Other screen roles followed, but none held the potential of *Gone with the Wind* (1939) in which Paulette *almost* starred. Selznick considered Goddard the likely finalist to play Scarlett O'Hara. However, there was a backlash from morality pressure groups who were upset by Goddard's ambiguous marital status. (In actuality, she and Chaplin had wed during a vacation to China in 1936 but would not confirm the fact.) As a result, she lost the coveted role. However, she had a featured part in MGM's all-female cast of *The Women* (1939). Also that year, she starred with Bob Hope in the screen comedy *The Cat and the Canary*, the first of their three hit pictures together and her first under a Paramount pact.

By the time *The Great Dictator* was released in 1940, Chaplin and Goddard (who had long been seeing other men) had separated. (They divorced in 1942.) One of her professional conquests in the new decade was filmmaker Cecil B. DeMille—he had a special fascination with her pretty feet—who cast her as the heroine of *North West Mounted Police* (1940), the first of several screen epics she made for him. Also in that busy year, Paulette made the Fred Astaire musical *Second Chorus*, where she met Broadway wunderkind Burgess "Buzz" Meredith. She was smitten with Buzz's intellect and offbeat humor. After a lengthy romance interrupted by his World War II military service (and her romance with such notables as Clark Gable), they wed in 1944. Meanwhile, Goddard—always more a dazzling, earthy screen personality than a true actress—surprised Hollywood by being Oscar-nominated as Best Supporting Actress for the women-in-war drama *So Proudly We Hail* (1943). Her finest performance at Paramount, however, was as the guttersnipe who rises to riches in eighteenth-century England in *Kitty* (1945).

The pictures that Goddard made with Meredith were unremarkable, and their helter-skelter marriage ended in 1949. That same year, she made her final Paramount release, a costumed turkey called *Bride of Vengeance*. In the 1950s, forty-something Paulette made several potboilers, the last being *The Unholy Four* (1954). She also did occasional theater and television projects, while remaining part of the wealthy international set. By then, she'd met German-born Erich Maria Remarque, the celebrated novelist of *All Quiet on the Western Front* (1929). Born in 1898, he had finally divorced his wife in 1951 after many notorious love affairs, including a serious one with Marlene Dietrich. Now an American citizen, Remarque spent part of each year in New York City, where he met Paulette. They married in 1958 and divided their time between Manhattan and Switzerland. He died in 1970. Thereafter, she made a final movie, the telefeature *The Snoop Sisters* (1972), costarring Helen Hayes and Mildred Natwick, and settled into a luxurious retirement.

During her last decades, she sold a lot of her prized art and jewelry collection at premium prices, toyed with writing her autobiography, and simplified her well-organized life. By now, her social drinking had turned into a severe alcoholic problem. Sadly, her final years were lonely, painful (she contracted cancer, had a mastectomy, and later suffered from emphysema), and full of repeated suicide attempts. She died of a heart attack in Ronco, Switzerland. Clutched in her manicured hand at the time of her death was a New York auction house catalog listing several of her famous jewelry pieces, which had sold that day for $1 million.

Melanie Griffith

[Melanie Griffith]

AUGUST 9, 1957–

At five feet, eight inches, blond and blue-eyed young Griffith was physically stunning, albeit possessed of a squeaky voice that grated on some listeners. As the daughter of actress Tippi Hedren—one of director Alfred Hitchcock's golden protégées—Melanie had an instant entrée into show business when she initially turned to the profession in the mid-1970s. In her first screen roles of substance (such as 1975's *The Drowning Pool*), she received solid reviews. It appeared her budding movie career was destined to take off successfully. But drug addiction, a seriously debilitating car accident, and a stormy relationship with actor Don Johnson messed up her early chances for industry success. By the late 1980s, she'd made a stunning big-screen comeback with her Oscar-nominated role in *Working Girl* (1988). She was again on the launching pad to further acclaim. Once again, drug addiction—and treatment—diverted her attention from career goals. By the late 1990s, the still striking actress was once more wavering back and forth between substance abuse and recovery. The question was—and remains—could Melanie, already in the mature leading lady category, reestablish her acting credentials? Or was her life destined to continue being a tumultuous soap opera played out in the tabloids?

She was born in 1957 in New York City, the daughter of Peter Griffith, an actor/real estate

A young Melanie Griffith in *Night Moves* (1975).
(Courtesy of Echo Book Shop)

developer, and Nathalie Hedren, a striking blond model. When Melanie was two, her parents separated; they divorced a year later. Nathalie took her daughter to Los Angeles, intending to build a career in TV modeling. Instead, she became Grace Kelly's replacement for director Alfred Hitchcock and, using the name Tippi Hedren, starred in his *The Birds* (1963) and *Marnie* (1964). By then, Hedren, who had spurned Hitchcock's romantic overtures, was on the master's bad list and it sealed her career fate in Tinseltown. (One of Melanie's most vivid childhood memories is receiving a macabre gift from the director on

her sixth birthday: a miniature coffin with a tiny wax replica of her mother lying inside.) In 1964, Tippi wed advertising executive/television agent-producer-director Noel Marshall and they moved to a suburban ranch. During the next several years, Melanie gained two half-siblings, Tracy and Clay. In 1970, the Marshalls flew to Africa to make a movie revolving around the wild animals of the bush. (The picture, *Roar*, was finally released in 1981.) When the clan returned to California, they brought several animals back to their Soledad Canyon ranch with them, including a lion, which became Melanie's pet. During these years, Melanie did modeling assignments.

While an extra on *The Harrad Experiment* (1973), sexually precocious Melanie fell instantly in love with castmate Don Johnson, eight years her senior. By then, the non-Catholic Griffith had been expelled from a Catholic high school because she had questioned religion. Not long thereafter, in 1974, the rebellious Melanie left her parents' ranch to move in with Johnson. He was a party-hearty playboy involved in the drug and alcohol scene. Their relationship aborted the following year when he married another woman. Meanwhile, Johnson obtained an interview for Melanie, which she thought was for a modeling job. It turned out to be an audition for a part in *Night Moves* (1975). She won the role of the man-crazy Hollywood child and had a topless scene in the picture. (Continuing her disrobing trend, the voluptuous newcomer appeared in a *Playboy* magazine layout in February 1976.) Still pining for Johnson, Griffith renewed her relationship with him when his marriage ended. In early 1976, the couple impulsively flew to Las Vegas and wed. The union proved shaky and they divorced in 1977. In the fall of 1978, Melanie, who suffered from substance abuse, was dropped from the short-lived TV series *Carter Country* even before it left the air that December.

One evening in 1980 after an inebriated Melanie left a trendy Los Angeles restaurant, she was hit by a drunk driver as she was crossing Sunset Boulevard. She suffered extensive injuries, including a broken leg and arm, hairline fractures, and a concussion (which left her with amnesia for several days). It took two months to recuperate from the severe accident. During that time, she attended Alcoholics Anonymous but soon fell off the wagon. Because the movie studios refused to consider her for roles (due to her substance abuse problems), she took whatever TV assignments she could find. While making the telefeature/pilot *She's in the Army Now* (1981), she met Cuban-born actor Steven "Rocky" Bauer. He convinced her to relocate to New York with him to study acting with Stella Adler. During this financially precarious period, pampered Melanie learned what it was like to be an average citizen. ("All of that was wonderful," she said. "It really kicked my butt.") The couple married in May 1983. Meanwhile, when Jamie Lee Curtis rejected the lead in the thriller *Body Double* (1984), Griffith convinced director Brian DePalma to cast her as the porn queen with a high IQ and received good notices.

Giving birth to son Alexander in August 1984 was an "amazing" experience for twenty-seven-year-old Griffith. Two years later, she had a career-making part as the kooky kidnapper in *Something Wild*. It gave her new acting credentials. She and Bauer divorced in 1987. In the spring of that year, Melanie appeared on an episode of Don Johnson's hit TV cop series, *Miami Vice* (1984–89). Their romance rekindled briefly but then sputtered out.

Melanie had four big-screen releases in 1988. Her best showcase was the Mike Nichols–directed *Working Girl*. During her research for this feature set in New York City, she became involved with Wall Street executive Liam Dalton and the duo lived together for a year. While making *Working Girl*, her drug and alcohol problems flared up again. At the urging of friends (including Don Johnson, who had been in detox programs), she entered a treatment program at the Hazelden Foundation in Center City, Minnesota. (Said Griffith, "It just had me where I couldn't stop it. And I wanted to. Really badly.") During her month-long stay there, Johnson phoned frequently and his calls helped her deal with her recovery program. Once released, she flew to Florida to be with Johnson, who ended his current relationship with Barbra Streisand to focus on his ex-wife. On June 26, 1989, Griffith and Johnson were remarried in Aspen, Colorado. It was her third and his fourth marriage. Less than four months later, Melanie gave birth to their love child, Dakota Mayi.

In 1990, Griffith reemerged professionally in three theatrical releases. The nadir of the trio was *The Bonfire of the Vanities*, while the most intriguing was the thriller *Pacific Heights*. She was badly miscast in *Shining Through* (1992) and the next year teamed with

Johnson for the failed remake of *Born Yesterday* (1993). During this unsatisfactory career phase, her marriage to Don was falling apart. He was again abusing alcohol and had returned to being a rowdy Hollywood playboy. When he had a near-fatal car accident, he went back into treatment. By spring 1996, he was starring in the San Francisco–based TV cop series *Nash Bridges*. By then, Melanie had fallen in love with handsome, Spanish-born actor Antonio Banderas while on location with him in Florida and Spain filming the screwball comedy *Two Much* (1996). Like Melanie, the three-year-younger actor was married to another at the time. Both got divorces and the couple wed on May 14, 1996 (reportedly after signing a prenuptial agreement in which Banderas would pay Griffith $1 million if their union ended). That September their daughter, Stella, was born.

Despite rejuvenating cosmetic surgery, middle-aged Griffith was finding it difficult to obtain A-grade features. Instead she accepted lesser fare such as the crime drama *Another Day in Paradise* (1998) and the far-out comedy *Crazy in Alabama* (1999), which was directed by Banderas. Much-touted plans for her to star in a CBS-TV sitcom, *Me and Henry*, fell through in 1998–99. In November 2000, Melanie, coping with career problems and the pressure of keeping her marriage to Banderas intact (he was constantly away on location where she couldn't check up on him), entered a rehab facility in Marina Del Rey, California. She was there to cut back on her addiction to painkillers prescribed for a neck injury. After much hoopla that the stay would turn her life around, she left the treatment center after eight days rather than remain for the typical month. Claiming to have her life under control, the actress charted her progress on her Internet website. By now she was using fertility drugs, anxious to provide Antonio with the baby boy he wanted so much.

In mid-2001 her father, Peter Griffith, with whom she had become close in recent years, died of cancer and emphysema. Meanwhile, she returned to filmmaking (including *Tempo*, released in 2002). However, by November 2001, Griffith was back in treatment at a Los Angeles hospital for a "refresher" in dealing with her substance abuse. According to the supermarket tabloids, there was growing friction in the Banderas household, with Antonio being upset about her constant financial help of ex-husband Steven Bauer, who had been in and out of several drug rehab programs. On her part, Melanie was reportedly highly stressed by concerns that Antonio would turn to a younger woman.

Once a Hollywood golden child, Melanie has self-destructed her promising career on several occasions, only to bounce back for yet another opportunity in the highly competitive business. Never shy about putting her private problems on public display, Griffith said in the new millennium, "I just try to be a good person. I'm not trying really to make any statement. If I'm brave enough to put myself out there, I have to be brave enough to handle what comes back at me. I just try to do it as elegantly as possible. I think we get more interesting as we get older, and our time shouldn't be wasted."

Jean Harlow

[Harlean Harlow Carpenter]

MARCH 3, 1911–JUNE 7, 1937

Legendary is an overused word in the Holly-wood vocabulary. However, in Harlow's case, it admirably summed up the gorgeous screen siren who had a penchant for not wearing bras or panties. She gained fame as the 1930s' "Blonde Bombshell," playing a brassy, pushy dame who lacked refinement but had a prover-bial heart of gold beneath that tough exterior. Jean's movie alter ego usually had a touching, vulnerable side, a trait that had been shaped by negative events in her own life: three bad mar-riages; the scandalous suicide of one of her mates; abortions; venereal disease; a greedy and controlling mother; and a parasitic, manipulative stepfather. If that weren't enough misery for one life, she died tragically at the height of her fame at the age of twenty-six.

Unlike many movie stars who became vicious in their struggle for success in the Hol-lywood jungles, Jean (known as "Baby" to many) had a good-natured personality. It led to her being well liked by coplayers and crews. On the other hand, her naïveté about some aspects of life made her an easy mark for spongers (such as her mother and stepfather, as well as the studio) who lived off her. Over the years, many men chased after the five-foot, two-inch actress, magnetized by her striking figure. Several of these pursuers obtained her sexual favors, while she used some of them for her own career advancement. As time wore on, she became increasingly reckless in her pursuit of fun, sexual gratification, and heavy drink-ing—all to help her forget how empty her sup-posedly glamorous, wonderful life had become.

Having physically matured as a young teen-ager, she had a lot of experience being the cen-ter of attention. But being a movie queen who was adored by the masses took it to a new level. On the MGM lot where she spent her stardom years, Harlow became a prized com-modity. If she did as her studio bosses dictated on and off the set, she was pampered and her whims became realities.

She was born Harlean Harlow Carpenter in Kansas City, Missouri, in 1911. Her father, Mont Clair Carpenter, was a well-known local dentist. Her mother, born Jean Harlow, was a reluctant homemaker, a grand schemer who hated being under any man's thumb. Compet-ing for the youngster's attention were her maternal grandparents, especially the domineering Skip Harlow, a successful real estate broker. In 1922, Jean divorced Carpenter. By the next year, mother and daughter were in Hollywood where Jean hoped her beautiful youngster could break into movies. After two fruitless years in Tinseltown, they returned to Kansas City. Skip Harlow had demanded that his granddaughter return to the Midwest or he would disinherit Jean. The latter had no choice but to return to the unpleasant fold.

Thanks to Dr. Carpenter, Harlean attended several private schools in her childhood. Meanwhile, Jean had encountered Marino Bello. He was swarthy, mustached, and dapper but unfortunately also a lazy schemer who mostly lived off others. Despite Skip Harlow's great disapproval of the man, he preferred that his daughter wed Bello rather than continue her scandalous affair with him. The couple complied in January 1927. During this period, Harlean was attending a private girls' school in Lake Forest, Illinois. On a fix-up date, she met twenty-year-old Charles Fremont McGrew II, who came from a wealthy family. Marriage to the heavy-drinking playboy seemed like a good means to escape boring school. It would also get her away from her controlling relatives. Because both sets of parents disapproved of the intended match, Chuck and Harlean eloped to Waukegan, Illinois, in September 1927.

A few months later, McGrew came into a portion of his sizeable inheritance. The newlyweds went to Los Angeles, where Chuck purchased a Beverly Hills home for them. He hoped the relocation would separate his child bride from her domineering mother. However, he underestimated Harlean's relatives, and soon Jean and Bello moved to Los Angeles.

Once on the West Coast, Harlean was enjoying a pleasant, somewhat decorous life as a young married socialite. Then, through a screen-struck pal, she met executives at Fox Films. Friends bet shy Harlean that she would not pursue Fox's offer to be in pictures. To win the wager, she registered at Central Casting (using her mother's maiden name of Jean Harlow) and made her debut in the silent feature *Honor Bound* (1928). Excited by the potential, Mama Jean and Bello pushed the reluctant screen newcomer to seek a movie career, and Jean did small screen bits at Paramount and other studios. Still unenthusiastic about show business, Jean was pleased to discover in spring 1929 that she was pregnant; this would allow her to give up acting. Again Mama Jean sprang into action, insisting that her daughter have an abortion, which Bello arranged. That June, Jean lost another family member when she and Chuck McGrew separated (and later divorced). Mama Jean and Bello moved into Jean's house to fill the void.

Forced to support her relations, Jean grew more serious about succeeding in films and gained a small speaking role in Clara Bow's *The Saturday Night Kid* (1929). Meeting agent Arthur Landau eventually led to Harlow joining the cast of Howard Hughes's World War I airplane epic *Hell's Angels* (1930). Cast as a British tart, Jean struggled with the role's demands. However, she came across so sexily on screen that critics and moviegoers alike took special notice of her bedazzling, offbeat presence. Hughes had the reluctant sexpot under contract, but, as he had no vehicle ready for her, he loaned her to MGM, where she teamed with Clark Gable in the gangland drama *The Secret Six* (1931). Other film loanouts followed, including Columbia's *The Platinum Blonde* (1931). In that, she was miscast as a snobbish socialite, but the picture's title stuck as a descriptor of her striking hair color.

By late 1931, MGM had acquired Jean's contract from Hughes. She costarred in yet another underworld melodrama, *The Beast of the City* (1932). She had also come under the influence of Paul Bern, a top MGM executive. The German-born Bern was thought to be a bachelor and was noted for his eruditeness, sensitivity, and willingness to help others. (He was known on the lot as "Little Father Confessor.") On the other hand, he was not attractive or manly; he was pudgy and bespectacled, had thinning hair and an effeminate look, and was rumored to have particularly small genitalia. Nevertheless, Jean was flattered that he seemed to care more about her emotional and intellectual growth than her sexy attributes, and she was impressed by his studio power. On July 2, 1932, Jean—whose latest picture, *Red-Headed Woman*, had showcased her well—wed the twenty-two-years-older Paul. Two months later, the mismatched union was over. Bern was found dead of a gunshot wound on the bedroom floor of their Benedict Canyon home. The "facts" in the media-hyped scandal generated great speculation for decades to come. However, the prevailing opinion today is that Bern had wed Jean in the

Jean Harlow, the 1930s' Blonde Bombshell.
(Courtesy of JC Archives)

hopes that his sexy bride would cure his impotence. She hadn't, and the couple's disintegrating marriage had nose-dived when Bern's secret common-law wife, an emotionally disabled woman named Dorothy Millette, had shown up at their home one day. From her, Harlow learned more about her strange husband than she cared to know. The next day, he killed himself. Between the studio cover-up to protect Harlow (who had purportedly been on the premises when Paul shot himself), yellow journalism, industry gossip, and so forth, the matter was not even laid to rest after the official inquest (which reached a decision of no foul play) or Bern's cremation. Adding insult to injury, Bern left Jean to cope with several of his debts.

Eventually Harlow returned to the studio to complete *Red Dust* (1932) with Clark Gable and then was part of the all-star cast of *Dinner at Eight* (1933). She had begun dating again and had developed an attraction for, among several others, boxer Max Baer who was acting in an MGM film. The torrid affair caused Metro great concern because the fighter was married and studio head Louis B. Mayer feared Harlow would be the center of another scandal. Thus, she was pressured to transfer her attention to Hal Rosson, the respected cinematographer who had worked with her on *Bombshell* (1933). (Ironically, Rosson bore a great physical resemblance to Bern.) The couple "eloped" to Yuma, Arizona, in September 1933. The studio milked the nuptials for all possible publicity, but not even MGM could make the mismatched marriage work. (Harlow complained that Hal spent too much time reading in bed and ignoring her.) Jean and the sixteen-year-older Rosson separated in a matter of months and were divorced by 1935. Meanwhile, an unhappy Harlow reluctantly joined Mama Jean and Bello in the Beverly Hills mansion paid for by her studio earnings.

If Jean didn't have the strength to fight her overbearing relatives, she did rebel against the studio, rejecting vehicles, being difficult, and accelerating her growing fondness for alcohol. She finally agreed to star in *Reckless* (1935), a musical drama whose plot had uncomfortable parallels to the tragic finale of her marriage to Bern. In the course of the tough production, during which she struggled to learn her dance steps and had to deal with her singing voice being dubbed, she became close with her dapper costar, the forty-three-year-old William Powell. He'd been married and divorced twice (his second wife being movie star Carole Lombard). Harlow and Powell developed a relationship while working on the movie and she came to believe that they would wed. However, ladies' man Powell (the star of the *Thin Man* movies) was in no hurry to remarry and kept postponing their talked-about nuptials.

During the shooting of *Saratoga* (1937), Jean's sixth vehicle with Clark Gable, Harlow looked increasingly pale and bloated. (Onlookers attributed this to her alcoholism.) She became seriously ill and had to leave the set. Her mother was also convinced that the ailing Baby was having an adverse reaction to her drinking problem. One of Jean's physicians misdiagnosed nephritis (kidney failure) as something else. When the wrongly treated star's kidneys shut down, she developed uremic poisoning. She died on June 7, 1937, after suffering horrendously during her final days. Again, there was a cover-up (of the doctor's wrong judgment). This situation was compounded by Mama Jean having used her Christian Science beliefs as an excuse to mask her know-it-all refusal to follow MGM's directives when Harlow became dangerously ill. These factors contributed to rumors that the movie star had died from her mother's refusal to allow her to have needed medical treatment—which was not the case. After the spectacle of

Jean's circuslike funeral at Forest Lawn Memorial Park in Glendale, California, on June 9, 1937, the studio completed *Saratoga* using a stand-in and a voice double for Harlow. The picture did well financially due to the public's morbid curiosity to see Jean's last film.

By the early 1960s, Jean Harlow's once-spectacular screen reputation had become a musty legend. However, a lurid book biography and a few trashy movies about her life reawakened public interest in the vintage sex symbol. These (fictional) re-creations did much to create many of the exaggerated myths that exist to this day about the reckless Hollywood "wanton" known as Jean Harlow.

Susan Hayward

[Edythe Marrener]

JUNE 30, 1917–MARCH 14, 1975

In life, she was feisty, gutsy, and explosive; on the screen, this beautiful five-foot, three-and-a-half-inch redhead radiated those same qualities. Hayward overcame tough odds in her Brooklyn childhood, and that determination and resiliency similarly helped her to stand out from the pack when she later tried her luck in Hollywood. Bette Davis, John Wayne, and Marilyn Monroe to one side, few performers had such a distinctive walk as Susan. When she strode into a room in one of her pictures, she was like a panther taking stock of the landscape and, once focusing on her prey, closing in for the kill. On-screen, Hayward was a remarkable example of a sexy, tough broad who rarely yielded an inch. Unlike most demure leading ladies in the pre-feminism era, her film alter egos never shied away from looking a person squarely in the eye and saying exactly what was on her mind. Off camera, her forthrightness was mingled with impulsiveness, competitiveness, and a resolve not to let anyone push her out of the limelight or discover her hidden vulnerability. All this led to rocky times for Hayward on and off the soundstage.

She was born in 1917 in a tenement flat in the Flatbush section of Brooklyn. Edythe was the third child of Walter (a redheaded Irishman, whose jobs ranged from Coney Island barker to subway guard) and Ellen Marrener (of Swedish extraction). Coming from a poor family in a tough neighborhood, Edythe learned to fight for what she wanted. At age six, she was hit by an automobile and suffered fractured legs and a dislocated hip. Clinic physicians insisted she'd never walk again; Edythe proved them wrong. By the second grade—through grit and painful exercise—she had learned to walk on her own without braces or crutches. As a youngster, she was a loner with a great love for movies. Her ambition after high school was to survive financially, perhaps as a secretary. To earn cash during high school, she modeled. Later, she became a professional model, and her picture in a *Saturday Evening Post* magazine fashion layout was spotted by an associate of movie producer David O. Selznick, who was then on a massive search for an actress to play Scarlett O'Hara in *Gone with the Wind* (1939). The

A sultry Susan Hayward in the 1950s.
(Courtesy of Echo Book Shop)

novice was flown to Los Angeles with her sister Florence. Edythe's inexperience lost her the coveted screen role, but once in Hollywood, she remained there. A talent agent later changed her name to Susan Hayward and negotiated a six-month Warner Bros. contract for her. She did bits in *Hollywood Hotel* (1937) and several other features.

Although Warner Bros. dropped Susan's option, Paramount was impressed enough to hire her. Hayward's first assignment at her new studio was *Beau Geste* (1939), a major production starring Gary Cooper. She handled herself adequately as the love interest of Ray Milland's character. Then, for no apparent reason, Hayward was demoted to appearing in run-of-the-mill products like *Our Leading Citizen* (1939). Convinced she was failing at the studio, she adopted an even stronger posture of self-assuredness that verged on egocentricity. If before she had mostly kept to herself on film sets, she now became a staunch loner who insisted she didn't need anyone's help. In developing this protective willfulness, she ignored suggestions from directors on her pictures or advice from other contractees. As she explained later, "The only way I knew how to protect myself was to try and scare people before they scared me." It worked! The aloof, frequently short-tempered actress who had no interest in small talk became extremely unpopular with the casts and crews of her films. On the other hand, she photographed well and the mix of her improved acting style and her strong presence translated effectively to the screen.

When Paramount announced an upcoming major production titled *Hold Back the Dawn* (1941), Hayward begged executives to be cast as the second female lead. Instead, the studio gave the part to the more established Paulette Goddard. Susan fumed. Not long after, Hayward was among the company talent trotted out at a studio sales convention meeting to be introduced to the nationwide sales staff. When she went to the microphone, Susan came out fighting. "Did anyone in the house ever hear of me before?" The sales force yelled, "No!" She responded, "You said it! But I'm drawing my salary every week. Is that economics?" The response was again "No!" She then shouted, "Anybody in the house like to see me in a picture?" The reply was an enthusiastic "Yes!" Amid the strong applause, she turned to a bemused studio executive on stage with her and said, "Well, how about it?" Without waiting for a reply, she strode off, leaving the sales force to clap, stomp, and whistle their approval of this spirited newcomer.

Thereafter, Susan's career dramatically picked up with roles in such features as Cecil B. DeMille's *Reap the Wild Wind* (1942); *I Married a Witch* (1942); and *The Fighting Seebees* (1944), the latter opposite John Wayne. Everything seemed to be improving in her career. In fact, Buddy DeSylva, the studio's production chief who had shown no previous interest in her welfare, summoned her to his office. She was told she was to be loaned to United Artists for a major drama, *Dark Waters* (1944). Susan was jubilant for days until she read in the trade papers that Merle

Oberon had been signed for the demanding role. When a crushed Hayward questioned DeSylva as to what had happened, he replied, "You've been rude, snippy, and uncooperative with stars and directors. Maybe this will teach you." He advised the humiliated actress she was next to support Loretta Young in *And Now Tomorrow* (1944). End of conference.

Meanwhile, with the United States' entry into World War II, Hayward had joined countless other screen talents in entertaining servicemen at the famed Hollywood Canteen. There she met Jess Barker, a New York actor under contract to Columbia Pictures. On their first date, she slapped him for getting fresh. It was a prelude of things to come. They dated on and off for the next nine months, while he still played the field, leading to verbal arguments and physical fights between them. Nevertheless, she wed him in July 1944 (Jess having signed a prenuptial agreement that kept her money hers). Less than two months later, she was ready to abandon the marriage. However, she was pregnant and, in February 1945, she gave birth to twin sons. The new arrivals in the household created another bone of contention between Susan and Jess as they battled over how to bring up the boys.

When Hayward was ready to return to work, she was no longer at Paramount but had signed with independent producer Walter Wanger. She was cast in the Western *Canyon Passage* (1946) and later in *Smash-Up, the Story of a Woman* (1947), the latter bringing Hayward her first Oscar nomination. If Susan had been behaving herself on the set in recent years, that fell apart while she was making *The Lost Moment* (1947). She became so irritated with director Martin Gabel at his "mishandling" of this period drama that one day, during a rehearsal, she picked up a ceramic lamp in a fit of anger and cracked it over his head.

By the late 1940s, Susan had moved up in the Hollywood hierarchy when Twentieth Century-Fox took over Wanger's contract with her. In the 1950s, she became one of that studio's major assets, starring in such varied vehicles as *David and Bathsheba* (1951), *The Snows of Kilimanjaro* (1952), and *Soldier of Fortune* (1955). Also in 1955, she starred in *I'll Cry Tomorrow*, winning her fourth Oscar bid. Offscreen she made a different type of headline. In April of that year, she was hospitalized for attempting suicide with sleeping pills. The cause was given as depression following a serious argument with ex-husband Barker, whom she had divorced in 1954. That November, she was back in the news when starlet Jill Jarmyn accused Susan of having smacked her with a hairbrush. This occurred when Jarmyn arrived at actor Don "Red" Barry's apartment and found Hayward there clad in pajamas. An argument ensued. Once that news story faded, Hayward briefly turned to dating producer John Beck and billionaire Howard Hughes. She had much better luck when she met former FBI agent Floyd Eaton Chalkley, who was now an attorney and based in Carrollton, Georgia. They wed in February 1957.

After years of moviemaking, Hayward finally won an Academy Award for playing condemned murderess Barbara Graham in *I Want to Live!* (1958). Her mentor Walter Wanger joked, "Thank God, now we can all relax. Susie finally got what she's been chasing for twenty years!" But what Susan now wanted was to enjoy her happy domestic life. She had that with Chalkley until his death from hepatitis in early 1966. Thereafter, she only made occasional forays back to Los Angeles for feature films such as *Valley of the Dolls* (1967) and *The Revengers* (1972). By late 1973, she had been diagnosed with inoperative brain tumors. Through tremendous willpower, she rallied enough to make an appearance at the April 1974 Academy Awards. She died at the home she'd purchased in Culver City, California, during her last years.

A few years before she passed away, Hayward said of her life in films, "I've enjoyed every minute of my career. It isn't art to me, it's work, and darn good work, but it's never been my life. There are other things vastly more important to me."

Rita Hayworth

[Margarita Carmen Cansino]
OCTOBER 17, 1918–MAY 14, 1987

She felt her great beauty was a curse because men chased after her body, never her inner self. Over the years, Hayworth was exploited by her father, by her studio bosses, and by each of her five husbands. Later in life, when she should have been enjoying the fruit of decades of moviemaking, she sank into a morass of alcoholism and accelerating Alzheimer's disease.

In earlier years, especially in the 1940s, she was at her most physically alluring. Rita was then a coveted screen goddess and, along with Betty Grable, a top pinup queen for millions of servicemen around the world. By 1946, with the release of *Gilda*, she was at the peak of her cinematic popularity. In this remarkable performance, she was a gorgeous siren whom men found exciting and unattainable. The celluloid role seemed a luscious reflection of the off-screen Rita, the movie star who *appeared* to have everything a woman might desire: beauty, fame, riches, power, and even a pretty young daughter. In reality, Hayworth was insecure, restless, and constantly searching for escape through sexual liaisons, alcohol, and self-indulgent behavior.

The future star was born Margarita Carmen Cansino in 1918 in New York City. Her father, Eduardo, had relocated there from Spain five years earlier and teamed with his sister in a vaudeville dance act. In Manhattan, Eduardo met Volga Haworth, a Ziegfeld Follies beauty who was of English-Irish ancestry, and they soon married. Besides Margarita, the Cansinos later had two other offspring, Vernon and Eduardo Jr.

Taught to obey her father, Margarita complied when he decreed that the four-year-old should take dance classes. She disliked the grind of the daily practice but hid her feelings. In 1926, she made her film debut as a member of the family act in a silent short subject. By 1927, the Cansinos had relocated to Los Angeles, where Eduardo taught dance steps to film performers at the studios. While attending school, young Margarita continued her dance training and took acting classes to gain poise and help her overcome her shyness. Her classroom studies ended in the ninth grade when her father decided his physically mature daughter should become his new dance partner. She made her professional debut in a stage prologue at a Los Angeles film theater, later dancing with Eduardo at resorts in Mexico and on a gambling boat off the California coast. During this period, when she was out of her mother's supervision, her father sexually abused her. It was the start of her lifelong role as a pawn to dominating, selfish men. (Later, she would observe of herself, "Basically, I am a good, gentle person, but I am attracted to mean personalities.")

Dark-haired, five-foot, four-inch Margarita, who had been pimped by her father to various movie executives who expressed interest in her, made her feature film debut at the Fox studio playing a Spanish dancer in *Dante's Inferno* (1935). Working in pictures gave the exotic young actress a semblance of independence, but she soon fell into the clutches of Edward Charles Judson, a former car salesman and con artist. She married the middle-aged man in May 1937, just about the time he negotiated a Columbia Pictures contract for her. To make Margarita more enticing to gruff studio boss Harry Cohn, Judson put his wife through a grueling physical transformation that included dieting, electrolysis to raise her hairline, and dying her hair auburn. She also adopted a new name: Rita Hayworth.

Crude, randy, married Cohn desired Rita and, although Judson pushed his wife in the direction of any industry executive who could help her career, Hayworth and Cohn never seem to have connected. Instead, for the next two decades, they carried on a sadistic cat-and-mouse game of seesawing power plays. (Fellow Columbia player Ann Miller once observed of Hayworth and the Boss, "Her whole life was running from him.") Rita's career eventually expanded, especially when she was loaned out to other film lots as with MGM's *Susan and God* (1940), Warner Bros.'s *The Strawberry Blonde* (1941), and Twentieth Century-Fox's *Blood and Sand* (1941). Back at Columbia, she teamed with Fred Astaire for two well-received musicals. Her star status was now assured. She ended her increasingly unpleasant marriage to Judson in 1943 after Columbia Pictures paid him not to besmirch Rita's reputation in the divorce proceedings. (He had vowed to reveal the names of the many industry men she'd slept with—ironically, at his insistence—to advance her career.)

Enjoying a burst of freedom, Rita dated muscle-bound actor Victor Mature. The press thought they'd marry, but she couldn't make up her mind about the good-looking hunk. She was far more drawn to actor/director Orson Welles, with his great intellect and sophistication. She also liked his reputation as the industry's bad boy genius. They wed in September 1943.

Rita soon discovered that Orson's insatiable appetites included more than fine wine and food: he had a roving eye for pretty women. To salve her ego and get even, Hayworth, the star of the very popular musical *Cover Girl* (1944), found her own dalliances—all the while staving off persistent Cohn. Hayworth thought of leaving Welles, but then she became pregnant. (Their daughter, Rebecca, was born in December 1944.) Unfortunately, parenthood did not cure the disintegrating marriage. Having already self-destructed his brilliant Hollywood career, Orson now imposed his will on Rita's. To please him, she agreed to have her famous tresses chopped short and the remainder dyed a brassy blond color. He then cast her as his leading lady in the murky, autobiographical drama *The Lady from Shanghai*, which didn't see release until 1948—and then did poorly at the box office.

Hayworth divorced Welles in November 1948. She soon fell under the spell of Prince Aly Khan, the son of the immensely rich Indian potentate Aga Khan III. Like her past spouses, Aly wanted the screen siren to be his trophy wife, but he didn't intend to abandon his dissolute ways. Again, passive-aggressive Rita played a game of romantic tag across continents as he pursued, she fled, and vice versa. When she found herself pregnant by Aly, they hurriedly arranged the wedding of the decade in May 1949. Five months and a day after the nuptials, she gave birth to Princess Yasmin. For a brief spell, Hayworth seemed content, but then it was back to bickering with philandering Aly and trying to avoid his intrusive hangers-on.

By the early 1950s, the long-doomed royal union had collapsed despite a few attempts at reconciliation. Her ego bruised and her bank account empty (thanks to Aly's rich lifestyle at her expense), Rita returned to Hollywood with her two daughters in tow. She had not made a feature since 1948's *The Love of Carmen*. Studio chieftain Harry Cohn slapped together *Affair in Trinidad* (1952) and reteamed Hayworth with her frequent leading man, Glenn Ford. By the time she made the 3-D musical *Miss Sadie Thompson* (1953), Rita was in her mid-thirties and looking frayed. Four years later, in the musical *Pal Joey*, in which Frank Sinatra and young Kim Novak were *the* stars, Rita appeared matronly. What had hurried the aging process was her short but stormy marriage to unstable singer Dick Haymes. Getting unhitched from the crooner in December 1955 cost the movie queen a good deal of her bank account and much of her remaining self-respect.

In *Separate Tables* (1958), Rita emerged as a character lead, showing a previously underused acting acumen. That same year, in February, she wed producer James Hill, a coupling that quickly failed. By September 1961, she was single again and dating Bette Davis's cast-off spouse, actor Gary Merrill. That destructive entanglement exhausted her until she ended it. Film offers were now few and far between, and most of them were dismal (such as 1972's *The Wrath of God*).

The one-time film goddess admitted to having a face-lift in the mid-1970s, and then there were embarrassing public spectacles such as her disembarking "drunk" at London's Heathrow Airport in early 1976. By the next year, it was medically concluded that she was suffering the results of chronic alcoholism, and a petition was filed to have her estate and personal matters controlled by a conservator. She ended up in a New England hospital to dry out, with daughter Yasmin appointed as her

The beguiling Rita Hayworth in the 1940s.
(Courtesy of Echo Book Shop)

guardian. In 1980, doctors finally concluded that Rita was suffering from Alzheimer's disease. Her last years were spent in a New York apartment suite where Yasmin could supervise her care. By the time Rita passed away in May 1987, she had retreated into her own world and could no longer care for her simplest body functions. She was buried at Holy Cross Cemetery in Los Angeles.

Once, when asked about her cinema fame, Hayworth explained, "I never really thought of myself as a sex goddess; I felt I was more a comedian who could dance." In life, she proved to be full of wry observations about herself (for example, "Orson Welles sometimes gave me cause to think that he married me so he could direct me. Off the set and, in particular, on it. If the film we did had been more successful with the public, our marriage might have lasted longer"). As for her high-octane life—full of self-damage and pathos—she had her own take on it: "I haven't had everything from life, I've had too much."

Sonja Henie

[Sonja Henie]

APRIL 8, 1912–OCTOBER 12, 1969

Several Hollywood moviemaking celebrities (including Johnny Weissmuller, Esther Williams, and Jim Brown) began their careers as athletes. One of the most popular—with her public but *not* her coworkers—was Scandinavian ice-skating champ Henie, who became a major American movie star in the late 1930s. On ice, she was a cute and bubbly blond bundle of skating joy who delighted her legion of fans around the world. Away from the rink, the dimpled darling was a cunning businesswoman and a major shrew with employees. Despite her riches, she was extraordinarily stingy. Her self-absorption and undiplomatic treatment of others (intensified by a drinking problem that

Sonja Henie, the Queen of Ice.
(Courtesy of JC Archives)

accelerated as she aged and lost the limelight) gave her a nasty reputation with insiders as the "Vicious Ice Queen." Then too, there were many who could not forget her friendship with dictator Adolf Hitler in the mid-1930s and labeled her dangerously naïve because of her associations with the Nazis before the outbreak of World War II.

She was born in Oslo, Norway, in 1912, the second offspring (there was an older brother, Leif) of Wilhelm and Selma (Nilsen) Henie.

Her father was a successful fur merchant and had been a champion bike rider in his youth. Before age six, she received her first pair of ice skates and began her lasting and passionate enthusiasm for the sport. In the ice-skating events at the 1924 Winter Olympics at Chamonix (France), the talented youngster came in third. Discouraged by the results, ambitious Sonja convinced her parents to permit her to undergo an ambitious training program, one that took her to Germany, Switzerland, Austria, and England. To further improve her poise and rhythm, she also studied ballet. By age fourteen, the perfectionistic miss had won the Norwegian skating championship. In 1927, she achieved her first world figure-skating prize. The next year, she won Olympic gold in women's figure skating, a success she would repeat in 1932 and 1936. Much as she cherished her victories on ice, her dream was to become a glamorous movie queen in America. (In 1927 she had appeared in a Norwegian silent movie, *Syv Dager for Elisabeth* [*Seven Days for Elisabeth*].) In March 1936, Henie ended her amateur skating career and turned professional.

Hoping to tempt the Hollywood film studios into signing her, Sonja craftily went to Los Angeles and hired the Polar Ice Palace for a three-day show at her own $28,000 expense. The investment not only paid off in ticket receipts but it also so intrigued Twentieth Century-Fox film mogul Darryl F. Zanuck that he offered the sexy five-foot, two-inch skater a movie contract. He suggested $75,000 per film; she demanded $125,000 for each picture *and* time off each year to tour in her skating show. Appreciating her astute negotiations,

Zanuck made the deal with the young woman, whose enchanting smile outweighed her thick accent. To ensure the success of her screen debut in *One in a Million* (1936), Sonja was supported in the lightweight romp by Don Ameche, Adolphe Menjou, Jean Hersholt, and the zany Ritz Brothers. The movie impressively grossed more than $2 million at the box office. (But all was not gold for Fox. What the studio chief had not reckoned with was Henie's demand that he honor a contractual clause in her filmmaking pact that she be paid an additional $7,000 per day for putting together the film's ice-skating elements. That added over $400,000 to her take on *One in a Million*.)

Her next picture, *Thin Ice* (1937), costarred her with handsome Tyrone Power, a fellow Fox star with whom she had already begun a passionate affair. (Power was physically similar to her frequent skating partner, Jackie Dunn, with whom she had had an on-again, off-again romance.) Used to getting what she wanted, Sonja was convinced that Power would eventually wed her. She claimed to be heartbroken when Tyrone (actually a bisexual) equivocated with her about marriage and then "suddenly" wed French-born actress Annabella in 1939. Meanwhile, Henie's beloved father died in May 1937. His funeral, with the much-grieving Sonja in attendance, was highly publicized by the studio, but her trip to the bank shortly after Wilhelm's death to grab the huge amount of cash in a safety deposit box she shared with him was not. The family plan was to avoid the skater having to pay tax on the $150,000, but once she had the money in hand, she had no intention of sharing it with her relatives.

On-screen, Henie breezed through such profitable fluff as *Happy Landing* (1938) and *Second Fiddle* (1939), her second and final picture with Power. Off camera, now that her father was not there to guide her, Sonja really let fame go to her head. She became increasingly capricious and stingy with beholden family members and employees, as well as greedy at the studio. For example, after she had completed one of her Twentieth Century-Fox pictures, Zanuck concluded the screen fare would benefit from an additional skating number. Although her renegotiated, lucrative contract did not specify that she would be paid for add-on work to her pictures, Henie refused to undertake the new routine unless the studio gave her an additional $25,000. The film factory eventually caved in to her demands.

When the world-famous skater made personal appearances or endorsements or performed on radio, she rejected the custom of accepting expensive merchandise in lieu of a cash fee. She reasoned gleefully, "I take the cash and buy my own things." At the same time, this big-money earner was very tightfisted, examining every deal to be sure she got the most from the situation. She also rarely tipped for services rendered and was renowned for stripping hotel suites clean of sheets, towels, and so forth when she departed.

By the end of the 1930s, Henie was earning a mighty $2 million a year from her movies and touring ice revues. She was nicknamed the "U.S. Mint," and it was joked that the star, who adored expensive jewelry, was swapping ice in the rink for ice on her fingers. As time passed, this wealthy celebrity became pro-gressively litigious, generally winning her lawsuits. (One that she lost was a $77,000 decision in favor of an ex-manager.) In July 1940, she wed twice-divorced millionaire sportsman Daniel Reid Topping. That year, she bought a swank home in Holmby Hills adjacent to Beverly Hills. Increasingly active in social circles, she was more popular with high society than with the film industry set because with members of the latter she was too frequently competitive and barely shielded her envious and mean-spirited nature.

After *Wintertime* (1943), Twentieth Century-Fox finally bid Henie farewell. Her annual ice show still gave the star great public exposure, and lesser Hollywood studios hired her for *It's a Pleasure* (1945) and *The Countess of Monte Cristo* (1948), both of which were disappointing entertainments. (Her final picture was an elaborate British musical travelogue, 1958's *Hello London*.) Her marriage to Topping soured long before their January 1946 divorce. In 1949, she wed aviation executive Winthrop Gardiner Jr., an unsatisfactory union that ended in divorce in 1956. (Knowing that the bad marriage was over, Sonja hastened to her husband's Long Island estate, which she had furnished. Joined by helpers, she removed everything that was not nailed down—including rolls of toilet paper.) A few weeks later, Henie married her childhood sweetheart, Neils Onstad, a Norwegian ship owner. As the years passed, the couple became ardent modern art collectors and, in 1968, bestowed an art center on Norway; the $3.5 million facility was built just outside of Oslo. A year later, the mercenary lady of the ice—one of the ten wealth-

One's character, it is said, is judged by the company one keeps. In 1936, as Henie was preparing for the winter Olympics, she gave an exhibition in Berlin. One night, Adolf Hitler and several key members of the Third Reich showed up to see her skate. When she entered the rink, Sonja gave the Fuehrer the Nazi salute. He returned the gesture by throwing her a kiss. When this exchange was reported in her native Norway, an angered Henie, only interested in career strategies, said, "Nazi-schmatzy. Hitler is the German leader. I was honoring Germany, not the Nazis. I don't even know what a Nazi is." It wasn't until Germany invaded Norway a few years later that she publicly had a change of heart about the dictator and his regime. However, even after she became a Hollywood movie star and before America entered World War II, she associated with pro-Nazi groups in the United States.

iest women in the world—died of leukemia while being flown by ambulance plane from Paris to Oslo.

Katharine Hepburn

[Katharine Houghton Hepburn]
MAY 12, 1907–

For much of her more than seventy years as an actress, she was a major star. Nominated twelve times for an Oscar, she won on four occasions. To some, this unique American marvel is Hollywood's most distinctive actress of its Golden Age. To others, the highly mannered, iconoclastic woman is a performer who received far *too* much recognition for being a dedicated eccentric, one who seemingly reveled in straying from the norm for its own sake. Whatever one's assessment of this opinionated performer, one has to be in awe of her talent in getting her own way throughout her

life and thumbing her nose at everyone who opposed her wishes.

Even as a novice performer full of insecurities, Hepburn presented a public front of self-confidence. She seemed a person who resolutely charged ahead, guided only by her own standards. From the start of her stage career in the late 1920s, many in the business found her high-toned, Yankee ways to be pretentious, odd, and abrasive. When she first started making movies in the early 1930s, she resisted becoming the media's pawn, insisting that her work must stand on its own. This smug standoffishness contributed to her being labeled box-office poison by movie theater exhibitors in the late 1930s. In the 1940s, however, she reemerged in Hollywood as—for a time—a softer, kinder Kate, one who was less haughty and far more accessible to the press. It was also during this period that she began a lengthy on- and offscreen relationship with married movie star Spencer Tracy. Although they never wed, the media respected their secret and didn't capitalize on the affair. Following Spencer's death in 1967, she became more reclusive when not working. When forced into a rare interview, the indomitable Kate could be testy. (She also had not softened in her dislike of worshipful fans. She loved to tell this story: "Once a crowd chased me for an autograph. 'Beat it,' I said, 'go sit on a tack!' 'We made you,' they said. 'Like hell you did,' I told them.")

Hepburn plowed into old age saying, doing, and working as she pleased. By then, she'd become an American institution whose individualistic (or, if you will, peculiar) ways were not only respected but revered by the public. For once, she was in agreement with the majority who now so resolutely admired her. Said no-nonsense Hepburn, "Cold sober, I find myself absolutely fascinating!"

She was born in Hartford, Connecticut, in 1907, one of six children of Dr. Thomas Norval Hepburn, a surgeon, and his wife, Katharine Houghton, a suffragette and campaigner for the dissemination of information about birth control. In this unconventional family, young Kate was no exception. She was an extreme tomboy in her youth, rambunctious and daring—a headstrong child who thought nothing of shaving her head, so her male playmates couldn't pull her hair. When she was twelve, her beloved older brother Thomas hung himself in the attic of a family home. The traumatic event affected her all her life.

At fashionable Bryn Mawr College, Hepburn continued her willful ways (which included the forbidden habit of smoking). By then, she had become devoted to theater work and only studied so that she would have the grades to stay in school and perform in class productions. After graduation, she began her professional theater life, unswayed by the fact that at five feet, seven inches, freckle-faced, bony, and with a heavily nasal New England twang, she was not an ideal candidate for leading stage roles. After being rejected by a stock company for lack of training, she took private lessons financed by her family. By the late 1920s, it was a common occurrence for Hepburn to be hired and then fired from a Broadway show because her presence and performance were too offbeat. Rather than retreat, she pushed forward, all the while entrenching her reputation as a rebellious and arty personality.

During this period, she had the notion of marrying, despite her mother's warning: "If you want to sacrifice the admiration of many men for the criticism of one, go ahead, get married." The groom, Ludlow Ogden Smith, was a Philadelphia aristocrat whom she'd met when she was still at Bryn Mawr. The couple wed in December 1928, but within three weeks Kate knew that marriage was not for her. Although they later shared a European vacation, they soon separated but were not officially divorced until 1934. It was Hepburn's one and only stab at marital bliss. (As to the fact that her decision meant not having children, Kate said, "I would have made a terrible parent. The first time my child didn't do what I wanted, I'd kill him.")

Single again, Hepburn continued in the theater. She finally had a Broadway success with *The Warrior's Husband* (1932). With her newfound stage status, Hollywood courted Kate.

Rather than be flattered, she reacted in an off-hand way, almost as if she couldn't be bothered with the offers. She made a screen test that showed she had a lot to learn before becoming a film actress and that her physical presence would never allow her to be a conventional movie star. However, her dashing agent, Leland Hayward (who became her lover for a time), negotiated a $1,500 weekly contract at RKO for his client. Kate's arrival in Hollywood marked her entire tenure there. Off camera, she dressed strangely (wearing slacks and favoring mannish clothes) and was standoffish to the point of rudeness. At the studio, the aloof Easterner refused to become part of the team. It was Kate against the Establishment.

Her first picture was *A Bill of Divorcement* (1932), starring aging matinee idol John Barrymore. Some accounts of the film's production insist that Barrymore was quite patient with the jittery newcomer as she adapted to the new medium. Others relate that the alcoholic leading man invited Kate to his dressing room, stripped naked, and tried to seduce her. Yet another report says that when filming ended, Hepburn told Barrymore, "Thank goodness I don't have to act with you anymore," to which a nonplussed John replied, "I didn't know you ever had, darling."

Alternating between stage and screen projects, Hepburn next made *Morning Glory* (1933) as a starry-eyed actress reaching for stage success. She won the Oscar. After making several weak dramas that only accentuated her special personality, Kate had another hit with *Alice Adams* (1935), for which she was again Oscar-nominated. During the making of

A resolute Katharine Hepburn in 1944.
(Courtesy of JC Archives)

Mary of Scotland (1936), she developed a strong rapport with married film director John Ford, which turned into a long-standing platonic relationship. When Hepburn became involved—as so many Hollywood actresses did—with idiosyncratic billionaire Howard Hughes, there was great speculation in the press that the two unusual personalities, who shared a mutual love of flying, golf, and privacy, might take their live-in situation to the next step—marriage. Eventually, Kate con-

multi-Oscar winner who enjoyed an extraordinarily long career, Kate was always set apart from the Hollywood mainstream. Frequently eccentric in wardrobe choices, she was an independent thinker who never overcame the initial impression she made on Tinseltown in 1932. She was snobbish, arty, and rebellious. Outspoken to a fault, her candor was biting even when she intended to compliment someone. Some of her more memorable observations include the following:

To director Dorothy Arzner:

"Isn't it wonderful you've had such a great career when you had no right to have a career at all?"

On Humphrey Bogart:

"He was a real man—nothing feminine about him. He knew he was a natural aristocrat—better than anybody."

On director John Ford:

"I liked working with Jack Ford very much; he and I were great friends. But he was as unsuited to that material [for 1936's Mary of Scotland*] as a director as I was unsuited to Mary of Scotland as an actress."*

On Greta Garbo:

"I'm a legend because I've survived over a long period of time and still seem to be master of my fate . . . whereas [Greta] Garbo has always been a mysterious sailboat who disappeared over the horizon the moment she felt she couldn't cope."

On Judy Holliday:

"She looks like a Monet model. And she's so—so defenseless. I like defenseless people. They're the best."

On Maggie Smith:

"She can act and she can overdo. It is becoming the style, you know, to attack the overdoers; so we overdoers have to stick together. But she hadn't the script she needed to protect her."

On John Wayne:

"He wasn't as clever as Spence [Tracy], but a brilliant actor nonetheless, bigger than life in his performance—and often when he didn't have to be."

cluded that Hughes, whom she found fascinating and extremely attractive, would never quit his philandering ways. Their romance ended, but they remained friends.

Anemic screen dramas such as *A Woman Rebels* (1936) and *Quality Street* (1937) shut Hepburn off from the moviegoing masses. Not even the entertaining screwball comedy *Bringing Up Baby* (1938), with Cary Grant, could lift Kate out of her box-office rut. Her RKO contract ended and, having burned her Hollywood bridges with her abrasive, above-it-all attitude, she returned East. Next, she starred on Broadway in *The Philadelphia Story* (1939), a tailor-made role that showcased her acting virtues and minimized her flaws. The romantic comedy was a hit. Having already acquired the screen rights to the vehicle (with funds provided by pal Howard Hughes), she negotiated a crafty movie deal with MGM that gave her great control over the film adaptation. The resultant 1940 picture was a hit (and she was again nominated for an Academy Award).

Hepburn's rejuvenated status in films was confirmed by *Woman of the Year* (1942), in which she teamed with Spencer Tracy. It was the first of seven features, including *Adam's Rib* (1949) and *Pat and Mike* (1952), they made together over the next decade. Much of her time with Spencer was spent coping with his alcoholism, his insecurities, his guilt complexes, and his self-centered desires. However, she threw herself wholeheartedly into the lopsided relationship, subjugating her personal life and career needs to his many whims. It was a strange love that brought her a fulfillment of sorts but at a great personal expense.

The high-caliber *The African Queen* (1951) began forty-something Hepburn's rash of whimsical spinster roles, which included *Summertime* (1955). By the early 1960s, with *Long Day's Journey into Night* (1962), Kate the survivor was specializing in heavy dramatic parts that kept her entrenched in the limelight. Despite her age and the tremors brought on by her advancing Parkinson's disease, she continued working in major screen roles while most of her contemporaries were forced into retirement. Shortly after 1967's *Guess Who's Coming to Dinner?* (for which she won her second Oscar), Tracy died. Thereafter, she mostly lived on the East Coast and carried on her sheltered life when not working. After earning her third Oscar for *The Lion in Winter* (1968), she pushed her limits by doing the Broadway musical *Coco* (1969) and performed in classy TV movies such as *The Glass Menagerie* (1973). She even turned up on the big screen as John Wayne's leading lady in the Western *Rooster Cogburn* (1975).

Teamed with Henry Fonda in *On Golden Pond* (1981), the veteran star won her fourth Academy Award. Occasionally, the grand old lady of show business—as irascible as ever—gave a TV interview or returned to the small screen for a telefeature (her last was 1994's *One Christmas*). She grew increasingly infirm as she reached her nineties but has not become docile in her later years.

She hated the fact of growing old ("It's a bore—B-O-R-E—when you find you've begun to rot"). Asked by an interviewer if she feared death, Hepburn shot back, "Not at all. Be a great relief. Then I wouldn't have to talk to you." As to her chosen career, she acknowledged, "Acting is a nice childish profession—pretending you're someone else and, at the same time, selling yourself." As to her accomplishments, this self-styled individualist has said, "With all the opportunities I had, I could have done more. And if I'd done more, I could have been quite remarkable."

Miriam Hopkins

[Ellen Miriam Hopkins]

OCTOBER 18, 1902 –OCTOBER 9, 1972

Beauty, wit, and talent are marvelous attributes for any actress. However, if she also boasts a volatile temperament, great impatience, and tremendous self-absorption, it can easily ruin her career. Southern belle Hopkins—the leading lady of such classic movies as *Dr. Jekyll and Mr. Hyde* (1932), *Trouble in Paradise* (1932), and *Becky Sharpe* (1935)—learned this lesson the hard way. In the 1930s, she used her comeliness, abilities, and charm to negotiate multipicture contracts at three (!) major Hollywood studios. Each time, Miriam undercut herself with her imperious ways. (Added to the self-destructive mix was her staunch belief in astrology, which led her to reject many plum roles.) As she worked her way through Tinseltown's film lots, she earned the enmity of many eminent movie moguls. Moreover, her domineering, self-indulgent ways won her no friends among her fellow actors and crews. Hopkins finally met her match when she battled Bette Davis in their two costarring screen vehicles (1939 and 1943). It led the mighty Davis, no slouch at being a virago on and off the movie set, to spit out in disgust years later, "Miriam Hopkins? She was a swine! . . . Unprofessional, born to upstage, not to act."

Miriam was born in Savannah, Georgia, in 1902, the second child of insurance salesman Homer Hopkins and his wife, Ellen (Cutter) Hopkins. On her mother's side of the family, Miriam and her two-year-older sister, Ruby, came from illustrious stock—one of their forebears had signed the Declaration of Independence. The Hopkinses fought constantly, and Ellen frequently took her daughters to stay with her mother in nearby Bainbridge. When Miriam was seven, her father vanished from the scene. Thanks to the generousity of Ellen's twin brother, the Hopkins girls were well educated. Miriam completed her secondary education at Goddard Seminary in Barre, Vermont.

By the time Miriam was in her late teens, she, her mother, and her sister were living in New York City. By then, the five-foot, two-inch blond Southerner had decided on an acting career. Enterprising Miriam talked herself into a chorus role in the *Music Box Revue* (1921). With her calculated Southern airs, she made no pals among the street-smart chorines, but she stayed the course. She later worked in stock, cross-country stage tours, vaudeville, and then back on Broadway in the musical farce *Little Jessie James* (1923).

In 1926, she impetuously wed Broadway leading man Brandon Peters. Shortly thereafter, she was hired to play Lorelei Lee in *Gen-*

tlemen Prefer Blondes but was dismissed for being too intellectual to play the flighty heroine. She turned this setback to her advantage, for she was now available to join *An American Tragedy* (1926), which enjoyed a long Broadway run. By the next year, she had separated from her spouse and begun an affair with established playwright Patrick Kearney. When he wanted to wed her, free spirit Miriam hid from him that she'd already quietly divorced Peters. This led to confusion in 1928 when she married playwright Austin Parker, and her seeming bigamy caused a furor in the press. That same year, she performed with a stock company in Rochester, New York. One of the lesser players in the group—with whom Hopkins did not get along—was young Bette Davis.

Miriam made her movie debut in Paramount Pictures's *Fast and Loose* (1930), shot at their Astoria, Long Island, facility. She filmed during the day, returning to her Broadway chores at night. Always deeply insecure, especially about her looks, she insisted to studio executives that her true love was the theater. (She hated getting up early to film and abhorred the grueling regimen required to shoot each scene.) However, when her next stage vehicle closed suddenly, she agreed to making Paramount's *The Smiling Lieutenant* (1931) opposite Maurice Chevalier. Her affair with the Frenchman helped end her union with Parker.

On accepting a Paramount term contract, Miriam relocated to Los Angeles. Before long, her demanding ways earned her the growing enmity of the Paramount regime. Her last good role at the studio was Ernst Lubitsch's sophisticated *Design for Living* (1933). Meanwhile Mims (as close acquaintances called her) impetuously adopted an infant boy. There were rumors that the child might be hers, but Hopkins explained her good deed with "I just felt, I suppose, that it was nicer to have a baby in the house than not to have a baby in the house."

By 1934, Hopkins had burned her bridges at Paramount, returned to the Broadway stage, and taken a new lover—theatrical agent Leland Hayward. Meanwhile, her West Coast representative negotiated an enticing film pact for her with iron-willed independent producer Sam Goldwyn. Her stay with Goldwyn, which included making *These Three* (1936) with Joel McCrea and Merle Oberon, was tumultuous. Off camera, Miriam had an affair with fading screen idol John Gilbert and later fell in love with Russian-born film director Anatole Litvak. Their romance flourished and she eloped with him to Arizona in September 1937.

With such unremarkable 1937 releases as *Wise Girl*, Miriam ended round two of her screen career. She returned East to star in *Wine of Choice* but quit the prestigious production during its pre-Broadway engagement in early 1938. That year, she won a New York newspaper's poll as the favorite choice to star as Scarlett O'Hara in *Gone with the Wind* (1939). However, those in charge of the epic wanted nothing to do with temperamental Miriam. Undaunted, Hopkins used her inestimable charms to win her husband directorial assignments at Warner Bros. In the process, the thirty-six-year-old actress negotiated a multipicture contract for herself with the Burbank film lot.

For 1939's *The Old Maid*, she paired with the lot's reigning star, Bette Davis. Throughout the making of the costume drama, egotistical Miriam used every acting trick she knew to draw attention away from her colead—and always with an air of feigned innocence. Davis's prediction, "She'll be trouble, but she'll be worth it," proved true and the Warner Bros. picture was a huge hit. Meanwhile, Miriam's marriage to autocratic Litvak fell apart; they divorced in 1939. Hopkins next found herself cast opposite a several-years-younger Errol Flynn in *Virginia City* (1940). She made it known publicly how much she despised being in this Civil War Western, even if the esteemed Michael Curtiz was its director. Thereafter, the studio lost interest in her and, by the early 1940s, she and her young son were back in New York City.

When Warner Bros. bought *Old Acquaintance* (1943) as a Bette Davis vehicle, Jack L. Warner shrewdly knew it would benefit from Miriam's presence in the cast. Nevertheless, he demanded she accept below-the-title billing. Never one to admit defeat, she did her best to steal Davis's thunder on camera, but the ever-vigilant Bette kept her from accomplishing this goal. The two actresses feuded openly during production. Everyone on the lot waited with great anticipation for the two veterans to square off in a crucial dramatic scene in which Davis's character slugs Hopkins's Millie Davis. That day, the set was crowded with onlookers. Davis recounted later, "It was rather like a prizefight ring. . . . We rehearsed this scene for

Miriam Hopkins in the early 1930s.
(Courtesy of JC Archives)

hours . . . but [eventually] stand still she did— and take her slap she did. To be sure, her eyes filled with tears of self-pity—but the camera couldn't see it. It was on her back!"

After the popular *Old Acquaintance*, troublesome Miriam was off the screen until 1949. Then she accepted a character role as the heroine's aunt in *The Heiress* (1949). During subsequent years, she alternated among the stage, television, and occasional supporting film parts. Her fourth and final marriage was in 1945 to *New York Times* foreign correspondent Ray Brock. They divorced in 1951. She continued to divide her time between New York and Los Angeles. There were rumors at this time that Hopkins had developed an overfondness for alcoholic beverages. One of her last public appearances was in 1972, when New York's Museum of Modern Art held a major retrospective of films made by Paramount Pictures. After sitting through a showing of her 1933 vehicle, *The Story of Temple Drake*, Miriam voiced her disappointment in the movies to her companion. Next, she headed to the ladies room where she found a long line. Still an impatient queen at heart, she quipped to the queued-up women, "I've suffered more than any of you. So let me in." They did.

Talented, garrulous, but self-defeating Miriam died of a massive coronary attack on October 9, 1972, in New York City. She was buried in her family's plot in Bainbridge, Georgia.

Whitney Houston

[Whitney Elizabeth Houston]

AUGUST 9, 1963–

Looking back on the early phase of her stellar singing career, Whitney Houston recalled, "Three women in my life who I grew up around and highly respected, Dionne War-

wick, Aretha Franklin, and Cissy Houston [her mother], they used to talk to me all the time. When I first hit, Dionne said to me . . . 'So, you wanted to be a star.' . . . My mother says it to me constantly. Aretha, in that Detroit drawl, says, 'So, you wanted to be a star.' That was the thing that they were saying to me. All of this stuff is cool, it's wonderful when you do something and people accept it and embrace it. But that fame is some crazy mess." As Whitney's fame increased, she learned more hard lessons about being wealthy and celebrated: "Money doesn't solve your problems. It creates problems. Fame doesn't solve anything. It just makes people more dangerous. You've got people who love you so much they hate you. Hate to love you. What kind of s*** is that? All I want to do is sing."

In the 1980s and early 1990s, Whitney, with her big voice and ability to shift from one musical genre to another, had huge across-the-board appeal to music lovers. Next, she made an impressive feature film debut in *The Bodyguard* (1992). In that flashy box-office hit, she demonstrated that—with more training and experience (plus a better screenplay and a loosening of her haughty demeanor)—the beautiful five-foot, eight-inch actress could become a true movie star. But that same year she married bad boy rapper Bobby Brown, known for his womanizing and street-tough ways. Since then, her life and reputation have never been the same. Subsequently, amid increasing reports of substance abuse, bizarre public behavior, brushes with the law, and rumors of a life spiraling totally out of control, Whitney became a prima donna in the worst sense of the phrase. As she showed up late for appointments, looking emaciated and spaced out, her once-mammoth career nose-dived.

She was born in 1963 in Newark, New Jersey, the third child of John Houston and Emily "Cissy" Drinkard. Her father worked for the city (he was later head of the Newark Central Planning Board). Her mother had a rich musical background. As a child, Cissy had been part of the family's gospel singing group, the Drinkard Sisters. Thereafter, Cissy and her cousins—Dionne and Dee Dee Warwick—created a trio, the Gospelaires. Later, Cissy organized the Sweet Inspirations, a rhythm-and-blues quartet that sang backup vocals for Elvis Presley and Aretha Franklin. Still later—at the time of Whitney's birth—Cissy was minister of music at the New Hope Baptist Church in Newark.

Two years after Whitney was born, the Houstons moved to nearby East Orange, New Jersey. As a child, Nippy (as Whitney was called) suffered from asthma and got into the typical mischief of a tomboy with two rambunctious older brothers. Cissy was away a good deal of the time on concert tours and recording sessions but sought to keep the household highly structured and well disciplined. Church played an important role in Whitney's youth, especially since she took a more active role in the choir there. When she was eight, she sang her first church solo. While Cissy trained her daughter for church singing, she had seen the downsides of working in show business and did her best to discourage the girl from becoming a professional singer. However, Whitney already had a mind of her own and

would sneak off to the basement and practice singing to the recordings of Aretha Franklin and Chaka Khan. She knew she wanted to perform in front of paying audiences.

In 1978, her parents separated and later divorced. The following year, sixteen-year-old Houston, more determined than ever to break into show business, was singing backup for some of Cissy's club and recording sessions. In 1980, Houston signed a management contract, and her controllers decided that if she gained exposure as a model it would help develop her stature and reputation. Before long, Whitney became a successful model. By the time she graduated from high school in 1981, she was taking acting lessons (in addition to modeling and singing). Her managers negotiated guest parts for her on such TV sitcoms as *Silver Spoons* and *Gimme a Break*. While singing at a Manhattan showcase in 1983, Whitney was heard by Arista Records producer Clive Davis, who signed her to a recording contract. Over the next few years, she was coached and her image carefully developed while she gained further experience by performing on concert tours. Davis invested an unprecedented $250,000 in ensuring that her debut album, *Whitney Houston* (1985), would be just right. After a slow buildup, the album rose high in the charts, as did such breakout singles as "How Will I Know" and "Greatest Love of All." The album sold thirteen million copies. Her follow-up album, *Whitney* (1987), led to a Grammy award for one of its cuts, "I Wanna Dance." Before the end of the year, Houston's first two albums had sold an amazing twenty-one million copies. In 1988, the increasingly popular singing star, who was racking up all sorts of awards, grossed $45 million.

As a major star in her mid-twenties, Whitney aroused a great deal of public interest. The media dutifully reported when she purchased a $2.7 million home in Mendham, New Jersey. The sprawling estate included an Olympic-size swimming pool, well-manicured tennis courts, and a thirty-two-track recording studio that the celebrity had custom ordered. On the social scene, strikingly beautiful Houston was seen with the likes of movie stars Eddie Murphy and Robert De Niro and TV personality Arsenio Hall. One relationship that particularly intrigued the press was Houston's longtime good friend, Robyn Crawford, who was the star's personal assistant but also resided in Whitney's New Jersey home. When *Time* magazine brought up the subject, Houston, who could be regal and testy at times, said, "People see her with me and they draw their own conclusions. Anyway, whose business is it if you're gay or like dogs? What others do shouldn't matter. Let people talk. It doesn't bother me because I know I'm not gay. I don't care."

In 1990, Houston's third album, *I'm Your Baby Tonight*, was released. It didn't fare as well as her earlier ones, but her mind was elsewhere. At the annual Soul Train Awards in 1989, she'd met Bobby Brown, the rap singer noted for his sexy, provocative image. The Massachusetts-born performer was several years younger than Houston. They became better acquainted in the months that followed. While others were shocked at the clash of their two images—wholesome, pure Whitney and

Whitney Houston at the center of media attention. (Photo by Albert L. Ortega)

down-and-dirty Bobby—she thrived on his dangerous-guy reputation. "Bobby knows the world," she explained. "Bobby helps me see things in myself I've never even thought about. He is the only man I've ever felt [that I was] myself with." Despite pressure from family and friends for her to find someone else, Houston continued to date him. She was pregnant with his child during the making of *The Bodyguard* but suffered a miscarriage in the spring of 1992. The duo drew closer to marriage when he signed a prenuptial agreement, which reportedly said that if the pair should split, she would keep her $70 million and he would retain his own $5 million. In mid-July 1992, the two Grammy winners were wed in a lavish ceremony at her compound. The bride wore a $40,000 wedding gown. After the celebration, the newlyweds, along with friends, flew to the Mediterranean where they boarded a triple-decker yacht. At a $10,000-a-day cost, the group cruised the French Riviera. By the time Whitney and Bobby returned and became full-time residents of her estate, Robyn Crawford had moved to her own place miles away. (In June 2000, Crawford quit her job as office manager of Nippy, Inc., Houston's New Jersey–based management company, and moved out of state.) In March 1993, Whitney gave birth to daughter Bobbi Kristina Houston Brown. (At this juncture, Bobby already had four other children by other women.)

The new mother, having lost the extra pounds put on during her pregnancy, talked to the media about her competitors: "People who go out and buy me, buy me for me. . . . They don't say I sound like Mariah Carey, they say Mariah Carey sounds like me, you dig what I'm saying? So I don't feel like I'm in competition with these people. . . . I've been out here since 1985, so whoever comes got to come after me." The pop diva, meanwhile, was gaining a negative reputation for outré behavior. Reportedly, she put her own needs before that of her young child while on the road, her marriage to Brown was said to be drifting, and there were newspaper rumors that she'd been hospitalized in Florida for an intentional overdose of diet pills. Meanwhile, extremely rich Whitney continued to thrive in material splendor, adding a

getaway house in Boca Raton, Florida, to her inventory.

After a world tour and raking in more music industry awards, she returned to film-making with *Waiting to Exhale* (1995) and *The Preacher's Wife* (1996). Meanwhile, she and Brown (whose career was stalling and who was allegedly in and out of rehab centers for substance abuse) announced that they were splitting, but they later reconciled. She suffered another miscarriage at the end of 1996, and her tempestuous married life continued to fascinate the tabloids. Her 1998 album (*My Love Is Your Love*), Houston's first in eight years, received good reviews but continued the downward trend of her record sales.

Houston remained the subject of sensational stories, true or false, and she lumped the accounts together, saying, "I don't deal with it because I know it's somebody treating me like a commodity." In a statement to *Newsweek* magazine that proved ironically prophetic, Whitney spit forth, "No, I'm not a drug addict, and neither is my husband. If that were so, you'd get a lot less work out of me. It would show in the performance and then in the work." In January 2000, Whitney was caught by security workers at an airport in Hawaii with a reported (up to) half ounce of marijuana in her handbag. She and Brown left for San Francisco before police arrived. (Eventually, the misdemeanor charge was dropped when a New Jersey drug counselor filed a statement with the Hawaiian court on her behalf in early 2001 that the singer did not need substance abuse treatment.) A few months later, Houston was "unable" to sing at the Academy Awards and failed to show up at her Rock 'n' Roll Hall of Fame induction. Meanwhile, her turbulent relationship with Brown continued and reputed attempts at intervention by family and friends failed. (In mid-2000, Bobby sat in a Florida jail for violating probation based on earlier drunk driving charges.) Insiders were suggesting that difficult Houston was no longer the victim being led astray by her trouble-prone husband but that she gave as good as she got.

In 2001, Whitney was one of the producers of the successful Julie Andrews screen comedy *The Princess Diaries* and signed a new recording contract worth $75 million. However, by September 2001, wild rumors were rampant that Houston had died of a drug overdose or been severely beaten by her supposed drug dealer. What was clear was that, when she was a guest that month on Michael Jackson's thirtieth anniversary celebration (a special televised in November), she looked gaunt and haggard and her voice seemed tremulous—not a bit like the former "Prom Queen of Soul."

By May 2002 Houston had recovered sufficiently to participate in VH1 cable's "Divas Las Vegas" charity fundraiser. Looking healthier than she had during the prior year, the thirty-eight-year-old singer was still not quite herself—missing her cue and having to rush on stage to join Mary J. Bilge to perform "Rainy Dayz." Thereafter, for reasons unknown, Whitney left the stage for the evening, choosing not to join the other divas for the event's star-studded finale. (Later the tabloids reported that Houston and Bilge had feuded the day before about a called-for joint rehearsal for their duet.) The next month, Houston was in the headlines again, this time when husband Bobby Brown had to be hospitalized in Virginia for an undisclosed infection. (The couple was returning in their tour bus to New Jersey from Atlanta, Georgia, where she had been recording her latest album.) After three days of treatment, he was released and the couple returned to their Garden State home.

Whitney Houston's terrible thirties bring to mind a statement she made once: "You're supposed to be partying in your twenties. I was on tour and making records. I sacrificed those years. When Bobby came along I started having a ball. He taught me how to have fun."

Betty Hutton

[Elizabeth June Thornburg]
FEBRUARY 26, 1921–

"Blonde Bombshell," "America's #1 Jitterbug," "Bounding Betty," and the "Blitzkrieg Blonde" were only a few of the laudatory descriptors applied to this multitalented five-foot, four-inch bundle of nonstop energy. In the 1940s and early 1950s, she cavorted in hit movies, Broadway musicals, and recordings and was enthusiastically applauded by audiences whenever she made personal appearances on stage and radio. In her heyday, husky-voiced Hutton was second only to Judy Garland in popularity as America's favorite female entertainer. Betty was but thirty-one when her spectacular show-business career began to implode. Thereafter, she made several teary announcements of her retirement, only to reemerge yet again to entertain audiences before she once more vanished from the public eye. Over the years, she consistently made bad decisions regarding her career and her soul mates, and she alienated many of her relatives and friends. Sadly, this gifted diva was her own worst enemy.

She was born in 1921 in Battle Creek, Michigan. Her unmarried mother (Mabel Lum Thornburg) was already the parent of nearly two-year-old Marion. (From the start, the two sisters competed for their mother's attention—the often-fractious sibling rivalry lasted until Marion's death in 1987.) Elizabeth June never knew her father, who had disappeared before her birth. (Purportedly, he was a railroad worker who committed suicide in 1937, leaving each daughter $100.) Uneducated and desperate to support her family, Mabel operated an illegal beer and gin club out of her tawdry apartment. The trio moved frequently, often just a step ahead of the police. Three-year-old Elizabeth gave her first public performances at her mother's joint, knowing that if she started to sing, the drunks would calm down and her mother would be safe from their physical abuse. The three later moved to Detroit. By then, Mabel was a confirmed alcoholic, and little Elizabeth had to patrol the local bars looking for her mom and singing songs to earn a few coins from her barroom audience. By age fifteen, she had quit school and made an unsuccessful trip to New York City, hoping to break into show business.

Fred Astaire and Betty Hutton in *Let's Dance* (1950). (Courtesy of JC Archives)

In 1937, the future movie star and her sister were singing in Detroit clubs. One night, famed bandleader Vincent Lopez heard Elizabeth perform and hired her as his new band vocalist at $65 a week. She almost lost the job when she developed stage fright on her opening night. In desperation, she gulped down a few drinks, got up on stage, and recklessly began belting out her songs as she danced a fractured jitterbug, acting boisterously with the audience and the band. She was a hit and stuck to this attention-gathering, bombastic style ever after. It was Lopez who renamed her Betty Hutton. (The more demure Marion, who also sang with Lopez before joining Glenn Miller's Orchestra, adopted the Hutton surname as well.)

Betty performed with Lopez's group in New York and elsewhere in clubs, on radio, and in vaudeville; she made her movie debut in four 1939 short subjects, including Paramount's *Three Kings and a Queen*. She left Lopez to appear in the Broadway musical revue *Two for the Show* (1940). Next, songwriter/stage/film producer Buddy DeSylva hired Hutton to support Ethel Merman in *Panama Hattie* (1940). On opening night, Merman insisted that Betty's splashy musical number be dropped from the show. A shocked Betty begged her protector (DeSylva) to intervene. He made her an offer: stay with the show for its run and then accompany him to Hollywood. He confided that he was about to become a top executive producer at Paramount and would make her a movie star! She agreed, and he lived up to his word. When she arrived at the studio in late 1941, the grapevine insisted she was DeSylva's girlfriend; Hutton claimed they were merely good friends. Whatever the case, her special status did not win her friends on the lot.

Unique for a film newcomer, Betty enjoyed a major role in her first feature, *The Fleet's In* (1942). Her supercharged presence and delightful hamming captivated audiences, as did her singing of the fast-tempo "Arthur Murray Taught Me Dancing in a Hurry." She mugged with Bob Hope in *Let's Face It* (1943) and played twins opposite Bing Crosby in *Here Come the Waves* (1944). In Preston Sturges's satirical gem *The Miracle of Morgan's Creek* (1944), she demonstrated that she could be effective on-screen without songs. By the time she made *The Stork Club* (1945), DeSylva was

being phased out of his Paramount post due to ill health. Meanwhile, big-headed, highly emotional Hutton was gaining an increasingly negative reputation on the lot. The high-voltage talent had a character actor dismissed from *The Stork Club*, and during the musical's production she was frequently late to the set—intolerable even for *the* star of the picture. Like Judy Garland, her big-screen counterpart at MGM, hyper Betty had developed the habit of taking prescription sleeping pills to help her sleep and other tablets in the morning to counter the grogginess from the nighttime medication.

In September 1945, Betty wed Chicago business executive Theodore Briskin. He wanted a stay-at-home wife, but she refused to abandon her movie career. Their marriage was filled with separations and reunions, during which they had two children (in 1946 and 1948). By early 1951, they were divorced. Hutton had a big hit with *The Perils of Pauline* (1947), but the high-salaried star drove the studio executives crazy when she rejected a slew of suggested pictures, including the title role in *My Friend Irma* (1949) and costarring with Bob Hope in *Fancy Pants* (1950). Instead, she insisted on appearing in the nonmusical *Dream Girl* (1948). On the shoot, she had a boss-lady attitude and was supported by a coterie of sycophants on her payroll. That film flopped and the next, *Red, Hot and Blue* (1949), was not a hit either. The studio wondered if Hutton was worth the continued aggravation.

Earlier she had nagged Paramount to buy the movie rights to Irving Berlin's massive

Broadway hit *Annie Get Your Gun*. However, MGM outbid them and Judy Garland was given the plum role. When Garland had a nervous breakdown and left the film, Hutton badgered studio executives to get the part. She prevailed, but making the 1950 musical was a nightmare for her. Almost everyone on the MGM production was a Judy supporter and angry with substitute Hutton. They gave her the cold shoulder throughout the shoot, which so unnerved the emotionally fragile Betty that it soured her on moviemaking.

While filming *Somebody Loves Me* (1952), she was so angry at Paramount for not hiring Frank Sinatra as her leading man that she only communicated with the picture's director through an intermediary. But at least the production netted her a new husband. He was dance director Charles O'Curran, with whom she eloped to Las Vegas in March 1952. However, things went from bad to worse. When the studio refused to let O'Curran direct *Topsy and Eva* later that year, Betty refused to make the technicolor biography of show business's Duncan sisters just weeks before it was to start. It was the final straw for the exhausted studio brass, and they allowed Hutton to buy out her remaining contract. Her prima donna actions made her persona non grata in Hollywood.

Thereafter, a distraught Betty jumped from filmmaking to one-woman concerts in the United States and abroad, club work in Las Vegas and elsewhere, highly publicized retirement bids, and two stabs at TV—a lavish spectacular (*Satins and Spurs*) in 1954 and the sitcom *Goldie* (also known as *The Betty Hutton Show*) from 1959 to 1960. On each of these projects she was dictatorial, territorial, capricious, and overwrought, and both were disappointments to her and audiences. Divorced again, she went through two more marriages and had a third daughter. She turned down playing Ado Annie in the movie *Oklahoma!* (1955), insisting the part was not big enough. However, she accepted the low-budget *Spring Reunion* (1957), her last feature.

Later in Betty's erratic career, there were brief returns to Broadway in already running shows. Her greatest visibility occurred in the mid-1970s when she was discovered as a rectory cook in Portsmouth, Rhode Island. It was revealed that she had gone through an estimated $11 million, endured years of drug and alcohol dependency, lost her mother in an apartment fire, was frequently estranged from her children, and had often contemplated and tried suicide. She announced that she had found herself by participating in the Catholic Church. As to her celebrated show-business past, she said, "I am not into nostalgia. Not at all. I'm not somebody from the past. The Paramount days were all terrific, all marvelous, and they're all gone."

Janet Jackson

[Janet Damita Jo Jackson]
MAY 16, 1966–

"You don't have to hold on to the pain to hold on to the memory," Jackson said once of her drama-filled life. She also noted, "We all have the need to feel special"; that wasn't easy for her, having such ultraeccentric siblings as Michael and LaToya Jackson and being part of the Jacksons, America's favorite dysfunctional family (once a close-knit unit, later a fractured entity). To date, the full dynamics of this bizarre celebrity household remain shrouded in intriguing mystery, for rarely has any clan member ever agreed on the specifics of growing up in that complex environment where physical abuse, adultery, and sibling rivalry endured.

As a youngster, cute little Janet was overshadowed by her older brothers, show business's the Jackson 5. However, by the time she was twenty and her album *Control* was enjoying a triumphant release, she'd demonstrated her own performance magnetism, reinforced by her successful concert act. Constantly reinventing herself over the years ("like a really successful software program," said *Time* magazine), Janet shared an affinity for plastic surgery, a love of animals, and an urge for great mystery when it came to marriage, along with her eccentric brother Michael. While establishing her own identity as a show-business icon, she was often in competition with him. After child molestation charges put his career into a decline in the 1990s, she became the most successful working Jackson. On the way to fame and fortune, the five-foot, four-inch dynamo became her own kind of control freak and demanding diva. Then too, as her tattoos, pierced body parts, and later song lyrics suggested, she had traveled a long way emotionally from being that endearing adolescent on the TV variety show *The Jacksons* (1976–77).

She was born in 1966 in Gary, Indiana, the ninth and final surviving child in the Jackson household. Janet Damita Jo was preceded by Maureen ("Rebbie") in 1950; Sigmund Esco ("Jackie") in 1951; Tariano Adaryl ("Tito") in 1953; Jermaine LaJuane in 1954; LaToya Yvonne in 1956; Marlon David in 1957 (his twin brother, Brandon, died within a day of birth); Michael Joseph in 1958; and Steven Randall ("Randy") in 1961. Her father was Joseph Walker Jackson, a former professional boxer, who loved music, played the guitar, and earned his livelihood operating a steel mill crane. Her mother was Katherine Esther Scruse, whose childhood bout with polio had left her with a limp and who had once dreamed of becoming a country music star. Katherine was also a Jehovah's Witness; in the Jackson household, she said, "I was strict; Joe was stricter."

When Janet was an infant, her elder brothers were already performing as the Jackson 5, supervised by the ever-present Joseph (none of the children ever called him "Father" or "Dad"). By 1969, the group had been signed by Motown Records, and accompanied by Joseph, they relocated to Los Angeles. Katherine, LaToya, Randy, and Janet followed them several months later. In 1971, as the Jackson 5 flourished with their multimedia appearances, the family moved into a $250,000, two-acre estate in Encino, located in the West San Fernando Valley. Little Janet had childhood thoughts of becoming a jockey, but her stern, controlling father had more ambitious plans. When she was seven, she joined the family act when they performed on a casino club stage in Las Vegas. She and brother Randy did celebrity impressions, sang, danced, and so forth. It was Janet's first move away from the shadow of her siblings into the limelight.

Young Janet grew up in front of TV audiences. From 1977 to mid-1979, she was part of the sitcom *Good Times*. Later, in the early 1980s, she played Todd Bridges's outspoken girlfriend on *Diff'rent Strokes* and then joined the cast of TV's *Fame* from 1984 to 1985. During this period, the Jackson 5 faded from prominence, but Michael—who had left the family compound—had achieved great fame with his solo album *Thriller* and had fired Joseph as his manager. Needing an ongoing cash flow and someone to manage, Joseph pushed a reluctant Janet into a solo recording career. Her first two albums (*Janet Jackson* in 1982 and *Dream Street* in 1983) sold adequately but didn't stir much industry fever. In 1984, desperate to break out of her smothering home life, Janet dated the slightly older James DeBarge, who was part of a singing family act. Jackson's family tried to break up the romance, insisting she was too young for such a relationship and convinced (rightly) that James had a serious drug problem. In an act of rebellion, she eloped with DeBarge in September 1984. (Then and later, she denied rumors that her weight gain at this time was the result of an alleged pregnancy—one which the rumor mill said ended in an abortion or a child being born and raised secretly in Europe.) Within seven months of the union, Janet admitted defeat, unable to deal with her husband's problems. The vulnerable teen returned to the Jackson compound. In November 1985, her marriage was annulled.

Rethinking her career and spurred on by Michael's success away from Joseph's micromanagement, Janet ended her working relationship with her father. She took on a new manager, hooked up with producers/writers Jimmy Jam and Jerry Lewis, and turned out her *Control* album in 1986. Among the disc's hit singles was "What Have You Done for Me Lately," which said a lot about the new persona of emancipated, tough, and introspective Janet. With album sales of more than five million copies, she was now rich, an ethnic role model, and very much her own woman. Brother Michael might have earned $65 million in 1989, but Janet had a hot-selling new album, *Rhythm Nation 1814*, in release. Filled with socially conscious themes, the funky— sometimes somber, sometimes romantic and upbeat—album was a big hit, as was her world concert tour in 1990.

By the start of the 1990s, Janet had a steady boyfriend in Rene Elizondo Jr., the son of a Spanish father and a Mexican mother. She had met him years earlier at her parents' home, and since then he'd danced in one of her splashy music videos, acted in another, and would later direct one of her short-form music films. With her impressive cash flow, she purchased a spacious $4.5 million home in Malibu and developed a circle of friends among whom she was the queen bee, just as she was on her stage tours. Only much later would it be revealed that Janet had convinced Rene to sign a prenuptial agreement in 1990 (each party would keep what they brought into the union) and that by the end of March 1991 they had secretly become husband and wife. Also during this period, she signed a three-album deal with Virgin Records, a pact that was worth a staggering $35 million to $40 million. (Not to be outdone, highly competitive Michael signed a $65 million deal with Sony Records a few days later.) By now, Janet—the lamb who became a tigress as she gained independence— was battling sister LaToya. The latter, who'd shocked her family with her 1989 *Playboy* layout, had authored a creative autobiography in 1991. That tome had deeply angered most of

A smiling Janet Jackson displaying her latest industry award. (Photo by Albert L. Ortega)

her family with its accusations, opinions, and "facts" about her bizarre life as a Jackson.

Vetoing the idea of being showcased in a musical feature film, Janet instead starred in *Poetic Justice* (1993), a romantic drama. While she claimed to have had little personal rapport with her on-screen leading man, rapper Tupac Shakur, she really loved playing a home girl from the hood. As a result, the chameleon-like singing star took on a layer of gritty toughness that became part of her persona. If her movie was not a big hit (although she was Oscar-nominated for the song "Again"), her new album, *janet*, was a major success. With songs like "That's the Way Love Goes"—and enticing music videos to boot—Jackson became a slinky sex goddess for the 1990s. Already her concert tours were major entertainment events, each one more heavily choreographed than the last, with her frenetic nonstop dancing the highlight of each outing. Fanatical about her body shape, she was compulsive about fitness training. Whatever parts of her anatomy didn't tone or shape to her expectations were rectified with cosmetic surgery. A dynamo in front of audiences, she had become a commanding businesswoman and a determined superstar, who pushed herself relentlessly to deal with competitors like Madonna, Mariah Carey, and (later) Jennifer Lopez.

By the release of her album *The Velvet Rope* (1997), filled with sexually explicit songs and numbers dealing with AIDS and homophobia, Janet had signed a new Virgin Records agreement, one reportedly worth $80 million. The rumor mill claimed that workaholic Jackson had suffered a strong bout of depression (or perhaps even a nervous breakdown), while the latest incarnation of Janet was proclaiming in interviews the many virtues of coffee enemas. She was paid $3 million to be Eddie Murphy's leading lady in *Nutty Professor II: The Klumps* (2000), and in music videos and concerts, she was the glitzy, hard-driving diva

who favored leather costumes. Her album *All for You* (2001) produced such hits as "Someone to Call My Lover" and documented the songster as a pulsating, sensual icon.

If it was difficult for the public to keep up with the many changing faces of Janet Jackson, it was even tougher for those close to the goal-oriented diva, who was voted one of "The 10 Sexiest Women of 2001" by *Black Men* magazine. By now, her hush-hush marriage to Rene Elizondo was public knowledge, as the couple had split in 2000. By the next year, they were in the first throes of a court battle in which Elizondo sought to overturn their prenuptial agreement and obtain a more than $10 million settlement. Having dated singer Johnny Gill as the new millennium dawned, Jackson was also seen with Matthew McConaughey in 2002. Said the hunky actor, "I met her at the Grammys and found her to be a very, very sweet lady. We swapped some good music and she's a dear lady. She's a sweetheart but we're not dating, we're just friends. That's about all there is right now," which in Hollywood-speak means "Think what ya wanna." McConaughey was but one of her recurrent escorts at the time.

As multimillionaire Janet looks to the future as a touring concert diva, the queen of pop, and a four-time Grammy winner, she continues to pursue her creed: "Always follow your heart, and never forget where you came from. Always extend your hand to help others." P.S., she says, "The sky is the limit!"

Grace Kelly

[**Grace Patricia Kelly**]

November 12, 1929–September 14, 1982

Alfred Hitchcock, who directed Kelly in three 1950s features, prized this patrician (but for him unobtainable) five-foot, six-inch blond beauty because of her "sexual elegance." Usually mild-mannered Jimmy Stewart admitted of his seemingly aloof movie costar, "Everything about Grace is appealing. I may be married, but I'm not dead!" Another of her beguiled leading men, Clark Gable, summed up Kelly's seductiveness—a mixture of childish innocence and brazen flirtatiousness—as being "like a baby cobra." Screenwriter John Michael Hayes noted with surprise during the making of *Rear Window* (1954), "There was an alive, vital girl underneath that demure quiet façade. She had an inner life aching to be expressed." Her *High Noon* (1952) leading man, Gary Cooper, was far more graphic in separating the real Grace from the ice princess illusion she projected on-screen and to the public: "She looked like she could be a cold dish with a man until you get her pants down and then she'd explode."

The dichotomy of Grace's Philadelphia main-line debutante façade and the actual earthy woman continues to intrigue the public many decades after her short, but stellar, movie career. In retrospect, there is a touching irony that this lusty leading lady should have married into European royalty but not have lived happily ever after as in children's tales. On the contrary, her Monaco years with Prince Rainier and their children were often filled with tedium and frustration. This led her into clandestine romances as well as overeating and drinking binges. Her unenviable reign ended in a fatal car accident.

She was born Grace Patricia Kelly in 1929 in Philadelphia, the third of four children of self-made, affluent construction contractor John Brendan Kelly (a former Olympic champion) and his strikingly attractive wife, Margaret Majer, a former model and the first woman to teach physical education at the University of Pennsylvania. Among Grace's relatives were Pulitzer Prize–winning dramatist George Kelly and Walter C. Kelly, a celebrated vaudevillian. As a youngster, Grace was bashful and had to vie with her siblings (Margaret, John Jr., and Lizanne) for the attention of their father, a gruff man's man who, when not busy with work, was off philandering with an assortment

Alec Guinness, Grace Kelly, and Louis Jourdan in *The Swan* (1956). (Courtesy of JC Archives)

attend college, enrolling instead at the American Academy of Dramatic Arts in New York City. Her annoyed parents finally agreed to pay for only one year's tuition, hoping that the stagestruck girl would come to her senses about a frivolous career in show business. To pay for her tuition thereafter, Grace became a fashion model. As part of her ongoing rebellion against her unsympathetic parents, she had an affair with a twenty-seven-year-old academy instructor. She was especially intrigued that her lover was Jewish and married (although separated from his wife), as she knew these factors would particularly annoy her snobbish parents when they found out (and Grace made sure they did).

The combination of having relatives in show business, refined good looks, and ambitions of making a name for herself helped Grace to find summer-stock work. She made her Broadway debut in 1949 and became active in the burgeoning TV industry then thriving in New York City. She was part of the ensemble appearing in the feature film *Fourteen Hours* (1951) shot largely in Manhattan. The producing studio (Twentieth Century-Fox) offered her a term contract, but she vetoed the standard deal. Instead, she negotiated to get the role of the Quaker spouse of ex-marshal Gary Cooper in 1952's *High Noon*. The Western became a hit, while off camera Kelly and the twenty-eight-year-older Cooper enjoyed a short-term affair. (It set the pattern for her romances with many of her leading men, all of whom were well established, much older than she, and sometimes married. Kelly's sexual aggressiveness, in an era before such behavior

of mistresses. Nothing Grace could do then—or thereafter in her success-crammed life—ever seemed to visibly impress him. The result was her lifelong search for substitute father figures. As for Grace's controlling mother, the offspring of German immigrants, she was exceedingly disciplined and dealt with her children according to stringent Teutonic principles.

After attending a nearby convent school until the age of fourteen, Grace enrolled at Stevens Academy in Chestnut Hill, Pennsylvania. Her chief concerns there were boys and the drama club. In a willful burst, she refused to

became commonplace for women, fascinated her many conquests.) After a brief return to Broadway, Grace flew to Africa to join Clark Gable and Ava Gardner for John Ford's *Mogambo* (1953), for which she was Oscar-nominated. During the location shoot, Kelly and Gable had a passionate affair, but he concluded that the big age difference put marriage out of the question. By this juncture, Grace was under MGM contract, but the studio was unsure how to showcase her refined beauty and clipped British accent on the big screen.

During the making of the thriller *Dial M for Murder* (1954), Kelly fell starry-eyed in love with her forty-nine-year-old costar, Ray Milland. The Oscar winner left his wife for Grace, which shocked Hollywood, and *Confidential* magazine published an exposé of Kelly's indiscreet comings and goings at Milland's new bachelor digs. MGM's publicity department did damage control to refocus the public's sympathies toward the actress. Eventually, a lovelorn Milland returned to his wife. Meanwhile, Kelly thanked MGM for its cover-up activities by refusing several studio properties suggested as possible vehicles. MGM reluctantly loaned her to Hitchcock again, this time for 1954's *Rear Window*.

Rebounding from the Milland debacle, Grace found consolation in the arms of French actor Jean-Pierre Aumont, fashion designer Oleg Cassini, and others. Media speculation about the extent of her relationships with several of these men disgusted her snobbish, domineering parents, but headstrong Grace went her own way. During the filming of *The Bridges of Toko-Ri* (1954), Grace had a fling

with married colead William Holden. Holden reteamed with Grace for *The Country Girl* (1954), but he gentlemanly stepped aside so that the film's other lead player, Bing Crosby, could romance Kelly. Bing proposed marriage, but Grace wasn't interested in a permanent situation with the too-staid Crosby. Meanwhile, she won an Oscar for her performance as the drab wife in *The Country Girl*.

After making *To Catch a Thief* (1955) with Cary Grant (who became a lifelong friend and occasional lover), Grace attended the Cannes Film Festival in May 1955. There she was introduced to thirty-one-year-old Prince Rainier III of Monaco. Almost immediately, the stocky monarch decided the elegant beauty should be his wife. Their engagement was announced the following January, by which time she had made the costumed fable *The Swan* and begun the musical *High Society*, both released by MGM in 1956. The wedding of the century occurred on April 18, 1956, in a modest civil service in the royal palace at Monaco followed the next day by an elaborate Catholic ceremony covered by an estimated sixteen hundred reporters. (Grace's father, finally appreciating the prestige of the royal marriage, had provided a nearly $2 million dowry to help seal the union.)

When she wed Prince Rainier, Grace never fully appreciated that doing so would signal the end of her film career. She was offered several screen roles over the years but was eventually persuaded that it would be unseemly for a princess to appear in such commercial ventures. She was permitted, however, to provide the narration for *The Children of Theatre*

Street, a 1977 documentary focusing on Russia's Kirov School of Ballet. During her early reign, she gave birth to Princess Caroline (in 1957), Prince Albert (in 1958), and Princess Stephanie (in 1965).

As the years passed, Grace grew increasingly lonely from being so far away from her American—and especially Hollywood—friends. Her relationship with Rainier became a formality in which the passion reportedly had nearly evaporated. As her pampered, spirited offspring grew to adulthood, they proved a handful, but being as obstinate as their mother, they usually persuaded Grace to give them their own way. For Kelly, even with the distraction of a lot of charity work, her royal duties became stifling. Now past forty and having gained weight, she had little illusion of returning to filmmaking, even if the opportunity arose. Purportedly, her royal highness had

occasional extramarital flings; one of the recurrent men in her life was Cary Grant. She found diversion in excessive eating and drinking, as well as in keeping somewhat current with the world of show business she'd left behind.

On September 13, 1982, Grace had a scheduled appointment with her Monaco couturier before traveling on to Paris that evening with daughter Stephanie. With Grace driving her Rover 3500 and her offspring in the passenger's seat, the two left Roc Agel, another family home situated a few miles from the royal palace in Monaco. A half hour later, on the twisting Moyenne Corniche road, the car crashed through a barrier and slammed down the steep hillside. When rescued, Stephanie had treatable injuries, but Grace was unconscious. At the Princess Grace Hospital, it was discovered that Kelly had suffered a stroke

On camera, she played the aloof, beautiful lady who spoke with a refined British accent. Off camera, the future princess of Monaco was a passionate man-killer. Early in her Hollywood years, she began having affairs with her leading men—most of them many years older than she. The notches on her belt included Gary Cooper, Clark Gable, William Holden, Bing Crosby, and Ray Milland. The latter was so besotted that he (temporarily) left his wife of over twenty years. Said one of the wronged wife's good friends, "Grace Kelly was a conniving woman . . . she was worse than any woman I'd ever known. She knew how to lead a man on." The scandal sheet *Confidential* magazine took note of predatory Kelly's effect on Oscar-winner Milland: "After one look at Gracie, he went into a tailspin that reverberated from Perino's to Ciro's. The whole town soon hee-hawed over the news that suave Milland, who had a wife and family at home, was gaga over Grace. Ray pursued her ardently and Hollywood cackled." After Milland eventually returned to his spouse, Kelly acknowledged to a friend, "It was a bad mistake." Years later, Grace, who had never struck people as being the naïve type, said of the Milland fiasco, "I really thought that the marriage was over. That is what he told me. I didn't know that he had many affairs and that I was just one of them."

prior to the accident. Although surgery halted her internal bleeding and her multiple fractures could be repaired, the attending physicians concluded that even if she did recover, she would be a helpless invalid. On September 14, her life-support equipment was turned off and Princess Grace died. The next week, she was buried in the Grimaldi family vault at the same cathedral where she had been married twenty-six years earlier.

So ended the tragic tale of regal, headstrong Grace who was always more than she seemed on the surface and who found that life was never enough for her.

Veronica Lake

[Constance Frances Marie Ockleman]

NOVEMBER 14, 1919–JULY 7, 1973

She may have been only five feet, two inches tall, but petite Veronica Lake carried a mighty chip on her pretty shoulder. As a shy, defensive teenager, she'd barely masked her growing distrust of and anger with the world. On blossoming as a Paramount Pictures star in 1941, the young blond with the gimmicky peek-a-boo hairstyle and those cold, blue-gray eyes embarked on a self-destructive course. Her studio status allowed her to indulge her jaded attitude about life and people (including family, studio bosses, and the public). She had no qualms about telling off anyone who annoyed her, whether it was a lofty costar, a powerful studio executive, or a soundstage crew member. Belligerent Lake became indifferent to bettering her craft, being diplomatic with those who controlled her future and respectful of movie coplayers, and accommodating her fans. (It was typical of Veronica to sit in her studio dressing room rummaging through her fan mail. She'd pick up a letter. If she felt a coin inside—sent to ensure the star would

mail the admirer an autographed picture—she'd tear open the envelope and drop the coin into a jar. If the missive had no coin bulge, she'd toss it unopened into the wastepaper basket.)

As Lake's dependency on alcohol to deaden her inner pain increased, so did her troublesome marital life, her complicated extracurricular loves, and her escalating inability to devote herself sufficiently to any of her three young children. A major movie star in the 1940s, by the 1950s, she was a Hollywood has-been.

Constance Frances Marie Ockleman was born in Brooklyn, New York, in 1919 (some sources say 1922). She was the only child of seaman/oil company worker Harry Ockleman and his wife, Constance Trimble. Following her dad's death in 1932, her mother wed Anthony Keane, a staff artist on the *New York Herald-Tribune* and she adopted her stepfather's surname. (The youngster had never gotten along with her father and this poor attitude carried over to her dealings with Keane.) As a child, she had a short attention span and was a tomboy who hated being made to wear frilly dresses. For a while, the rebellious youngster attended convent school in Montreal, Canada, but was expelled for unruly behavior. When

Veronica Lake and Richard Widmark in *Slattery's Hurricane* (1949). (Courtesy of JC Archives)

Constance was fifteen, Mrs. Keane took her troubled daughter to talk with a psychiatrist, but none of the several she tried could break through the teenager's emotional wall and she finally gave up on such therapy. (There were indications that the girl suffered from schizophrenia.) In 1937, the family relocated to Miami, Florida, where Constance attended (but did not graduate from) high school. In a state beauty competition, shapely Constance was named Miss Florida. However, she was disqualified because she was underage.

During the summer of 1938, Constance accompanied her parents and cousin to the West Coast. Hoping to overcome the girl's shyness, Mrs. Keane enrolled her offspring in an elocution/acting class. Later, Constance accompanied a friend to a casting audition at RKO Pictures, and it was Constance who won a bit part in *The Wrong Room* (1939). By the time she made Eddie Cantor's *Forty Little Mothers* (1940) at MGM, the newcomer had adopted her over-the-eye hairstyle, which reportedly came about by accident when it cascaded over one eye while she was filming a sequence.

The summer of 1940 found Constance being hired by Paramount Pictures for its aviation drama *I Wanted Wings* (1941) and being christened with the new professional name Veronica Lake. During the making of the picture, she feuded with Constance Moore, who accused the novice of being a cocky brat and trying to steal the limelight. Months before starting the picture, Veronica had begun dating MGM art director John Detlie, age thirty-three. After the shoot finished, they married in September 1940, choosing not to alert anyone—let alone the studio—of her rash act. Thankfully, when *I Wanted Wings* was released, it was a big success and Veronica, with her novel hairstyle, captured both the critics' and the public's fancy. Thus Paramount forgave her for being so undisciplined on and off the set.

During the making of *Sullivan's Travels* (1942), Lake was pregnant, a fact that came to the studio's attention and almost caused her to be removed from the picture. However, the movie's director, Preston Sturges, intervened and saved the actress's job. (Veronica's daughter Elaine was born in August 1941.) Paramount had been having difficulty locating diminutive leading ladies to pair with rising contract player Alan Ladd, who was only five feet, four inches. This was a key factor in assigning Veronica to play opposite him in *This Gun for Hire* (1942). The film noir entry proved to be enormously popular and led to several other Lake-Ladd screen teamings. In *I Married a Witch* (1942), Lake demonstrated a knack for comedy. She also battled with her randy leading man, Fredric March. She detested him for his arrogant, woman-chasing ways and his scorn of her fledgling acting skills. On the home front, Veronica and her husband were constantly bickering; he was fed up with being known as "Mr. Lake." Even when he joined the army and was based in Seattle, Washington, the couple still managed to feud.

On the final day of shooting *The Hour Before the Dawn* (1944), pregnant Veronica tripped over a soundstage cable and began to hemorrhage. Her condition was stabilized and her child, William Anthony, was born in July 1943; he died a week later due to uremic poisoning. Before the year ended, Lake and Detlie had divorced.

Paramount was growing increasingly weary of troublesome Veronica and she was offscreen for much of 1944. She used her free time to party and date such men as billionaire Howard Hughes and millionaires Aristotle Onassis and Tommy Manville. Rather than marry one of these well-heeled candidates, she instead wed Hungarian-born film actor/director Andre De Toth in December 1944. Their son, Michael, was born the following October and their daughter, Diana, in October 1948.

In the mid-1940s, Lake (who was still riding high at the studio because of the public's infatuation with her) was earning $4,000 a week. But she aggravated her bosses by rejecting projects or, when she finally agreed to an assignment, by sleepwalking through the part. (She often showed up for her morning makeup call looking the worse from a rough night on the town or from another of her

She may have been pint-sized, but diminutive Lake was fearless—and foolhardy—when it came to her career. Early in her stay at Paramount Pictures in the 1940s, an executive chastised the star-in-the-making for disappearing from the studio for nearly three days. Unshaken, Lake said, "I didn't ask to work for you, remember. You sent for me. I'll hand in my notice right away." On one of her later pictures, the self-destructive and troublesome Veronica bragged to a crew member about her calculated affair with the film's producer. Said Lake, "They're not giving me what I want. But so-and-so gets in on the plane at seven o'clock. So, by eight o'clock, I'll have him in bed and by nine o'clock I will have anything I want."

Damn-the-world Veronica also played fast and loose with reporters, uncaring that alienating the media could eventually do her career damage. One of the journalists she lied to in an interview later went to work for Paramount's publicity department. Years afterward, the individual recalled, "She was circulating all sorts of crap in order to get me fired because she didn't feel comfortable with me since I knew what kind of person she was."

increasing battles with her physically and emotionally abusive spouse.) Bad at managing finances, Veronica was having severe money problems by 1948. The situation was aggravated by her free-spending husband De Toth, who "allowed" her to finance much of their lifestyle. In midyear, Lake's mother sued her daughter not only for back support (under a prior agreement) but to have the sum raised from $200 to $500 a week. The nasty proceedings made headlines that further tarnished Veronica's waning reputation in Hollywood and disillusioned her decreasing number of fans.

After the unimaginative *Isn't It Romantic?* (1948), the studio dropped Lake's contract and her career went into a free fall. When De Toth directed *Slattery's Hurricane* (1949) at Twentieth Century-Fox, Veronica accepted the second lead. By then, she and her disciplinarian husband were estranged, and they filed for

bankruptcy. They separated that year and were divorced a year later, sharing custody of their children. With no roles being offered, the former screen siren abandoned Hollywood for New York.

Her professional descent continued on the East Coast, slowed only temporarily by occasional TV and stage roles. She lived in a run-down Greenwich Village apartment. In 1955, she married rough-and-tumble songwriter Joseph McCarthy. He liked to drink as much as Veronica and they clashed constantly. They divorced in 1959. As for her children, they were bandied back and forth between Lake in New York and her West Coast–based ex-spouses.

In 1960, a reporter came across Veronica working in Manhattan as a barmaid and hostess at the Martha Washington Hotel for Women, where she was living in obscurity. The discovery, along with an account of Lake's poststardom years, made worldwide headlines.

The accompanying photos showed how alcoholism and tough times had weathered and bloated her once-beautiful features. In the summer of 1963, she took on the role of a fading cinema queen in an off-Broadway revival of the musical *Best Foot Forward*. Two years later, she was in the news when she was arrested for drunkenness in Galveston, Texas (where her current boyfriend lived). Later, after her lover died, she relocated to her hometown of Miami, where she performed onstage in stock. She accepted a meager $10,000 to do the Canadian-made movie *Footsteps in the Snow* (1966), but it had a scant release. Her final screen work was in the Florida-shot *Flesh Feast*, but the sloppy horror entry did not reach theaters until 1970.

Lake was in England in 1969 to promote her just-published (ghostwritten) autobiography and then stayed on to star in *Madame Chairman*. The stage comedy expired before reaching the West End. In 1971, she was back in the States touting the American publication of her life story. Her promotional book tour took her to Hollywood for the first time in years. She visited her old studio stomping grounds and displayed a rare vulnerability when she admitted that she was very upset to witness how Paramount and Tinseltown had radically changed in her long absence.

The following year, in June, the Florida-based Lake wed Robert Carlton-Munro, a retired British sea captain. Before long, the mismatched couple were living in England, where their domestic disharmony and boozing continued. She returned to America alone. In late June 1973, Veronica was visiting friends in Burlington, Vermont. She was in ill health and was soon hospitalized for acute hepatitis. With her body worn out from years of alcohol abuse, she died on July 7. She was cremated and her ashes were scattered at sea near the Virgin Islands—a locale she and a former boyfriend had once enjoyed visiting.

Years earlier, when reminiscing on her screen career, Veronica had stated, "I wasn't a sex symbol, I was a sex zombie. I was never psychologically meant to be a picture star. . . ." As for her often-stormy life, Lake acknowledged, "I wouldn't live it any differently than it was. How would I learn to be a person otherwise?"

Hedy Lamarr

[Hedwig Eva Maria Kiesler]
NOVEMBER 9, 1913–JANUARY 19, 2000

It is a wonderful asset for a budding movie actress to be blessed with breathtaking beauty. However, when the woman is both gorgeous *and* very smart it can, sadly, be dangerous to the welfare of her screen career. This was especially true during Hollywood's Golden Age, when studio bosses ruled their rosters of contract players with iron fists. It is no secret that in those days—and to a degree even today—the casting couch syndrome determined the rise or demise of many beautiful actresses, who were expected to provide sexual favors or, at the very least, be consistently flattering to their industry mentors. The danger was intensified, in that era of gender inequality, if a gorgeous female under contract was more intelligent than her supposedly all-knowing studio bosses. This inevitably led to battles of will that, generally, the actress could not win. Such was the unfortunate case with Austrian import Hedy Lamarr.

There was much more to five-foot, six-inch Hedy than her well-proportioned 120-pound frame, her shimmering brown hair, and her incandescent blue eyes. When this intelligent beauty arrived in late 1930s Hollywood, she envisioned a bright future at Metro-Goldwyn-Mayer where she could develop into an actress of dimension. She hoped that mogul Louis B. Mayer (and his studio underlings) would see beneath her veneer of beauty and treat her career goals with respect. In that, she was naïve, for she was always regarded as nothing more than an eye-grabbing mannequin best used as pretty decoration in MGM products. Soon disillusioned, she not only stopped dreaming of becoming a real performer but she became openly petulant and rebellious. Already narcissistic, self-absorbed, and very self-indulgent in her private life, she grew increasingly uncooperative, demanding, and disinterested on the studio lot. It led Lamarr to conclude that all that was expected of her was to "stand still and look stupid."

She was born to George and Gertrude Kiesler in Vienna, Austria, in 1913. Her Jewish father, a well-to-do banker, was disappointed at not having a son. Even in her youth, bright and creative Hedwig wanted more than to be pampered by her indulgent (albeit strict by today's standards) parents. Eager for self-expression, she fastened on show business as an outlet. At fifteen, she abandoned school to become a script clerk in a small Viennese film studio. This led to her appearing in the 1930 film short *Geld auf der Strasse* (*Money on the Street*). By 1931, she'd relocated to Berlin, where she studied acting with the great Max Reinhardt, appeared on the stage, and made three additional films. Then came the 1933 Czech-Austrian picture *Symphonie der Liebe* (*Symphony of Love*), better known as *Extase* (*Ecstasy*). The simplistic plot concerned an impotent man, his much-younger bride, and a young man who spies on her while she's swimming in a small lake. In her lakeside sequence, as well as in her sprint through the woods, she is nude. The picture was banned in Germany because its leading lady was Jewish. However, the titillating film did sizeable box-office business elsewhere.

Also in 1933, twenty-year-old Hedy married. Her husband, Fritz Mandl, a munitions manufacturer, was extremely wealthy and much older. Possessive Mandl sought unsuccessfully to purchase and destroy all prints of the racy *Extase* because it riled him that others should see his gorgeous wife naked. By 1937, Hedy had grown bored with her stifling marriage and was upset by her spouse's politics, which favored Nazism. She fled to Paris, where she divorced him that year. To escape Hitler's advancing troops, she moved on to London. There she met MGM studio boss

Louis B. Mayer. He was attracted by her great beauty but hesitated to sign her to a studio pact because he feared that the notorious *Extase*—which had been released in the United States in 1937—might have made her inappropriate to join the prestigious MGM stable of stars. However, when he sailed back to America, he discovered Hedy aboard. By the end of the transatlantic trek, he had signed the highly erotic young woman to a seven-year deal that started at $500 weekly.

At MGM, Mayer pondered on how to present the glamorous newcomer, who had been renamed Hedy Lamarr. Meanwhile, he loaned her to producer Walter Wanger for the exotic romantic tale *Algiers* (1938), opposite Charles Boyer. The United Artists' movie and its costars were great hits. Now enthusiastic about his new catch, Mayer matched Hedy with Spencer Tracy in *I Take This Woman* (1939). However, Louis B. interfered so much with the film's progress—wanting to outdo *Algiers* in showcasing Lamarr—that the movie dragged on for many months. (When finally released, it was a mess.) Meanwhile, Metro assigned her to *Lady of the Tropics* (1939) as a half-caste, with handsome Robert Taylor as her leading man. Both of these releases were box-office disappointments, leading fickle Mayer to lose interest in his import. Lamarr had to fight to be cast in *Boom Town* (1940) with Clark Gable and Claudette Colbert.

By now, fun-loving Hedy was a fixture on the Tinseltown social scene, where her intellect and wit were better appreciated than on her home lot. In 1939, Lamarr met and immediately fell in love with screenwriter Gene Markey (who had previously been married to movie star Joan Bennett and who would later wed another screen leading lady, Myrna Loy). They wed on a quick trip to Mexico that March. Independent-minded Lamarr and ladies' man Markey were not a good match and the union soon fell apart, although their divorce didn't occur until September 1940.

In 1941, the year she gave her best screen performance in *H. M. Pulham, Esq.*, she adopted an infant boy named James. On the

Hedy Lamarr at the height of her beauty in the 1940s. (Courtesy of JC Archives)

soundstages, Lamarr had already gained a reputation for being difficult and more concerned with her personal life than her screen career. The well-mounted *Tortilla Flat* (1942) was her third screen teaming with Spencer Tracy and far superior to the claptrap *White Cargo* (1942), which presented her as another half-caste jungle temptress. This entry signaled the end of MGM's concern for Hedy as, by now, the studio had decided to focus its attention on another sexy contract player, Lana Turner. Lamarr married again in 1943, this time to British actor John Loder. Again, it was an impetuous decision that she soon regretted. However, they remained together to have two children: Denise, born in 1945, and Anthony, born in 1947. By the time of the latter's birth, Hedy had already filed for divorce from Loder.

When Lamarr made MGM's *Her Highness and the Bellboy* (1945), she was paid $7,500 weekly. Hedy was fed up with the studio bosses (as were they with her temperament and the cost of her productions versus the bottom-line profits), so she negotiated a release from her contract. She formed her own production company, but neither *Strange Woman* (1946) nor *Dishonored Lady* (1947)—both of which cast her as a femme fatale—were box-office winners. Her career revived when Cecil B. DeMille showcased her in the Biblical epic *Samson and Delilah* (1949). Despite the picture's popularity, Hedy received the Sour Apple Award that year for being Hollywood's least cooperative actress. For *My Favorite Spy* (1951), she played straight woman to screen quipster Bob Hope. Hedy was now approach-

ing forty, and her Hollywood career was nearly over.

In June 1951, headstrong Hedy married restaurateur Ernest "Ted" Stauffer. They split up less than a year later, with Lamarr claiming that he'd beaten her on several occasions. Next came Texas oilman Howard Lee, whom she made her fifth husband in 1953 (only to divorce him in 1959). Meanwhile, she made the lackluster *The Female Animal* (1958), playing a mature screen star competing with her daughter (Jane Powell) for a man's affections. Her sixth and last marriage was in 1963 to Los Angeles lawyer Lewis W. Boies Jr. When they went their separate ways in 1965, she said that he had threatened to hit her with a baseball bat. She also noted that $500,000 of her funds went to maintaining their lifestyle during their stormy union.

Lamarr was announced to make her screen comeback in *Picture Mommy Dead* (1966). Her $10,000 fee for the cameo was paltry when compared to her past screen salaries, but the former star was then broke. However, before the shoot began, she was arrested on shoplifting charges. She was in police custody for five hours before being released (the charges were later dropped). Tinseltown was shocked, and Hedy was replaced in the feature by Zsa Zsa Gabor. Financially strapped, Hedy agreed to "write" her autobiography, *Ecstasy and Me: My Life as a Woman* (1966). It proved to be another painful episode in her life. She became so upset by her ghostwriters' alleged misrepresentations and the extreme tawdriness of the sexcapades presented in the text (including several romantic encounters initiated by lesbian acquaintances) that she sued the publisher and the book's writers. She lost and the highly erotic memoir was published to much notoriety (and embarrassment to Lamarr).

Hedy was long out of the news until 1991, when she was accused of shoplifting $21 of merchandise in a store near Orlando, Florida. Lamarr insisted the incident was a big mistake—a result of her forgetfulness and poor vision (she was legally blind at the time). Again, the charges were dropped, but the tabloid newspapers featured stories of Hedy's pathetic decline. On the plus side, in 1997, she finally received public acknowledgment for the antijamming device she had created in 1941, one geared to thwart German radar during World War II. (She and her partner had offered their patented apparatus to the U.S. War Department, but it had been rejected. Years later, after the patent expired, the invention was used by a major corporation as a tool for American ships during the Cuban blockade of 1962.) The ailing Lamarr sent her son Anthony to accept her accolade in San Francisco.

Her final years were a trial for Hedy. Now a great-grandmother with her failing eyesight much worse, she hardly ever left her Florida residence in Atamonte Springs. When she died of natural causes in early 2000, she left an estate worth over $3 million (of mostly tied-up assets). Not many months before she passed away, the ex–film goddess told a reporter that, in looking back on her life, she realized that a guiding principle for her career should have been "Do not take things too seriously." If she had followed this advice and her studio

employers had done the reverse, they all might have had a more profitable working relationship on the soundstages.

Jennifer Lopez

[Jennifer Lopez]
JULY 24, 1970–

When Brazil's Carmen Miranda and Mexico's Lupe Velez became movie stars during Hollywood's Golden Age, they were largely pigeonholed on-screen into racial minority stereotypes. Such was *not* the case with Lopez when she rose to box-office popularity in the late 1990s. This cinema star (who also recorded albums) enjoyed crossover lead roles that were not ethnic specific. Like movie celebrities of any race who achieve major stardom, she has had to be sharply focused and aggressive to push through the ranks. Says Jennifer, "I have this attitude . . . that you have to fight for things you want." She also has a good memory for how people treated her on the difficult path to success: "There are certain people that are marked for death already. I have my little list of journalists that have treated me unfairly. Like, I was totally happy, totally confident with my work in *Selena* [1997], but out of the seven hundred reviews— and I read every single one—I can quote the [bad] one. . . . I definitely have my list of people that are going to get their justice."

On her way to fame, the voluptuous five-foot, five-inch actress discovered that "Everybody *thinks* that you're the one that changes, but it's the way people treat you that changes. You see them looking at you weird. It's like, 'Why are you looking at me weird?' I'm still Jennifer . . . and my mother's still Lupe and that's the way it is. Why are you freaking? People have a thing. That's why we make the money we do, I guess." One of the things she has had to change is expressing her undiplomatic opinions too freely. For example, in some all-too-candid interviews—especially with *Movieline* magazine in February 1998— she made rancorous remarks about past costars and/or filmmaking rivals. Regarding Jack Nicholson (of 1997's *Blood and Money*), she said, "A legend in his own time and in his own mind—like the rest of us are peons." As for Mexican-born Salma Hayek, who often vied with Jennifer for the same parts: "She's a sexy bombshell and those are the kinds of roles she does. I do all kinds of different things. It makes me laugh when she says she got offered *Selena*, which was an outright lie. If that's what she does to get herself publicity, then that's her thing." When such unvarnished remarks created negative feedback for Lopez, she was persuaded to make public apologies.

The beauteous J. Lo (as she is called) also has had problems in knowing what to say or not to say to the media about the men in her life, as well as those wanting to be part of it. For example, there was Wesley Snipes, her costar in *The Money Train* (1995). When Jennifer, who had a boyfriend at the time, rebuffed the actor's overtures, she didn't mind telling the press about Wesley: "He wouldn't talk to me for two months." Then there was her unholy alliance with bad boy musician Sean "Puffy" Combs and her attempts first to convince the media that there was no romance and later to say that the nonrelationship was over. In the meantime, she made an effort to distance herself from him after a night on the club circuit led to both of them being arrested. Such reversals of position and facts didn't help her credibility with the media or the public. But then again, Jennifer, noted for being demanding and controlling in much of her life, seems to be unrestrained when it comes to affairs of the heart: "When I fall in love, it's so sick. I just can't deal . . ." She has also said, "I don't fall in love easily, but when I do, it's intense."

She was born in 1970 in the Bronx, the second of three daughters of David and Guadalupe Lopez. Both her parents had immigrated to New York from Puerto Rico and were devout Catholics. Her father was a computer specialist for a Manhattan insurance company, while her mother was a monitor at Holy Family School, which Jennifer attended. (Later, Mrs. Lopez would become a kindergarten teacher.) The Lopez family lived in the borough's tough Castle Hill section. As a youngster, feisty Jennifer loved the creative arts—especially dancing—and dreamed one day of becoming a movie star like her idols Rita Hayworth, Ava Gardner, and Marilyn Monroe. Her role model, however, was Puerto Rican American Rita Moreno, whose Academy Award–winning role was in *West Side Story* (1961), a movie that a fascinated young Jennifer watched repeatedly. At Mrs. Lopez's urging, all three of her daughters took dance lessons.

Even as a youngster, the future movie star had no qualms about standing up for herself. In the fourth grade, she became friendly with a female classmate who was the best pal of another girl. The latter got jealous and told Jennifer that her new pal was talking about her behind her back. Jennifer confronted the girl, who denied it, and a rumble ensued. Said Lopez years later, "It was pretty ugly and although I'm not proud of the event, I did win the fight. Nobody ever messed with me after that, and I graduated from school unscathed." In high school, Jennifer performed in class musicals. She even had a tiny role in the little-seen movie *My Little Girl* (1986). Her passion for show business—especially dance—led to a showdown with her parents. They had dreamed and planned that she'd attend college and go on to become a lawyer. However, after one semester at Baruch College in New York City, Lopez quit; she was intent on becoming a professional dancer. Her disappointed parents protested, and Jennifer moved out.

After the usual struggles, Jennifer began getting show-business work in the late 1980s. She worked in regional theater, doing musicals like *Jesus Christ Superstar*. She performed in Japan (as a dancer, singer, and choreographer) in the musical *Synchronicity* and appeared in Europe in a tour of the revue *Golden Musicals of Broadway*. In the process of winning these roles and losing others, she learned a survival mentality: "If you're gonna make it in this business, you need the kind of personality that you have to do it or die, there's no alternative."

Lopez was one of two thousand who auditioned to be a dancer on a new satirical TV variety show, *In Living Color*, conceived by and starring Keenen Ivory Wayans (and featuring several of his siblings). She was hired in 1991 as one of the Fly Girls, a chorus of comely young women who decorated the hip program. By the time her work on this series ended in 1993, she was dancing in music videos. She went on to become a cast member of *Second Chances*, a late-1993 TV show starring Connie Sellecca, and was featured in two short-lived 1994 small-screen series. She won a part in *My Family* (*Mi Familia*, 1995), a saga of several generations of a Mexican family.

The 1995 actioner *Money Train* first brought Jennifer to moviegoers' attention, but it was starring in *Selena*, the 1997 biography of the late singer, that made Lopez a nationally known entity. It was one of her three features that year, which also included the action picture *Anaconda*. During much of this period, she lived with David Cruz whom she'd dated since she was in tenth grade back in the Bronx. But in a typical Tinseltown scenario, she'd outgrown her homeboy. While she became prominent, he'd worked as a production assistant in the industry. By the mid-1990s, their relationship had ended and he'd returned to the East Coast. Said Lopez of her onetime true love, "Careerwise, we weren't in the same place. He just didn't know what he wanted to do. But I had a fire under my ass. I was so fast, I was like a rocket; he was like a rock."

While making 1997's *Blood and Money* in Miami, Lopez dined at Larios on the Beach, the Miami Beach Cuban restaurant co-owned by singer Gloria Estefan. She spotted a cute young waiter, Cuban-born Ojani Noa, and told her dining companion, "That's the man I'm going to marry." Eventually the two were introduced and began a passionate romance. While she was on location in Texas filming *Selena* in late 1996, Noa often joined his girlfriend. At the picture's wrap party at the Hard Rock Café in San Antonio, he grabbed a microphone and proposed to her in Spanish. In February 1997, the couple wed in Miami at a ceremony that included over two hundred relatives and friends. After a week's honeymoon in Key West, Lopez returned to filmmaking.

By the time of 1998's thriller, *Out of Sight*, costarring George Clooney, Jennifer had become Hollywood's highest-paid Latina film actress and her per-film fee would soon escalate past the $9 million mark. She had also been named one of its "Fifty Most Beautiful People in the World" by *People* magazine. Only months after her wedding to Noa, the tabloids were chronicling that the couple were having public disputes. She denied the reports, but soon the high-profile couple were going in different directions. He was now the manager of the Conga Room, a Los Angeles Latino club in which Lopez was a backer. At the March 1998 Oscars, well-toned Jennifer, wearing a revealing sexy ensemble, appeared without her spouse. Already Lopez's attention was elsewhere. She had signed a recording contract with Sony Music. As she prepared her debut album, Jennifer turned increasingly to hip-hop artist/record industry mogul Sean "Puffy" Combs. (She'd already appeared in his 1997 music video "Been Around the World.") The media duly noticed the growing alliance between married Lopez and Combs (whose

Jennifer Lopez in the late 1990s.
(Photo by Albert L. Ortega)

prior girlfriend had recently given birth to their son). Then it became known that Jennifer and Ojani Noa had been separated since early 1998 and had divorced that March. Noa now told the press, "She wanted the divorce. She also gave me money and paid for my lawyer. She wanted her career, so everything with us went out the window. . . ." He added, "I'm in pain. I loved her a lot." (The hurt obviously healed somewhat, because in 2002 he was one of the managers of Madre, a restaurant that Lopez opened in Pasadena, California.)

In 1999, Jennifer's album *On the 6* was released and was a hit, especially the single "If You Had My Love." Late in the year, she and Combs acknowledged their romance. However, weeks later, on December 27, the couple—along with the rap entrepreneur's entourage—were at a New York club where one of Puffy's associates was allegedly involved in a shooting. Jennifer and Sean beat a hasty retreat in his SUV. They raced through ten red lights before being apprehended by the police. In arresting the celebrity couple and his chauffeur and bodyguard, police confiscated a stolen, loaded nine-millimeter gun. Lopez was handcuffed and detained for fourteen hours before being exonerated and released. By the

time the high-profile debacle was resolved in 2001, Jennifer and her trouble-prone boyfriend had announced they were no longer an item. By now, Jennifer a veteran of the Hollywood jungle, had gained her own bad rap as being a difficult diva. In reaction to the negative reports, she said, "Who cares? I don't. I'm just being who I am. I don't try to be nice. . . ."

In 2001, sultry Jennifer starred in the thriller drama *Angel Eyes* and her second album, *J. Lo*, was released to good sales. Already she had a new man. While filming the music video "Love Don't Cost a Thing" in October 2000, she'd met dancer Cris Judd, who was a year older than she. At the March 2001 Oscars, Judd was her attentive date. By August of that year, the couple announced their engagement at a fancy bash at a posh Tinseltown restau-

When asked what had broken up her first marriage, Lopez answered, "I think wealth got in the way. The success." Her ex-husband, Ojani Noa, on the other hand, observed that when she quit him after ten months, she said, "You're not the man I married." He added, "We'd only been married six months. I hadn't changed—it was she who had changed. All she thought about was work." He might also have added that her thoughts included the material benefits from stardom. While Jennifer frequently and proudly referred to her roots in a rough Bronx neighborhood, she had become famous for traveling with a sizeable retinue and requiring such perks as a limousine painted in a preferred color. Once, when she planned to dine at a posh London restaurant, she sent her security squad ahead to check out the establishment. The offended management suggested she eat elsewhere. When Lopez was promoting her new film, *The Wedding Planner* (2001), in Australia, future husband number two Cris Judd accompanied her. She had her heart set on a particular suite at a classy hotel. Miffed that the $5,500-a-night accommodation was unavailable, she settled for another hotel. To soothe her ruffled feathers and put herself back into a romantic mood, she had $16,000 worth of candles (in her favorite scent) placed about the suite, along with a "request" that the bathtub be filled with several dozen rosebuds each time she and Judd used it.

rant. In late September 2001, they wed in Calabasas, a Los Angeles suburb in the West San Fernando Valley. The lavish ceremony was attended by 170 family and friends. Word had it that the exacting bride-to-be was very specific about how everything should operate on her big day. In November, *Jennifer Lopez in Concert: Let's Get Loud* aired on national TV. Jennifer's spouse was listed as its creative director. When the special was panned by several critics, it supposedly accentuated the reportedly growing dissension between the newlyweds. Then came gossip in 2002 that Lopez and twenty-four-year-old rapper Ja Rule—who did two duets with Lopez on her album *J to Tha L-O! The Remixes* (2002)—were an item. Lopez denied the rumors.

In early June 2002, self-willed Lopez announced that she and Cris Judd, her husband of eight months, had separated a few weeks before and were now planning to end their marriage. While the Hollywood rumor mill wondered if it was true that Judd was receiving a $1 million settlement for terminating the union, speculation ran high whether the new bachelor girl was planning to reunite with ex-love, Sean Combs. But Combs was *not* the "new" man in her life, *nor* was singer Marc Anthony (who had made a music video with Lopez and was discussing with her the possibility of costarring in a film biography about salsa singer Hector Lavoe), *nor* was the mystery man British actor Ralph Fiennes, her very friendly costar in the then currently shooting film *The Chambermaid* (2002).

The new man in Jennifer's life proved to be Ben Affleck, who had enjoyed a fun flirtation with Lopez early in 2002 when they shot *Gigli* (2003). At the time they had denied anything serious about their noticeable special on-set rapport, even when in March 2002 Affleck placed an ad in the trade paper *Variety* gushing about Jennifer's "graciousness of spirit, beauty and courage, great empathy, astonishing talent, real poise and true grace." By June 2002, however, the now-single Lopez and the two-year-younger Affleck were spotted by the media spending quality time at one another's homes and at assorted fashionable dining establishments. The next month, in late July, Ben was a special guest at Jennifer's thirty-second birthday party at New York City's trendy Park restaurant where he presented her with an 18-karat gold bracelet composed of white and yellow diamonds. By this point, he and Lopez had contracted to continue their togetherness by costarring in the big-screen romance entry *Jersey Girl* (2003). Although the show-business couple du jour had not decided if they'd solidify their bond by marriage, Jennifer had recently begun telling the press that she wanted to settle down: "I come from a great, loving family and one day I would like to have the same thing."

Meanwhile, Lopez, now earning $12 million per film, was the star of a new thriller, *Enough* (2002). Made at a cost of $38 million, the middling suspense-action yarn garnered a little more than that amount during its summer domestic release.

With some of the income from her various enterprises (which included—besides her films, recordings, and concerts—an extremely lucrative clothing line, a signature fragrance, a greeting card line, and a Latin-themed restaurant), Jennifer bought a $9.5 million Miami villa as a getaway from the new Los Angeles estate she was having constructed.

Despite her many accomplishments to date, determined Lopez, a classic type A personality, has her eyes set on bigger goals. "I still wake up thinking about everything that I want to achieve . . . feeling that I can't stop . . . that I have to win an Oscar . . . make better movies . . . sing in big arenas . . . Every day I wake up with that anxiety."

Jeanette MacDonald

[Jeanette Anna MacDonald]

JUNE 18, 1903–JANUARY 14, 1965

Even during the first half of the twentieth century, when operettas—and even operas—were far more popular with the general public than they are today, being a singer associated with such musical genres suggested that the vocalist was most likely a cultural snob, not a person of the people. Similarly, in Hollywood's Golden Age of the 1930s and 1940s, those on-screen vocalists famed for singing *not* popular ballads but selections from operettas and operas were often regarded by studio coworkers as cultural elitists. This certainly applied to Metropolitan Opera star Grace Moore, who made several movies in the 1930s, as well as to Jeanette MacDonald.

MacDonald earned her diva label with studio coworkers not only because she was a lofty cinema operetta star but also because on-screen—and especially in her concertizing—she preferred singing operatic numbers. Added to this, pretty five-foot, four-inch Jeanette had a naturally regal bearing that made her seem slightly pretentious. (Some who were less than

charmed by her thought she was outright snooty.) What earned this redhead with blue-green eyes her stripes as a prima donna was the fact that, beneath her refined exterior, she was as determined as Joan Crawford or Bette Davis to advance her career. Frequently that meant fighting with the studio hierarchy. When it came to negotiating her picture fees, being allowed time off from the soundstages to give concerts, or being able to select her next leading man, Jeanette was extremely tenacious. Thus, there was good reason why MacDonald was known in the film industry as "The Iron Butterfly" (not to be confused with Loretta Young's label, "The Steel Butterfly").

She was born in Philadelphia in 1903 (some sources say 1901; MacDonald preferred 1907), the third daughter of Daniel MacDonald and his wife, Anna Mae Wright. Her father was a salesman for a small local factory that made windowsills, mantelpieces, and so forth, and it was a struggle for him to support his family. Nevertheless, her determined mother (who was from a blue-collar background but was very culture minded) saw to it that her three musically inclined girls had training in singing, dance, and drama. One of Jeanette's earliest professional performances was in a 1909 Philadelphia production of *Charity*, a chil-

Jeanette MacDonald in the early 1930s.
(Courtesy of JC Archives)

Magic Ring (1923). Her first starring role in a Broadway musical was in *Bubbling Over* (1926), followed by such stage projects as *Yes, Yes Yvette* (1927) and *Boom-Boom* (1929). During the run of the latter, film star Richard Dix saw Jeanette perform and urged his studio (Paramount) to test her for a screen role at their Long Island facility. However, MacDonald did not want to abandon her stage career and turned down the film offer.

Later in 1929, moviemaker Ernst Lubitsch was preparing a musical for Maurice Chevalier at Paramount. He saw Jeanette's test footage and convinced her to be the leading lady of *The Love Parade* (1929), a sophisticated boudoir musical comedy, in which she played the pert queen of Sylvania who weds a prince (Chevalier) with a shocking past. The risqué film was quite successful, and the new studio contractee moved to Hollywood, where she lived with her widowed mother. Meanwhile, Jeanette remained in constant touch with a friend based in New York City. The friend was Bob Ritchie, a decade older than Jeanette. He was a fast-talker from New Jersey with a penchant for fictionalizing his past and present. He moved in various strata of New York life, jumping from one financial opportunity on Wall Street to another. He intrigued the more conservative MacDonald and their relationship continued for several years, even after he married and divorced another woman. Not trusting this ladies' man on an emotional level, MacDonald nevertheless allowed him to become her personal business manager. (In the 1930s, Hollywood wondered if MacDonald and slick-talking

dren's opera. As a teenager, MacDonald went to New York City to visit her older sister Edith (known as Blossom MacDonald and later billed as Marie Blake and Blossom Rock). At the time, Blossom was working in the chorus of *The Demi-Tasse Revue*, the stage show that accompanied films being shown at the Capitol Theater. Jeanette was hired to join the chorus. After being a chorine in *The Night Boat* (1920)—and adding to her income with modeling assignments—Jeanette had parts in such Broadway productions as *Irene* (1921) and *The*

Ritchie were actually married. When asked, Jeanette always denied it with a bright smile, which added to the mystery.)

After she made several films for Paramount, including *Monte Carlo* (1930), the studio terminated MacDonald's contract—not only because musicals had outworn their box-office welcome but also because studio officials were tired of Jeanette's constant gripes about how she thought Paramount should be treating her. For example, company executives were annoyed that she refused to promote her screen work unless she was paid additional income. On top of that, irritating Ritchie was always complaining on the set about what should be done to make things better for Jeanette.

MacDonald negotiated a pact at Fox Films, where bosses felt that her screen image as the insouciant queen of chic lingerie comedy would bring verve to their products. However, Jeanette found dealing with pedestrian studio head Winfield Sheehan beyond endurance, and she suffered through a trio of pictures, including *Oh, For a Man* (1930). Ernst Lubitsch engineered her return to Paramount, where she was cast in *One Hour with You* (1932). In this saucy musical, she was reteamed with Chevalier (who had little love for MacDonald because of the attention she got from viewers). The popular stars were reunited again for *Love Me Tonight* (1932). Thereafter, the Paramount hierarchy chose not to continue its working relationship with hard-to-please Jeanette.

Through MacDonald's cultivated friendship with Norma Shearer, the queen of MGM, and her husband, top studio executive Irving Thalberg, it was arranged for Jeanette to join MGM at a starting salary of $4,000 weekly. Rags-to-riches studio head Louis B. Mayer thought the cultured Jeanette was an ideal woman, and, if she were too refined to submit to his casting couch, he could still enjoy a paternalistic relationship with her on the lot. (His favoritism toward Jeanette soon upset many at the studio, a situation aggravated by her taking advantage of his partiality when she played studio politics.) Her debut feature was *The Cat and the Fiddle* (1934), a stale, song-filled entry in which she and her fellow castmate, Broadway veteran Vivienne Segal, feuded. (Segal later insisted that Jeanette had deliberately had Vivienne's role minimized in the film and that when the two first met on the set, MacDonald had said airily, "Hello, Viv. Have you seen your part? It stinks!") Following *The Cat and the Fiddle*, Jeanette appeared in the expensively mounted *The Merry Widow* (1934). In this bubbly confection, she was paired with her old nemesis Maurice Chevalier. (Thereafter, the Frenchman refused to work with her again.)

Cinema history was made when MGM paired MacDonald with baritone Nelson Eddy in *Naughty Marietta* (1935), which was followed by another operetta, *Rose-Marie* (1936). Jeanette appreciated the public's enthusiasm for the new screen twosome, but she disliked being defined as part of a team, especially with such an unaccomplished actor as Nelson. She had already sold MGM the story of *San Francisco* (1936) and demanded that Clark Gable be her leading man in the screen adaptation. Initially, he refused the assignment, aware of her unflattering reputation as a "star." He was finally persuaded to accept the part and the movie proved to be an enormous hit. After joining with wooden Eddy in *Maytime* (1937), MacDonald was thrilled to be teamed with the more robust actor/singer Allan Jones in *The Firefly* (1937). That same year, in June, much to the dismay of die-hard fans of the MacDonald-Eddy movie team, Jeanette wed actor Gene Raymond in a lavish Beverly Hills church wedding.

Jeanette's close working relationship with Louis B. Mayer began deteriorating when she promoted Jones over Eddy to be her *Girl of the Golden West* costar. When Mayer refused to break apart the established love team for this movie operetta, she went over the executive's head to get her way. However, Eddy won out and worked with the reluctant MacDonald on this musical as well as in *Sweethearts* (1938). By now, the bloom was off MacDonald's status as Mayer's darling.

By the early 1940s, World War II had closed off some of the MGM markets in Europe that responded well to movie operettas. Thus, Mayer became far less a champion of the difficult-to-control Jeanette. Her and Nelson's films were expensive to produce and, when *I Married an Angel* (1942) registered a sizeable loss, MacDonald left MGM (as did Eddy). A few years later, with all forgiven—at least on the surface—Jeanette returned to the lot to make the popular musical *Three Daring Daughters* (1948) and the dramatic *The Sun Comes Up* (1949). The latter was an entry in the studio's Lassie series. After that, MacDon-

ald, who was approaching fifty, chose to make no more features.

In her postfilmmaking years, she did concerts and an occasional stage tour and made a few TV and nightclub appearances. When Louis B. Mayer—long since deposed from his MGM throne—died in 1957, she sang at his funeral. The actress was plagued by heart problems in her final years and died in January 1965 following open-heart surgery in Houston, Texas. At her funeral at Forest Lawn Memorial Park in Glendale, California, Nelson Eddy sang one of the team's most popular duets, "Ah, Sweet Mystery of Life." Even in death, the Iron Butterfly could not escape her erstwhile leading man.

Madonna

[Madonna Louise Veronica Ciccone]
AUGUST 16, 1958–

She is one of the great pop culture fabrications of the twentieth century, a celebrity who has craftily reinvented her striking image on a periodic basis, so her fans would always stay intrigued. From the start, the public wanted to place this brash, unique talent in some easily definable category, such as a Marilyn Monroe wannabe. But, insisted iconoclastic Madonna, "I'm not the new Marilyn. I'm me! Do I look like Marilyn?" She didn't, but what the then newcomer lacked in striking beauty or appealing vulnerability, she made up for with chutzpah. The self-promoting singer explained her

The ever-changing Madonna.
(Photo by Albert L. Ortega)

ter aspect of her persona in the late 1980s, Madonna was having a friendship (and later the reverse) with abrasive comedian Sandra Bernhard. Controversy-adoring Madonna maintained, "Whether I'm gay or not is irrelevant. Whether I slept with [Sandra Bernhard] or not is irrelevant. I'm perfectly willing to have people think that I did."

At another juncture in her lengthy show-business career, the brittle and manipulative star scoffed, "I know the majority of Americans think I walk around my house [with] jodhpurs on and a whip . . . that I eat men for breakfast and send out my limousine driver to pick up bushels of young men and women, and I let everybody else make my business decisions for me. Even really successful, intelligent men are so f****** scared of me and buy into the hype." Having sent so many mixed messages to her fans over the years, she nevertheless claimed to be hurt by the misconceptions running rampant about her: "Most stars are misconceived by the public. People make up their mind. They give you one attribute and that's all you're allowed to have. You're not allowed to have a full life."

She was born in 1958 in Bay City, Michigan, to Silvio (Tony) Ciccone and Madonna Louise Fortin. She was the third of six children. Her father was a design engineer for Chrysler/General Motors. When Madonna was six, her mother succumbed to breast cancer. Mr. Ciccone moved with his children to Pontiac, Michigan, where three years later he was remarried—to the family's housekeeper. Madonna, the eldest of the three Ciccone girls, rebelled at the changes in the household. As a

mind-set as follows: "I grew up with a lot of brothers and sisters. I did all I could do to really stand out and that nurtured a lot of confidence and drive and ambition." It also bred a great deal of boundary breaking from the once-sweet, young Catholic girl. She boasted, "I lost my virginity as a career move." She also wasn't afraid to be raunchy to make her point (for example, "P**** rules the world"). In addition, she thrived on pushing limits, especially when it came to such topics as her status as a bisexual. When she was indulging this lat-

child, she thought she wanted to become a nun, but by the time she was in junior high school, she enjoyed performing in class plays. However, her great delight was dance and it became her passion throughout her teen years. When she was fourteen, she met Christopher Flynn (more than two decades her senior), who became her best friend and mentor. The gay man helped her develop her skills as an exhibitionist on the dance floor. After high school, she won a dance scholarship to the University of Michigan where she studied jazz dancing. Then after a year or so on campus, she dropped out to make a career for herself in dance.

By the summer of 1978, she was in New York, living in very meager surroundings in the East Village. To survive, she did figure modeling, worked in a donut shop, and so forth. In 1979, she made *A Certain Sacrifice*, a soft-core porn film. (The picture resurfaced once she became famous in the mid-1980s.) Meanwhile, Madonna joined the third company of the Alvin Ailey Dance Troupe but left after a few months. Later, she met rock musician Dan Gilroy at the apartment of an ex-lover (Norris Burroughs). With Dan (who became her new boyfriend) and his brother Ed, she formed her first band, the Breakfast Club. She dropped out of this Queens-based group to start a new-wave rock group called the Millionaires (also known as Emanon, Emmenon, and Emmy). Determined to have a solo career, she frequented trendy rock discos where her attraction to rap and dance music developed. She became friendly with (and the lover of) deejay Mark Kamins, who in turn introduced

Madonna to executives at Sire Records. They signed her to a recording contract. Her first album, *Madonna*, was released in mid-1983. Before long, two of the disc's singles were in the top ten and the video for one ("Lucky Star") became a popular item on MTV. Soon the strutting sex kitten with her trademark provocative outfits was well-known to TV viewers. With such album cuts as "Material Girl," Madonna became an international attraction. Her second album, *Like a Virgin* (1984), containing its highly controversial title song, confirmed her reputation as a major star.

She made her mainstream feature film debut in *Vision Quest* (1985) singing "Crazy for You" in a club sequence. This appearance added to her growing reputation as the "in" thing. She became a national craze, as popular for her controversial postures as for her music. With her lead role in the movie *Desperately Seeking Susan* (1985), the singer–turned–actress gained additional acclaim. That same year, she made her cross-country *Like a Virgin* concert tour. It was an enormous success. In August 1985, she wed moody, intense actor Sean Penn in Malibu, California. Their volatile union was punctuated over the following years by their public fights with one another and his explosive behavior with paparazzi. She and hot-tempered Sean ended their punishing relationship in 1989. During her Penn years, she continued to record, do her funky concert tours, and heap up a huge bank account that let her indulge her every whim.

She signed to play Breathless Mahoney in the big-screen edition of *Dick Tracy* (1990). During production, she began a much-hyped relationship with the movie's director/star, Warren Beatty. By the time the star-studded picture was in release, Madonna and the much-older Beatty had gone their separate ways, and she was back on the road with her *Blonde Ambition* tour. Preparation for and performances from this concert trip were the subject of a feature-length documentary, *Truth or Dare* (1991). The well-received entry gave fresh insight into the many worlds of controlling, emotional, savvy Madonna.

Always eager to titillate her public, she published *Sex* (1992), an expensively mounted book containing soft-core erotic photography (including shots of herself, other female celebrities, and Madonna in tandem with such past boyfriends as rapper Vanilla Ice). The volume created the desired controversy and, despite scathing reviews, did what it was geared to do—sell extremely well. Her disc (*Erotica*) was issued at the same time as *Sex* but sold a relatively modest two million copies.

Madonna had a burning ambition to be a great movie icon, but such offerings as 1993's *Body of Evidence* and *Dangerous Game* greatly diminished her chances of achieving her Tinseltown dream. She lost out to Sharon Stone to play opposite Robert De Niro in Martin Scorsese's *Casino* (1995) and wisely turned down a role in *Showgirls* (1995), another picture dealing with Las Vegas. Finally her persistence paid off when she beat out such earlier contenders as Meryl Streep to take on the demanding title role in *Evita* (1996). Made on a $55 million budget, the screen musical only grossed $49.994 million in domestic distribution. Many reviewers considered Madonna, now in her late thirties, too mature to effectively play the ambitious wife of Argentinean dictator Juan Peron.

The star overcame the anticlimax of *Evita* by becoming a mother in 1996. With typical disregard for convention, she did not bother to wed the biological father (her personal fitness trainer, Carlos Leon). The baby girl was named Lourdes Maria Ciccone Leon, and the singer thrived on her latest image—a pushy, single parent. Again reinventing herself professionally, Madonna went in a new direction for *Ray of Light* (1998), her first album of new songs in four years. The disc emphasized high-tech production values and did well with both critics and the public. Two years later, the star reunited with *Ray of Light* producer William Orbit to turn out *Music*. It too performed nicely in the marketplace.

Over the years, free-spirited, unconventional Madonna had a wide variety of lovers who included rap musician Vanilla Ice, bizarre basketball star Dennis Rodman, porn actor Tony Ward, and actor/writer Andy Bird. Then in the late 1990s, she met British filmmaker Guy Ritchie. Ten years her junior, he became the father of her son, Rocco, born in August 2000. Four months later, the couple wed in a high-toned wedding in a medieval castle in Skibo, Scotland. Already having made England her home base (and having become increasingly affected with her acquired British accent), Madonna, Ritchie, the two children, and the family's retinue became a familiar sight about London. If her romantic comedy *The Next Best Thing* (2000) earned her poor reviews, she proved she was still a major concert star

Whether performing onstage or in films, the singing superstar never received the acclaim she felt was her due; in fact, the critics sometimes savaged her screen appearances (as with 1993's *Body of Evidence*). Perhaps part of her creative problem was her "casual" approach to the acting craft:

"Acting is just another kind of performing. It's just an expression, it's just being honest with your audience. So to me it's just an extension of what I do already."

"To me, a script is a skeleton that I have liked enough to hang my skin on."

"What's a 'trained' actress? I think that in living the life I live I've paid my dues."

Or perhaps it was more a matter of ego and control. After appearing in Woody Allen's film *Shadows and Fog* (1992), Madonna noted that the "whole process of being a brushstroke in someone else's painting is a little difficult."

when she undertook her highly successful *Drowned World* tour, which concluded in Los Angeles in September 2001. Her next movie was the romantic comedy *Swept Away* (2002), directed by husband Ritchie. Also in 2002, Madonna made her London West End theater debut in *Up for Grabs*. She received very mixed reviews for her performance.

As hyperactive, rich, powerful, and inventive Madonna, who owns the Maverick record label, nears her fifties, she is no less aggressive or self-indulgent than when she was a show-business newcomer. Looking back on her spectacularly high-profile life, in which her self-promoting ploys often overshadowed her talent, she said, "I sometimes think I was born to live up to my name. How could I be anything else but what I am, having been named Madonna? I would either have ended up a nun or this." Like any queen, she has been given to pontification over the years, such as her self-

absorbed creed for life: "When I'm hungry, I eat. When I'm thirsty, I drink. When I feel like saying something, I say it."

Jayne Mansfield

[Vera Jayne Palmer]
APRIL 19, 1933–JUNE 29, 1967

In the United States, the 1950s was a decade of conformity, stereotypes, and contradictions— particularly regarding sexuality. Sex was on everyone's mind, but it was *not* to be discussed openly in polite company. Women were prized for their sex appeal, but they were *not* supposed to flaunt it. Men thought themselves the masters in the game of sex, and women were supposed to be brainwashed into being their compliant followers. Voluptuous Mansfield was both a product of and a rambunctious rebel against this era's dichotomies and hypocrisies.

Initially regarded as an aspiring Marilyn Monroe type, Mansfield was far more blatant and crude in promoting her mesmerizing physical assets—especially her overly ample breasts. Not a dumb blond, Jayne was nevertheless naïve regarding many aspects of life, especially with her childish, misplaced reliance on many of the men with whom she became involved. In fact, her need for the opposite sex was so strong that her attorney, Greg Bautzer, once quipped, "She was like Will Rogers. She never met a man she didn't like."

Jayne was never a polished actress, but she brought gusto to her screen roles. She did, however, excel at the art of self-promotion. She was a natural publicist who instinctively understood how—especially in the confining 1950s—to grab the most publicity possible for her exceptional cleavage, her pouty lips, her luxuriant white-blond hair, her eye-grabbing wiggle, and that squeaking joke of a voice. In her fledgling campaigns to promote herself, she gathered a wide variety of contest/honorary/promotional titles, including "Miss Photoflash," "Miss Queen of the Chihuahua Show," "Miss Texas Tomato," "Miss July Fourth," and so on. She said later, "I think the only thing I ever turned down was a chance to be Miss Roquefort Cheese because it didn't sound right."

Unfortunately, in the process of achieving her place in Hollywood as an aggressive sex symbol, Jayne became a caricature of herself. By the late 1950s, Tinseltown and America had moved on to the next level of sexual explicitness and sophistication. As a result, Mansfield's blatant sexual teasing seemed out of date and somewhat ridiculous. Unable (or unwilling) to refine her established image, Jayne grew desperate to recapture the success she'd enjoyed during the fifties. If she had been self-oriented, hard to control, and capricious in her Hollywood heyday, she was more so in the sixties. Then fate intervened and her years of fame seeking came to a crashing finale.

She was born Vera Jayne Palmer in 1933 in Bryn Mawr, Pennsylvania, to Harry Palmer, an attorney, and Vera, an elementary school teacher. When the youngster was three, her father died of a heart attack. In 1939, her mother married sales engineer Harry "Tex" Peers, and she and her daughter moved to Dallas, Texas, where he was based. During high school, the aspiring actress with fantasies of becoming a movie star fell in love with another student. She and Paul Mansfield were married secretly in January 1950. When young Vera became pregnant, her parents hosted a second, public wedding. That November, their baby girl, Jayne Marie, was born. By now, Paul was at the University of Texas in Austin, while Vera was employed as a dance studio receptionist and was working at the Austin Civic Theater.

Paul was called to active duty during the Korean War. Suddenly on her own, the young mother headed to Los Angeles, leaving Jayne Marie with her grandmother. Once on the West Coast, Vera Jayne enrolled at UCLA and entered the Miss California Contest (hiding her marital and parental status). She was a local winner in the competition, but a con-

Ray Walston, Jayne Mansfield, and Harry Carey Jr. in *Kiss Them for Me* (1957). (Courtesy of JC Archives)

cerned Paul made her quit the pageant. Before reluctantly returning to the Lone Star State, the voluptuous blond had a tiny movie role in 1951's *Prehistoric Women*.

Back in Texas—and with Paul still in military service—Vera attended college in Dallas, studied acting, and even appeared on a local TV show. When Paul returned to civilian life in 1954, he kept an earlier promise to take his wife to Hollywood, so she could try her luck again in pictures. Her brunette hair was dyed platinum blond. She soon found an agent, and the twenty-one-year-old adopted a new screen name (Jayne Mansfield). She was hired for a small role in the movie *Female Jungle* (not released until 1956). However, Paul was unhappy with Hollywood life and found he had little in common with the "new" Jayne. Thus, the disheartened husband returned to Texas alone, and their divorce was finalized in January 1958.

Mansfield's enthusiastic young press agent, James Byron, used his ingenuity to elevate his statuesque, pliant client into a well-known commodity, relying on her well-endowed figure and her attention-grabbing walk and talk to do the rest. On a press junket to Silver Springs, Florida, Jayne craftily gained media attention by posing in a skintight red bathing suit. Her *Playboy* magazine spread in February 1956 left little doubt about Jayne's impressive physical assets, and she soon maneuvered a term contract at Warner Bros. In her studio assignments, such as *Illegal* (1955) and *Hell on Frisco Bay* (1956), she typically played a moll.

When her brief studio tenure expired, Jayne inherited the lead (rejected by several others) in a 1955 Broadway sex comedy titled *Will Success Spoil Rock Hunter?* The risqué romp was popular, and Mansfield tirelessly maximized her publicity opportunities on the East Coast as "Broadway's Smartest Dumb Blonde." She also became a prima donna at the Belasco Theater, not arriving until nearly curtain time, walking around backstage in the nude, making a nuisance of herself with the stagehands, and generally being too full of herself. Meanwhile, she met Hungarian-born muscleman Mickey Hargitay (a former Mr. Universe), who was then part of Mae West's club act and was considered the veteran star's personal property. Jayne stole the larger-than-life Mickey away from the much-older West, with the two women choreographing their

tug-of-war to achieve the maximum (mutual) publicity.

Twentieth Century-Fox hired Jayne to be one of several threats to its resident blond bombshell, Marilyn Monroe. Mansfield's first movie at the studio, *The Girl Can't Help It* (1956), was an amusing satirical comedy and showcased her well. Next came the screen adaptation of *Will Success Spoil Rock Hunter?* in 1957. This was followed by John Steinbeck's *The Wayward Bus* (1957), which Mansfield had cajoled the studio into letting her do. To her credit and Fox's surprise, she rose to the occasion by stretching her acting abilities. On January 13, 1958, five days after her divorce from Paul Mansfield was official, Jayne and Hargitay married in Portuguese Bend, California. They had three children: Miklos Jr. (born in 1958), Zoltan (born in 1960), and Mariska (born in 1964).

Dedicated to increasing her fame, Jayne (with Mickey as part of her act) began performing in Las Vegas clubs, exploiting her statuesque dumb-blond comedic appeal. Fox shipped her to England for the comedic Western *The Sheriff of Fractured Jaw* (1958). She remained in the United Kingdom to do two other low-budget entries that proved unmem-

Sometimes sudden fame swells a person's head but not in the case of the curvaceous Mansfield. At the time of making *Illegal* (1955), her spectacular measurements (40-21-35) already adorned her chair on the soundstage. Later, when one magazine referenced her stats and did not give Jayne her busty due, she griped, "They treated me as if I were only a thirty-six. Marilyn's [Monroe] only a thirty-eight! I'm a forty!" However, while stopping off in London a few years later, Jayne exclaimed that she was "41-18-35 and tanned over every inch of me!"

orable. Traveling to Italy, she and Hargitay teamed for *The Loves of Hercules* (1960). By now, it was clear even to Jayne that Twentieth Century-Fox had lost interest in her; this made her more desperate, which in turn made her dealings with her studio bosses more stressful for all concerned.

If the public was tiring of revealing photos of her famous curves, Jayne got a lot of promotional mileage from showing off her new pink, Spanish-style Beverly Hills mansion at 10100 Sunset Boulevard. With its heart-shaped bed, bathtub, and pool, the tacky setting amused the media and intrigued the public. In 1962, Fox, embarrassed by Jayne's over-the-top promotional gambits and her increasingly wild and exhibitionistic off-camera sex life, dropped her option. Two years later, Mr. and Mrs. Hargitay divorced.

Having lost the career structure provided by a studio contract, Jayne drifted professionally. She made the sordid sexploitation entry *Promises, Promises* (1963) and posed nude once again for *Playboy*. She continued her publicity stunts, but they no longer seemed fun or spontaneous. She made several negligible movies abroad and then married twenty-eight-year-old film director Matt Cimber in 1964. Their son, Anthony, was born in 1965. Despondent over her career crash, Mansfield relied increasingly on alcohol to ease the pain, which gave her a bloated look. In the midst of this, she and ex-husband Mickey had media-covered battles over the custody of their children.

Relying on Cimber's advice—which turned out to be bad—Jayne vetoed the role of Ginger on the TV sitcom *Gilligan's Island* (1964–67), which did so much for actress Tina Louise. Instead, Mansfield made low-caliber movies, appeared in stock productions (including *Bus Stop*, directed by Cimber), and wondered where her fame had gone.

In 1966, Matt Cimber divorced his heavy-drinking wife. Thereafter, Jayne become infatuated with San Francisco attorney Samuel S. Brody. He sacrificed his career to be at her beck and call as she undertook an unsuccessful tour of sleazy club engagements in Sweden, England, and Ireland. By now, Mansfield was gaining headlines for having drunken scuffles with Brody and for being cited in a messy divorce suit by Brody's wife. Back in California, career-stricken Jayne, who had become intrigued with the church of Satan, earned additional bad press coverage when Jayne Marie, her sixteen-year-old daughter, was put into protective custody because her mother and Brody were allegedly mistreating her.

In 1967, after touring Vietnam to entertain the military, Mansfield undertook a club engagement in Biloxi, Mississippi. On the trek, Jayne was joined by Sam Brody and her three children by Mickey. In the early morning of June 29, 1967, they were traveling by car from Biloxi to New Orleans for an interview. Their auto smacked into the back of a stopped trailer truck. Jayne's young driver, Brody, and Mansfield were killed instantly. Her children, asleep in the backseat, escaped any serious injury. After a memorial service in Beverly Hills, Jayne's body was shipped to Pen Argyl, Pennsylvania, for burial in the family plot.

As Martha Saxton noted in *Jayne Mansfield and the American Fifties* (1975), "She wanted rapturous love, not a sex object, but a romance-object, a man who would outdistance her and be more to her than she was to herself. Her career, as she saw it, was simply a backdrop for a love affair. She never expected that her career would become her most stable love affair."

Liza Minnelli

[Liza May Minnelli]
MARCH 12, 1946–

"I think she decided to go into show business when she was an embryo, she kicked so much!" said Judy Garland of her first offspring, Liza Minnelli. In subsequent years, Liza was forced to be a nursemaid to her emotionally fragile, drug- and alcohol-addicted mother. By then, the teenager had entered show business as an entertainer. Soon she found herself competing professionally with Mama—as in November 1964, when she joined Garland in concertizing at London's Palladium. To the girl's astonishment, Judy proved highly competitive on stage, frantic not to be outshone by her teenaged daughter. "Working with her was something else," Liza admitted. "I'll never be afraid to perform with anyone ever again after that terrifying experience."

In June 1969, forty-seven-year-old Garland died of an (accidental) overdose of prescription medication. Coping with her mother's death, Liza—whose look, voice, and mannerisms so readily recalled the legendary Judy—

swore she'd avoid her mother's pitfalls: career instability, substance abuse, and bad romances. But sadly, vibrant, talented Liza emerged a carbon copy of her famous parent regarding the difficulties in her professional and private life. Also like Judy, Liza has bounced back many times from the brink of professional disaster and physical ruin. Her pilgrimage over the years has been all the more amazing because she has had to cope with the heavy baggage of her dysfunctional childhood and the career obstacle of living in the shadow of her well-remembered mother.

She was born Liza May Minnelli in Los Angeles in 1946. She was the only child of the beloved Metro-Goldwyn-Mayer singing star and Garland's second spouse, MGM movie director Vincente Minnelli. At age two, Liza made her screen debut playing Judy's daughter in the closing sequence of *In the Good Old Summertime* (1949). By 1951, Judy had been dismissed by her studio, attempted suicide (again), and divorced Minnelli. The following year, the superstar wed promoter Sid Luft, who guided her through comebacks on the concert stage and in films. Garland and Luft had two children (Lorna and Joey) and spent rocky years together and apart before divorcing in 1965. In coping with Garland's turbulent life, Liza grew up (too) quickly emotionally, which left her unprepared to handle her own problems in the future.

By 1961, five-foot, four-inch Liza worked as a summer stock theater apprentice on Cape Cod. The following year, at Scarsdale High in suburban New York, she starred in a school production of *The Diary of Anne Frank*.

Unable to avoid following in her mother's show-business footsteps (which included Judy's starring role in 1939's *The Wizard of Oz*), Liza recorded the voice of Dorothy in a cartoon feature version of *Journey Back to Oz* (not released until 1974). In 1963, Minnelli made her off-Broadway debut in a revival of *Best Foot Forward*, and she appeared on Broadway in the musical *Flora, the Red Menace* (1965). Already, she'd begun her vocal recording career.

Judy was unable to fix her own out-of-control life in the 1960s, but she did intervene on her daughter's behalf. She used industry connections to get Liza considered for a small role in the British-made *Charlie Bubbles* (1968). (During its filming, Minnelli became involved with her leading man, Albert Finney.) It was Garland who brought Liza together with Australian-born entertainer/composer Peter Allen. (He had previously been part of Judy's club act, teamed with his good friend Chris Bell.) Minnelli debated about wedding Allen—who had an alternative lifestyle—but in March 1967, she and Peter wed. In the next few years, Liza was Oscar-nominated for *The Sterile Cuckoo* (1969), organized her mother's funeral, played the club circuit (including Las Vegas), and starred in a TV special for $500,000.

The year 1972 was hectic for fast-living, high-strung Liza. She and Allen divorced (although they remained good friends), and she became involved in a high-visibility romance with the son of Lucille Ball and Desi Arnaz, Desi Jr. He was seven years younger than she. The couple got engaged, but then the union ended suddenly. Also that year, she starred in the movie *Cabaret* (for which she won an Oscar) and earned an Emmy for her TV special (*Liza with a "Z"*). Jumping on a romantic merry-go-round, Minnelli garnered much media coverage for her attachments to Peter Sellers, Edward Albert, Ben Vereen, Assaf Dayan, and others. But it was none of these men that substance-abusing Minnelli wed. It was, instead, film/TV producer Jack Haley Jr., twelve years her elder and the son of the performer who'd teamed with Garland as the Tin Man in *The Wizard of Oz*. Setting a precedent for her future, Liza and Jack had a huge wedding gala hosted by Vincente Minnelli and Sammy Davis Jr. at Ciro's on Hollywood's Sunset Strip. The marriage, however, ended in divorce in 1978. (Liza remained on good terms with Jack and, when he died in April 2001, she spoke at his memorial tribute.)

When the movie musical *New York, New York* (1977) flopped at the box office, it was Liza's third screen failure in a row and her once-promising movie career appeared to be over. As her mother had done when her own film career waned, Minnelli returned to the stage. The vehicle was *The Act* (1977), and she won a Tony in the process. In December 1979, Liza took husband number three—Mark Gero, a former stage manager–turned–sculptor, who was seven years her junior. During the next several years, she suffered numerous miscarriages, and her increasingly shaky marriage turned into an in-name-only situation. The pair finally divorced in 1992.

Thanks to the comedy *Arthur* (1981), Liza was in a smash hit movie. But the success was

Liza Minnelli in *Cabaret* (1972).
(Courtesy of Echo Book Shop)

attributed to her leading man (Dudley Moore), so she still had no movie marquee clout. She returned to the stage in *The Rink* (1984). Minnelli departed the musical during its run to enter the Betty Ford Center in Rancho Mirage, California, for treatment of alcohol and Valium abuse. Accompanied to the facility by stepsister Lorna Luft and cheered on by Ford Center alumnus Elizabeth Taylor, Liza admitted publicly, "I've got a problem and I'm going

to deal with it." But her much-hyped recovery was followed by a cycle of relapses.

Liza's father died in mid-1986 and left her $1 million from his estate. The following year, she did a PBS-TV tribute to him titled *Minnelli on Minnelli*. In May 1987, she had a hugely successful three-week engagement at Carnegie Hall. In movies, however, she couldn't get a break, floundering in such weak fare as *Rent-a-Cop* (1988) and *Stepping Out* (1991). In fall 1991, it was rumored that Minnelli would wed Billy Stritch, a much younger pianist who had been part of a cabaret trio; however, the much-speculated-on union never happened. She returned to Radio City Music Hall with her act, followed by a Carnegie Hall engagement in June 1993 with French singer Charles Aznavour, her good friend from previous years.

By the early 1990s, Liza was most frequently in the news due to health problems (including hip- and knee-replacement surgeries). Recovered from those afflictions, she made a TV movie, *West Side Waltz* (1995), and revisited the club circuit. The tabloids continued to speculate on her life as a party animal, her boy toys, and her dependency on drugs and drink. In January 1997, she replaced Julie Andrews for a month on Broadway in the musical *Victor/Victoria*.

Now past fifty, Minnelli went through yet another substance abuse recovery, informing the press, "I want the people who care about me to know I'm taking care of myself." Having slimmed back down to her usual svelte figure, it seemed this was the "new" Liza. She insisted, "I've got a good life, and I don't think anything can rock that anymore." In late 1999,

For ordinary people, the expression "third time's the charm" applies. But VIP celebrities require the stakes to be upped a bit. When Minnelli wed her fourth husband, event planner David Gest, in 2002, the celebrity guest list for the nuptials and the caliber of the bountiful all-night reception made it the extravagant wedding of the decade. The media spared the public no detail about the bizarre event or the complex arrangements leading up to the glittery spectacle. Accustomed to sharing such intimate details of her rocky life as her ups and downs in show business, substance abuse rehabilitation, and assorted romances with the press, Liza also chose to tell the world about her sex life with Gest. "I have a husband who loves me in every way a woman dreams of being loved," insisted Minnelli. "We have the best sex ever. It makes me feel alive." Meanwhile, the newlyweds broke away from their global honeymoon to appear on *Larry King Live*. The cable TV talk show host asked the groom about "the talk about your sexuality and the like." Gest—noted for his plucked eyebrows, wearing heavy-duty facial bronzer, and adding heel lifts to his shoes—replied ambivalently, "I know who I am. That's the important thing. She knows who she is and we're so in love we've got our own world." Adding to her (tacky) tell-all frenzy, the singer later boasted to a New York newspaper, "I know many of my husband's ex-girlfriends will agree that if every man was as good in bed as David, there would be a lot of happy women in the world. We moved in together one week after we met, that says it all."

she was back on Broadway, this time in *Minnelli on Minnelli*, a tribute to her father's movies. The show later went on tour but was cancelled in May 2000 when the star was hospitalized for a severe hip condition. By that September, she was in Fort Lauderdale, Florida, planning to purchase a home. The next month, however, she was admitted to a local hospital for viral encephalitis and nearly died. Her near-fatal experience led to a reconciliation with sister Lorna after several years of noncommunication. Spring 2001 found problem-plagued Liza submitting to additional hip and back surgery.

While participating in the TV special *Michael Jackson: 30th Anniversary Special* (2001), the diva met event planner David Gest,

seven years her junior. To everyone's amazement, the seemingly odd couple were soon announcing they planned to wed. While this was nothing unique for impetuous, madcap Liza, their ostentatiously circus-style wedding was by anyone's standards! The ceremony of the new millennium was held on March 16, 2002, at Marble Collegiate Church on New York's Fifth Avenue. (By then, the bride-to-be had been through further substance abuse treatment and had shed ninety unwanted pounds.) The wedding party consisted of such matrons of honor as Elizabeth Taylor (the ring bearer) and Liza's *Cabaret* teammate Marisa Berenson. The two best men were Michael and Tito Jackson. Assisting at the formalities were thirteen bridesmaids, thirteen groomsmen, two flower girls, and two flower boys. Among the conglomerate attending the service were Donald Trump, Rosie O'Donnell, Sir Anthony Hopkins, Janet Leigh, Mickey Rooney, Celeste Holm, Alan Cummings, Arlene Dahl, Jill St. John and husband Robert Wagner, and Robert Goulet. (Also present were the bride's half-brother Joey Luft, half-sister Christiana Nina Minnelli, and stepfather Sid Luft. Lorna Luft, who had attended Liza's engagement party in Los Angeles the month before, was not at the wedding. She claimed a prior commitment to sing in Australia.)

During the pomp and circumstance–type ceremony, Natalie Cole sang "Unforgettable." Most noteworthy at the ceremony was the groom's breath-sucking kissing of the bride. Said Donald Trump, "I have been to many weddings, and I have never seen a kiss like that before." When the hour-long service ended, the bride, who wore a Bob Mackie–designed empire gown, exited the church wearing a floor-length, white mink coat, a recent gift from a friend. Such guests as Kirk Douglas, Lauren Bacall, Mia Farrow, Joan Collins, Dionne Warwick, Andy Williams, and David Hasselhoff were also on hand at the lavish, gaudy, and expensive reception gala at the Regent Wall Street Hotel.

Liza being Liza, hardly had she and her spouse departed for their honeymoon when the bride's ninety-four-year-old stepmother, Lee Anderson Minnelli, was suing for breach of contract and elder abuse. The plaintiff complained that since Liza was executor and trustee of her late father's estate, she was obligated to maintain the six-bedroom home for her stepmother and not try to evict her. Court papers stated that Liza had refused to pay for the utilities or household staff since she had begun efforts to sell the house six months earlier. While those unfortunate headlines were breaking and the embarrassing situation was being resolved, Liza returned to the concert stage both abroad and in the United States.

Still gushing about the joys of their recent marriage, Liza and Gest agreed to star in a fall 2002 reality show on VH1 cable. The format of the outing would have the couple entertaining guests at weekly dinner parties in Manhattan during which Liza and some of the visitors would entertain with songs and such. Said the typically hyper Minnelli of this bizarre entertainment vehicle, "Yes, of course I'm going to cook, if there's time."

One can only speculate what flabbergasting events will crowd the next years of Liza's chaotic, hectic, and always fascinating life.

Marilyn Monroe

[Norma Jeane Mortensen]
JUNE 1, 1926–AUGUST 4, 1962

Probably the most adored and (over-) analyzed pop-culture icon of the twentieth century, Monroe still remains a luscious enigma, despite the many books and film documentaries that have dissected every aspect of her life and career.

The terribly insecure beauty admitted once, "I always felt I was a nobody, and the only way

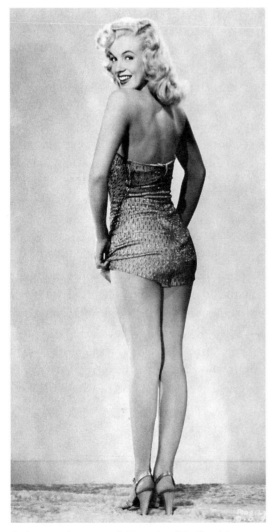

A cheesecake pose of the young Marilyn Monroe in the late 1940s. (Courtesy of JC Archives)

much fun as dreaming of being one." After she attained status as a great cinema siren, she realized that fame was a mixed blessing: "That's the trouble, a sex symbol becomes a thing. I just hate to be a thing. But if I'm going to be a symbol of something, I'd rather have it be sex than some other thing they've got symbols of."

As five-foot, five-and-a-half-inch Marilyn gained stature in the film industry, she admitted, "Being a sex symbol is a heavy load to carry, especially when one is tired, hurt, and bewildered." Mounting insecurities led her to arrive continuously late to her movie sets and do many other disconcerting things. She often subconsciously invented reasons to lag behind in her dressing room, anything to avoid the frightening prospect of facing the cameras and perhaps failing to meet her own and others' expectations. Acknowledging her notorious habit of being tardy, she said, "I guess people think that why I'm late is some kind of arrogance and I think it is the opposite of arrogance. . . . The main thing is, I do want to be prepared when I get there to give a good performance or whatever to the best of my ability . . . [Clark] Gable [her costar in 1961's *The Misfits*] said about me, 'When she's there, she's there. All of her is there! She's there to work.'"

Billy Wilder directed Monroe in two features (1955's *The Seven Year Itch* and 1959's *Some Like It Hot*) and had to cope with her increasingly unprofessional behavior, emotional baggage, and quirks that made working with her both frustrating and harrowing. Perhaps witty Wilder said it best when explaining

for me to be somebody was to be—well, somebody else." The alter ego she chose was that of a film performer. However, she discovered later that "Being a movie actress was never as

why studios and coworkers put up with her upsetting conduct: "Marilyn Monroe was never on time, never knew her lines. I have an old aunt in Vienna. She would be on the set every morning at six and would know her lines backward, but who would go to see her?"

She was born Norma Jeane Mortensen (but listed as Norma Jeane Mortenson on her birth certificate) in Los Angeles in 1926. Her mother, Gladys Pearl Monroe Mortensen, was a photo lab technician and her father, Martin Edward Mortensen, a baker who abandoned Gladys during her pregnancy and filed for divorce, although it had not yet become official when Norma Jeane was born. (Martin, who died in a motorcycle mishap in 1929, is thought by many sources *not* to have been Norma Jeane's real father. Her biological dad was believed to have been C. Stanley Gifford, who worked with young Gladys at Consolidated Film Industries in Hollywood and had an affair with her.)

Emotionally unstable, Gladys spent much of her daughter's youth in mental institutions. As a result, Norma Jeane had a dismal childhood in a succession of foster homes and orphanages; she was raped when she was only eight years old. One of the results of those bleak early years was Norma's tendency to stutter.

To avoid being shipped to yet one more foster home, sixteen-year-old Norma Jeane wed twenty-one-year-old James Dougherty, an aircraft factory worker, in June 1942. While the groom was away from home during World War II serving in the merchant marines, Norma Jeane worked for a time at a San Fernando Valley defense plant. She started posing (usually in form-fitting sweaters) for local photographers, which led to photo layouts in major girlie magazines. In July 1946, she was screen-tested by Twentieth Century-Fox and signed a $75-a-week contract. She was given a new name—Marilyn Monroe—and divorced Dougherty.

Monroe had a few bit parts at Fox (including 1948's *Scudda Hoo! Scudda Hay!*), but her option was dropped. At Columbia Pictures, she was signed to a six-month contract and had a starring role in the low-budget *Ladies of the Chorus* (1948). By now, she was dating vocal coach Fred Karger. When he moved on to another girlfriend, she tried to kill herself. Then, thanks to high-powered talent agent Johnny Hyde, who became her new boyfriend, Monroe won flashy, small screen parts in *The Asphalt Jungle* and *All About Eve* (both 1950). That same year, Hyde, who negotiated a new Twentieth Century-Fox contract for Monroe, died at age fifty-five.

Using casting couch tactics and shrewd self-publicity, Monroe made herself known to studio higher-ups, and the studio finally began promoting her as their new blond bombshell. As Marilyn gained prominence with her film roles, her 1949 nude calendar photo surfaced. Instead of ruining her mainstream movie career, the notorious pose boosted her popularity. In *Don't Bother to Knock* (1952) and *Niagara* (1953), Marilyn showed a knack for drama. By the release of *How to Marry a Millionaire* (1953), she had become the studio's top female box-office attraction. Already her escalating emotional frailties were causing her to be late to the set and to reveal flashes of temper. She was under the professional control of acting coach Natasha Lytess and listened only to her on the set, ignoring her film directors. It was just another of the annoyances that the studio accepted, ever mindful of Marilyn's great box-office appeal.

Now an established entity, Monroe began rejecting studio projects. Marilyn claimed it was for artistic reasons; Fox felt she was just being temperamental. She turned down *Pink Tights* (1953) with Frank Sinatra and was placed on suspension; the film was shelved. Later, she refused to make *The Girl in the Red Velvet Swing* (1955), and Joan Collins replaced her. Fox next cast the reluctant star in *How to Be Very, Very Popular* (1955), but she was in the midst of forming Marilyn Monroe Productions with photographer Milton Greene and said no to the lead part. Sheree North was substituted. North also took over for Marilyn in the comedy *The Lieutenant Wore Skirts* (1956), and it was equally busty Jane Russell who accepted Monroe's cast-off title role in *The Revolt of Mamie Stover* (1956).

In January 1954, the sex goddess wed Joe DiMaggio, the popular baseball player. The thirty-nine-year-old athlete wanted her to give up show business to become a homemaker. Instead, he was forced to become "Mr. Monroe," and the humiliation of it all fanned his

The effect of an idolized sex goddess on even a movie king can be deadly. While many men over the years had fixations on Monroe, she had an obsession with film star Clark Gable. As a child, Marilyn's mother had shown her a photo of her father (likely C. Stanley Gifford, a Gable look-alike). For a time, Marilyn thought Gable was her dad. In 1960, she costarred with him in *The Misfits*. Monroe was thrilled, but the combination of shooting the film on location in the Nevada heat, her fast-disintegrating marriage to playwright Arthur Miller, and her addiction to prescription drugs made her a dazed nightmare on the set—when she showed up. During the troubled shoot, she overdosed on pills and, after her stomach was pumped, she was taken to a California hospital to recover. Meanwhile, the rest of the cast and crew were stuck in Nevada. Clark, anxious to get back to Los Angeles to his pregnant wife, began drinking and smoking heavily—both of which aggravated his questionable health. He also insisted on doing his own stunts for the film. Eventually Monroe returned to the set and the picture wrapped by mid-October. Three weeks later, Clark had a heart attack and died six days later. The press played up the fact that Monroe's problems on the set had led to Gable's death. Marilyn was devastated and cried for weeks. A few months later, Gable's widow, knowing of the rumors, asked Marilyn to the christening of infant John Clark Gable. Monroe attended the event, even holding the baby in her arms. All was forgiven, but the King was still dead.

frustrations and jealousies. They divorced in September of that year. By early 1955, a rebellious Monroe had fled Fox and gone to New York, where she established her film production company and took classes at the famed Actors Studio. There she studied with Lee Strasberg, and his wife, Paula, became Marilyn's new acting coach and controller.

When Marilyn returned to filmmaking at Fox, she received excellent reviews for *Bus Stop* (1956). It increased her demand as a performer, but her problematic behavior on the set and clashes with the studio continued. At the same time, her substance abuse (pills and liquor) was running rampant. In June 1956, she wed famous, much-older playwright Arthur Miller. A few months later, she suffered a miscarriage, as she did again in 1957 and 1958. During this period, she went to England to make *The Prince and the Showgirl* (1958) with Laurence Olivier. The picture bombed, but she had great success with the 1959 comedy *Some Like It Hot.*

By 1960, complicated and confused Marilyn was seeing psychiatrists regularly. Her affair with Yves Montand, her *Let's Make Love* (1960) costar, had ended when he returned to France and his actress wife, Simone Signoret. Monroe proved to be excessively out of control while making *The Misfits* (1961), a vehicle written for her by Miller. In late October 1960, she and Arthur agreed to a divorce (it was given in Juarez, Mexico, in January 1961). Because Monroe was now exhibiting such suicidal behavior, analyst Marianne Kris convinced her to enter Manhattan's Payne Whitney Psychiatric Clinic in February 1961. After three days there, the distraught actress begged Joe DiMaggio to rescue her and he arranged for her release.

In 1962, Marilyn became involved with President John F. Kennedy; had bought a modest bungalow-style home in Brentwood, California; and was continuing her psychiatric therapy. After many months away from filmmaking, Monroe returned to Twentieth Century-Fox in April 1962 to start the romantic comedy *Something's Got to Give*, which teamed her with Dean Martin. While well physically, she was falling apart emotionally. On the few days she showed up on the set, director George Cukor often found her to be incoherent and unable to remember her lines. In years past, the studio would have coddled her, but Fox was currently in severe financial straits. Having lost over $61 million in unrewarding film releases over the past few years, it had staked its future on the epic *Cleopatra* (1963) being shot in Rome. As the budget on that Elizabeth Taylor–Richard Burton saga spiraled ever upward, panicked studio executives back in Los Angeles refused to let *Something's Got to Give* become another potential financial nightmare. Outrageous behavior accepted from Taylor in Italy was not tolerated from Monroe on the home lot. Fox management showed little patience when Marilyn was absent from the set due to alleged illness. During one of these truancies (in mid-May 1962), she flew to New York to sing "Happy Birthday" to President Kennedy at Madison Square Garden. The studio was enraged. Things calmed down, however, when she returned to the West Coast and was more accommodating than usual on the soundstage.

On June 1, Monroe celebrated her thirty-sixth birthday with a party on the set. Six days later, the star was dismissed from the film due to "unprofessional antics." Fox filed a $750,000 lawsuit against their former bread-winner. Then, thinking better of its hard-nosed attitude, the studio relented and suggested that once colead Dean Martin had completed other screen commitments, the project would be reactivated with Monroe still the leading lady. On August 1, 1962, Fox signed Marilyn to a new contract at $250,000 per picture. But that was to never be, for in the early morning of August 5, she was found dead in her bedroom. (Her death late the previous evening was attributed to a lethal overdose of Nembutal and chloral hydrate.) Three days later, the movie star was interred in a crypt at Westwood Memorial Cemetery, a few miles from where she had worked at Twentieth Century-Fox. Then and later, many conspiracy theories arose: Some claimed that Marilyn's alleged suicide was murder; others insisted she had taken an accidental overdose of pills and that it was not a suicide.

In death, vulnerable, self-doubting Marilyn became a legend. While her diva behavior as a movie star was not forgotten, it was now forgiven. She was placed on a pedestal where each sad fact of her life and her excessive behavior became part of her myth. As *Time* magazine noted so aptly, "Marilyn Monroe's unique charisma was the force that caused distant men to think that if only a well-intentioned, under-standing person like me could have known her, she would have been all right."

Maria Montez

[Maria Antonia Africa Gracia Vidal de Santo Silas]
JUNE 6, 1912–SEPTEMBER 7, 1951

Sustained self-confidence is a great asset to screen newcomers as they cope daily with rejection, discouragement, and bewilderment. But too much self-assurance can, at some point, become a liability. An arsenal of manufactured assurance, poise, and buoyancy can easily turn off the very people intended to be impressed. Such was the case with lovely Maria Montez. She was an exotic personality whose amazing attractiveness did much to compensate for her lack of acting finesse. However, her colossal ego—her towering belief in herself—killed Maria's career after her relatively brief but colorful reign in 1940s Hollywood.

She was born in 1912 in Santo Domingo in the Caribbean. Her father, Ysidoro Gracia, was the Spanish consul and embassy delegate to the Dominican Republic; her mother, Teresa, was the offspring of political refugees. Maria was one of the couple's ten children. She was educated at a convent school in Santa Cruz, the capital city of Tenerife (one of the Canary Islands), which was the family's homestead. As a student, Maria rebelled against the strict discipline at the Sacred Heart Convent and was glad when, as a teenager, she was allowed to rejoin her family. By 1937, the clan was residing in Belfast, Northern Ireland, where her father was on a new diplomatic assignment. That summer, Maria impetuously married a wealthy Irishman, William McFeeters, an officer in the British army. Of a tempestuous and impatient nature, the young bride soon became bored living with her aristocratic in-laws, especially as her husband was away so often on military duty. She solved her ennui with trips to London, Paris, and later New York City. Once in Manhattan, she quickly became part of the chic set and decided it was her destiny to remain in America. Thus, when her perplexed spouse came to reclaim his wife, she advised him that their marriage was over. A divorce was arranged, much to the chagrin of her staunchly Catholic father.

Now fully on her own, Maria embarked on a carefree life among the café set. Before long, the society sections of New York newspapers were full of pictures of the five-foot, seven-inch, auburn-haired beauty, a captivating young woman who spoke broken English with a fetching accent and punctuated her delicious chatter with sparkling brown eyes. For fun (and welcome income), she accepted modeling assignments for print ads and with prominent painters. Meanwhile, ambitious, fiery Maria had hatched a new plan. With her beauty—unmatched, in her opinion, by anyone in Hollywood—she *must* be in the movies. She owed it to filmgoers.

A genius at self-promotion, she arranged to lunch at a swank Manhattan restaurant where

Maria Montez, the exotic star of *Cobra Woman* (1944). (Courtesy of Echo Book Shop)

the head of RKO Pictures was scheduled to dine one day. As anticipated, the film executive invited the fetching Maria to his table and, before long, he was inquiring whether she would consider undertaking a screen test. "Moving pictures?" She shrugged. "What harm can it do?" Soon after, crafty Maria, with her thirty-six-inch bust and thirty-six-and-a-half-inch hips, was auditioning before the movie cameras. RKO offered her a $100-a-week salary. Universal Pictures executives had also seen her screen audition and suggested a $150 weekly deal plus a studio-paid trip to Hollywood. She quickly accepted the latter pact.

Once in Tinseltown, Maria quickly chose a new surname, one in tribute to the nineteenth-century adventuress/dancer Lola Montez. Newly anointed Maria Montez, she undertook photo sessions for publicity photos with relish. A sharp senorita, she swiftly perfected the finer points of playing the studio politics game, including the grand art of making an eye-catching entrance at the studio commissary during the crowded lunch hour. Soon Universal's publicity flacks were infatuated with this gorgeous newcomer with her attention-getting exotic looks, heavy accent, and supreme self-confidence. (Montez could not have picked a better time to arrive in Hollywood, for the studios were catering to all things South American—an interest fueled by the American government, which wanted the public to embrace its south-of-the-border neighbors in the World War II era.)

Universal promptly thrust Montez into tiny roles in its assembly line features (such as 1941's *The Invisible Woman*) and loaned her to Twentieth Century-Fox. There she appeared very briefly in *That Night in Rio* (1941), a musical that spotlighted the "Brazilian Bombshell," Carmen Miranda. Back on the home lot, Maria changed her hair color to blond for *Raiders of the Desert* (1941). She was in the news for arousing the ire of the film industry's self-censorship organization due to her cheesecake poses, in some of which she appeared not to be wearing a bra.

Maria's big-screen break occurred with 1942's *Arabian Nights*, a simplistic fantasy adventure filled with action, scantily clad actresses, and gorgeous color photography. In this confection, she costarred with Jon Hall and Sabu, and the movie appealed mightily to escapist-minded audiences (and especially to war-weary servicemen). The picture grossed $2 million and Montez was suddenly a major asset at Universal. The celluloid formula was repeated with equal success in *White Savage* (1943), *Ali Baba and the Forty Thieves* (1944), and *Cobra Woman* (1944), a camp classic in which she played twins.

As Montez moved from one exotic picture to the next, her self-absorption escalated. On camera, it gave an added dimension to her regal posturing and mouthing of the inane dialogue of her sex-and-sandal excursions. She intensely believed the garbage she was uttering and portrayed her clichéd situations so earnestly that moviegoers and even reviewers—those not satisfied by her beauty alone—tended to take her more seriously. One particular man who took the new movie queen very sincerely was Jean-Pierre Aumont. The handsome, French-born actor had made his Hollywood film debut in 1943, and his first encounter that year with Maria was love at first sight. They wed that July. A few months later, he went overseas to serve with General de Gaulle's Free French Army in Africa. While her husband was away, Maria pined for him, made sure to keep her name and photo in the news, and turned out *Sudan* (1945).

As World War II drew to an end, Maria, who took her pronouncements as items from on high, announced that her secret for maintaining her 125-pound weight was a daily steam bath. She acknowledged that some of her past films were "stinkers," that she was writing a romantic novel, and that she composed songs in her "spare" time. She also informed the studio that she had outgrown her stereotypical desert-and-romance roles; she wanted to do more dramatic screen projects.

Universal executives knew what Montez did not. With the end of the war, tastes were changing fast and her vogue was quickly passing. More important, they already had a backup player in the studio bullpen waiting to take over the title of "Queen of Technicolor." Her name was Yvonne De Carlo; the Canadian-born actress had far greater acting talent than Montez and was far less demanding (at the time) regarding salary and acting assignments. Meanwhile, Aumont returned from the battlefront and in February 1946, Montez gave birth to a baby girl. In *The Exile* (1947), Douglas Fairbanks Jr. was the picture's star and Maria merely had an extended cameo. Her studio swan song was that year's *Pirates of Monterey*.

Egged on by her husband, Maria had made no effort to make peace with Universal bosses. She was convinced she did not need them. Her new screen project away from the lot was starring with Jean-Pierre in *Siren of Atlantis* (1948). The Aumonts sank a great deal of their own money and time into the trouble-plagued picture, which did not reach most theater screens until 1949. The public proved indifferent to the confused romantic adventure and it was a complete flop. By then, the couple had relocated to France, where Jean-Pierre built a strong screen career. Occasionally he costarred with Maria in pictures such as *Hans Le Marin* (1949). But none of her European-made features recaptured her former screen glory.

In September 1951, Maria returned from picturemaking in Italy. She was in her Paris home with her sisters, Anita and Teresita, as houseguests. On that fateful day, she adjourned to her daily (extremely) hot midday bath to soak in reducing salts. When Montez did not reappear in a reasonable length of time, her siblings investigated. They found her submerged in the tub, with only her forehead above water. She had suffered a fatal heart seizure. (Unsubstantiated rumors have persisted over the decades that Maria, fearful of growing old, committed suicide.)

So ended the legend of narcissistic Montez, who had exclaimed on more than one occasion, "When I look at myself I am so beautiful I scream with joy." A diva in life and on-screen, her creed was "You must always act as if you are the most beautiful and desirable woman in the world. You must demand to be treated as a queen, and you must not let any directors intimidate you because the public has the last word."

Demi Moore

[Demetria Gene Guynes]
NOVEMBER 11, 1962–

In the early twenty-first century, such Hollywood actresses as Julia Roberts were claiming whopping $20 million paychecks per movie

Demi Moore at the Academy Awards in 1992.
(Photo by Albert L. Ortega)

star husband Bruce Willis were one of the movie colony's most powerful couples. The duo had expensive, elaborate pads in Los Angeles; Hailey, Idaho; and New York City. They reveled in the lavish lifestyle of the super rich and famous, buoyed by a large support staff at their beck and call.

At her popular peak, Moore was considered one of the American film industry's most influential women. It seemed there was nothing that control-happy Moore couldn't obtain. Exceedingly ambitious, she was nicknamed in the film colony "Gimme Moore." (She was also known for being abrasive, demanding, and temperamental. Explained Demi, "Certain people say I'm a real bitch, but I don't care because I know that what I fight for is something I feel strongly about.") At the time, it appeared likely that she would climb even higher in the entertainment business. She was already thinking of directing films as well. The five-foot, five-inch, smoky-voiced actress acknowledged, "I want it all."

The future star was born in 1962 in Roswell, New Mexico. Her mother, Virginia King, had been abandoned by Charles Harmon after a two-month marriage and, three months after infant Demetria's birth, she married Daniel Guynes, a newspaper advertising salesman. (Moore would not learn these facts about her parentage for years to come.) Named for a product in a beauty magazine, she would have one younger sibling, brother Morgan. Her teenaged parents nicknamed their skinny daughter Demmie. Because of Daniel's gambling and drinking habits, the family moved more than thirty times in the

assignment. However, when Moore received a $12.5 million salary for *Striptease* in 1996, she became Tinseltown's then highest-priced female luminary. As such, she and her super-

coming years, living largely in poverty. In childhood, Demmie suffered from recurring kidney infections and, at twelve, she had corrective surgery to repair a crossed right eye. In the mid-1970s, Virginia (who also often drank too much) and Daniel divorced. The couple remarried soon after but divorced again in 1977. (In 1980, Daniel committed suicide.) Meanwhile, Virginia took her daughter to live in West Hollywood, California.

Demetria, who had condensed her name to Demi (French for "half") and insisted that it be pronounced DUH-mee, entered Fairfax High, where she sampled such pastimes as smoking marijuana, drinking liquor, and downing prescription drugs. She quit school at sixteen, moved in with a boyfriend named Tom, and worked for a collection agency. Soon she was pursuing a new romance with Freddy Moore, a married musician who was fourteen years her senior. By now, she dreamed of becoming an actress and took acting lessons. She also modeled, which included showing "a little cleavage" for the cover of *Oui* magazine. In 1980, Demi and Freddy Moore wed and she became Demi Moore.

She got her first acting break on an episode of the TV series *Vega$* in 1980. This led to work in the low-budget feature *Choices* (1981). Then Moore beat out many other actresses for the role of Jackie Templeton, a feisty young reporter, on the daytime TV drama *General Hospital*. She made a strong impression on viewers and gained prominence on the show. Her husband claimed later that during this period Demi was hardly ever home and that she drank too much in her off-hours. Already

restless for "the next thing," Demi left *General Hospital* in the spring of 1983. She flew to South America to make *Blame It on Rio* (1984), in which she had a topless scene on a beach. By the time *No Small Affair* (1984) was released, she and Freddy Moore had divorced.

Director Joel Schumacher first spotted Demi riding her motorcycle in Los Angeles, and he tested and then hired her for *St. Elmo's Fire* (1985). In ironic casting, Moore's character was heavily into drugs. At the time, Demi was having her own substance abuse problems and Schumacher soon fired her from the picture. She begged for a second chance, promising she would immediately go into rehab. He agreed and she was back in the production. When released, the picture was the ultimate Brat Pack showcase, and Moore joined the privileged company of Rob Lowe, Ally Sheedy, Andrew McCarthy, Judd Nelson, and other twenty-somethings popular at the time. She began a three-year relationship with Emilio Estevez, another of the Brat Packers in the film. The couple announced their engagement, but their marriage was postponed repeatedly. The relationship ended in August 1987 after Emilio introduced Demi to an actor friend, Bruce Willis. She and Bruce (seven years her senior and the costar of the TV series *Moonlighting*) quickly became an item.

Besides appearing in such films as *About Last Night . . .* (1986) with Rob Lowe, workaholic Moore made her stage debut in the off-Broadway production of *The Early Girl* (October 1986). Demi and Bruce wed in Las Vegas in November 1987. Two weeks after their civil ceremony at the Golden Nugget Hotel-

Casino, they were remarried on a soundstage at the Burbank Studio. Rock 'n' roll singer Little Richard officiated at the ceremony. (The shindig was said to have cost $875,000.)

Before long, the newlyweds moved into a $2 million, two-story home on Malibu's Carbon Beach. They became favorites of the supermarket papers, with no part of their personal life sacred from tabloid coverage. Their first child, Rumer Glenn, was born in August 1988. Demi was constantly seen breast-feeding her child in public.

In the unmemorable film *We're No Angels* (1989), husky-voiced Moore sported a becoming new short hairstyle. The following year, she and Willis (his career in high gear thanks to 1988's *Die Hard*) bought an $8 million triplex penthouse apartment in Manhattan overlooking Central Park West. Within the fourteen-room expanse, she housed her $2 million

*B*eing a star with clout has its perks, as illustrated by these incidents from Demi's career:

- When Demi was asked to participate in the New York premiere of *A Few Good Men* (1992), the studio volunteered to send a private jet to Idaho to take Moore to Manhattan. Because of her large number of bags—none of which could be stacked on top of one another—the producers had to order a second plane for her luggage.

- Conscientious to a fault, when Moore screened footage of her project *The Scarlet Letter* (1995), she concluded that she was a victim of a bad hair day. She insisted the sequence be reshot—at a cost of $50,000.

- During the making of the animated feature *The Hunchback of Notre Dame* (1996) at the Disney Studio in Burbank, California, Moore—who was providing the voice of the heroine, Esmeralda—informed the producers that it was necessary for her to participate in an upcoming PTA gathering. The executives readily agreed to supply her with round-trip transportation to the meeting. Only then did it come to light that the PTA get-together was back in Idaho. The shuttling cost the studio $4,500 for a private jet.

- Demi also had air-control problems during the making of *G.I. Jane* (1997). Her personal retinue included several nannies for her children; a cook; a hairdresser; a makeup artist; and, of course, a personal assistant. Her support staff was so huge that the studio hired a second jet to accommodate everyone.

collection of antique dolls. In addition, the famous duo acquired an abode in the mountains near Hailey, Idaho. Also in 1990, Demi costarred with Patrick Swayze in the feel-good love story *Ghost*. She was, according to its director, "difficult and frustrating" on the set. The tearjerker became a huge success, and her fee per picture jumped to $2.5 million. By the end of the year, *People* magazine named Demi (pregnant with her second child) and Bruce "Hollywood's Hottest Couple."

Rated "a tough broad" by the film community—one who is "gutsy enough to take on all comers"—she coproduced *Mortal Thoughts* (1991) with Willis as her costar. During filming, she had the initial director discharged because "what he's getting was not what I was wanting." On *The Butcher's Wife* (1991), the coscripter said of Demi, "She had a strong conception of her role that wasn't up for discussion." Much more noteworthy than her film appearances that year was her daring pose for the cover of the August 1991 issue of *Vanity Fair*; she was naked, except for an earring. The very pregnant celebrity had one hand covering her breasts and the other beneath her bulging belly. The controversial shot made Demi the talk of America. Meanwhile, she had given birth in July 1991 to her second daughter, Scout LaRue.

By now, Moore was widely known as being a perfectionist and totally goal oriented. She played the female leads in *A Few Good Men* (1992), *Indecent Proposal* (1993), and *Disclosure* (1994). In 1994, she and Bruce became parents of their third daughter, Tallulah Belle.

While Demi was rapidly climbing the Hollywood ladder, her mother was tumbling down the social scale. Frequently arrested on drunk-driving charges, getting into barroom arguments and worse, she'd posed nude in 1993—at age forty-nine—for a girlie magazine, trading on her daughter's famous cover pose. After that episode, Demi stopped speaking to her mother for five years, reconciling only shortly before Virginia's death in mid-1998 of lung cancer.

Moore was seen infrequently in Hollywood in 1995, but she was highly visible in Idaho. Outside Hailey (population 5,500), she and Bruce had a twenty-five-acre estate. In the old mining town, the celebrity couple owned and renovated the only movie house; built a retail and office center building; and earmarked $1.5 million to renovate a honky-tonk bar into The Mint, a restaurant/club where Bruce often jammed with visiting musicians. Among other envisioned projects was a doll museum to house Demi's prized collection. To celebrate Bruce's fortieth birthday in 1995, Demi spared no expense to fly in over one hundred (close) friends, so the celebrities could tour the couple's estate and town and toast the actor at a big party.

While she was busily ruling over her Idaho fiefdom, things were not going well with her movie career. She made Nathaniel Hawthorne's *The Scarlet Letter* (1995), changing the classic's famed ending to a happy one. She reasoned, "Not many people have read the book." The film was a bomb. Next she played a stripper in the much-lambasted *Striptease*

(1996), which revealed quite a bit of her amazingly buff figure, but moviegoers stayed away. Moore shaved her head for *G.I. Jane* (1997), but the service drama did not justify its $50 million budget.

On the home front, following years of rumored breakups and reconciliations, Bruce and Demi separated in June 1998. They halted their Hailey projects and ended some of their operations. Willis bought his own house not too far from the couple's original spread. It required nearly two years to reach agreement on the division of the pair's estimated $150 million holdings. By the time of their October 2000 divorce, each party was dating others. Also by then, Demi's long-completed new picture, *Passion of Mind* (2000), a psychological romantic thriller, had opened in limited release. However, the movie was panned and disappeared quickly from theaters.

By the start of the new century, her high-flying film career seemed shot, a victim of the growing backlash against her public pronouncements, her conspicuous lifestyle consumption, and a string of box-office disappointments. Increasingly, she was perceived by Hollywood and the public as an ungracious diva, one who had made blatantly bad choices in recent screen vehicles. Her punishment was to be dethroned to make way for new Tinseltown queens.

Then, growing tired of being away from filmmaking, Demi made a foray back into show business. Now she was no longer the queen bee of the film colony and had to be more flexible about her career choices. As such, she reprised her role as the voice of

Esmeralda in the direct-to-video animated feature, *The Hunchback of Notre Dame II* (2002). Moore also signed to play a villainess in the big-budget actioner *Charlie's Angels 2* (2003) as a "fallen" Angel who navigates on the wrong side of the law. On the domestic scene, Demi and ex-husband Willis, who had remained "friendly" after their divorce a few years earlier, were now being seen together increasingly in Idaho and elsewhere, usually accompanied by their three children. By this point, each of the couple's recent romances had fallen by the wayside. As had been true for the past fifteen years, Moore and Willis remained one of Hollywood's most unpredictable duos.

Mae Murray

[Marie Adrienne Koenig]
MAY 10, 1889–MARCH 23, 1965

Today she is but a sad footnote to Hollywood history, but in the early 1920s, Murray was a famous silent screen personality. Promoted as "The Girl With the Bee-Stung Lips" (suggested by the contour of her naturally puckered lips) and "The Gardenia of the Screen," she was at the pinnacle of her popularity when she teamed with John Gilbert in the extravaganza *The Merry Widow* (1925). By then, she'd already built a reputation with the public for leading an extravagant lifestyle and within the movie industry for being highly temperamental.

By the early 1930s, Mae was washed up in movies, broke, and left with distorted memories of the golden times. As time passed, she became a homeless specter who refused to acknowledge her harsh fate. In her mind, she was still at her career peak. For Murray, that long-ago *Merry Widow* waltz when she swirled ever so gracefully with John Gilbert through the crowd of soundstage extras was just yesterday.

From her earliest professional years, she played fast and loose with the facts, determined to reshape her life to fit her grandiose vision of what it should have been. She was born Marie Adrienne Koenig in 1889 (some sources claim it was 1885; she insisted the year was 1894) in Portsmouth, Virginia. She was the daughter of immigrants: Her mother was from Belgium, her father from Austria. (Later, she maintained that her dad had been Irish and her mom Italian.) Her father, an artist, died when Marie was four and her mother disappeared, perhaps returning to her homeland. The little girl was shipped to New York City to live with her grandmother, who in turn sent the youngster to convent schools. (Fanciful Mae later suggested fashionable boarding schools in Europe had been part of her youth.) Bored by the classroom, Marie dreamed of a career as a professional dancer. To fulfill her destiny, she left the boarding school near Chicago that she was attending and joined a touring show as a dancer.

In 1906, now known as Mae Murray, the five-foot, two-inch performer appeared in a Gus Edward revue. By 1908, she was part of the *Ziegfeld Follies*. In September of that year, in Hoboken, New Jersey, she wed young, wealthy William Schwenker Jr. The marriage was over by 1909. Mae returned to her first love—dancing. In and around New York City, she performed in clubs and at ballroom exhibitions. Later, she sailed to France to learn the latest dances. Back in New York, Murray performed at the Sans Souci cabaret in 1913 and 1914. In the latter year, she was hired to substitute for Irene Castle in the Broadway revue *Watch Your Step*.

When not dancing on Broadway, Mae was performing in popular cabarets. One of her frequent dance partners and good friends at the time was future film idol Rudolph Valentino. While appearing in the *Ziegfeld Follies of 1915*, she was spotted by movie executive Adolph Zukor, and he hired her to be in movies for the Jesse L. Lasky Feature Play Co. Her debut was in *To Have and to Hold* (1916), a historical drama that teamed her with handsome Wallace Reid. At age twenty-seven (or thirty-one), Mae was mature—by silent film industry standards—to be starting out as a leading lady. More important, she lacked any real training in acting and had to learn on the job. By the time she did *The Plow Girl* (1916), her screen presence had been refined by director Robert Z. Leonard, with whom she made several pictures.

A week before Christmas in 1916, Mae made headlines not for her screen work but for a bizarre marriage. On December 18, she impetuously wed New York playboy and stockbroker Jay O'Brien in front of a justice of the peace in Pasadena, California. The love match lasted a day before she called it off and

Jay returned to New York. Later, creative Mae would insist that she had been kidnapped at gunpoint from the set of *The Primrose Ring* (1917) and forced to wed O'Brien. According to her, she'd only been saved from her unwanted groom when she had fled from their wedding banquet at a Los Angeles hotel and gone into hiding. O'Brien denied the fanciful account.

By late 1917, Mae and Leonard had moved their production unit to Universal, where she made such films as *The Bride's Awakening* (1918). In June 1918, while filming *What Am I Bid?*, she and Leonard wed. The couple lived for a time in New York, where she continued her career and was now noted for playing glamour roles on screen. Her weekly salary soon skyrocketed from $1,200 to $10,000. In 1922, she and Leonard formed the Tiffany company and released their product through Metro (soon to merge into Metro-Goldwyn-Mayer). If *Peacock Alley* (1922) was a high point of her film career, she was playing an even more exciting role off camera. She and Leonard had developed a reputation as Hollywood's saucy, fun couple who entertained their friends lavishly. Murray would describe herself and Leonard as being "like golden dragonflies suspended over a swamp."

Now considered Metro's top star, Mae was teamed with John Gilbert in 1925's *The Merry Widow*. It was directed by Erich von Stroheim, a taskmaster for whom no costly production whim was too great. He and Mae clashed on a daily basis, and their escalating feud had to be mediated by the harassed studio brass. Eventually the way-over-budget,

trouble-plagued project was completed. When released, the epic and its stars were huge hits. After vacationing in Europe, Mae returned to the studio to make *The Masked Bride* (1926). By now, fame had swelled her ego to such an extent that she became nearly unmanageable and made life miserable for everyone involved with her.

During her May 1925 trip abroad, Mae had divorced Leonard in Paris, claiming he had been treating her with "marked disdain and haughty contempt." Before long, Murray met Russian David Mdivani, who claimed to be a Georgian prince. After knowing the gigolo for only three weeks, she wed him in a lavish ceremony in Beverly Hills in June 1926. Their son, Koran, was born in 1927. During this period, imperious Mae, egged on by her parasitic spouse, had walked out on her studio contract. She went abroad where, thanks to Mdivani, she went through most of her sizeable funds.

Returning to Hollywood in 1930, Mae was nearly broke. She found that because of her reputation as a troublemaker who had left her employers in the lurch, none of the major studios would deal with her. She used her remaining funds to finance a remake of *Peacock Alley*, but the new 1930 version—a talkie released independently—was poorly received. Her old pal actor/director Lowell Sherman cast Mae in *Bachelor Apartment* and *High Stakes* (both 1931 releases), but thereafter there were no more screen offers.

With Mae down on her luck and no longer of use to Mdivani, the couple divorced in October 1933. He refused to support their child, and Mae could barely make ends meet from her occasional vaudeville or radio appearances. She demanded child support from her ex-spouse and the nasty battle of wills caught the media's attention. Eventually she put her son in the keeping of a doctor and his wife, and they later won full custody of him. (By then, the boy had renounced any allegiance to Mae.)

By the late 1930s, the destitute actress was often sleeping in Central Park. Occasionally during this bleak period, she was suggested for a stage assignment, but she proved so difficult that she would be discharged. More years passed, and the much-heavier Murray, with her bleached blond hair and heavy makeup to hide the ravages of time, was still at very desperate ends. Returning to Tinseltown, she somehow became acquainted with actor George Hamilton, who helped to establish her in a modest apartment. Mae's ghostwritten, fanciful autobiography (*The Self-Enchanted*) was published in 1959.

In summer 1960, Mae had a stroke. It left her even more detached from reality as she rode busses back and forth between Los Angeles and New York, insistent that she was still a major luminary. In early 1964, she took refuge in a St. Louis Salvation Army shelter, thinking she was once again in Manhattan. The shelter paid for Murray's return to Los Angeles, where she was admitted to the Motion Picture

Mae Murray and Roy D'Arcy in *The Merry Widow* (1925). (Courtesy of JC Archives)

Country Home. Still engulfed in self-delusion, she passed away in March 1965.

Through her last decades, delusional Murray insisted she was still a celebrity. She reasoned, "You don't have to keep making movies to remain a star. Once you become a star, you are always a star." Years earlier, when she saw *Sunset Boulevard* (1950) with Gloria Swanson as a faded silent film legend who went mad, Mae supposedly remarked, "None of us floozies was ever that nuts."

Vera Ralston

[Vera Helena Hruba]

JUNE 12, 1919–

According to Vera Ralston in 1950, "A girl in the Olympics was jealous of me. She put laxative in my food. . . . I saw one star pull a knife on another. . . . They put needles in your skates, they foul up your zippers, they take nickels and dull your blades so that you'll break a leg, maybe. Everything goes—even spiders in your underwear. It's Hades, darling." Even decades ago the world of competitive figure skating was a deadly jungle. (For example, when asked what would have happened if she and more famous skating rival Sonja Henie had ever been on the same ice rink together, Ralston retorted, "They would have to lock us in separate cages—like tigers.") Having grown up in the cutthroat world of sports—not to mention standing up to Adolf Hitler at the 1936 Olympics in Germany—Vera should have been inured to Tinseltown's fierce dog-eat-dog lifestyle. However, she learned the hard way about the lurking viciousness in the film business when she transitioned to moviemaking in 1941 and became the long-term pet project of a Hollywood movie mogul. She endured endless scoffs and cruel jokes behind her back from coworkers. They and others whispered that only her special relationship with Republic Pictures's studio head Herbert Yates accounted for her remaining in pictures year after year after year. The fledgling screen personality quickly gained the reputation as "the actress most damned by the critics." Later, she became the subject of a virulent, highly publicized attack by stockholders angered by her (in)direct cost to the studio's financial bottom line. Vera, who loved diamonds and furs, chose to ignore the grapevine and "bravely" smiled (some thought her mode was haughty) in the face of continuing criticism about her acting abilities and her frequently unprofitable screen vehicles.

She was born Vera Helena Hruba (pronounced roo-BAH) in 1919 (she insisted the year was 1923) in Prague, Czechoslovakia, the daughter of wealthy jeweler Rudolf Hruba and his wife, Marie. (The couple's firstborn, Rudolf, was two at the time.) As part of the Catholic girl's privileged upbringing, she took ballet lessons. Although she was double-jointed, it did not help her to become a better-than-average dance student. In 1932, her brother taught her to ice skate. She became obsessed with perfecting her skills in the sport. Meanwhile, as the Nazi regime grew more dangerous to European peace, her politically minded father instilled in his children a fierce pride in being Czech. Hoping that Vera's skating talents would reflect well on their country, he spared no expense in paying for the best teachers. During the summers of 1934 and 1935, she trained in London, where she not only won prizes but also learned English.

Teenaged Vera was her country's entry in the skating events of the 1936 Olympics, which were held at Garmisch-Partenkirchen. As host of the Olympics, German Fuehrer Adolf Hitler was embarrassed that the fatherland lacked a top-notch woman figure skater. The dictator sent for Vera, asking her to represent Germany by skating under his country's flag. She looked the feared leader in the eyes and bravely said, "I would rather skate *on* it than *for* it." Later, during the preliminaries, when she passed by his reviewing box, she refused to offer the expected "Heil Hitler" salute, instead giving him a token nod. In the events, it was Norway's Sonja Henie who won the gold medal, while Vera received the silver.

In 1937, Rudolf Hruba chaperoned his daughter to the United States, where she appeared successfully in ice revues along the eastern seaboard. While performing in New York City, RKO (eager to duplicate Twentieth Century-Fox's success with Sonja Henie pictures) offered her a film contract. She refused because she was going home to wed one of her wealthy suitors. However, back in Prague, the engagement fell apart because his Jewish family and her Catholic parents did not approve of the interfaith love match. In the winter of 1939, the Germans moved into Czechoslovakia and soon occupied Prague. Vera and her mother fled on literally the last plane to leave the city. (Her brother was later smuggled out of the country; her father was incarcerated and tortured by the Nazis but was later released when a signed photo of the Fuehrer posing with Vera was uncovered and it was assumed Hruba was pro-Nazi after all.)

The nearly penniless Vera and her mother made their way to America. Hruba found work in figure skating and eventually joined the Ice Capades. The revue was hired by meat-and-potatoes Republic Pictures to appear in a film. Thus, as part of the troupe, Vera made her screen debut in *Ice-Capades* (1941). This was followed by *Ice-Capades Revue* (1942). With her longish nose, thin face, thick lips, athletic build, and thick accent, she was not ideal screen material. However, sixty-three-year-old studio chieftain Herbert J. Yates was smitten with five-foot, five-inch, blue-eyed Vera and put the fair-haired Slav under long-term contract, grooming her for stardom. She took acting and diction lessons and acquired the new surname Ralston (borrowed from a popular breakfast cereal). She appeared in *The Lady and the Monster* (1944), but it was legendary screen villain Erich von Stroheim who provided the feature's chief interest. *Dakota* (1945) was the first of her several Westerns for the studio, which specialized in horse operas. (Although she learned to ride horseback, stunt doubles always performed her perilous riding stunts.) Her final movie to have a skating theme was *Murder in the Music Hall* (1946).

Vera Ralston and John Wayne in *Dakota* (1945).
(Courtesy of JC Archives)

That same year, she removed Hruba from her professional name, tired of people calling her everything from "rumba" to "rhubarb."

Occasionally, she had a good screen showcase (as with 1948's *I, Jane Doe*), but many of her movies (for example, 1948's *Angel on the Amazon*) were unredeemable clinkers in which she was badly miscast as the fetching American heroine. It was bad enough that the critics were often merciless to her, but her lack of acting acumen and her reputation for appearing in stinkers made several leading men avoid being teamed with her on camera. For instance, Yates had to bribe John Wayne, who had gritted his teeth through *Dakota*, to make *The Fighting Kentuckian* (1949) with her. After that, nothing could induce the Duke to make another picture with Vera. But Ralston seemingly didn't mind; she was under a lucrative long-term contract and in her rosy-tinged view of life, everyone—cast, crew, and the public—really loved her.

Vera called Yates "Baby" and to him, she was "Sweetie." However, it was not until 1947 that Herbert separated from his wife of thirty years (by whom he had four children). Meanwhile, not since William Randolph Hearst made actress Marion Davies his protégée and mistress, had Hollywood seen such a lavish case of favoritism. Nothing was too good for Vera, who became the recipient of a grand lifestyle. By 1952, Yates had finally negotiated a divorce and then, as he phrased it, he "signed a new contract with his favorite cinemactress." Despite what the film colony or the public thought, Vera insisted then and later, "To me, he was everything. He was my boyfriend, my lover, my husband, and my left hand." The movie crowd was also amused that high-stepping Vera, who lived in a mansion filled with art treasures (many of them first having appeared in Republic pictures), had a thrifty side to her nature: "I don't believe in throwing money around. I buy half a cow and put it in the deep freeze. That way I save twenty cents on a pound of beef. . . . My home in Hollywood is entirely floored in marble. This way I save on carpets."

In 1955, not long after the release of *Jubilee Trail*, the elaborate 1954 Western that featured

Ralston, disgruntled stockholders of Republic Pictures Corporation demanded a committee be appointed to examine the company's financial operations. At the annual stockholders' meeting, the rebelling investors snidely wondered if true information could be obtained since nepotism ran so rampant at the studio, extending "even to Yates's actress wife." In October 1956, two minority stockholders filed suit against Yates and his studio executives claiming, among other charges, that Republic was promoting Ralston "to the loss and detriment of the company." (It was alleged that most of her pictures had failed to earn back their costs.) The embarrassing suits dragged on for years. Meanwhile, in 1958—shortly after Vera's latest celluloid showcase dud, *The Man Who Died Twice*, opened and closed—Yates severed all connections to Republic and its affiliate businesses, gaining a favorable settlement in the process.

He and Vera (now retired from pictures) relaxed at their Sherman Oaks and Santa Barbara, California, homes and enjoyed a privileged life, including trips abroad. The couple temporarily separated in 1962 but later reconciled, and she was with him when he died of a heart attack in 1966. Thereafter, she moved permanently to Santa Barbara where, in June 1973, she married a local businessman. The couple proudly grew avocados, which she jubilantly sold each year for a small profit.

Looking back on her generally undistinguished but lucrative film career, Ralston would say, "If you give a cook an egg and water what can she do with it? Not very much. It's the same thing with an actress."

Joan Rivers

[Joan Alexandra Molinsky]
JUNE 8, 1933–

As the women's movement began promoting gender equality in 1960s America, Rivers burst onto the entertainment scene. She was then a rarity, a woman in the man's world of stand-up comedy. Her persona of choice was that of Jewish American Princess (JAP), a comical extension of her ethnic upbringing in the New York suburbs.

A stereotypical JAP is a pampered, status-conscious girl whose self-indulgence knows no boundaries. In extreme cases, this type of shallow diva is a spoiled brat, a materialistic female who, from cradle to grave, never knowingly lifts a finger to help another—in short, someone to be avoided at all costs and typically *not* funny at all. However, Joan smartly riffed on the caricature. On stage, she posited herself as an unmarried Jewish miss whose physical flaws and poor application of JAP tenets made her a wallflower (for example, "My parents had a big sign, 'Last girl before thruway' "). As Joan gained increasing favor with amused audiences, the line between Rivers the real person and Joan the JAP blurred. For many, this funny lady became synonymous with the worst characteristics of the Jewish American Princess.

By the 1970s Rivers was an international favorite, which gave her great confidence in the limelight. In her stand-up act—and in her gigs as a TV talk show host—the five-foot, two-inch talent became more caustic about others, especially when skewering the negative characteristics of celebrities. For example, "You know, once they're dead, death just scrubs [celebrities] clean. Everybody says, 'Oh, they were wonderful.' Suddenly, Grace Kelly didn't drink." Or "Liz Taylor should be grateful to me—my jokes are one of the reasons she went on a diet. It was embarrassing. When I took her to Sea World and Shamu the Whale jumped out of the water, she asked if it came with vegetables." Thus, the Jewish American Princess, who was constantly refining her look through plastic surgery and diet, had become a biting jokester who no longer used herself as her chief target. Audiences knew that when "The Mouth" said her rhetorical "Can we talk?" they were in for a barrage of funny but stinging commentary. Rivers had become a diva with fangs.

Joan Alexandra Molinksy was born in 1933 in Brooklyn. She was the younger of two daughters (the older was Barbara) born to Meyer Molinksy, a physician, and his wife, Beatrice Grushman. Both parents were Russian Jewish refugees. Joan's sense of humor—and she needed one to deal with her parents' constant bickering—came from her father. As a toddler, she learned to make people laugh with imitations of her dad's patients. Meanwhile, even though money was tight for the family in the Depression years, her determined mother made sure that both daughters took piano, violin, and elocution lessons. To overcome shyness and a sense of being an outsider, Joan joined the school drama club and tried

acting classes. She knew that entertaining others would be her life's work. When Joan learned a movie (1951's *Mr. Universe*) was to shoot partially in New York City, she wangled an extra's role for herself.

By the time Joan graduated high school, her family had relocated to suburban Larchmont. After graduating from Barnard College in 1954 and being pressured by her parents to become financially self-sufficient, she put her show-business ambitions on hold to work in the department store retail business. In 1957, although she really loved an ex-boyfriend, she married James Sanger, the son of the merchandise manager at Bonds, the store where she was employed. However, as she quipped later, "Our marriage license turned out to be a learner's permit." The union was annulled after six months. She then began her show-business career in earnest.

Initially, Joan had no luck with her auditions for Broadway shows. Instead, she turned to stand-up comedy to pay her bills. Later, however, she made her Broadway debut in the revue *Talent '60* (1960). The following year, she joined the Chicago-based Second City improvisational troupe. Thereafter, back in New York City, she performed her comedy routines in clubs. Her gigs were interspersed with steadier work as writing comedy material for Phyllis Diller, Zsa Zsa Gabor, and others. Finally, after many failed attempts to be booked on TV's *The Tonight Show Starring Johnny Carson*, she appeared there successfully on February 17, 1965. It started a long working association with Carson and his late-night forum. During this upbeat period, she met British-born film and TV writer/coordinator/producer Edgar Rosenberg. He was not only bright and cultured but the forty-year-old also respected her talents and enjoyed pampering her. They married in July 1965 and he became her agent and manager. In between club work, appearing on national TV variety shows, and recording her first comedy album, she gave birth in January 1968 to a baby girl the couple named Melissa. That fall, Joan headlined the syndicated TV program *That Show Starring Joan Rivers*, which lasted into 1969.

Joan coauthored and also starred in a short-lasting Broadway comedy (*Fun City*) in 1972. She had greater success playing major clubs in Las Vegas and elsewhere. By 1973, the Rosenbergs had purchased a twelve-room residence in swanky Bel-Air, California. At home, Rivers was waited on hand and foot; on the comedy trail, she was treated with deference and audiences everywhere gave her the best gift of all—they laughed heartily at her jokes. She authored the bestselling *Having a Baby Can Be a Scream* (1974), the first of her several books and memoirs. Joan directed and coscripted the movie *Rabbit Test* (1978), did TV commercials, had her own line of acerbic comic greeting cards, and was named permanent guest host of *The Tonight Show Starring Johnny Carson* in 1983.

Edgar had a massive heart attack in 1984 and he was never the same afterward. The stress on Joan and their daughter was tremendous. Two years later, Rivers was offered her

Joan Rivers in the late 1970s.
(Courtesy of JC Archives)

own talk show on the fledgling Fox TV network. She accepted not only for the $5 million annual salary but also as a project to keep her husband (as the program's executive producer) occupied. When Johnny Carson learned of her defection from *The Tonight Show*, he refused to ever speak with her again. The feud accelerated and, to many onlookers who didn't know all the facts, it seemed that an ungrateful Joan had been grossly unfair to the benevolent Carson. Trying to offset the unflattering publicity from the feud, Joan quipped, "I've been a tabloid tootsie"; claimed, "There's *no* fight"; and wailed, "I wanted it to end nicely—I'm a lady, my mother brought me up right."

The Late Show with Joan Rivers debuted on October 9, 1986, and initially was popular with TV viewers. However, when the novelty wore off, the program's viewership base slipped. As the ratings dropped further, Joan grew increasingly tense and worried. When her bosses pulled away more artistic control from her and Rosenberg, Edgar retaliated with counterdemands on Joan's behalf (as well as his own notions). By spring 1987, Joan was given an ultimatum: Either Edgar goes or you both go. She chose the latter and was fired on May 15, 1987.

Adding to her woes, Rosenberg committed suicide three months later in his hotel room while on a business trip to Philadelphia. On the audiotape he made for his wife shortly before overdosing with pills, he said, "I know you'll get through this, Joan, because you're strong. I know you'll be just fine." But Rivers was not so sure. When the shock from Edgar's death wore off, she discovered that (1) daughter Melissa had turned her grief and anger at her father's "desertion" against Joan, (2) her major club bookings had dried up because no one wanted to present a comedian whose spouse had just killed himself, and (3) her finances were in a sorry state.

As described in Joan's 1997 book, *Bouncing Back*, her return to mainstream success was slow and painful. At the time, much of the public had a perception of Rivers as a middle-aged Jewish American Princess. They felt that, although she'd suffered bad breaks recently, she was still a coddled celebrity living a plush existence. It took time for her to live down this negative image. She rebounded with the syndicated daytime TV talk show *The Joan Rivers Show* (1989–93). This was followed by a cable TV gossip program and a successful showcase on a shopping cable network for her line of manufactured jewelry. She had long since sold the Beverly Hills mansion and now had a chic Manhattan apartment. She and daughter Melissa reconciled and forged a relationship as "best friends." In fact, they frequently cohost TV fashion commentary specials and celebrity interviews attached to entertainment industry award shows. Having regained financial security, Joan gifted her daughter with a very pricey wedding in December 1998. (By 2002 that union had soured and the couple, parents of a baby boy, had filed for divorce.)

During the period after Joan was widowed, she quipped, "At my age, I don't really go out anymore. It's not nice." However, over the following years, she did date an assortment of older men but didn't have a permanent relationship. She has continued her privileged lifestyle and undergone further plastic surgery, and still performs her comedy act in prime venues. Of her roller-coaster professional life, Rivers has said, "Nothing has ever come easily for me. My whole career has been just hard, hurting little steps." As to her many setbacks in life, she noted, "Whatever doesn't kill you makes you stronger. And always remember: Surviving is the best revenge." Regarding her decades-long reputation as an extremely demanding person (in front of and away from audiences), she observed, "I've yet to meet one person who got to the top with generosity."

Julia Roberts

[Julia Fiona Roberts]
OCTOBER 28, 1967–

When one earns $20 million per picture—the highest paid to date to a female Hollywood star—and has won an Academy Award (plus two other nominations), a celebrity must have more than mere talent and beauty. She needs grit to push through the Tinseltown jungle to such success. In developing her hard shell, touchy Roberts has said, "I don't like having to explain myself. I resent having to make it comfortable for other people to understand. My job is not being in the public eye. My job is acting."

Over the years, Julia has displayed volatility on and off the set. (For example, she was nicknamed "Tinkerhell" when she played Tinkerbell in 1991's *Hook*.) Roberts also fostered an ongoing rebellious streak: "My mannerisms and whatever I do is spontaneous and unaffected. It will not be controlled by what people think or say, or what they like. If somebody tells me they like something I probably won't do it anymore." Having achieved fame, the toughened luminary admitted, "I don't question the reasons for my success. I'm not curious about it. I don't need to know that and I don't concern myself with that." (She also didn't question when she felt "a hostile

moment coming on" and snapped at journalists in the pressroom at the 2002 People's Choice Awards.)

She was born in Smyrna, Georgia, in 1967, the youngest of three children (two girls and one boy) of Walter Roberts and his wife, Betty Lou Brademus. Both parents wanted to be actors and, by the time of Julia's birth, were operating the Actors and Writers Workshop in the Atlanta area. By 1972, Walter and Betty Lou, worn out by their career struggles and personal problems, had divorced. Lisa and Julia lived with their mother, who became a secretary, while Eric remained with their father, who became a vacuum cleaner salesman at an Atlanta department store. While both her siblings knew immediately they wanted to become actors, Julia thought of becoming a veterinarian. However, in high school, she developed an interest in film as an art form and decided to pursue acting. A few days after graduation, she moved to New York City and stayed with her sister. Five-foot, nine-inch Julia, with her toothy, radiant smile, took modeling assignments to support herself and attended acting classes. In 1986, Roberts got her first screen assignment thanks to brother Eric, who had been making movies for seven years. She played the small role of his sister in the low-budget entry *Blood Red*, which did not see release until 1988. (In subsequent years, Julia and Eric—who had a reputation as an explosive, angry young man—stopped speaking and she would no longer discuss him or his part in her early film career.) A few TV assignments followed, leading to the movie *Satisfaction* (1988). During the making of this lightweight entry, she began a relationship with a coplayer, Irish-born Liam Neeson, who was fifteen years her senior. The romance ended after several months, remaining a painful chapter that Neeson refuses to discuss publicly.

Meanwhile, also in 1988, Julia had a breakthrough role in *Mystic Pizza*. Her high visibility in that sleeper hit led to her being cast in *Steel Magnolias* (1989) as the dying daughter of Sally Fields's character. Despite a cast that also included Shirley MacLaine and Dolly Parton, it was Roberts who stood out in *Steel Magnolias* and she received a Best Supporting Actress Oscar nomination. She also found a new romance with rising young actor Dylan McDermott, who played her husband in the screen drama. The couple got engaged. Then suddenly, the relationship ended.

By the time of 1990's *Pretty Woman*, a role Julia fought hard to get, she had already begun participating in the Hollywood ritual of hiring and firing representatives, citing the usual "We'd outgrown each other." With *Pretty Woman*, she won an Academy Award nomination—this time in the Best Actress category—for portraying the Hollywood hooker with a heart of gold melted by leading man Richard Gere. In her other 1990 release, *Flatliners*, she found a new boyfriend in costar Kiefer Sutherland. They were a couple by the time the shoot was over, but soon afterward workaholic Roberts was off making another picture. She then visited him in New Mexico, where he was filming *Young Guns II* (1990). On her birthday, she stopped by a tattoo artist to have a design (a red heart inside a Chinese word picture) etched on her skin. Roberts insisted, "My love for Kiefer will last as long as this tattoo." By then, he'd finalized his divorce from his current wife, an actress, with whom he'd had a daughter.

As of *Sleeping with the Enemy* (1991), Julia's career was picking up speed. Already in her rush to success, she'd developed a reputation for being one tough cookie. Said a coworker, "You can always tell when Julia's really mad because her eyes narrow down and her chin juts out. Believe me, if she's angry, you know it." She was also accustomed to getting her way. For example, while filming a tough sequence for the suspense picture, she had to spend several hours in front of the cameras in only bra and panties being repeatedly doused with water and then dried off as the scene was shot over and over. Worn out by the situation, she demanded that anyone in the crew who wouldn't strip down to his or her underwear could leave the set. She got her way.

Having bought a $1.5 million home in the Nichols Canyon area of Los Angeles, her live-in companion there was Kiefer. When interviewed on Barbara Walters's pre-Oscar special in March 1991, Roberts told the famed TV personality, "Kiefer is probably the most wonderful, understanding person I have ever met." Soon, however, there were rumors of a rift in their relationship, although the couple announced they would wed that June 14. Meanwhile, the gossip continued that Sutherland was having an affair with a Hollywood stripper he'd met while Roberts had been out of town filming. Nevertheless, plans for the nuptials to be held on a soundstage at Twenti-

Syndicated columnist Liz Smith once wrote of Roberts, "I think it would be great if she concentrated on her career and not on the men in her life." At the time of Julia's great romance with actor Kiefer Sutherland in the early 1990s, the radiant actress insisted that this was "Forever love. I believe in that, and I believe this is it. We live together and we are happy and we are in love with each other—isn't that what being married is?" Perhaps, but the couple decided to wed anyway. However, a few days before the planned nuptials, one or the other or both had a change of heart and called off the wedding. Two years later—during which time she'd dated actors Jason Patric and Daniel Day-Lewis—Roberts was scheduled to marry country music star Lyle Lovett. With her past track record, members of the groom's family were worried. "Oh Lord," said Lovett's cousin "Please don't let her back out because that'd break his heart." Even the bride-to-be didn't trust herself and convinced the groom to move the wedding up a few days. The union ended less than two years later.

By late 1997, Roberts was dating Benjamin Bratt, a colead on TV's *Law & Order*. She gushed, "I realized immediately that he is someone who will always challenge me in that great way that keeps you moving forward in your life. His presence raises the quality of my life." However, forever was not forever and the couple split in June 2001. Her batting average in real-life romance and marriage seems remarkably similar to those of her on-screen heroines in *My Best Friend's Wedding* (1997) and *The Runaway Bride* (1999).

Given that Roberts had used superlatives before to describe her man of the moment, it was no surprise when, after marrying cameraman Danny Moder in July 2002, she extolled her recently-divorced-beau-turned-groom to the media as "a man among men, unselfish, and all-encompassing." The superstar insisted that she and Danny were fated to be together and effused, "I hope that there are people who agree that I have done some good, kind things in my life, but to really, ultimately, stand fully in a moment of realizing that I was born to love and to be the wife of this man. . . . " When asked about the rumors that Moder's ex-wife, a makeup artist, had been very reluctant to give him a divorce, Julia acknowledged that the situation had been "terribly complicated." (The tabloids had already suggested that a liberal financial settlement—mostly from Roberts's funds—had been made for the former Mrs. Moder to free Danny to wed Julia.)

eth Century-Fox went ahead, and the celebrity guest list was completed. Everything was set for the big event, from elaborate decorations to the bride-to-be's expensive gown. A few days before the much-anticipated union, the couple went out of town—but separately (he to his ranch in Montana, she reportedly with her bridesmaids to a fancy spa in Tucson). She was back in town on June 11, when it was announced that the wedding was now off. (The grapevine insisted that Roberts had either had a representative call the prospective groom with the news or that he had to find out from news reports. She insisted later that the breakup had been mutual and that, in fact, Kiefer had instituted it.)

Things got spicier for Julia. On the day the wedding was to have occurred, she enjoyed a cozy dinner at a trendy West Hollywood restaurant. Her companion was Sutherland's good friend, actor Jason Patric. The next day, the new couple flew to Dublin, Ireland. Their romance continued over the following months, but now Roberts refused to discuss her personal relationships with the media. By mid-January 1993, the Julia-Jason connection was broken, following a loud fight the agitated couple had inside and then on the street outside his Hollywood duplex. Reputedly, the split was triggered by his jealousy over rumors that she and actor Daniel Day-Lewis had become cozy in the autumn of 1992 when the two were negotiating to star in *Shakespeare in Love* (which was repackaged with another cast for a 1999 release).

Although Julia and country singer Lyle Lovett each had cameos in *The Player* (1992), they met while she was filming *The Pelican Brief* (1993) in New Orleans. Craggy, low-key Lyle was noted for his musicianship, not his good looks. This made his sudden marriage to beautiful, high-energy Julia in late June 1993 all the more surprising to both the media and the public. Rather than embark on a honeymoon after the ceremony, she returned to the set of her current picture. Her next offering was *I Love Trouble* (1994), which truly described the lack of rapport on the set between Julia and costar Nick Nolte. When

Julia Roberts promoting *Ocean's Eleven* (2001). (Photo by Albert L. Ortega)

released the problem-plagued feature tanked. Her personal life also hit a low point. On March 28, 1995, she and Lyle issued a statement about their recent split, insisting, "We remain close and in great support of one another." Many observers said the union was doomed by her heavy-duty career orientation, which left too little time for them to be a couple.

By 1997, Julia's film career was back in high gear with the romantic comedy *My Best Friend's Wedding* and the thriller *Conspiracy Theory*. She also began a relationship with actor Benjamin Bratt, then costarring in the TV series *Law & Order*. From a close-knit family, Bratt grew up in San Francisco where he became a dedicated actor. Said Roberts, "He's very good-looking, and his handsomeness pales in comparison to his kindness." In 1999, before he left his series to concentrate on feature films, Julia guest-starred on an episode of *Law & Order*. In 2000, when she had such a major success in *Erin Brockovich*—she won an Oscar for Best Actress—she said about her relationship with Benjamin, "I'm happier than I've ever been in my life." On the other hand, the industry rumor mill insisted that Bratt, who wanted to start a family, was pushing for marriage and Julia was resistant.

Then, while filming *The Mexican* (2001), Julia met cameraman Danny Moder, the son of producer Mike Moder. Reputedly, Roberts and Moder had an instant attraction despite the fact that she was dealing with her faltering relationship with Bratt and Danny was a married man (since 1997). In June 2001, Roberts and Bratt had a much-publicized split. (Benjamin went on to wed actress Talisa Soto in 2002.) Thereafter, Julia and the year-younger Danny became an open item, spending a lot of time together at her New Mexico ranch and in Hollywood. In the meantime, he was negotiating a divorce from his wife.

Orchestrating a quiet wedding to surprise her friends and family and confound the media—not to mention evening the score for ex-beau Benjamin Bratt having beat her to the marriage altar by several weeks—Julia jumped into action. She arranged to marry the now-divorced Moder just after midnight on July 4, 2002, at her secluded fifty-one acre ranch in Arroya Seco, New Mexico, near Taos. Fifty guests gathered in a tent on the spread for the late-night ceremony, which occurred during a gentle rainstorm. Later in the day the newlyweds hosted a barbecue and softball game at the ranch. Days later when she talked with the media, an unusually talkative Roberts bubbled that she and Moder "want to have a family, and we will have a family in due course and whether it's a gaggle . . . I don't know. It'd be great." Thereafter the couple drove back to Los Angeles where she was promoting her new picture 2002's *Full Frontal* and he was shooting a fast-food commercial. Once they had fulfilled their work obligations, the duo embarked on a real honeymoon—a two-night stay at a cottage at the San Ysidro Ranch in Santa Barbara.

Although career junkie Roberts—at the top of her game—continued to make new films (2002's *Confessions of a Dangerous Mind* and 2003's *Mona Lisa Smile*), she now insisted, "For the first time my personal life's going to take priority over my professional life. I've made plenty of films, now I want to make babies. They're going to be on my production schedule for the next four years."

Roseanne

[Roseanne Cherrie Barr]
NOVEMBER 3, 1952–

When this overweight stand-up comic—who stands five feet, four inches tall—burst onto the national scene in the mid-1980s, she was a refreshing newcomer. Touting herself as a domestic goddess (that is, a homemaker) who had gripes with family and life in general, she was a humorous spokesperson for the blue-collar class. She referred to herself as "trailer trash" and entertained audiences with her wry perspective on the battle of the genders. That robust persona came before her makeover into Roseanne, the furious center-of-attention of the hit TV sitcom *Roseanne* (1988–97).

In the 1990s, the world was treated to a "new" Roseanne, the notorious arbiter of bad taste—especially during her stormy, headline-grabbing marriage to stand-up comic Tom Arnold. But changes of guise should not have surprised her public. After all, as the poster lady for tackiness informed the world, she suffered from multiple personality disorder and there were over two dozen "real" hers. The comedy diva also insisted publicly that as a child she had been abused by both her parents (although this was strongly denied by her parents and some relatives). Still later in the 1990s, Roseanne emerged as a TV talk show host, but she quickly wore out her welcome with many home viewers. Despite whatever career setbacks she's had in recent years, this extremely rich, self-focused celebrity has continued on her merry way. She has always seemed unfazed that she seems to be taking on the whole world. Said the acerbic luminary, "Some people hate me 'cause I'm so ahead of my time. But I don't think I was born too soon. I think the backward people were born too late."

She was born in Salt Lake City, Utah, in 1952, one of four children of Jerry and Helen (Davis) Barr. Her parents, both Jewish, sometimes sold crucifixes door-to-door to feed their family. When Roseanne was five, she hit her head on the side of a coffee table, which led to facial paralysis. When Jewish prayers brought no improvement in her daughter's condition, Helen consulted Mormon religious authorities. After they prayed over the ailing youngster, she recovered. Mrs. Barr decided that, from then on, the family would follow Judaism from Friday to Sunday morning, while subscribing to Mormon tenets on Sunday afternoon, Tuesday, and Wednesday. This split set of beliefs confused Roseanne. (Later in life she learned that her strange ailment was Bell's palsy and that it often disappears as quickly as it comes, as in her case. The revelation increased her cynicism about life.)

Being part of one of the few Jewish families in a largely Mormon community, Roseanne felt isolated and different as a child. As an antidote to this sense of alienation, she found comfort in watching stand-up comics on TV, an enthusiasm her father shared as well. Roseanne was close to sister Geraldine and they dreamed of going to Hollywood one day to become famous in show business. Meanwhile, the future star grew up to become a teenager from hell. Rebellious and promiscuous, she constantly overstepped the boundaries set by her permissive parents.

One day in 1968, out-of-control Roseanne was walking through a traffic-congested thoroughfare in Salt Lake City. She was hit by a car and the vehicle's hood ornament pierced the back of her head. The accident left her with memory loss, a susceptibility to nightmares, and an even more rebellious attitude. Her overwhelmed parents admitted her to the Utah

State Hospital in Provo. She spent eight months at the mental institution, during which she railed against God and her parents. On release, the teenager soon dropped out of high school and, three months later, found that she was pregnant. Her parents shipped her out of conservative Salt Lake City to a home for unwed mothers in Denver, Colorado. There, in May 1971, she gave birth to a baby girl who was put up for adoption. Five days later, Roseanne returned to Salt Lake City to gather her belongings, pocket $300 in savings, and leave home.

By the fall of 1971, the roaming teenager arrived in Georgetown, Colorado, an old hippie haunt. There she met soft-spoken Bill Pentland, a night clerk at a local motel. They began a relationship and later made their home in a log cabin (complete with outhouse). Roseanne found odd jobs in town. The couple lived a bohemian existence, including smoking pot and hitchhiking around the area. They finally wed in February 1974 and moved to a low-rent trailer park, one of several homes they had in the next few years. They became the parents of Jessica in 1975, Jennifer in 1976, and Jake in 1978.

As a mother of three, Roseanne grew increasingly depressed about her life. She developed agoraphobia—a fear of public places—and went on a crash diet. By 1981, she had overcome her problems enough to go back to work, this time as a waitress in a Denver restaurant/tavern. Customers were amused by her wisecracks and urged her to try her luck with stand-up comedy at open-mike night. She liked being in front of an audience and pursued

Roseanne fielding questions at the 1994 People's Choice Awards. (Photo by Albert L. Ortega)

this vocation. Meanwhile, sister Geraldine, who was now staying with the Pentlands, became Roseanne's professional sounding board, as well as her educator about feminism. Before long, these views became part of Roseanne's act and she was winning gigs in mainstream venues. By 1983, Roseanne—who had gained a good deal of weight—was on the road, performing on the comedy club circuit.

The year 1984 found Roseanne and her family (including Geraldine) in Los Angeles, where she was booked at the Comedy Store.

This led to her debut on *The Tonight Show Starring Johnny Carson* on August 23, 1985, and subsequently to a major comedy club tour. (Husband Bill became Mr. Mom and stayed home to take care of their children.) In September 1987, she headlined her own HBO cable special, which in turn brought her to the attention of the Carsey-Werner Company. The Los Angeles–based production firm signed Roseanne to star in a new TV sitcom about a midwestern blue-collar family. *Roseanne* went on the air in October 1988 with John Goodman costarring as her hefty husband.

Roseanne was suddenly part of a big operation turning out a weekly TV show. There were immediate clashes between the brutally direct star and the program's producer, whom she felt didn't have a clue about what the show needed creatively. The clashes escalated and Roseanne vowed to make big changes once the show became a hit. When the groundbreaking comedy became a success in short order, the emboldened Roseanne told management either the producer went or she did. The executives sided with her. Now, there was no holding Roseanne back. Her battles became the talk of the TV industry, and the public was kept abreast of everything in candid, behind-the-scenes articles in major publications. Soon Roseanne was a staple of the tabloids.

In 1989, the star made her feature film debut in the little-liked *She-Devil*. That year she held a record for being on more magazine covers in one year than any other celebrity in history. However, much of the coverage exposed the rough edges in the comedian's life. She couldn't

---

During her stormy marriage (1990–94) to comedian Tom Arnold, she and Tom were dubbed "The Terrible Two," for their ongoing public war with the producers and crew of her sitcom (*Roseanne*), the media, and one another. Once the boorish couple split for good after several reconciliations failed, the comedy queen let fly her wrath at her ex-groom. Her vitriol knew no bounds, as evidenced by these pronouncements:

"Yeah, I did marry beneath me. Doesn't every woman?"

"My life would be ruined if I continued in this abusive relationship."

"Tom Arnold's penis is three inches long. Okay, I'll say four, 'cause we're trying to settle."

"I'm not upset about my divorce. I'm only upset I'm not a widow."

How did Arnold act in the "War of the Rosies"? At one point during the breakup, he told her, "Let's not have the divorce get in the way of closeness." Later, as things got really nasty between them, he took offense at her repeated allusions to the supposedly small size of his genitalia. Said Tom by way of comparison, "Even a 747 looks small when it lands in the Grand Canyon."

understand why she'd become "the most hated woman in America." Rather than undertake any self-examination, she just maintained strong resistance to the media and continued her combative ways.

On the domestic scene, she and Bill Pentland divorced in January 1990, and one of her children underwent treatment at a substance abuse center. There was also the reunion of Roseanne and her teenaged daughter Brandy, brought about when a tabloid discovered the long-ago adoption and arranged the meeting to gain exclusive coverage.

She had first met stand-up comic Tom Arnold in 1983. When her TV series went on the air, he moved to the West Coast, hoping she'd deliver on an earlier promise to find him work on the program. She did and he joined the writing staff, leading to increased dissension in that department. In the fall of 1989, Roseanne and the younger Arnold became engaged. To those around the couple, he seemed to bring out the worst in her. When she insisted her frenetic boyfriend become a recurring character on *Roseanne*, things worsened. Before long, he was not only clashing openly with others on the show but with the star herself. Part of Arnold's problem was his drug addiction. She made him go into recovery and, after he was released, they wed in January 1990. The Arnolds' wedding gift to the sitcom was to drastically overhaul the show's crew. Among the casualties was Roseanne's sister Geraldine.

Adding fuel to her usual controversy was her guest performance at a San Diego Padre baseball game in July 1990. Partway through her ragged rendition of the national anthem, she chose to counter the audience's negative response to her "singing" by scratching her crotch and spitting—like ballplayers do. Her actions, taken as very unfunny, created a national furor.

In the 1990–91 TV season, powerful Roseanne became an executive producer of her sitcom. She also changed her professional name to Roseanne Arnold. In June 1991, after Tom converted to Judaism, the couple remarried. Bragged Tom, "We're America's worst nightmare: white trash with money." By now, the Arnolds had become the couple America loved to hate, with Roseanne posing as a perpetual victim. Meanwhile, she underwent an assortment of cosmetic surgeries, including breast reduction and a face-lift. In the fall of 1993, she received her first Emmy. A few months later, there were rumors of Tom having an affair with his young production assistant, Kim Silva. The Arnolds insisted that actually the trio planned to wed. But by April 1994, Roseanne, amid new rumors of a special rapport between Tom and Kim, fired both of them from her show and filed for divorce. Saying her only regret was that she wasn't a widow, she changed her show-business name to just Roseanne.

Not appreciating the single life, Roseanne wed her fourteen-year-younger bodyguard/driver, Ben Thomas, in February 1995. Their son, Buck, was born that August. For a time, Roseanne seemed to calm down. She was busy packaging a new TV variety series (*Saturday Night Special*), which left the air after only six weeks in 1996. In April 1997, *Roseanne*'s long run ended, a ratings victim. Next, Roseanne took on the role of the Wicked Witch of the West in a stage production of *The Wizard of Oz*. Industry observers said the part was typecasting.

In January 1998, Roseanne announced she would host a new daytime talk show. She also acknowledged that she and Ben Thomas were divorcing. (They had a temporary reconciliation but divorced in March 2002.) Her gab outing fizzled in 2000. By then, she was studying Kabala (a mystical way of interpreting Scripture), had debuted as a screeching rock singer with Roseanne and the Dicks, and set up her own production facility south of Los Angeles. In the new millennium, her visibility on the entertainment scene tapered off greatly. She did, however, make an appearance on David Letterman's late-night TV talk show in May 2002. Blond and svelte, she told the host that she'd spent much of the past six months housebound, "Because I'm crazy!" She also talked about her romantic life: "I didn't know being in a relationship meant you had to be nice. I thought it meant you had to hack away at the other person until they were beaten down and then were too afraid to leave!"

Over her several years in the limelight, an outspoken, abrasive, and unique Roseanne has often washed her professional and domestic dirty linen out in the open. Sometimes the public has found these outbursts amusing or revolting (or, more frequently, baffling). Perhaps the star was quite serious when she suggested once that she wanted the following carved on her tombstone: "What the Hell Was I Thinking?"

Diana Ross

[Diane Ernestine Ross]
MARCH 26, 1944–

Over the years, several famous singing acts have been pulled apart by jealousy among members or by the poor health or death of one or more of the group. Such breakups of successful musical entities have been well depicted in films (for example, 1976's *Sparkle* and 1991's *The Five Heartbeats*). Like *Sparkle*, the 1981 Broadway musical *Dreamgirls* dealt with an African American vocalist team very similar to the Supremes. In the case of the Supremes, who became great role models for many young blacks in the 1960s, the breakup and bitterness can be charted from events leading up to the group changing its name to Diana Ross and the Supremes. By then, Ross had decided her professional future lay in becoming a solo act. Her "me-first" career move led to much bitterness among the singers, and the acrimony can still be felt today. For many fans and observers, the breakup of the Supremes was just another instance of ambitious, often-snobbish Ross exhibiting the negative sides of her character.

She was born in Detroit, Michigan, in 1944, the second of six children of Fred Ross, a brass factory worker, and his wife, Ernestine Earle. (The name on the future singer's birth certificate was meant to read Diane Ross but by error was recorded as Diana.) The family lived in a Detroit ghetto, where Diane was a tomboy. While she was still quite young, her parents separated and her mother moved her family to a government-subsidized housing project. At fourteen, Diane entered Cass Technical High School where she focused on fashion, costume design, and cosmetology. After school, she worked part-time at a Detroit department store cafeteria.

In the late 1950s, two of Diane's friends and neighbors, Florence Ballard and Mary Wilson, formed a singing group called the Primettes, which Diane joined, as did Betty McGlown (later replaced for a time by Barbara Martin). The quartet sang at social functions, on street corners—wherever they could. Through Smokey Robinson, a former neighborhood friend of Diane's, who was recording with his group at Detroit's Motown Records (one of the first African American–owned recording firms in the United States), the Primettes auditioned for the label. They were rejected, partly because they were so young. Later, Diane got a short-lasting clerical position at Motown and began a budding friendship with the company's married owner, Berry Gordy Jr. As this personal relationship developed, she persuaded Gordy to let the Primettes sing background for Motown vocalists during recording sessions. By 1961, the singing group consisted of Florence, Mary, and Diane, and Gordy began grooming the trio for success. He changed their name to the Supremes and Ross became known as Diana.

Already there was friction in the group as Diana vied with Flo over who should sing lead. With Gordy favoring Diana, she soon took over as the chief vocalist. After several flop singles, they had a number-one hit with "Where Did Our Love Go" (1964). More chart-toppers

followed, and before long Gordy was (temporarily) serving as their personal manager. He further refined the trio into a winning package of glamour, glitz, and harmony, with emphasis on promoting Diana's sexy image and her breathy, coy singing style.

As the balance of power shifted within the Supremes, the other two women learned to deal with Miss Ross's aggressiveness and her ladylike airs in which appearance, not reality, counted for everything. Wilson said later of pushy Diana, "She craved attention, and in her attempts to get it, she could seem almost ruthless. Sometimes she would throw a childish tantrum." More rivalry occurred when Mary became engaged to marry, and it seemed envious Diana wanted Wilson's man. (Mary won the competition and wed her suitor.) Further discord arose among the trio when Ballard was raped at knifepoint by a man she knew. The traumatizing event left her morose and paranoid. It also killed part of her drive to succeed. This gave Ross a strategic advantage. In the mid-1960s, the vocalists became known as Diana Ross and the Supremes.

In summer 1967, a disillusioned Flo officially dropped out of the act and was replaced by Cindy Birdsong. In Ross's mind, she had done nothing to cause the vulnerable Ballard to quit the group. (Flo became a solo act, but by the mid-1970s, she was at a low point in her life and career. She died of a heart attack in February 1976. Although Ross took center stage at Flo's funeral service—which was widely covered by the media—she did not show up at the cemetery for the private burial, as did Mary Wilson and Flo's friends and relatives.)

As the 1960s ended, Diana displayed a dedication to success that superseded anyone else's well-being. Said singer Carmen McRae, "She'll defer to men or flirt with them or ignore them. With other women, she'll ignore them or arch her back like a cat." Sometimes Ross would attack her "rivals" verbally; other times she used her friendship with Gordy to get her way. Performers learned to steer clear of the volatile Diana or face the consequences of her wrath.

On January 14, 1970, at the Frontier Hotel in Las Vegas, the "original" Supremes performed for the final time. Ross introduced Jean Terrell to the audience as her replacement. That fall, Diana, finally a single act, had her first solo hit—appropriately titled "Ain't No Mountain High Enough." Even then, the rivalry between Ross and the Supremes did not die; it was continuously fanned by one side or the other making biting comments to the media or friends.

In January 1971, Diana married twenty-five-year-old, white public relations executive Robert Ellis Silberstein. For many, the Las Vegas wedding came out of nowhere, and some observers noted a coolness between the couple, even in the first blush of marriage. Within a few weeks of the ceremony, Diana announced she was pregnant. A few weeks later, the couple separated but later patched up their relationship. (They had three daughters, then divorced in 1976. Many years later, the long-held rumor that Gordy was the first child's father was confirmed.) In 1972, Diana had a hit movie with *Lady Sings the Blues*, a feat that far outshone her two later pictures (1975's *Mahogany* and 1978's *The Wiz*). *Mahogany*

Diana Ross in *Lady Sings the Blues* (1972).
(Courtesy of JC Archives)

costar Anthony Perkins later described Ross by saying, "This is not a person who shares" and revealed that on the film set she was constantly "trying to make clear to me that I'm in *her* movie, and I'd better not do anything to detract from her in our scenes together." Meanwhile, Ross's recording career was dipping in popularity, particularly in the late 1970s when the disco craze swept the United States. Among Ross's boyfriends at the time was actor Ryan O'Neal.

By the fall of 1981, the ultrarefined—her detractors just said uppity—Diana had departed from Motown, one more step in detaching herself from her past. She signed with RCA Victor Records. When not recording, she continued to concertize and do TV specials. Often her elaborate costumes (and frequent changes) received more critical notice than her singing. Socially, she dated Gene Simmons of the rock group KISS. In 1983, Diana was reunited with Mary Wilson and Cindy Birdsong for an NBC-TV special honoring Motown Records and its twenty-five-year history. On the show, Ross pushed Wilson away from the microphone and then later repositioned herself on the orchestra platform so that she would clearly be the center of attention. These had-to-be-seen raw moments (many edited from the TV special) rekindled the ongoing debates about Ross versus the Supremes, which had already received new impetus from the 1981 Broadway musical *Dreamgirls*. In 1986, Mary Wilson published *Dreamgirl: My Life as a Supreme*, the first of two autobiographies. Its depiction of the rise and fall of the Supremes provided an unflattering portrait of Ross. Diana's reaction to the matter was to drop Wilson totally from her life.

Meanwhile, on a romantic level, in May 1985, Diana met Norwegian multimillionaire shipping magnate Arne Naess in the Bahamas, where they were each on holiday with their children (he had three from his prior marriage). Five months later, the couple wed in New York in a civil ceremony, but on February 1, 1986, they remarried in an elaborate mil-

lion-dollar ceremony in Switzerland. The couple eventually had two sons: Ross, born in 1987, and Evan, born in 1988. The family resided in a well-fortified mansion in Greenwich, Connecticut. Obviously, Diana had reached her supreme goal of attaining the good life. But there was one thing amiss. Across the Atlantic, in the United Kingdom, there was another Diana grabbing the spotlight—the Princess of Wales, who had married England's Prince Charles. Said Ross, seemingly more miffed than amused, "I used to be the most famous Diana, [before] the princess. When your first name is almost a trademark, you don't get to keep it to yourself for very long."

In 1988, the Supremes were elected to the Rock 'n' Roll Hall of Fame. However, Ross did not bother to attend the ceremonies in New York City. Later, a hurt and angry Mary Wilson observed, "Since she left the group . . . she's gone out of her way to pretend that the Supremes never existed and that our phenomenal success was hers alone." By 1989, Ross was again part of Motown Records, this time as part-owner of the firm that Berry Gordy Jr. had sold to others. Ross's new album, *Workin' Overtime*, showcased a star desperate to be considered hip, relevant, and on a par with such newer and better-selling artists as Whitney Houston.

The year 1993 witnessed the publication of Diana's autobiography, *Secrets of a Sparrow*. *Entertainment Weekly* carped that the tome was a "gassy, mind-numbing affair" that depicted the singer as "deeply shallow, pretentious, self-involved. . . ." In 1994, Ross reemerged as an actress in the telefeature *Out of Darkness* and the next year began her first American concert tour in more than four years. There was no question who was in charge when Diana hosted the TV special *Motown 40: The Music Is Forever* in 1998. Perhaps deciding that, if she couldn't beat them (that is, new talents), then she would join them, she teamed with young singing star Brandy for the telefeature *Double Platinum* (1999). In April 1999, Ross and Naess announced the end of their marriage. (The official divorce occurred in the Dominican Republic in February 2000.) In September 1999, the aging diva was much in the news when she was arrested for allegedly assaulting a security officer at Heathrow Airport in London. It seemed Ross had set off a metal detector as she was about to board a plane. When a female guard attempted to search Diana, she supposedly brushed against the celebrity's breasts, leading to Ross's claimed retaliation. Diana was detained at a police station for some hours before being issued a warning and then released.

In early 2000, it was announced that Ross, along with Mary Wilson and Cindy Birdsong, would reunite for a summer tour. By that April, however, Wilson and Birdsong had exited the project and two other women who had briefly been with the Supremes were substituted. After a few concert dates in June, the remainder of the tour was cancelled for lack of sufficient ticket sales. A disappointed Ross insisted, "I would sing if there were ten people in the audience or ten thousand. I love the music and the fans, and I will find a way to reconnect with them."

In May 2002 the flamboyant fifty-eight-year-old Diana retreated to Promises, drug and alcohol rehab center based in Malibu, California, to "clear up some personal issues" and to prepare for a new concert tour both abroad and in the United States. Her press representative explained that Ross had voluntarily entered the treatment clinic because, "She wanted to be in great shape because she is someone who feels a sense of responsibility to her family and her fans."

In late July 2002 Diana was back performing before audiences—in London and then in Boston—and was receiving solid reviews. Just a week later, however, she cancelled the remainder of the American leg of her tour, with health issues being cited for her not fulfilling her concert obligations.

Looking back over a long and sometimes turbulent career, the rarely humble Ross complained once, "As a world-class singer, people didn't often give me enough credit as an actress." She also had another gripe as well: "People don't know about the human part of me that really cares about the world. For instance, I don't know what I feel about wearing my furs anymore. I worked so hard to have a fur coat, and I don't want to wear it anymore because I'm so wrapped up in the animals. I have real deep thoughts about it because I care about the world and nature." She also noted, "A reporter once asked me if I ever cried. I wonder if people think I'm just as hard as a rock and have no emotions at all."

Meg Ryan

[Margaret Mary Emily Anne Hyra]

NOVEMBER 19, 1961–

In the early part of the twentieth century, screen star Mary Pickford was known as "America's Sweetheart." Decades later, the title was bestowed on Ryan, the pert five-foot, eight-inch blond star of such romantic comedies as *When Harry Met Sally . . .* (1989), *Sleepless in Seattle* (1993), and *You've Got Mail* (1998). Such major box-office hits elevated her into the $15 million plus salary range but left the blue-eyed beauty dissatisfied. She was tired of being a dreamy screen heroine. "It starts to get irritating, you know," she explained. "It's not been easy wearing the mantle of America's sweetheart for so long."

But by the beginning of the new millennium, there was even more to upset the movie actress, who had reached her fragile forties, had a reputation for being stringent with production assistants and household staff, and who admitted, "I can be very relentless when I'm making a point and sort of alienate people." Her ten-year marriage to film star Dennis Quaid had ended. Overlapping that breakup was her high-profile romance—while she was still married—with her *Proof of Life* (2000) costar Russell Crowe. Even more embarrassing was the messy end of that highly publicized affair, with the film colony divided as to who had instigated the split and for what reason(s). It all showed that being rich and famous (also the title of Ryan's first feature film) did not always ensure getting one's way or a happy ending.

She was born in Fairfield, Connecticut, in 1961, the second of four children of Harry Hyra, a high school math teacher, and Susan Duggan, an aspiring actress. When Peggy (as Margaret was called) was twelve, the family moved to Bethel, where her father continued to teach high school math and coach student basketball and baseball teams. In 1976, the couple divorced. Because Susan was the one who wanted the change, it was agreed that the four children would remain with Harry while she explored job options. Once she was settled, her offspring would come to live with her. Peggy was a high school sophomore when the traumatic split occurred. She was so upset and embarrassed by the situation that she never mentioned it even to her best friends. She hid her misery in high academic achievement and a bevy of extracurricular activities. By spring 1976, Susan, now using her own mother's maiden name of Ryan, had abandoned substitute teaching and relocated to New York City to pursue acting and work as an assistant to a casting agent. Struggling to make end meets, she often bunked down at friends' apartments but made sure she saw her children on weekends.

During her high school years, Peggy modeled for local print ads and debated between a career as an international journalist or joining the Peace Corp. Through her mother's connections, she did a few TV commercials, earning her Screen Actors Guild card in 1978. (She registered for the union as Meg Ryan, using her grandmother's maiden name.) Meg was enrolled at the University of Connecticut in Storrs when her mother wangled her an audition for an upcoming movie, *Rich and Famous* (1981). Meg won the small part of Candice Bergen's daughter. The experience further intrigued her interest in acting, but she continued her college education as a journalism major, transferring to New York University to be closer to acting opportunities. As time passed, she spent most of her days making the rounds of casting agents. Eventually it led to her major part as Betsy Montgomery on the daytime soap opera *As the World Turns*. She played the role from 1982 to 1984. During this period, she put her college career on hold and dealt with both her mother's mastectomy and Susan's new love interest, journalist/novelist Pat Jordan. Meg's inability to get along with Jordan added another wedge in her already complicated relationship with her mother. By 1984, feeling confined by her job on *As the World Turns*, Meg quit the show, ended her NYU studies, and went off on a European holiday.

When Meg returned to the United States, she moved to Los Angeles to undertake a role in a new TV series, *Wildside* (1985). After the Western show faded after six episodes, she moved on to a small but showy role in *Top Gun* (1986). In this very popular picture, she was cast as Anthony Edwards's wife and made an impression with filmgoers. Offscreen, the two actors became a couple for a time. Later, on the set of *Innerspace* (1987), Meg became friendly with costar Dennis Quaid. However,

Quaid, seven years her senior, was involved with actress Lea Thompson at the time, while Ryan was still seeing Edwards. The next year, Ryan and Quaid were teamed in the thriller *D.O.A.* (1988). By then, each was a free agent and they began a romance.

As their relationship developed, Meg found it hard to deal with Dennis's stardom. However, in the months ahead, she gained major recognition as Billy Crystal's love interest in *When Harry Met Sally . . .* By 1989, Ryan and Quaid were having a getaway house built for themselves in Montana. That fall, they were engaged and celebrated with a small Thanksgiving dinner at their Montana digs to which Meg invited her mother and her now-husband Jordan. Time had not healed the personality differences between Pat and Meg nor the growing schism between Meg and her mother. The tense situation escalated when Susan and Pat became convinced that their future son-in-law had a serious drug problem. It was a subject Meg made clear she did not wish to discuss with her relatives.

Months later, in 1990, Ryan and her mother had another stressful conversation on the subject of drugs. Meg was scheduled to wed Dennis in July. Reportedly, the chat exasperated Ryan. That night, she phoned her mother to say the wedding to Quaid had been called off. Reputedly, it was the last time that mother and daughter ever spoke. Later, Susan would write—some said whiningly—of her frosty relationship with Meg in several national magazine articles. On the other hand, Ryan refused to discuss the situation publicly. As she informed one major magazine, "If I talk about

Meg Ryan and her then-husband Dennis Quaid in mid-1990s' Hollywood. (Photo by Albert L. Ortega)

it then they get to talk about it, and it'll never end. Certain things, in my opinion, are not for sale, and that includes the complex relationships we have with our families."

In this tense period, Quaid purportedly had taken his role as the rambunctious, boozing singer in *Great Balls of Fire* (1989) so seriously that he had become an alcoholic, which didn't help his mounting attraction to drugs. Eventually, even love-blind Meg had to deal with the reality of her fiancé's addictions. Supposedly, that was a key reason their July 1990 wedding got postponed. Soon after, Quaid

entered a substance abuse program that lasted a month. When released, he took time off to regroup, while Ryan made *The Doors* (1991). Finally, on February 14, 1991, in a spontaneous moment, the couple wed at the Bel-Air Hotel in Los Angeles at a small ceremony with Dennis's older brother Randy and his wife as their witnesses. In April 1992, Meg and Dennis's child, Jack Henry, was born.

Much later, Quaid would say, "We tried to be very good parents, so Meg would go off and do a film and she'd come home, and I'd do a film, and that's not exactly conducive to building a close and healthy relationship. There wasn't a lot of togetherness there. In the process of being good parents, I think we forgot about us." The couple did star in one more film together—the murky drama *Flesh and Bone* (1993)—but in the 1990s, her career was escalating, while his was diminishing. She mixed making comedies (such as 1995's *French Kiss*) with action dramas (including 1996's *Courage Under Fire*) and romantic fantasies (like 1998's *City of Angels*). Occasionally, she took on a really different type of role, such as that of the prostitute in *hurlyburly* (1998). As the 1990s ended, she signed to make the action thriller *Proof of Life*. Set in Latin America, she was cast as the frantic wife of a man kidnapped by drug lords. In trying to save her spouse, she comes to rely on a tough negotiator-for-hire (played by Russell Crowe).

In hindsight, Ryan would say her marriage was already failing when she went on location to Ecuador, England, and elsewhere to make *Proof of Life*. During the shoot, she and her New Zealand–born leading man, a few years her junior and single, began their affair. Perhaps what attracted media attention was that it was the newest fling for Crowe, the freewheeling star who had just completed the epic *Gladiator*. Or it could have been because Ryan, with her wholesome screen image, was noted as a devoted wife and mother off camera. In any event, the love match captured the press's fancy and became top news around the world. Photos of the happy "couple" were published everywhere and, before long, it was too well documented for anyone to deny anymore.

By mid-2000, Quaid had filed for divorce from Meg, although there was a point where a reconciliation was briefly hinted at by the media. By the end of the year, Ryan was no longer top priority with Crowe, who was back in the company of actress/friend Peta Wilson at his New Year's Eve bash in Australia. Thereafter he went back to dating former girlfriend Danielle Spencer, an actress-singer. (Rumor had it that Russell thought Meg was "too Hollywood" and felt overly pressured by her supposed insistence on their settling down together and having a child.) By May 2001 the Quaids were divorced and, in subsequent months, divided their joint property, which included putting their Manhattan residence on Fifth Avenue up for sale at a $6.3 million asking price. Dennis had gone on to new romantic interests, while Meg was spending time in Los Angeles—and later on the Toronto location of her *Against the Ropes* (2003)—with Broadway/TV actor Craig Bierko, age thirty-seven. Ryan and Bierko later ended their friendship, reputedly because she was still in love with Crowe.

Having gained celebrityhood from playing flighty celluloid sweethearts, the real-life Ryan, serious and down-to-earth, admits, "[Fame] is also a test of character at times. . . . Sometimes I pass the test, sometimes I'm a pain in the a**." She also notes that contrary to what the tabloids published during her romance with Crowe, she has not changed for the worse. "I'm not so unreachable," she insisted to *Satellite Direct* magazine. "I think I'm the most available person there is."

Norma Shearer

[Edith Norma Shearer]

AUGUST 10, 1902–JUNE 12, 1983

In the classic film noir *Sunset Boulevard* (1950), Gloria Swanson's Norma Desmond exclaims of silent movie stars, "We had faces then!" Shearer, who made several silent features before enjoying greater success in talkies, certainly had a striking countenance. However, it was slightly flawed by a cast in one eye that she took great pains to divert from viewers' attention. (In addition, her orbs were a bit tinier and closer set than normal.) Actually, Norma was an excellent practitioner of deflecting moviegoers' gaze from her physical "failings," which included chubby legs and a rather ordinary figure. Her shortcomings were minimized by constant exercise (of her walleye and her body) and through careful makeup, lighting, and costuming in front of the cameras.

Once she had maximized her physical potential, Norma—a tireless perfectionist and great controller of situations—did *not* stop there. She understood that a true movie star must radiate both great presence and self-confidence to have high-voltage charisma. Thus, Shearer developed a range of calculated emotional responses that were emphasized by crafted vocal inflections (especially that lilting, mocking laugh) and practiced body gestures. With constant practice, she appeared to be a captivating sophisticate, a glamorous and daring cinema free spirit ready to embrace the world and enjoy all that it offered. The persona became her stock-in-trade, as exemplified in her Oscar-winning role in *The Divorcee* (1930). She also used such calculated artifices away from the soundstage, and those in frequent contact with her were soon alienated by the unceasing pretense.

Shearer reigned in the late 1920s and 1930s in the kingdom known as Metro-Goldwyn-Mayer. One of Norma's greatest rivals on the studio lot was Joan Crawford, who lost many prestigious screen assignments to the regal Shearer. Envious Joan was convinced that only one thing accounted for these professional defeats: "Norma gets all the good parts . . . she sleeps with the boss." Shearer did indeed—she was the wife of Irving Thalberg, the studio's top production executive who was both the right hand and nemesis of MGM's chief, Louis B. Mayer. Certainly if Norma had not married

Norma Shearer in *Marie Antoinette* (1938).
(Courtesy of Echo Book Shop)

this schizoid situation as a cost of doing business. However, it made her a constant trial for costars, crews, and executives.

She was born Edith Norma Shearer in 1902 in Montreal, Quebec, the third child of Andrew and Edith (Fisher) Shearer. Her father was preoccupied with his thriving lumber company and Edith, consumed with her own ambitions and frustrations, pushed her children to excel in social graces and the creative arts. Soon after World War I, Mr. Shearer's business failed, plummeting the family into dire financial straits. The untenable situation led the domineering Edith to formulate a plan: Her two pretty daughters would become successful actresses. Thus, the three women traveled to New York City, leaving the meek father and diligent son behind. Edith especially targeted her younger daughter for success. When stage producer Florenz Ziegfeld rejected Norma for his new show because of her physical shortcomings, the girl (as well as her sister) did modeling and then appeared in bits in silent movies being shot in the New York area.

In 1923, Irving Thalberg, who had first spotted Norma in a 1920 movie (*The Stealers*) and tried unsuccessfully to track her down, was now working with Louis B. Mayer at Metro Pictures (soon to become Metro-Goldwyn-Mayer). He again came across Norma while searching for new talent and arranged a contract for her. With her mother and sister in tow, Norma relocated to Los Angeles. Through loanouts and projects on the home lot—especially *He Who Gets Slapped* (1924)—Shearer's popularity with the public began to grow. She and Irving eventually

Thalberg in 1927 her career might not have reached the peaks it did, but with her great ambitions, polished talents, and sharp smarts, it would still have hit a high plateau.

As Thalberg's wife—and then his widow after his death in 1936—ever-calculating Norma's greatest performances were reserved for off-camera situations. There she smartly navigated the choppy waters of studio favoritism by accepting her powerful MGM connection as her due and, at the same time, pretending that she was no different from any other studio leading lady struggling to reach and stay at the top. She accepted the strains of

dated, although Norma had to cope with Thalberg's romantic interest in others, as well as the sickly young man's ultrapossessive mother. Finally, in September 1927, after Norma had converted to Irving's Jewish faith, the couple married. (The Thalbergs had two children: Irving Jr. in 1930 and Katherine in 1935.)

With her exalted political connection at the MGM plant, Shearer soon had her choice of scripts and directors and undertook a wide variety of roles to avoid being typecast. In 1929, she made her first all-talking picture, *The Trial of Mary Dugan*, sporting a cultivated speaking voice and a chic new bobbed hairdo. She starred in the 1930 racy drama *The Divorcee*, and her Oscar-winning performance confirmed that she was one of the studio's top female stars, along with Greta Garbo, Joan Crawford, and Marion Davies. On the lot, she became known as "Queen Norma" who, according to one of Shearer's studio contemporaries (Anita Page), was a "great lady . . . [and one] you didn't just walk up and say hello to."

At a Christmas party in 1932, thirty-three-year-old Thalberg, in frail health since childhood, suffered a serious heart attack. He and Norma went abroad for his lengthy recuperation. When he returned, he found that a good deal of his studio power had been yanked away by Mayer. However, the studio still needed him and he was placed in charge of his own film unit. One of his top priorities was selecting and guiding vehicles for his wife. After the sophisticated *Riptide* (1934), he showcased her in *The Barretts of Wimpole Street* (1934), for which Norma won her fourth Oscar nomination. (Marion Davies had badly wanted the role, and when she lost the cherished part, she and her paramour, newspaper tycoon William Randolph Hearst, gave up trying to best Shearer and moved Marion and her huge star bungalow to Warner Bros.)

At age thirty-four, Shearer was certainly too mature to play the tragic teenaged heroine in *Romeo and Juliet* (1936), but the production was so sumptuously mounted and had such a superior supporting cast that moviegoers forgave the miscasting of Norma and her forty-three-year-old Romeo played by Leslie Howard. For this Shakespearean outing, Norma won yet another Oscar nomination. That September, Irving died of pneumonia. The grieving widow was off the screen for two years, and it was rumored she might retire, despite her studio contract still being in effect. Concerned that the wealth and MGM stock she inherited from Irving might be used against him, Mayer negotiated a new six-film deal with Norma at $150,000 per movie.

Her first was the long-in-preparation extravaganza *Marie Antoinette* (1938). Despite its enormous costs, the movie was a hit, and Shearer received her sixth and final Academy Award bid. In *Idiot's Delight* (1939), her oversized theatrical performance was appreciated because it mimicked how Lynn Fontanne had done the part on Broadway. *The Women* (1939) assembled an all-star cast of female talent, with Norma as the noble, wronged wife. The picture's highlight was the confrontation between Shearer's heroine and Joan Crawford's husband stealer. It expressed on camera the years of real-life deep envy and dislike that these two stars had for one another. At the film's sumptuous wrap party hostessed by Norma, Joan was conspicuous by her absence. On the other hand, witty filmmaker Ernst Lubitsch quipped to Rosalind Russell (another of the coleads in *The Women*) as she began dancing with George Cukor (who had directed the picture), "If you want all your close-ups to stay in the picture, better dance with Norma." As the good lady-in-waiting she was, Roz immediately told this to Norma, who was amused. A few moments later, Russell and Shearer twirled by Lubitsch, dancing cheek to cheek.

Shearer was too human to go into permanent widow's mourning. There were rumors that she had a brief fling with Tyrone Power, her young leading man in *Marie Antoinette*. That was a bit cheeky, but Louis B. Mayer was apoplectic when he discovered that Norma was having a liaison with the studio's pint-size star, eighteen-year-old Mickey Rooney. The mogul demanded that it stop. Then Shearer began seriously dating ex-hoofer–turned–movie star George Raft. Other lesser powers at the lot were amused by this odd match of regal Norma and the former thug (who still had many gangster pals), but Mayer was not. While pretending to go along with this whim—even to allowing a projected costarring vehicle to be announced for the duo, he counted on the fact that the Catholic Raft would never divorce his wife, who was demanding a huge divorce settlement. Eventually, Shearer and her tough guy beau went their separate ways.

In the early 1940s, it became apparent how much Norma had relied on Irving Thalberg's judgment to handpick her roles. Among other offered vehicles, she turned down *Pride and Prejudice* (1940), *Susan and God* (1940), and *Mrs. Miniver* (1942), all of which were hits for other actresses. Instead, she made such inept pictures as the outdated *We Were Dancing* (1942). At this juncture, Norma retired from the screen, leaving Greer Garson to inherit her studio throne. Instead, Shearer found contentment in marrying (in August 1942) the much-younger Martin Arrougé. For this ski instructor, she converted to Catholicism.

As the decades passed, Shearer drifted into semiseclusion, plagued by periods of great emotional instability (a problem that haunted her older sister) and occasional suicide attempts. Her final years found her a patient at the Motion Picture Country Home in the West San Fernando Valley. In her final months, she was nearly blind and mostly out of touch with reality. She kept thinking each knock at the door of her small quarters was announcing the arrival of her long-dead Irving. She succumbed to bronchial pneumonia in mid-1983 and was buried next to Thalberg at Forest Lawn Memorial Park in Glendale, California. The reign of the former MGM queen had come to a sad end.

Cybill Shepherd

[Cybill Lynne Shepherd]
FEBRUARY 18, 1950–

Patrician, blond, and five feet, seven inches tall, Shepherd has said, "The one false rumor I'd like to correct is that I'm difficult to work with, because I'm not. I have that reputation because if you stand up for your rights you're considered a b****. Bette Davis said it all in this area and I love her two quotes on it. 'If a man stands up for his rights, he's admired. If a woman stands up for her rights, she's a b****.' Also she [Davis] said once, 'If you've been in the business more than two years and you're not considered difficult, you're probably not very talented.'" For her own part, Cybill has observed, "When someone is beautiful, that gives people an excuse to go out of their way to be mean, as if someone who's beautiful isn't really deep, doesn't really hurt, and isn't really a human being."

Shepherd has been part of the entertainment industry for more than three decades, and in three key stages of her career—the Peter Bogdanovich phase (the 1970s), the *Moonlighting* years (1985–89), and the *Cybill* period (1995–98)—she antagonized the media, and/or the industry, and/or the public. As a result, the bright, outspoken feminist became the frequent target of cruel remarks, vicious reviews, and industry put-downs. She quickly earned the title of "the most clobbered actress in Hollywood." At one point—in the late 1970s—she was driven out of Hollywood by studio executives who regarded her as box-office poison, a cocky female, and a pain in the butt on shoots. It was a tough reputation to endure, let alone live down. Over the years, the sexy gal with a dirty sense of humor, who loved to shock her listeners, developed a hard shell to protect herself. Part of her resiliency was to shrug off what the press thought of her or her work and what gossip the tabloids published about her.

Cybill candidly admitted that initially she did not adjust well to movie fame: "I went through a period where I yattered on like an idiot. Then I went through a period where I didn't say anything because I was too dignified to speak. And then finally I became comfortable with being myself." This attitude led the often-flippant actress to quip about the crucial process of celebrities meeting with media, "Interviews are like therapy. You don't get the same kind of feedback. But it's cheaper."

She was born in Memphis, Tennessee, in 1950, the second of three children of William Jennings Shepherd, a former gridiron player who managed the family-owned home appliance business, and his homemaker wife, Patty Shobe. (The future star's first name was derived from "Cy," her grandfather, and "Bill," her dad.) As a child, she was a tomboy who loved sports, sang in the church choir, and wanted to become a singing movie star or swim the English channel. Large framed and with broad shoulders, she participated in sports at East High School. Despite her athletic prowess, she failed gym class for talking back to the instructor. In 1966, a cousin entered her name and photo in the Miss Teenage Memphis contest. Uncertain about her looks, Cybill had to be convinced by her mother to try the competition. She won, but in the subsequent Miss Teenage America competition, she only claimed the Miss Congeniality award. During this teenage period, pretty Cybill, considered a man-killer in town, met Elvis Presley. She and the King dated for about a month—she even pursued him to Las Vegas. Eventually, however, she was turned off by his drug dependency, hangers-on, and (especially) his ever-present bodyguards.

After graduating high school in 1968, Cybill planned to attend Louisiana State University at New Orleans. However, she entered the Model of the Year competition, which was nationally televised. As the winner, she received a $25,000 prize, making her completely independent of her now-divorced parents. She moved to New York City, where she quickly became a top model and magazine cover girl. She was earning $500 a day and was much in demand for such major TV commercials as those for Breck shampoo. Despite its benefits, Shepherd disliked being a mannequin and wanted to one day study art history in Italy. Meanwhile, she took night courses at various New York colleges.

Young filmmaker Peter Bogdanovich spotted Shepherd's picture on a magazine cover and asked her to star in *The Last Picture Show* (1971). He offered her the key role of Jacy Farrow, a spoiled teenage brat in small-town Texas. She was concerned about the character's nude scene, but the director reassured her it would be done tastefully. (Nude shots taken of her on the set ended up in *Playboy* magazine, leading Shepherd to file a lawsuit that took years to settle.) The movie and Cybill were big hits and she moved to Hollywood to be with her lover, the eleven-year-older Bogdanovich. Before long, Bogdanovich's wife, Polly Platt (a well-respected set designer/writer) and their two daughters vacated the Bel-Air mansion

and Shepherd moved in. Reveling in fame, riches, and bright futures, the lovers assumed the movie colony would embrace them warmly. Instead, because their success had come so "easily" and because they seemed so arrogant and pretentious, they were met with great hostility. A few of Peter's friends ignored the animus, including moviemaking genius Orson Welles, who helped Cybill gain confidence in her abilities.

After making the popular *The Heartbreak Kid* (1972) for director Elaine May, Shepherd went abroad to star in *Daisy Miller* (1974), produced and directed by Bogdanovich. The period drama was a box-office bomb. Meanwhile, offscreen, the actress was studying with an opera coach and later moved into her own Tinseltown digs. Her mentor/puppet master Bogdanovich guided her through her first record album (1974's *Cybill Does It . . . to Cole Porter*), but critics severely panned the record. Adding to her mounting career woes, Shepherd costarred with Burt Reynolds in Bogdanovich's *At Long Last Love* (1975). The period screen musical was a dud. Nevertheless, Peter next intended to costar Cybill in *Nickelodeon* (1976), but the studio said no (Stella Stevens got Shepherd's part).

In a career downslide, she accepted a supporting role in Martin Scorsese's *Taxi Driver* (1976), where her icy blond persona was well used. Thereafter, she made junk features such as 1978's *Silver Bears*. That same year, the *Playboy* matter was resolved, with Shepherd receiving a cash settlement plus a half-interest in the movie rights to the novel *Saint Jack*

(1973), which she'd wanted to film. Before Cybill left Tinseltown and Bogdanovich, she gave those rights to Peter, whose career was now floundering as well.

After a devastating response to her singing engagement in New York City, twenty-eight-year-old Cybill returned to Memphis. There she met David Ford, an auto-parts manager, who was three years her junior. They wed in November 1978 and their daughter, Clementine, was born the following year. After making the sci-fi junk *The Return* (1980), Cybill formed a jazz band (the Memphis All-Stars). Her husband left his job to play guitar, book the group, and manage her singing career. She recorded another album (*Vanilla*) in 1979 and worked in regional theater to improve her acting skills. Her marriage to Ford soured, and the couple soon divorced. "We outgrew each other," said Shepherd. Meanwhile, Cybill's prestigious talent agent (Sue Mengers) announced, "Cybill, you've been in Memphis for four years, you might as well be dead." By 1982, she was back in Los Angeles. The actress got another agent and a lead role in the TV series *The Yellow Rose*. Although it only lasted a season (1983–84), Cybill earned good reviews. It began her comeback.

In March 1985, Shepherd debuted as the leading lady of the screwball comedy teleseries *Moonlighting*. Her costar was relative newcomer Bruce Willis. Viewers, especially yuppies, loved the show and it became a top-ten program. Her popularity restored with critics and the public, Cybill made TV movies (including 1985's *The Long Hot Summer*) dur-

Cybill Shepherd in *The Last Picture Show* (1971). (Courtesy of JC Archives)

ing summer breaks. She also found time for a romance with Larry McMurtry, author of *The Last Picture Show*, who was working with her on a screenplay (eventually made as the cable movie *Memphis* in 1991).

With Cybill's fame revived, gossip columnists awaited the chance to pounce on her. It came when rumors spread of mounting dissension on the *Moonlighting* set, as she and Bruce reportedly developed an enmity toward one another. It didn't help Shepherd's standing that, in the accelerating skirmishes, management often sided with Willis. (Cybill was given the unflattering nickname of "Snivel" by some of the cast and crew for her alleged constant whining on the set.) By now, free-spirited Shepherd was having a romance with Los Angeles chiropractor Dr. Bruce Oppenheim. When she became pregnant, the couple wed in March 1987. Because of the difficult pregnancy, Shepherd's doctors ordered her to take a leave of absence from the TV show. This six-month furlough further turned the *Moonlighting* producers against her. She gave birth to twin sons in October 1987. Eventually, Cybill returned to her series, but the magic was gone and the on-set bickering went into high gear. When the show was cancelled in May 1989, Shepherd was relieved: "It was like being trapped in a gilded cage together [with Bruce Willis]." She and Oppenheim divorced in February 1989. She gave him a cash settlement, reasoning "I had money and he didn't."

On the big screen, forty-year-old Cybill reunited with cast members from *The Last Picture Show* and director Bogdanovich in making the sequel, *Texasville* (1990). Thereafter, she was largely stuck making TV movies until she broke out of the rut with a TV sitcom, *Cybill*. With Shepherd cast as a wisecracking actress and single parent, the series debuted in January 1995 and captured the public's fancy. But once again rumors arose of trouble on the set, supposedly engendered by

Shepherd's outspokenness and her vision for the program. Additionally, there was rumored conflict between Cybill and her series sidekick, Christine Baranski, the latter receiving more critical kudos and awards than the star. By 1998, the show was dead. Away from the soundstage, Shepherd had settled into a relationship with musician Robert Martin. They announced their engagement in early 1996, but the relationship ended in October 1998 when he told her it was over during a couples' therapy session.

In October 2000, Cybill turned up as the host of the TV talk show/news magazine *Men Are from Mars, Women Are from Venus*. She quickly learned just how difficult it was to host a gab program, and when ratings proved anemic—amid rumors of dissension on the set—she was unceremoniously replaced on the program. Undaunted, the very vocal actress found other forums to promulgate her opinions, including her frank memoir, *Cybill Disobedience: How I Survived Beauty Pageants, Elvis, Sex, Bruce Willis, Lies, Marriage, Motherhood, Hollywood, and the Irrepressible Urge to Say What I Think* (2000). She also acted in such feature films as the TV movies *Due East* and *Falling Off the Verge* (both 2002). In addition, the flinty Shepherd dealt with a skin cancer scare when it was discovered she had a growth on her back, which proved to be benign.

With her accustomed resiliency, it seems inevitable that ambitious Shepherd will bounce up again in the world of show business. One can only wonder what staunch diva Cybill will do then to become grist for the media mill.

Britney Spears

[Britney Jean Spears]

DECEMBER 2, 1981–

What's not to like when you've earned $50 million before you're twenty-one, are the idol/role model of millions of preteen girls, and have a huge, ardent fan base of males of many ages. For one thing, it has been very difficult for this poster child of squeaky clean living to maintain her pure reputation, especially when she's a pretty five-foot, four-inch blond with the natural urges of a maturing young woman and a penchant for wearing ultrasexy ensembles on camera. The challenge was especially hard for Spears (variously known to relatives and friends as Brit, Brit-Brit, or Pinky) when, for a time, she shared a West Coast home with another bubblegum-set singing favorite, Justin Timberlake (of the 'N Sync group). For another thing, how was it possible to maintain a sane perspective of herself and life when she had become the epicenter of a merchandizing blitzkrieg—including an interactive video game, a line of 4-Wheeler sneakers, a trendy restaurant, and a personal line of clothing and accessories? Then too, there was the realization on the part of this emerging adult that she had the fame, riches, and power to declare her independence from family and managers—which some observers insist she did with very firm, aggressive methods. Welcome to the world of Britney Spears.

In the highly competitive music business, staying on top is tough—you have to contend with such rivals as Christina Aguilera, Mandy Moore, and Jessica Simpson, who are eager to become the new top choice in the public's affections. Such career tension is enough to give even the most bubbly personality a few hard edges. Southern Baptist Britney also picked a really tough, confrontational career model for herself. Said Spears, "I would really, really, really like to be a legend like Madonna. Madonna knows what to do next, and when she's performing, the audience is just in awe of her." Will Spears become the Material Girl for the twenty-first century?

Britney was born in 1981 in the Louisiana town of Kentwood (population 2,500), the second of three children of Jamie Spears, the foreman of a construction company, and Lynne, a school teacher who ran a day-care center. When Britney and her brother Bryan (born in 1977) were young, the Spears had a rough time financially. Jamie had to relocate to Memphis to find work, coming home periodically to visit his family. As a little girl, Spears had a predilection for singing, whether at home or at the Baptist church the family attended. When she was four, she gave her debut public performance singing "What Child Is This?" for her church's Christmas service.

In her constant desire to entertain family and visitors to their home, the youngster would frequently do flips across the room. Her mother encouraged Britney's agility by enrolling her in dance classes, driving her back and forth to New Orleans for sessions in jazz, tap, and ballet. At school, Britney's teachers suggested the girl was good enough to train seriously in gymnastics. Her parents found the

Britney Spears at the Teen Awards in 1999.
(Photo by Albert L. Ortega)

of her friends had heard that the Disney Channel's *The Mickey Mouse Club* (MMC) was auditioning new talent to join the cable TV program. Mrs. Spears took Britney to the auditions in Atlanta, Georgia. While the show's scouts were impressed with the girl, they concurred that she was too young to keep up with the daily grind of a TV series. However, they referred Spears to a New York talent agent and to a Manhattan-based show-business lawyer. This resulted in Britney (accompanied by her mother) spending three summers in Manhattan. There, the fledgling entertainer studied at the Performing Arts School and the Dance Center. In 1991, Spears auditioned for and won the role of the replacement lead in *Ruthless*, an off-Broadway musical satire based on the movie *The Bad Seed* (1956). She stayed with the show for several months. During these training years, Britney also did TV commercials.

By the start of the 1990s, Britney had settled back into a routine at home, attending Park Lane Academy and baby-sitting for her recently born sister, Jamie Lynn. At this time, she was accepted as a contestant on Ed McMahon's TV talent showcase, *Star Search*. She won the first round, but the following week lost to a male competitor. Not long before her eleventh birthday, she reauditioned for *The Mickey Mouse Club*. This time she was accepted and joined the musical variety/comedy sketch program for its 1993 TV season. With her mother as chaperone, Spears moved to an apartment in Orlando, Florida, near the Disney/MGM Studios theme park. Among her castmates were Justin Timberlake (who would

means to start her in lessons. She became so proficient that she was sent to a gymnastics training camp in Houston, Texas. However, by that time, Spears was developing a mind of her own and soon decided she didn't want to become an obsessive gymnast. For her, the training was no longer fun, and she deemphasized the sport as part of her regimen.

By age eight, Britney was convinced she wanted a career in music. The mother of one

play a greater role in Britney's later years), Christina Aguilera, and Ryan Gosling. Spears remained with the series until it went off the air in 1994.

The MMC veteran spent the next year back in Kentwood attending school. Later, one of her TV series pals, Nikki DeLoach, told her about a new girl singing group that was being formed in Orlando, Florida. Not long before her fifteenth birthday, Britney auditioned for Innosense. However, Spears later decided against joining the group because she really wanted to be a solo performer. Firm in her conviction, she began a home-study school program, so she would have more time to reach her career goals. Britney made demo tapes to send to record labels. Through her entertainment lawyer in New York, she was introduced to Jive Records, which signed her to a recording contract. The label soon flew her to Sweden to work with Eric Foster White who would write the songs for her debut album.

By June 1998, the disc (. . . *Baby One More Time*) was ready. To launch its new vocalist, Jive established an Internet website for Britney, created a toll-free number for listeners to call in to hear snatches of her songs, and so forth. Spears flew to Singapore, where she gave her first live concert. The label then sent her on a tour of shopping malls around the United States so that her potential public could meet her face-to-face. By now, Lynne Spears had relinquished her role as Britney's chaperone, and a family friend took over the chore. The newcomer's first single, the title track, was released to radio stations in early November 1998 and was an immediate success. (The single eventually sold over 900,000 copies.) The music video to ". . . Baby One More Time" was soon airing on TV and became a viewer favorite. The album itself was issued in early 1999 and became a smash hit.

While Britney's CD was doing its thing, she was signed to be the opening act for 'N Sync's new tour. On the road, she renewed her friendship with fellow MMC alumnus Justin Timberlake, a key member of the hot boy band. At her eighteenth birthday party in December 1999, the couple got closer. In 2000, Spears, who had a successful second CD (*Oops! . . . I Did It Again*) in release, was an enormous favorite with preteen audiences and magazines. She insisted publicly that, although she and Justin kissed when they were on dates, she intended to remain a virgin until she was married. Meanwhile, the media had a field day with her supposed brief attachment to Britain's Prince William, a relationship that was actually just an exchange of friendly E-mails.

By the end of 2000, pert and shapely Spears was showing a new gyrating, sexy side of herself in her lucrative Pepsi TV commercials. She and Justin went on holiday together, first to Palm Springs, California, and then to Vail, Colorado. By January 2001, the couple were sharing a spacious three-story home in the Hollywood Hills. Midyear, she was insisting to her public that it was "hard to wait" to have sex, but in another media session, she said that it was nice to wake up in the morning next to Timberlake. With her third album, *Britney* (2001), in release Spears, who favored bare-midriff ensembles, was displaying a sassy, smoldering look that put her at odds with her

*H*aving incredible success while still just a teen can easily blow one's mind. After all, when your record company gives you a diamond necklace for your eighteenth birthday, how can it not distort your everyday values. Meanwhile, jaded civilians might take the following words of wisdom from Spears with a pinch of salt:

On her career choice:
"I'm so lucky. I get to do exactly what I love to do, each and every day—and they pay me for it!"

On being a role model:
"If I am, then I'm proud to be one, but I'm not doing anything different with my life because kids are looking up to me."

On industry award shows:
"I love the recognition—don't get me wrong—but even more fun than accepting an award has been getting to meet my childhood idols face-to-face."

On night life:
"I am so not the party animal that it's kind of embarrassing."

On those who suggested others shaped her career and persona:
"They think that people come in and put my clothes together or put me together. I come up with the concept for all of my tour ideas, all of my videos. It's just so lame that people would say that."

established image as a sweet virgin of the bubblegum set. (Also, having once made a big deal of informing her teenybopper fans that she never smoked, gossip columnists were quick to report that Spears now had been spotted puffing a cigarette on her hotel balcony in Sydney, Australia, as well as at clubs and so forth.)

The singer had also taken another step closer to becoming the next Material Girl with lavish spending on gifts for family (for example, a $1.5 million loft space in Manhattan for

brother Bryan); a plush Florida pad for herself on Miami's Key Biscayne; luxury cars for others and herself; and such trinkets as a $250,000 friendship ring from Justin. She also added a $3 million, 6,000-square-foot Los Angeles home to her growing inventory.

In early 2002, Spears, wanting "to see if I could do something different," made her feature film debut in *Crossroads*, a mindless road picture that showcased its star as less than morally perfect but still a pleasant screen personality, despite too many mechanical movements and moods on her part. Made for $12 million, it grossed over $37 million in domestic distribution, which meant that Britney would definitely return in future movie vehicles. At the end of February, she and Justin attended the Grammys together in Los Angeles. By March, their relationship was over, although they consistently denied it for a time. Rumor had it that heartthrob Timberlake had broken up with Spears by phoning her the bad news one evening in March 2002, just before he and 'N Sync hit the concert stage in Tacoma, Washington. But the gossip columns reported that Britney was not in mourning, for she was seen dancing her heart out on the Manhattan club scene and in rehearsal for her next tour. Supposedly, the fact that Britney's career had soared ahead of Justin's (who was now planning to become a solo act) had accentuated other relationship issues: lack of commitment; jealousy; and separate, high-pressure touring schedules.

As Spears prepared for her mid-2002 world concert tour, she learned that her parents were having marital problems and that her father had decamped from the $4.7 million mansion she'd built for them in Kentwood, Louisiana. Although they assured Britney that her career and the pressures it generated were not to blame for their domestic problems, she held herself accountable for their breakup (which ended in their divorce). While coping with this emotional turmoil, the pop superstar was making a music video of "Boys" to be used in the third Austin Powers' screen adventure *Goldmember* (2002). A zebra and a peacock were employed as atmosphere for the shoot despite the fact that animal rights groups had previously asked the young celebrity to stop using live animals as props in her video productions. All this came at a time when the media was reporting on her supposed wild nightclub partying, done—reportedly—to make ex-boyfriend Timberlake jealous. With such party-hearty behavior, there was an increasingly widening gap between the superstar's squeaky-clean professional image and the "new" real-life Spears. (It led some of the tabloid press to label the famed performer a "pop tart.")

Managing only to be mildly controversial with her very exuberant on- and offstage behavior during her international tour, things turned sour for Britney when she reached Mexico for the last lap of her performance trek in late July 2002. At the airport near Mexico City, photographers and the gasping public caught her flipping the bird in "a universally recognized gesture." The crowd of Mexican fans convinced that they were the target of Spears's unwarranted anger understandably took umbrage. Spears later explained that her finger gesture had not been aimed at her adoring public but at the intrusive paparazzi who had hounded her at the air terminal. Said Britney, "I'm human too. I get mad like everyone else." Two days after her belated public apology, she performed at Mexico City's Foro Sol baseball stadium. However, at her second concert at this venue—in front of 52,000 fans—she suddenly left the stage after the fifth song. Her only comment to the assemblage was, "I'm sorry, Mexico. I love you. Bye." The dismayed audience was none too pleased—some patrons reportedly began hurling Britney merchandise at the stage as they chanted, "Fraud. Fraud." The next day the promoters said the concert had been cut short because of security and safety concerns due to an approaching thunderstorm. The disappointed audience was offered a refund for their tickets, but that did not erase the negative memories of Britney's recent stopover in Mexico.

Once back in the United States, Spears announced unexpectedly that she intended to take a sabbatical professionally. Her publicist explained, "She is taking six months off. She has been working for four years straight and she is taking a break." Reportedly, during her downtime she would socialize with family and friends, write music, travel, and read scripts. (By this time she'd already made an agreement—through her recently formed movie production company—to do a film project in conjunction with the NASCAR racing circuit. In the untitled project, she was to play the daughter of a NASCAR team owner who inspires a racing champ to return to the track.)

Soon, an annoyed Spears was telling the press: "I'm taking a break, so people are writing that I'm having a meltdown. I don't get it. I need this break to rejuvenate and to just play." She also commented on her still much-discussed breakup with singer Justin Timberlake, which had included an attempt at a reconciliation: "[The split] was horrible. Very upsetting, and it took a lot out of me. He was my first real love, and I doubt I'll ever be able to love anyone like that again." As to her once squeaky-clean image that had come under

increasing media scrutiny, she noted blithely, "I drink. Smoking, drinking, sex—why is it such a big deal with me? As you . . . grow up, you experiment. I never wanted to hide who I was, but until about a year ago, I was trying to fit an image and trying to be someone I wasn't."

What effects Britney's abrupt career hiatus would have on her music industry standing—where highly competitive newcomers are always striving to topple the established talent—only time would tell. Meanwhile, Spears remained high up on the show-business ladder. Weeks before her unpopular, erratic behavior in Mexico City, *Forbes* magazine placed the young notable at the top of its Celebrity 100, a list based on stars' fame and fortune. Britney had supplanted Tom Cruise in the *Forbes'* ranking. The publication noted, "She doesn't have Steven Spielberg's pull, but in the last year she arguably had a bigger impact on pop culture."

Sharon Stone

[Sharon Stone]
MARCH 10, 1958–

Most of her life she wanted to be a big movie star—the next Marilyn Monroe. Then when it finally happened, Stone learned there was a big price to pay: "Because of my fame I had to really look at myself. I had to really look at what I was doing. . . . And I had to think about the part of me that was still naïve, the part of me that was open. Maybe that's the hurtful part. Now I have to be careful in a way that you don't have to be as careful if you're not a target." In addition, she discovered, "It was very confusing and very overwhelming. I started thinking about my life in terms of just one day at a time, because it was just too much."

She also acknowledged, "When I first got famous, the image of the movie [1992's *Basic Instinct*] really protected me. Everyone thought I had so much bravado and was so wild. So I could continue to be that. It was a blast. As the time has gone by and I had to continue to cope with it, things start to integrate with your own personality. I could bring it down and bring more of myself to the party. It's a learned thing."

In the process of getting and staying famous, Stone developed an enduring reputation as a tough cookie, leading to the nickname "Sharon Stones." (Bragged the actress, "I've got the biggest balls in Hollywood. It's good that they're scared of me. The longer they stay scared, the longer I keep my job.") She also achieved a reputation as a man-killer who got almost whomever she wanted. It led her to say, "Any man in Hollywood will meet me if I want that. No, make that any man anywhere." Some of her targets found the experience excruciating. Stone herself allowed that "My ex-husband used to say I was a combination of Zsa Zsa Gabor and Arnold Schwarzenegger. I think he was right." Former boyfriend, actor Hart Bochner, said of Stone, "She's the Antichrist." Proving she could give tit for tat in the dating game, after breaking up with

Sharon Stone as a rising film star in the 1980s.
(Courtesy of Echo Book Shop)

country music star/actor Dwight Yoakum, Sharon referred to him as a "dirt sandwich."

Explaining her forceful, sometimes-abrasive behavior, Sharon said on one occasion, "If I was just normally intelligent I could probably get away with it—but I'm fiercely intelligent, and that's threatening." Another time, she voiced a different theory, "If I was a petite, brunette, ethnic lawyer, then my behavior would be totally acceptable. But we Barbie dolls are not supposed to behave the way I do."

She was born in Meadville, Pennsylvania, in 1958 to Joe and Dorothy Stone, who were both employed at a local tool-and-die company. The second of four children, Sharon felt like an outsider as a youngster because of her extremely high (154-point) IQ. The shy tomboy became a loner who loved to read and dreamed of one day becoming a film star. When she was thirteen, she was riding a neighbor's horse when it suddenly charged a row of bedsheets her mother was drying on a clothesline in the backyard. As the animal tore through the sheets, Sharon's neck was badly cut by the rope, leaving deep open wounds. It took many months for the scars to diminish. (A few years later, she had cosmetic surgery to complete the recovery process.) By the time Stone was fifteen, she was spending half her day in high school classes and the other half taking courses (thanks to a scholarship) in English and drama at nearby Edinboro University. By the twelfth grade, the introverted teenager had reinvented herself and blossomed as an attractive young woman. She began winning local beauty pageants.

In 1976, Stone moved to New York City where she became a model for the Eileen Ford Agency. One day, she answered a casting call for extras in Woody Allen's *Stardust Memories* (1980). Eventually, she was hired for a silent cameo as the sparkling girl who kisses the window of a train. Sharon recalled that while doing the small role she suddenly felt that "Life makes sense."

Sharon relocated to Los Angeles to further her career, winning small parts in films like *Deadly Blessing* (1981) and the short-lived TV series *Bay City Blues* (1983). As she recalled later, "I looked like an inflatable Barbie doll and nobody wanted me to play anything too edgy." This frustrated her because "I never thought that I looked on the outside like I was on the inside. On the inside I feel like a dark, Semitic girl with curly hair. I have never felt blond." During this apprenticeship period, in August 1984, she wed TV producer Michael Greenburg. By January 1987, they had divorced. Meanwhile, she made several action films, including the inept African adventure yarn *King Solomon's Mines* (1985) and its equally bad sequel. Bored with her career rut in B movies and concerned that she would soon be thirty (and perhaps too old to break into leading roles in major pictures), she concentrated her energy on classes with acting coach Roy London. She found great satisfaction in acting exercises that required her to play nongender-specific roles and display the same power as a man. It gave her increased self-confidence.

Stone's breakthrough role was playing opposite Arnold Schwarzenegger in the sci-fi thriller *Total Recall* (1990), a part that demanded she do physical battle with the former Mr. Universe. On-screen, it looked as if she gave as good as she got in their fight to the finish. A week after completing the picture, Sharon was in a bad car accident on the Sunset Strip. It required an arduous recovery period, during which she rethought her career focus. Deciding she now needed a sexy, edgy image, she posed for *Playboy* magazine (July 1990). Shots of her hanging daringly off the side of a tall office building made an impact and gave her the desired fresh presence with casting agents.

Paul Verhooven had directed *Total Recall* and Stone begged him to let her audition for the thriller *Basic Instinct* (1992). She did so, but leading man Michael Douglas wanted a big name as his leading lady. When several major actresses rejected the role because of the required on-screen nudity, Stone won the part. Her (in)famous scene involved her character being questioned by the police. As she sat in the interrogation chair, she spread her legs wide—revealing a distinct lack of under-wear—and the attending cops are agog. In what became typical Sharon style, she at first insisted to the media that she was tricked into doing this revealing scene. Later when the sequence made her an "overnight" star, she put a new spin on the situation—she had thought of it. Meanwhile, the director, who allowed that Stone was a hard-edged person-ality to work with, insisted that the idea for the scene had actually been his all along.

Now a major Hollywood player, Stone tackled her love life anew. She claimed that in the past men had "put her on a pedestal, then never come to visit." That proved far from the case with her next romance. While making the erotic thriller *Sliver* (1993), she had problems on the set with leading man William Baldwin. However, she developed a strong rapport off the set with the film's coproducer, William J. MacDonald. The problem was that he was recently married. He left his wife for Stone, while his spouse became involved with the pic-ture's producer/scripter. Labeled a home wrecker, Sharon lived with her new amour (after she had him sign an agreement that he

could never publicly discuss their relationship). Following months of togetherness, Stone can-celled wedding plans and sent him packing. Thereafter, since the nondisclosure ban did not apply to her, she bad-mouthed him frequently to the media.

Sliver had not done well at the box office, a fate equaled by *Intersection* (1994), *The Spe-cialist* (1994), and the Western *The Quick and the Dead* (1995). Sharon's reputation of being outspoken, controlling, and sometimes para-noid on film sets accelerated as her career fal-tered. The downslide reversed itself when she joined Robert De Niro in Martin Scorsese's *Casino* (1995), for which she won a Golden Globe and an Oscar nomination. Thereafter, her choice of vehicles—including *The Mighty* (1998) for her own production company (Chaos) and *Gloria* (1999)—put the forty-year-old star in professional jeopardy.

Meanwhile, the mature bachelor girl (who had been dating men like the CEO of Guess Jeans, as well as the much-younger Dweezil Zappa, son of Frank) abandoned her single status. Sharon met San Francisco–based news-paper editor/executive Phil Bronstein while she was making *Sphere* (1998). The couple mar-ried on Valentine's Day 1998. His work kept him in the Golden Gate City a good deal of the time, while she was preoccupied in Tinsel-town. As a result, the couple had a difficult period of adjustment. In the midst of all this, they adopted a baby boy (Roan) in June 2000. The following year, her husband nearly lost a toe to an aggressive Komodo dragon lizard at the Los Angeles Zoo. Later in 2001, Sharon suffered a ruptured brain aneurysm, which required extensive surgery to repair and a long recuperative period.

After a two-year layoff, Stone returned to picture making by costarring with Dennis Quaid in the thriller *Cold Creek Manor* (2003). Next she was scheduled to make *Liar's Club* and *A Different Loyalty*. In the latter, she'd be seen as the wife of Kim Philby (to be played by Rupert Everett) who infiltrated British intelligence on behalf of the Russians before defecting to Moscow in 1963.

Her ambitions still very much intact, the Stone of the new millenium puts Hollywood on alert: "I identify with the risk-taking element of things. It's much more thrilling to me to take the risk of playing something new than it is to just do the thing. . . . I want to do more. I want to try more. I want to be more of an artist than I was the year before."

Gene Hackman and Barbra Streisand in *All Night Long* (1981). (Courtesy of JC Archives)

Barbra Streisand

[Barbara Joan Streisand]

APRIL 24, 1942–

"It's a very male-chauvinist word. I resent it deeply," she told *Playboy* magazine in 1977. "A person who's a b**** would seem to be mean for no reason. I'm not a mean person. Maybe I'm rude without being aware of it—that's possible." She also denied that she was swellheaded: "To have ego means to believe in your own strength. And to also be open to other

people's views. It is to be open, not closed. So, yes, my ego is big, but it's also very small in some areas. My ego is responsible for my doing what I do—bad or good." And when doing her thing, "I just don't want to be hampered by my own limitations."

At a height of her popularity in the 1970s, Barbra asked rhetorically, "Why am I so famous? What am I doing right? What are the others doing wrong?" Often those "others" told the media exactly what Streisand was doing amiss. For example, her *Hello, Dolly!* (1969) leading man, Walter Matthau, judged, "The trouble with Barbra is she became a star long before she became an actress. Which is a pity, because if she learned her trade properly she might become a competent actress instead of a freak attraction—like a boa constrictor." Said Peter Bogdanovich, who directed Barbra in 1972's *What's Up, Doc?*, "She's a real kvetch . . . always moaning about something or other, a really hard-to-please lady." Her *Nuts* (1987) movie director, Martin Ritt, concurred, "She is not as selfish as she's made out to be. Except as a performer; then it's me-me-me-me . . . the demon diva." Even actor Elliott Gould, her spouse from 1963 to 1971, admitted, "My toughest job was being married to Barbra Streisand."

While few critics or the public ever seriously questioned Barbra's talents as a vocalist, her New York–style aggressive personality has made her vulnerable to attack over the years. But then, even she was conflicted about her behavior: "A large part of me is pure nebbish— plain, dull, uninteresting. There's a more flamboyant part, too. Obviously." Another time, she described her proclivity for (undiplomatic) directness and strongly voiced opinions with a roundabout apology of sorts: "I knew that with a mouth like mine, I just had to be a star or something."

As a star, the "Great Voice" gained legions of admirers. Entertainer and TV talk show host Rosie O'Donnell, who rivaled diet guru Richard Simmons as Barbra's greatest fan, told her idol on national television, "You were a constant source of light in an often-dark childhood, and you inspired me and gave me the courage to dream of a life better than the one I knew." On the other hand, the songster aroused ire in other celebrities. For example, Omar Sharif, who costarred with Streisand in

Funny Girl (1968) and *Funny Lady* (1975) and who had a dreamy relationship with her for a time, later scorned his leading lady: "I think her biggest problem is that she wants to be a woman and she wants to be beautiful, and she is neither." Cogently summing up the anti-Streisand camp, Zsa Zsa Gabor, a sparkling personality on the Tinseltown circuit for decades, said, "Darling, she's so distasteful!"

She was born Barbara Joan Streisand in Brooklyn in April 1942. Her father, Emanuel Streisand, was a teacher with a Ph.D. from Columbia University; her mother, Diana (actually born Ida) Rosen, was a homemaker. The Streisands' first child, Sheldon, had been born in 1935. When Barbara was only fifteen months old, her dad died of a cerebral hemorrhage. Her mother returned to bookkeeping and the family struggled to survive. Young Barbara escaped into a world of fantasy, imagining herself becoming a movie star one day. By the time she graduated from high school in 1959, she was intent on becoming a stage actress. She moved to Manhattan.

The fledgling talent had many obstacles to overcome. With her prominent nose, she lacked the conventional look required by most casting agents. She also had a thick Brooklyn accent and had become a nonconformist kook who dressed in an oddball variation of a beatnik. Despite these roadblocks, in 1961, she was singing at Greenwich Village clubs and began appearing on New York–based TV talk shows. (By now, she had changed her first name to Barbra.) She made her professional stage debut that October in the off-Broadway revue

Another Evening with Harry Stoones. That show folded after one night, but her next, *I Can Get It for You Wholesale* (1962), had a decent run on Broadway. She had one big number in it that showcased her well, and she was nominated for a Tony Award. After joining in recording the cast album, Streisand was signed to a contract by Columbia Records. Meanwhile, she was living in a tiny New York apartment with *Wholesale*'s leading man, Elliott Gould.

In February 1963, Barbra's debut solo album was released and rose high on the charts. It also won Barbra her first Grammy Award. Soon she was appearing at major clubs around the country and was a guest on TV variety programs. That September, Streisand and Gould wed. By the following year, after she starred in the Broadway musical *Funny Girl*, Barbra had superseded her husband in fame, and her look and mannerisms were becoming popular. She starred in a spring 1965 TV special, then, after repeating her hit role in the London edition of *Funny Girl* in late 1965, she headlined another small-screen showcase in America. In December 1966, she gave birth to son Jason. Whether she performed live in concert (as in Central Park in June 1967) or on albums, her acclaim continued to grow.

For $200,000, Streisand starred on-screen in 1968's *Funny Girl*. On the set, she didn't hesitate to instruct multi-Oscar winner William Wyler on how their picture should be made, and her war with Hollywood was on. Despite production contretemps, the movie was a hit and she won an Oscar. Much in demand, she was now paid $750,000 plus a percentage of the profits to do *Hello, Dolly!* (1969). Her perfectionistic, brazen behavior during the shoot angered director Gene Kelly and made her the target of costar Walter Matthau's wrath. Later, ego problems between Streisand and leading man Yves Montand were reflected in their lack of chemistry in *On a Clear Day You Can See Forever* (1970). In that picture, Jack Nicholson, featured as Barbra's on-screen sibling, was more than unhappy when his celluloid role was reduced in the final print, as was Montand's.

Now a full-fledged Hollywood movie star, Streisand divorced Elliott Gould in 1971. She had a romance with leading man Ryan O'Neal while making *What's Up Doc?* (1972) and would have been happy to do the same with Robert Redford in 1973's *The Way We Were*, but her costar was not interested. That picture was a big success, as was her singing of the theme song, "Memories." In 1974, Barbra began a long-term relationship with hairstylist/entrepreneur Jon Peters. He produced—and she executive produced—*A Star Is Born* (1976). Her costar on this distended musical was Kris Kristofferson, who allowed, "Working with Barbra Streisand is pretty stressful. It's like sitting down to a picnic in the middle of a freeway." The film was hated by critics but did decently at the box office. Throughout the rest of the decade, whether in movies (such as 1979's lamebrained *The Main Event*) or in music (for example, *ButterFly* in 1974), Peters was a major force—for better or worse—in her creative decisions.

The men's club in Hollywood power circles has never dealt well with women who grab commanding industry positions. Thus Barbra almost failed when she fought and wheedled to get the musical *Yentl* (1983) made. She wore several hats on this pet project: producer, director, coscenarist, and star. Her obsessive, meticulous methods drove many on the picture to distraction, including distinguished author Isaac Bashevis Singer, who wrote the short story on which the musical was based. Said the disillusioned Singer when the film was completed, "I must say that Miss Streisand was exceedingly kind to herself [in the film]. The result is that Miss Streisand is always present, while Yentl is absent." Snapped Barbra, "If a writer doesn't want his work changed, he shouldn't sell it."

Stinging from the ordeal of getting *Yentl* made, it was four years before the celebrity returned to the screen, this time playing the emotionally distraught prostitute in 1987's *Nuts*. Off camera, the forty-something star gained public attention when she had a relationship in the late 1980s with hunky Don Johnson, then the star of TV's *Miami Vice*. To her chagrin, he dumped her to remarry former wife Melanie Griffith. Barbra's ex-boyfriend Jon Peters (now head of a film studio) greenlighted *Prince of Tides* (1991), which she directed and costarred in with Nick Nolte. Also that year, the ever-surprising Streisand dated tennis star Andre Agassi, who was three years younger than her son Jason. When that

W hile championed by many over the decades for her artistry as an entertainer, Streisand has had her share of detractors, including the following:

"There's a market on late-night TV shows for anti-Streisand anecdotes. She scares people. She could be Madame Guillotine the way some people speak of her."

—London's *Sunday Times*

"I had no disagreements with Barbra Streisand. I was merely exasperated at her tendency to become a complete megalomaniac."

—Walter Matthau, costar of 1969's *Hello, Dolly!*

"Miss Streisand is possibly the only fishwife ever to become a star. She has broad abrasive theatricality, and she sings well, though without much individuality. But since Funny Girl, *her performances grow repellent."*

—Stanley Kauffmann, reviewing 1970's *On a Clear Day You Can See Forever*

"This summer may go down in history as the summer of horror movies, but none of these can match Barbra Streisand and her latest offering."

—critic John Simon on 1979's *The Main Event*

alliance vaporized, Streisand, an ardent Democrat, became a center of attention for her enthusiastic support of Bill Clinton in his 1992 run for the U.S. presidency.

She proved she was still a major recording presence with her 1993 *Back to Broadway* album. At the end of that year, she returned to the concert stage after a twenty-two-year absence. The concert's enormous success led to other such engagements, including her 2000 tour, which she insisted was her last. During this period, she starred in and directed the much-lambasted *The Mirror Has Two Faces* (1996). In July 1998, she and actor James Brolin, a year her elder, wed in an elaborate ceremony at her Malibu, California, compound. Late 2001 saw the release of her *Christmas Memories* album. In fall 2002, Barbra broke her two-year retirement from live concert giving by performing at a Democratic fund-raiser in Hollywood.

As a show-business queen, Streisand's reign has been supreme and unique. But much more so than another much-loved singing great, Judy Garland, Barbra always seemed to have a proverbial chip on her shoulder; she was always ready to battle anyone in her path. Sometimes her attitude has been more damning than her deeds, as when she said while making *Nuts*, "I want so much to be liked and understood. But I have to be in control because so much of the world is so stupid!" Also typical was the famous encounter between Brooklyn's own Barbra and the Italian cinema sexpot Sophia Loren. The latter enthused to Streisand, "I would give anything if I could sing like you." To which Barbra responded, "If I could look like you, I wouldn't even want to talk!" Promises, promises.

Gloria Swanson

[Gloria May Josephine Svensson]
MARCH 27, 1899–APRIL 4, 1983

During Hollywood's silent era, Swanson was a magical screen personality. She gravitated from Cecil B. DeMille's saucy dramas of the upper crust in the second decade of the twentieth century to an output of exceedingly popular features in the 1920s, in which her array of movie heroines included gamines, shop girls, society matrons, and—in *Sadie Thompson* (1928)—a prostitute. Offscreen, the four-foot, eleven-and-a-half-inch, dark-haired movie diva enjoyed an oversized life that encompassed a spectacular Los Angeles mansion, a fleet of cars (including a leopard-upholstered Lancia), and a procession of husbands and lovers. Among her six spouses was Henri, Marquis de la Falaise de la Coudraye. That gave the divine Gloria the rare distinction of being the first Hollywood movie star to wed European royalty, just as a prior union had produced a daughter and made Swanson one of the first of Tinseltown's megastars *not* to hide the fact that she was a mother. But then, at the studio or away from it, Queen Gloria was way above normal standards. She had such smarts and acting talent and so much public adoration that her least whim (and there were ever so many) was someone's command to accomplish on the studio set, in fashionable Hollywood society, or at home in her grand private life.

On the other hand, extravagant Swanson was not so daring (or foolish) that she didn't feel it necessary to camouflage indelicate situations. One was her late-1920s romance with Joseph P. Kennedy, the married Massachusetts banker, film distributor, and father of three future politicians (John, Robert, and Edward). Like so many of the men she allowed into her privileged life, he took advantage of her physically, emotionally, and financially. That she let this happen repeatedly with her consorts was not really a case of "love is blind." Rather, it was her belief that no matter how famous, rich, and powerful she was, there *must* be a man to hopefully shelter, guide, and control her. In that respect, Swanson was very old-fashioned.

Later in life, Gloria made a tremendous return to pictures in *Sunset Boulevard* (1950). In that classic drama, she played a deranged superstar from silent films who pathetically dreams of a great screen comeback. Swanson was so effective in her performance as the demented, homicidal Norma Desmond that forever after the public merged the role with the actress herself.

She was born Gloria May Josephine Svensson in Chicago in 1899 (some sources cite 1897 or 1898). She was the only child of Joseph Svensson, of Swedish descent, and Adelaide Klanowski, whose forebears came from Germany. Her father was an army officer, and as a military brat, Gloria attended an assortment of schools before the family resettled in the Windy City when she was in her early teens. At one juncture, she dreamed of becoming an opera singer, but a chance visit to the local Essanay movie studio in 1913 changed all that. She began working in the company's silent short subjects. At the film factory, she met burly Wallace Beery. When Beery went to California in 1915 to improve his career options, she soon followed. He signed on at Mack Sennett's Keystone studio and persuaded the slapstick comedy king to hire Gloria, whose screen surname was now Swanson. She and Beery eloped in March 1916, but from the start they were not a good match. He was crude, abusive, and uncaring. (He raped her on their wedding night; at a later date, he tricked her into swallowing medication that caused her to abort their baby.) The Swanson-Beery union terminated after only a few unpleasant months.

By 1918, Gloria, who hated lowly slapstick, had graduated to leads in weepy dramas at Triangle Pictures. The next year, she transferred to Paramount where, under the tutelage of indulgent film director Cecil B. DeMille, she appeared in *Don't Change Your Husband* (1919), the first of her polished, titillating bedroom tales. Gloria was soon beloved by filmgoers—particularly shop girls, who fanatically mimicked her hairstyles and outfits and thrived on movie magazine reports that revealed snatches of her privileged and sophisticated lifestyle. With her $3,500-a-week salary, the actress purchased a twenty-four-room home that required a minimum of eleven servants.

Decorated lavishly, the mansion became one of Beverly Hills's six great showplaces. This extravagant abode was part of her ambitious life plan: "When I am a star, I will be every inch and every moment the star. Everyone from the studio gateman to the highest executive will know it."

In December 1919, Swanson wed Herbert K. Somborn, the former head of Equity Pictures, who owned the local Brown Derby restaurants. Their daughter, Gloria, was born in October 1920. Somborn was twice Swanson's age and she had married him hoping for emotional and financial security. Instead, he took over managing her business deals, and she ended by paying *all* their bills. To make matters worse, "I felt no strong passion for him; he had given me no cause." They separated in spring 1921 and their divorce occurred two years later. Not long after the split, Gloria adopted a baby boy she named Joseph after her father. It was gossiped that the infant might be her own child, a rumor she emphatically denied. Meanwhile, Gloria continued to indulge her rich lifestyle. It was not uncommon for her to spend, in a given year, $9,600 for silk stockings, $25,000 for furs, and $50,000 for gowns. (Years later, looking back on such whimsical extravagance, Swanson reasoned, "In those days they [the fans] wanted us to live like kings and queens . . . so we did. . . . We were making more money than we ever dreamed existed, and there was no reason to believe that it would ever stop.")

On her own, Swanson wrangled a new Paramount deal. The new agreement provided her with $6,500 weekly and permitted her to shoot most of her new pictures in New York, where she found the cultural climate more to her liking. Desperate with fear of losing their big box-office winner, the studio complied. Her first picture made on the East Coast was *Zaza* (1923); later came the hugely successful *Manhandled* (1924). Next, she had the notion of making the elaborate *Madame Sans-Gêne* and again the studio acquiesced, undertaking this lavish $700,000 feature to be shot on locations in France. While making the high-profile production, she required a translator on the set. Dashing Henri, Marquis de la Falaise de la Coudraye was hired, and soon the couple were lovers. They wed in January 1925 in Paris. But she had little time to rejoice. Gloria was pregnant, but to have a baby so soon after her marriage would destroy her box-office standing. So the next day she had an abortion, during which she contracted blood poisoning and later nearly died. On her recovery, the couple returned to the United States. She wired Paramount, "Am arriving with the Marquis tomorrow. Please arrange ovation." The studio heads followed her dictates. There was a glorious premiere for *Madame Sans-Gêne* in New York City, followed by an even more spectacular debut of the film in Los Angeles. The streets were jammed with fans anxious to see their beloved Gloria—now royalty—make her triumphant return to Tinseltown. But shrewd Swanson told herself that evening, "It should be happening when I'm fifty. I'm only twenty-six. What's left? How can I top it?"

Gloria made the four remaining features on her Paramount contract. She hedged about resigning, and the terrified studio offered her a

Gloria Swanson displaying her world-famous profile in *Fine Manners* (1926).

(Courtesy of JC Archives)

staggering $1 million annually to remain with the company. She declined, choosing to form her own production company for which a new friend and soon-to-be lover, Joseph P. Kennedy, raised the needed funds. (Meanwhile, Swanson's spouse had been given an industry job, one that would keep him largely in Europe and out of Gloria's path.) The star had success with *The Love of Sunya* (1927) and *Sadie Thomp-*

son (1928), winning an Academy Award nomination for the latter, but failed badly when she invested nearly $1 million of her own funds in *Queen Kelly* (1929), a salacious tale of debauched characters. Kennedy eventually convinced Gloria to fire its director, Erich von Stroheim, and to close down the silent picture (which was shelved for years, except for showings in Europe and South America). Making the debacle even worse, Kennedy soon ended his affair with Swanson and returned to his wife and family. The final insult occurred when Gloria discovered that Joe had largely used her funds to finance their incredibly expensive fling together.

Her career and finances in near ruin, Gloria made a comeback with her first sound film, *The Trespasser* (1929), and was Oscar-nominated. She and Henri divorced in 1930, and Swanson married Irish-born sportsman Michael Farmer the following year. Their daughter was born in 1932; two years later, the pair divorced. After doing 1934's *Music in the Air* freelance, Gloria—considered passé by the film colony and deserted by her vast public—did not make another movie until 1941's negligible *Father Takes a Wife*. To fill the slack in her life, she became a businesswoman with multiple interests. She took on husband number five, retired businessman George W. Davey, in January 1945. They separated some six weeks later and divorced in 1946.

The eternal Swanson made another screen return in 1950's *Sunset Boulevard*, which provided her with her third and final Oscar bid. Her movie projects thereafter were occasional, ranging from an Italian-French coproduction in 1952 to her final picture, *Airport 1975*, in 1974. She received acclaim on Broadway and on tour in *Butterflies Are Free* in the early 1970s and made infrequent appearances on TV talk shows. Her last marriage was in 1976 to William Dufty, the author of a book on the evils of sugar addictions. Gloria's memoir, *Swanson on Swanson* (1980), was a fascinat-ing chronicle of her career. She died from a heart ailment in New York in 1983.

Until the end, energetic, inquisitive, and queenly Gloria, who once ruled a film studio and enjoyed an incredibly bountiful life, never looked back on her resplendent past. "I always look ahead. I never regret. I have excitement every waking minute."

Elizabeth Taylor

[Elizabeth Rosemond Taylor]

FEBRUARY 27, 1932–

Many detractors called the actress a pushy dame long before Queen Elizabeth II named her Dame Elizabeth Taylor in late 1999. But British-born Taylor, often termed Hollywood's last great movie star, has long been a controversial figure, inspiring conflicting reactions to her high-drama, indulgent life. For example, although many moviegoers labeled her as the world's most beautiful woman, Richard Burton—one of Liz's seven husbands and the only one to marry her twice—once said of his five-foot, four-inch better half: "[She] has a double chin and an overdeveloped chest, and she's rather short in the legs. So I can hardly describe her as the most beautiful creature I've ever seen." And for those who thought the glamorous, much-coveted Taylor was someone to envy, superstar Joan Crawford had a different estimation of the much younger Elizabeth: "Miss Taylor is a spoiled, indulgent child, a blemish on public decency."

Crawford's scathing assessment was issued in 1962, when thirty-year-old Liz was at the peak of her box-office popularity, having won her first Oscar for 1960's *Butterfield 8*. At the time, the travails and scandal surrounding the making of *Cleopatra* (1963) were grabbing top headlines around the world. Probably never before and never again would one actress hold the fate of a major movie studio in her gem-adorned hands. Her indulgent behavior would set not only a giant film company on its ear but establish a new precedent in Hollywood for out-of-control behavior and lavish coddling. The fantastic events that transpired off camera during the production of this saga made the resultant opulent film pale by comparison. Most likely, if the real-life Cleopatra (69–30 B.C.) had been alive to witness Taylor's reign of gluttonous extravagance, the Egyptian queen would have bowed in deference to this twentieth-century diva.

The chaos began innocently enough when veteran film producer Walter Wanger bought the screen rights to Charles Marie Franzero's *The Life and Times of Cleopatra* (1957) for $15,000. Soon after, he made a deal to produce films at Twentieth Century-Fox and, in September 1958, suggested to Spyros Skouras (president of the studio) that he wished to make *Cleopatra*. The Greek-born executive was old enough to recall that, back in 1917, the

Larry Parks and Elizabeth Taylor in *Love Is Better than Ever* (1952). (Courtesy of JC Archives)

studio had made a lavish silent feature starring Theda Bara as the Egyptian monarch and the picture had done very well at the box office. He green-lighted the project, hoping the costume drama could turn the tide for the beleaguered studio, which had been on a losing streak for years.

Almost immediately, everything went expensively haywire. Skouras intended to use a studio contract player (such as Joan Collins, Joanne Woodward, or Suzy Parker) in the lead or, if the casting went out of house, then perhaps Susan Hayward, Audrey Hepburn,

Shirley MacLaine, or Sophia Loren. Wanger insisted that it must be Elizabeth Taylor. He was not dissuaded, even when Taylor in a facetious mood stated that her fee must be $1 million. (At the time, no Hollywood megastar was earning such a magnificent salary.) She was surprised when Wanger agreed to the sum.

Fox was aghast at Liz's demand, but she didn't care. For one thing, after making one more picture under her MGM contract, she would be free to accept many other lucrative movie offers. Then too, the widow Taylor (whose third husband, Mike Todd, had died in a plane crash in March 1958) was preoccupied with a new amour. She was involved with Todd's best friend, singer Eddie Fisher, then married to America's sweetheart, movie star Debbie Reynolds. (When a gossip columnist questioned Liz about the propriety of dating so soon after the tragedy, Taylor snapped, "Mike's dead and I'm alive. . . . What do you expect me to do—sleep alone?") While negotiations dragged on regarding *Cleopatra*, Liz and Eddie wed in May 1959. Then, with her bridegroom/gofer in tow, she went to London to make *Suddenly, Last Summer* (1959), directed by Joseph L. Mankiewicz.

On September 1, 1959, Taylor agreed to do *Cleopatra*, but Liz had additional demands: The film was to be shot in England; she required $4,500 weekly living expenses for herself and Fisher; they had to have a penthouse suite at London's swank Dorchester Hotel; a Rolls-Royce limousine was to shuttle her back and forth to the set; and she had final say as to hairstylist and costume designers. Also, the picture must be shot in the Todd A-O process developed by her late husband Todd, in whose company she owned stock. Finally, Taylor was not required to film during the first two days of her menstrual cycle.

In the understatement of the century, Skouras told Wanger that he was worried about the studio working with Taylor because "she'll be too much trouble." Nevertheless, by mid-1960, it was finalized that Elizabeth would do *Cleopatra*, with the film to be shot largely in England. In further negotiations, she was to receive $50,000 per week after the initial sixteen weeks, as well as 10 percent of the gross income of the movie. She also demanded that actor friend Roddy McDowall be given a role in the film and that she was to receive a complimentary 16-mm print of the completed feature.

On August 31, 1960, Liz and Eddie arrived in England, where they pushed through a huge crowd of onlookers at the London airport. She refused to stop for photos, still angered that the British press had treated her so harshly during the filming of *Suddenly, Last Summer*. Production was to start on September 30. Rouben Mamoulian was to direct, with Peter Finch cast as Julius Caesar and Stephen Boyd to play Mark Antony. By now, the production budget was up to $7 million. The initial days of shooting had to film around Taylor. First she was suffering from a cold; then she was distraught when Fisher had to fly back to California on business. Even with these delays, the production lacked a satisfactory script and the massive period sets were still being built (at overtime costs). Over the next few months, the star's health remained marginal. Her persistent cold turned into a viral infection, and she took days off to vacation in warmer climes. By January 19, 1961, Mamoulian had quit as director and, with Liz's approval, Joseph L. Mankiewicz was hastily substituted. The new director discarded most of the expensive earlier screenplay versions and begin rewriting the epic (while filming other scenes).

On March 4, 1961, Taylor was rushed to the hospital and it was feared she was dying of pneumonia. An emergency tracheotomy was performed to help her breathe. Surviving the ordeal (during which she died four times), she announced, "I felt I touched God." On the twenty-ninth of the month, she flew back to Los Angeles with Fisher to recuperate. On April 18, thanks to a sympathy vote, she won her *Butterfield 8* Academy Award. When Liz finally returned to work on September 1, the filming had been switched to the Cinecitta Studios in Rome (with only ten minutes of footage salvaged from the extremely expensive England shoot). Because of other commitments, Finch and Boyd were gone, replaced, respectively, by Rex Harrison and Richard Burton. To entice Taylor to come to Italy, the studio had met her new set of demands. Besides a huge entourage (including a Greek chef they had encountered on a vacation cruise), family, pets, and so forth, Taylor and Fisher insisted on a sizeable villa for their personal use. She wanted her personal physician to come to Rome for six weeks at a $25,000 fee. There was also the question of her dressing room accommodations. For this, Fox ordered that an entire building at the studio be designated for her use, and it was redesigned to encompass space for her personal room, a wig room, a makeup room, and facilities for helpers.

On September 25, 1961, *Cleopatra* got under way in Rome. By mid-November, with the shooting going at a snail's pace, Taylor casually told Skouras (who was now in fear of being ousted from his corporate post by the Fox stockholders), "What do you care how much *Cleopatra* costs? Fox pictures have been lousy. At least this one will be great—though expensive." By now, the budget was over $17 million. The insurance firm Lloyds of London had finally settled for $2 million regarding the losses suffered during the British debacle; that sum covered only a portion of the losses Fox sustained.

Toward the end of January 1962, most of Rex Harrison's sequences with Taylor had been completed and on January 22, Liz and Burton (he had been sitting idle in Rome for many weeks) did their first scene together. When Liz had first encountered the married actor in 1952, he had been in Hollywood shooting *The Robe* (1953) for Twentieth Century-Fox. She was then wed to actor Michael Wilding, and Burton was legally tied to Sybil Williams. Taylor had not thought much of him then nor had he of her. (In fact, before arriving in Rome to make the spectacle, he'd crudely referred to his costar as "Miss T***.") But she—and soon, he—had a dramatic change of heart. Burton, the father of two, appeared on the set with such a bad hangover that he couldn't stop his hands from trembling. His vulnerability made him suddenly appealing to Liz. Only a few days later, the distressed director was issuing an SOS alert to company higher-ups: "Liz and Burton are not just playing Antony and Cleopatra."

Soon the explosive romance was the gossip of Rome and the international media was frenzied to confirm the affair. The studio tried to play down the love match. Before long, however, the truth was out about the torrid affair, with Eddie and Sybil victims caught in the wake. Liz's only concern now was being with Richard. As the domestic merry-go-round spun faster, Taylor feared Burton might return to Sybil out of guilt. By February 21, she was physically distressed and announced, "My heart feels as though it is hemorrhaging." Before long, a Vatican City publication, among others, was denouncing the costars' scandalous behavior.

By April 21, with the Taylor-Burton alliance the juiciest talk of the world, the two lovers disappeared for a brief holiday at Porto Santo Stefano, some sixty miles north of Rome. Days later, when Liz reappeared in Rome, she had a black eye and a bruised nose. She insisted her injuries were the result of her chauffeur having to stop the car suddenly and her having fallen forward. It was estimated it would take three weeks for her to be in shape to film again. Meanwhile, a distraught Eddie and Sybil flew in and out of Rome, making statements as to

Taylor, the first female Hollywood star to earn $1 million per picture, had an extremely expensive hobby: collecting *real* jewels. (In 2002 she authored *Elizabeth Taylor: My Love Affair with Jewelry*.) Regarding her addiction to gems, she said, "'The more the better,' has always been my motto." She also preferred that others do the buying.

In the late 1940s, athlete Glenn Davis, her boyfriend of the moment, gifted her with a necklace of sixty-nine graduated pearls. Mike Todd, her future third husband added to her collection with diamond earrings, a pearl ring, and a twenty-carat diamond engagement ring. A few weeks before they wed in 1957, Todd also presented her with a gold necklace. Said Taylor, "I love being surrounded by beautiful things and I love being looked after." Once married, Mike surprised her with a magnificent necklace of diamonds and rubies with, of course, matching earrings. Husband number four, singer Eddie Fisher, gave Elizabeth such baubles as an oversized diamond ring. While she was in Rome filming *Cleopatra* (1963), he made her the owner of "a bracelet of sapphires, diamonds and green stones, set in gold and platinum, designed like a delicately woven coronet." Remarked the actress, "He knows how to please me."

During Taylor's first marriage to Welsh actor Richard Burton, the British-born actress acquired a $65,000 40-carat blue sapphire brooch, the 33.19-carat Krupp diamond worth $305,000, and the 69.42-carat Cartier diamond costing $1.5 million. Later, when divorcing Burton the first time, she dated used-car salesman Henry Wynberg, who purchased a lavish coral necklace for Elizabeth. He ordered the jeweler to "Make it bigger." To celebrate his second marriage to Taylor, Burton presented her with a 72-carat diamond wedding band. Her next husband, John Warner, the gentleman farmer–turned–politician, gave her a remarkable engagement ring made of diamonds, rubies, and sapphires. When asked if he could support her in her accustomed lavish lifestyle, Warner replied that "if I can't, perhaps she will support me." In 1982, a Mexican attorney named Victor Gonzalez Luna was Taylor's temporary beau. He presented her with a diamond and ruby ring. Later that year, she returned the $250,000 trinket to Luna when they called off their engagement. A few years later, she gifted herself with a $623,000 brooch that had once belonged to the duchess of Windsor.

whether or not there would be divorces. In the midst of all this—in mid-May 1962—Taylor received a letter threatening her life and those of her children. Special police were detailed and the matter died down.

Between bad weather, Taylor having dental problems, and infighting among studio executives, efforts to have Elizabeth finish her filming by June 1 did not happen. The desperate situation intensified when in June, back in Los Angeles, Fox fired Marilyn Monroe for her prima donna actions, which had delayed an orderly filming of *Something's Got to Give*. Said a Fox spokesperson, "No company can afford Monroe and Taylor." As production on *Cleopatra* crept into July, those in charge debated about deleting battle sequences to be shot in Egypt. Elizabeth suddenly decided if the company went to Egypt, she wanted to join them. However, since she had converted to Judaism for her marriage to Fisher, Egyptian officials did not want her there. Finally, on July 23, 1962, Taylor shot her last scene on *Cleopatra*.

Over succeeding months, Darryl F. Zanuck replaced the now-ousted Spyros Skouras as studio head. He ordered certain battle scenes to be reshot and fired and then rehired Mankiewicz, who was editing the many hours of footage down to five hours. The director begged to have the picture released as two films, but Zanuck vetoed the notion because he feared the Taylor-Burton liaison might be old news by the time the second part could be issued. By the time *Cleopatra* was distributed in mid-1963, the cost for the epic had risen to $44 million. Released in a 243-minute road

show version (later cut to 194 minutes), the movie grossed $26 million in domestic distribution. With foreign distribution and later ancillary sales, it finally turned a marginal profit of $5.5 million. The picture earned nine (mostly token) Oscar nominations and won four Academy Awards (none for its actors).

As for Taylor, she later insisted the worst humiliation of making the lavish film that almost sank a studio was having to see the picture. She claimed that after screening it, she threw up. (Many filmgoers who sat through the lugubrious epic could empathize with Liz's reaction to the celluloid saga.) In her personal life, on March 5, 1964, she divorced Eddie Fisher. Burton, untied from his wife, wed Taylor in Montreal, Canada, nine days later. Their first union, full of extravagant living, drunken binges, separations, and reconciliations ended on June 26, 1974, when she divorced him in Switzerland. Unable to resist one another, they remarried on October 10, 1975, in a tiny village on a Botswana game preserve in Africa. That match lasted only several months, and by July 30, 1976, Burton had divorced Taylor again. Years passed, and Liz and Dick—each of whom had had other spouses and lovers in the interim—reunited in 1983 for a stage production of *Private Lives*. He died of a brain hemorrhage in August 1984 at age fifty-nine.

The indomitable actress and mother of three offspring went on to spearhead (to her great credit) a major fund-raising drive to find a treatment and cure for AIDS. Later, she married and subsequently divorced burly blue-collar worker Larry Fortensky, survived more life-threatening surgery, underwent repeated treatment for substance abuse, and maintained an odd friendship with singer Michael Jackson. In December 2002 Taylor was among the five notables who received the Kennedy Center Honors for their lifetime achievements in the creative arts.

Surviving a lifetime of pampered living, freewheeling Liz has said of herself, "You can see through celluloid, and it is brittle. Neither of those things is true about me." As for the infamous picture that caused so much gossip, havoc, and financial loss, Taylor admitted years later, "I really don't remember much about *Cleopatra*. There were a lot of other things going on." However, she allowed, she had learned something from the ordeal. "You find out who your real friends are when you're involved in a scandal."

Lana Turner

[Julia Jean Mildred Frances Turner]
FEBRUARY 8, 1920–JUNE 29, 1995

Once when Turner was asked who should star in her life story if it were ever filmed, she snapped back, "She hasn't been born yet!" The name "superstar" was correct, for Lana (most famously known as the screen's "Sweater Girl") was a one-of-a-kind luminary in an era crowded with screen goddesses created by the Hollywood studios.

She was a unique fabrication both on and off camera. A five-foot, three-and-a-half-inch blond with fetching blue eyes and a 35-23-35 figure, the 110-pound Lana was a stunner. She may not have been the world's best actress, but what she lacked in dramatic subtlety she made up for with a magical screen presence. In pictures like *The Postman Always Rings Twice* (1946), *Peyton Place* (1957)—for which she was Oscar-nominated—and *Imitation of Life* (1959), Lana provided larger-than-life performances that were convincing to moviegoers because she so earnestly believed in her celluloid characterizations.

Away from the soundstages, Turner was an equally legendary personality—a truly nonstop party girl. She was (in)famous for the impetuous whirlwind romances she initiated with movie stars and "civilians," all undertaken with little concern for her movie career or her studio employers. Some of these amours she wed, but her legalized unions all ended in divorce. In her later years, when she reflected on her marital track record, luscious Lana said, "In my wildest dreams I never, never thought that I would have seven husbands [actually eight, for she wed Stephen Crane twice]. . . . I thought at the time that each marriage would last forever. You see, with one bitterly painful exception [Tyrone Power], when I fell in love, I married."

During the course of Lana's tempestuous love life, which included several hushed-up abortions and at least one miscarriage, she had one child, daughter Cheryl. The latter would have her moment in the limelight when Turner's then-lover, minor gangland figure Johnny Stompanato, was stabbed to death in April 1958, purportedly by teenaged Cheryl to protect her mother from him.

She was born Julia Jean Mildred Frances Turner in 1920 (although she later claimed 1921 as her birth year) in Wallace, Idaho, a tiny, grimy mining town. Her dad, Virgil, a roving worker from Alabama, had met Mildred Frances Cowan, a beautician, in Wallace. They soon eloped and later became parents to Julia (who was nicknamed Judy). By the time Judy was eight, the Turners were living in San Francisco. On December 15, 1930, Virgil Turner, after winning big in an all-night craps game, was found murdered. (His assailant was never apprehended.) A few years later, Mildred and young Judy relocated to Los Angeles where the teenager enrolled at Hollywood High School. Already the girl had a spectacularly adult physique.

One day while cutting classes, Judy was sipping a coke at the Top Hat Café located near her school. She caught the attention of Billy Wilkerson, publisher of the *Hollywood Reporter*. He thought the pretty youngster with the long auburn hair should be in pictures. He introduced her to a talent agent who found the teen a job as an extra in *A Star Is Born* (1937). Thereafter, producer/director Mervyn LeRoy hired Judy to appear in a screen drama, *They Won't Forget* (1937). One of her few scenes required her to strut down a backlot street wearing a snug skirt and a form-fitting sweater. Her noteworthy screen stroll caught moviegoers' interest and LeRoy signed her to a personal contract at $50 weekly. In 1938, he transferred to MGM and took Judy with him. At her new studio base, she adopted the screen name of Lana Turner and wore bright red hair. Her MGM debut was in Mickey Rooney's *Love Finds Andy Hardy* (1938), and she and Mickey had a romance that supposedly led to an abortion.

While making *Dancing Co-Ed* (1939), self-absorbed Turner was unimpressed with arrogant, highly intellectual costar Artie Shaw. Later, she changed her mind about the famed bandleader. When her then-boyfriend, attorney Greg Bautzer, stood her up one night, she agreed to go out with Artie instead. During their date, the couple impulsively decided to fly to Nevada, where they wed on February 13, 1940. Realizing she'd forgotten to inform her mother where she was, Lana telegraphed her parent: "Got married in Las Vegas. Call you later. Love, Lana." Seven months later, Turner and Shaw divorced. The film colony speculated that a studio-arranged abortion had played a decisive role in their split.

With her striking performance in *Ziegfeld Girl* (1941) and then her dynamite chemistry on-screen with Clark Gable in *Honky Tonk* (1941), Lana became a full-fledged movie star. It led MGM to pamper, control, reassure, and rebuke their resident sexpot as over the years she rampaged through love affairs, abortions, and indulgent behavior on the film sets. She went from claptrap entries like 1945's *Keep Your Powder Dry* to glossy drama in the same year's *Week-end at the Waldorf*, reaching a peak with her erotic film noir entry *The Postman Always Rings Twice* (1946). She was lovely decoration as the villainess in the costumed adventure *The Three Musketeers* (1948), but her most striking performance was in *The Bad and the Beautiful* (1952), a classic insider's look at the Hollywood dream factory.

Lana Turner and Clark Gable in *Homecoming* (1948). (Courtesy of JC Archives)

There were many men in Lana's wild life. She wed restaurant owner Stephen Crane in 1942. Their daughter, Cheryl, was born in July 1943, but the couple divorced in April 1944. She dated exotic actor Turhan Bey, but the great love of her life was bisexual star Tyrone Power. He was married but played the field, and he did not want to be tied down to Lana. (It was he who urged her to abort their love child.) Four years later, she wed a wealthy Connecticut sportsman, Henry J. (Bob) Topping. In early 1949, their baby was stillborn. When the couple returned to Los Angeles, it was to a Beverly Hills mansion that Lana purchased with her own money because her husband was experiencing financial reverses. (They were divorced in 1952, not too long after

her suicide attempt, when petulant, generally depressed Lana cut her wrists.) The following September, turbulent Turner married hunky actor Les Barker, one of the screen's Tarzans. Barker later claimed that his and Lana's best times together were before they wed. The mismatched couple divorced in June 1957. (Later, it was revealed that Barker had reputedly sexually abused Lana's daughter.)

In the studio's latest economic wave, coddled Lana found herself adrift from MGM after *The Prodigal* (1955) and *Diana* (1956). Now in her mid-thirties and with no paternalistic studio to guide and protect her, she was at loose ends (but still had a cache of sorts at other studios). She rebounded with her Academy Award–nominated performance in 1957's

Journalist Adela Rogers St. John observed, "The real Lana Turner is the Lana Turner everyone knows about. She always wanted to be a movie star, and loved being one. Her personal life and her movie star life are one." But, while being a cinema star might seem glamorous, the perks had their price, according to Turner:

"The more famous an actress becomes, the less she's allowed to eat. Unless she wants to play people's mothers. And in bad clothes, yet."

"Until you're forty, you can coast on your looks. After that, as I've had to find out, you'd better develop your acting muscles!"

"I thank God that neither I nor any member of my family will ever be so hard up that we have to work for Otto Preminger!" (The director and Lana collided in preproduction on 1959's *Anatomy of a Murder.* She was replaced by Lee Remick.)

Peyton Place for Twentieth Century-Fox. Then came the scandal involving her gangland gigolo, Johnny Stompanato, who was stabbed to death with a butcher knife at Turner's Beverly Hills home in April 1958. Lana's long-ago beau, Jerry Geisler, was the defense attorney at the highly publicized trial where Cheryl received a jury verdict of justifiable homicide. (The Hollywood rumor mill still insists that it was Lana who wielded the deadly knife on that fatal Good Friday.)

A born survivor, Lana regained much of her screen popularity with 1959's *Imitation of Life* and such follow-ups as *By Love Possessed* (1961) and *Madame X* (1966). She married department store millionaire Fred May in 1960, but that coupling lasted only two years. Her next spouse was author Robert Eaton, who was out of her life by 1969. That spring she wed for the final time—to hypnotist and dietitian Robert Dante. After they divorced in

December 1969, Lana, who was nearing fifty, decided against any more walks down the aisle.

As film roles dried up for the aging screen siren, she tried a TV series, *The Survivors* (1970), but it was short-lived. She toured in the romantic drama *40 Carats* and ended her screen career with such features as the trashy *Witches' Brew* (1980). She bounced back yet again playing the chic Jacqueline Perrault on TV's *Falcon Crest* from 1982 to 1983.

In her final years, Lana lived in a condo in Century City, built on part of the backlot of Twentieth Century-Fox where she had made feature films decades earlier. Her autobiography was published in 1982, and one of her final TV appearances was a guest shot on *The Love Boat* in 1985. In 1992, Turner, who had been a heavy smoker all her life, was diagnosed with throat cancer. Treatment provided a remission, but the disease returned in 1994. It led her to becoming very religious. She died at her condo with Cheryl and a maid/companion in attendance. Turner requested that there be no funeral service and that she be cremated.

Once when examining her love life, the twentieth-century's great playgirl said, "You know, to love and to be loved are two very different things. I always thought I was being loved for myself. It was only later I found out I wasn't. If they're clever and if they give me the right story, I take the bait. Then I get kicked in the teeth again." It sounded remarkably similar to her love-hate relationship with studio bosses during her many years at MGM during its—and her—heyday.

Lupe Velez

[María Guadalupe Vélez de Villalobos]
JULY 18, 1908–DECEMBER 13, 1944

Decades before the current popularity of Jennifer Lopez and Salma Hayek, another female Latin sex symbol reigned in Hollywood. Velez may have only been about five feet tall, but this dark-haired beauty was a highly sexed and volatile personality who stormed through Hollywood (and life). During her heyday, the outgoing, peppery Lupe (known variously as the "Mexican Spitfire," the "Queen of the Hot-Cha," the "Hot Tamale," and the "Mexican Wildcat") tantalized lovers, caught the imagination of filmgoers, and captivated the amused press. On the other hand, with her oversized self-absorption and volcanic temper, she was often the bane of show-business coworkers.

If movie studios stereotypically placed the petite Lupe into repetitious, exotic celluloid roles, she proved to be a creative dynamo when it came to earning public attention. At a moment's notice, she could gain reporters' attention by expounding loudly in a heavily accented barrage about her latest enthusiasms or pet annoyances in life. Unlike other talents

who found it necessary to reinvent their public image every few years, Velez remained her same excitable, flamboyant self to the end—an untimely one, at that.

She was born María Guadalupe Vélez de Villalobos in 1908 in San Luis de Potosi, a suburb of Mexico City. According to legend—which may or may not be true since there is little surviving documentation of her early life—her father, Jacob Villalobos, was an officer in the Mexican army. Her mother, Josefina, had been an opera singer. (There were also three other children—Emigdio, Mercedes, and Josefina.) Reportedly, Maria attended a convent school in San Antonio, Texas, where she quickly displayed a rambunctious, willful nature. After her father's death a few years later, she returned home to help the family survive financially. With her striking features, shapely figure, and extroverted nature, it was not a stretch when she turned to show business. Before long, she was cast in the musical revue *Ra-Ta-Plan* (1924).

With blazing ambition, the young woman moved to Los Angeles, hoping to make a career in silent pictures. She was broke when she reached Hollywood in 1926 but promptly found work dancing in the *Music Box Revue*, a local production starring the famed Fanny

Brice. With a knack for drawing attention to herself, the teenager was soon being offered Broadway jobs. However, she was determined to become a movie actress, wanting to follow the path of another captivating Mexican talent, Dolores Del Rio. Lupe, as she called herself, made a comedy short with producer Hal Roach, but she was far more effective playing an untamed mountain girl in swashbuckling Douglas Fairbanks Sr.'s *The Gaucho* (1928). She made her talkie film bow in *Lady of the Pavements* (1929), demonstrating that her thick accent and rapid speech would not hinder her box-office future.

During the making of *Wolf Song* (1929), tempestuous Velez was kept busy juggling her relationships with three men involved in the project. Crooner Russ Columbo, who had a part in the movie, was a past love; the picture's director, Victor Fleming, was a current flame; and lanky Gary Cooper, her costar, was soon to become her lover. Handsome Cooper may have been more than a foot taller than diminutive Lupe, but he was overwhelmed—and even afraid—of the spitfire. He adored her zest for life, but her sexual insatiability and her jealous tantrums wore him out. When angry, she thought nothing of lurching at him with a drawn knife (one time even stabbing him). On another occasion, when the emotionally exhausted man attempted to flee Los Angeles, she learned of his departure and arrived at the station just as the train was leaving. She shot at him, narrowly missing her target.

On her own again, Lupe turned to heavy-drinking John Gilbert, the one-time movie matinee idol. Gilbert did not have the energy to keep up with the highly charged Velez and they separated. Much more appealing to her was tall, muscular, young swimmer Johnny Weissmuller, who was making a major name for himself as the star of *Tarzan* movies at MGM where Lupe was under contract. The couple married in October 1933, but their ill-matched union was one of constant public fights, breakups, and emotional reunions, often orchestrated by Lupe to gain fresh publicity for herself. The duo would finally divorce in 1938.

In pictures like *East Is West* (1930), *The Squaw Man* (1931), and *Cuban Love Song* (1931), Velez played characters of assorted nationalities but essentially always with the same oversized spitfire persona. If Lupe was hard to handle on the soundstage, she was dynamite when rehearsing or performing in Broadway musicals. In *Hot-Cha!* (1932) and *Strike Me Pink* (1933), she was a determined scene-stealer who wrecked havoc with the script and song lyrics and repeatedly drove many of her fellow cast members to desperation. But she was such an entertaining bundle of personality that audiences adored her, the press loved her for providing colorful interviews, and harried producers tolerated her constant shenanigans because they brought patrons into theaters.

When Lupe's promising MGM contract ended after such screen disappointments as *Laughing Boy* (1934) with Ramon Novarro, she went abroad to make pictures in England and appear on the London stage. She was back in Hollywood by 1938, where she made *Girl from Mexico* (1939) at RKO. The picture had

Lupe Velez and Lee Tracy in *The Half-Naked Truth*
(1932). (Courtesy of JC Archives)

been shaped to Lupe's hot-blooded public image and she was abetted by veteran Leon Errol, the rubber-legged comedian who was great at milking laughs out of any stale script. The unpretentious entry proved to be a surprise hit and led to seven later installments of what became known as the *Mexican Spitfire* series. Velez was a viable screen personality once again.

Now in her thirties, Lupe seemed on the surface to be the same fun-loving, explosive creature as always. But underneath she was feeling vulnerable about her age and having to compete with younger actresses for movie roles. Moreover, she was very disappointed that she hadn't fulfilled her potential to become a respected dramatic actress. In her private life, she was tiring of the strain of supporting her extended family and longed for a man to take care of her; she also wanted to become a mother. At this juncture, the susceptible actress met twenty-seven-year-old Harold Ramond, an unemployed Frenchman who claimed to be an actor. Their relationship was filled with emotional peaks and valleys; her friends kept telling her that he was using her. Somehow, stubborn Lupe could not break free of this unproductive romance.

She went to Mexico to make *Nana* (1944), hoping the picture might open up new acting horizons beyond the Spitfire series or such derivative fare as *Redhead from Manhattan* (1943). When *Nana* did not prove to be that magical career-changer, Velez refocused even more intently on her affair with Harold. In late November 1944, she announced that she and Ramond would marry. A few weeks later, however, the unpredictable Velez insisted that the planned nuptials had been called off. Unknown except to a few relatives and friends, the movie star was four months pregnant and in an emotional tailspin. A lifelong, devout Catholic, she was appalled at the thought of her child being born illegitimate; on the other hand, she no longer believed that Harold sincerely cared for her as anything but his meal ticket. At one juncture, the hysterical actress considered having the child and then allowing one of her sisters—who lived with her—to claim the baby as her own. Being Catholic and given the moral standards of the day, having an abortion was out of the question for Velez.

On December 13, 1944, after attending the Hollywood opening of *Nana* with her good friend, actress Estelle Taylor, Lupe returned to her Beverly Hills mansion. Her sisters were away at the time, and a depressed Lupe took an overdose of sleeping pills. The next morning, she was found dead by her maid. At the nondenominational church service for Velez at Forest Lawn Memorial Park in Glendale, California, Johnny Weissmuller, Arturo de Cordova, and Gilbert Roland served as pallbearers. Later, Lupe was buried in a Mexico City cemetery.

Perhaps the actress's friend, journalist Adela Rogers St. Johns summed up Velez best: "Lupe was the epitome of joyous, uninhibited lust for life. Never was there a more effervescent, earthy female Latin personality. She was as colorful and explosive as the Fourth of July."

Mae West

[Mary Jane West]

AUGUST 17, 1893–NOVEMBER 22, 1980

Delightfully unique, West enjoyed a lengthy and successful show-business career. Her performance venues included vaudeville, Broadway, nightclubs, and movies, with occasional but memorable forays into radio (for example, her 1937 "Garden of Eden" skit) and TV (such as her sensational duet of "Baby, It's Cold Outside" with Rock Hudson on the March 1958 Academy Awards). In addition to writing plays, memoirs, and screenplays, the one-time shimmy dancer recorded vocal albums. Besides her performances, her greatest contribution to twentieth-century pop culture was demystifying the topic of romance. With an insouciant arching of an eyebrow, an exaggerated wiggle of her hourglass figure, or a well-timed witticism, she poked fun at the subject of sex so amusingly that afterward audiences were hard-pressed to take the once-taboo topic quite so seriously.

In contrast, Mae took herself extremely seriously. Her supreme narcissism about her looks and sexual prowess, her self-absorption in her show-business activities, and her reverence about her writings were part of her great attraction.

Over many years, vain Mae pontificated on many topics, but none so eloquently as her theories on sex (both having and not having it). "You've got to conserve your sex energy in order to *do* things," she insisted. On the other hand, she advised, "An orgasm a day keeps the doctor away." To help with the latter, she had a distinct regimen to keep in shape: "I massage my breasts . . . because the muscle under the arm doing the massaging holds the bust up and keeps the breasts firm. Breast exercises stimulate the whole body and glands and everything else, you know."

To ensure that the public understood that Mae's preachments derived from an extremely special person, West pointed out, "I come from a very good family, descendants from Alfred the Great." She also allowed, "I was born with sophistication and sex appeal but I'm never vulgar. Maybe it's breeding." She was boastful of her credentials as a bawdy babe: "I'd be insulted if a picture I was in didn't get an X-rating. Don't forget, dear, I *invented* censorship."

But there was a mortal side to this unorthodox love goddess. She could be arrogant and

Mae West at the zenith of her movie fame in the mid 1930s. (Courtesy of JC Archives)

Patrick II.) From an early age, Mae—as she became known—gravitated to show business and as far away as possible from the confining classroom. At six, she made her stage bow in a Brooklyn theater, performing a song-and-dance routine on amateur night. This led to working with a local stock company and then becoming a strong woman in a Coney Island acrobatic act. By age fifteen, she was touring in vaudeville.

When West was thirteen, she lost her virginity to her twenty-one-year-old music teacher. Thereafter, she insisted, she was never "without a man for more than a week." (Her array of lovers over the decades would include men from many professions, but she had a penchant for well-toned boxers.) In April 1911, she wed jazz singer Frank Wallace in Milwaukee, Wisconsin. Months later, West had second thoughts about matrimony and separated from him. However, the couple did not officially divorce until 1943, after he'd made national headlines by revealing his long-ago relationship with the veteran sex symbol. She never remarried.

Mae made her Broadway debut in 1911, quickly developing a reputation as an avant-garde, risqué entertainer. In 1920, she auditioned for the lead opposite boxer Jack Dempsey in the Pathé movie serial *Daredevil Jack*. In her screen test, she advised the heavyweight champ, "Hold me tighter. I can take anything you can throw." Although she did not win the screen role, she and the fighter enjoyed a brief fling. A few years later, in 1926, West jolted Broadway when she starred in *Sex*, a play she'd written. Morality groups per-

petty about her competitors and successors: "[Barbra] Streisand [in 1969's *Hello, Dolly!*] has the unmitigated gall to imitate me. Garbo does more thinking than talking, Theda Bara had a nice mean quality, and Clara Bow had cute sex. Lana [Turner] did very well, too. But," concluded La West, "there's nobody in my class."

She was born Mary Jane West in 1893 in Brooklyn, the child of John Patrick West, a prizefighter, and German immigrant Matilda Delker Doelger, a corset designer. (Later, the Wests would have Mildred [Beverly] and John

suaded the authorities to shut the production down and to have its star arrested. She was sentenced to ten days in jail and a $500 fine. Less notorious but more successful was her *Diamond Lil* (1928), a Broadway show dealing with a rambunctious gold digger.

Ex-gangland thug George Raft had become a movie star in the early 1930s. He suggested Mae, a past hot romance, for *Night After Night* (1932). She only had a featured role in this Paramount release, but the five-foot, two-inch West was the film's best attraction. Moviegoers were agog at this mature blond (she was nearing forty at the time) as she sashayed through the proceedings, rolling her eyes, swaying her hips, and stopping long enough to punctuate conversations with her "ahs." Delighted studio executives offered West over $100,000 and top billing to make a starring vehicle for them. She added a few demands of her own. The film, *She Done Him Wrong* (1933), was to be based on her *Diamond Lil*, and that entitled her to an additional $25,000 for creating the screenplay. Having the run of the Paramount lot, she handpicked handsome contractee Cary Grant to be her leading man. The result was a box-office bonanza. Almost single-handedly, she saved the studio from bankruptcy. As such, everyone there was in awe of Mae. That included exotic Paramount star Marlene Dietrich, who came to West's dressing room one day and volunteered to wash the new movie star's hair. According to Mae, "I had to turn her down—I was afraid she didn't mean the hair on my head."

"It's not the men in my life," West often quipped, "but the life in my men." Usually the bawdy queen of the double entendre liked to boast about her gentleman callers but not about vaudevillian Frank Wallace, whom she'd wed in 1911. They'd separated soon after but had never divorced. When the marriage came to public light in 1935, Mae was afraid it would hurt her image as a wisecracking, unmarried femme fatale. In a dilemma, West made a bad decision. Going against her image as a dame who was "on the level," she lied. She told the press, "I never heard of the guy." Even after diligent newshounds interviewed the down-and-out Wallace in New York City, Mae still denied that they'd ever been legally tied. "I'm glad if some New York hoofer has been able to get a job out of all this publicity," she allowed. "But personally, I've had enough of it." (So had Frank's second wife, whom he had bigamously wed in 1916. She left him.) Wallace went on the road with a new act billed as "Mr. Mae West." Sticking to her guns, sashaying West announced, "I'm a single gal with a single-track mind." By 1937, Wallace's legal action to claim part of her wealth had reached the courts. She finally admitted in her statement to the court that she was his wife, but (1) they'd never lived together as man and wife, and (2) he had since wed another woman without getting a divorce. The matter dragged on until summer 1943 when, in exchange for a divorce, she gave Frank a healthy settlement. But the press never forgot that she had fibbed to them.

For *I'm No Angel* (1933), Mae again starred and wrote the innuendo-filled screenplay. She received a whopping $200,000 for her double duty. By the time *Belle of the Nineties* (1934) was released, West was in conflict with assorted morality groups, including the Catholic Legion of Decency. The censorship battles escalated and Mae was increasingly forced to tone down her characterizations and plot lines, which diminished her uniqueness on-screen.

With 1938's *Every Day's a Holiday*, a very diluted vehicle, Mae had worn out her box-office welcome for the time being. Two years later, she returned to the screen, teamed at Universal Pictures with another one-of-a-kind talent, W. C. Fields. The resultant mock Western, *My Little Chickadee*, was fun but not prime West. However, it was a gem compared to the Columbia Pictures fiasco *The Heat's On* (1943), in which she looked overweight and (rightfully) distressed.

If Hollywood didn't want Mae, Broadway did. She starred in *Catherine Was Great* (1944), her take on the randy Russian empress. She was back on the New York stage in a revival of her *Diamond Lil* in 1949. During its run, West gained a lot of publicity from her offstage affair with one of the show's leading men, the much-younger Steve Cochran. In 1954, she headlined her own club act in Las Vegas, where her chorus line consisted of nine musclemen. Among the beefcakes was Mickey Hargitay. When the show moved to New York City, Hungarian-born Mickey came under the spell of buxom movie actress Jayne Mansfield, who was forty years Mae's junior. The two women, each mavens of self-promotion, pub-

licly battled over the hunky Hargitay. Newspapers had a field day with the blonds' tug-of-war, which saw the muscleman leaving Mae's act to be with (and later marry) Mansfield. Although the tiff had been great publicity, West was not one to quickly forgive a rival—especially a blond one.

Mae inaugurated a new play, *Sextette*, in mid-1961 at Chicago's Edgewater Beach Playhouse. Her leading man was Jack LaRue, a past lover who had been in West's 1928 edition of *Diamond Lil*. LaRue wasn't the only one to hang around Mae's life for decades. Paul Novak, a muscleman in her nightclub act in the mid-1950s, became her faithful companion for the last twenty-seven years of her life. He was half her age but totally devoted to the legend.

West had many film offers over the years, but it was not until 1970's *Myra Breckinridge* that the septuagenarian returned to the big screen. She was given $350,000 for ten days of work in this labored sex comedy. Knowing that the studio (Twentieth Century-Fox) and the public were expecting her to be a diva, West didn't disappoint. The fireworks started when statuesque twenty-nine-year-old Raquel Welch came for a preproduction introduction to the divine Mae at West's fabled Los Angeles apartment. The two were polite but wary. It certainly didn't help their future rapport when Raquel presented Mae with a bouquet of flowers and said, "I've admired you for a long time."

For her role as a man-hungry talent agent, Mae insisted on tailoring her dialogue to suit the character, which she envisioned as a sexy *young* thing. In addition, West demanded that another old hand, Oscar-winning Edith Head, design her—and no one else's—costumes for the picture. It was also decreed that only West could wear outfits in the film that used a black-and-white color combination. This did not sit well with Welch. Raquel, who had her own diva reputation, did an end run around Mae's dictate by having one of her own on-camera outfits made up in black and a very, very pale shade of blue. The battle lines had been drawn and the two actresses glared at one another for the remainder of the shoot.

It was eight years before Mae appeared in another movie and that starring vehicle, *Sextette* (1978), was her cinema swan song. In July 1980, West suffered a stroke. That November, she died of natural causes while resting peacefully in a chair in her living room. She was survived by her sister, Beverly, with whom Mae had long feuded.

In life, Mae remained an enigma on many subjects even to those who knew her well. However, on one topic she was always quite candid, "I never loved another person the way I loved myself."

Shelley Winters

[Shirley Schrift]
AUGUST 18, 1922–

In her screen heyday of the late 1940s and 1950s, she sometimes took on a strongly dramatic role (such as in 1951's *A Place in the Sun*), but she was much more firmly entrenched in moviegoers' minds as a svelte blond bombshell (as in 1949's *South Sea Sinner*). Years later, Winters carefully pointed out, "It's not merely talent that bring them [decision-making studio executives] your way in Hollywood, but being noticed and talked about. I discussed it with my press agent and quite cold-bloodedly we invented this personality—a dumb blond with a body and a set of sharp sayings." (A typical anecdote was "I had to go and see this guy, very important man, and everyone said: 'Watch out, Shelley, the second you get into his office, he'll tear your dress off.' 'I'll remember,' I said, 'I'll wear an old dress.' ")

Later in her career, Shelley used her screen fame and growing dramatic acumen to play character leads, often of the loudmouthed, colorful type (as in 1966's *Alfie* and 1976's *Next Stop, Greenwich Village*). In the process, she won two Best Supporting Actress Oscars (for 1959's *The Diary of Anne Frank* and 1965's *A Patch of Blue*). Even then, the tireless self-promoter still wisecracked to please listeners. For example, when asked what she thought of nudity on the screen, Winters responded, "I think it's disgusting! Shameful! And damaging to all things American. But if I were twenty-two with a great body, it would be artistic, tasteful, patriotic and a progressive, religious experience."

During her many decades in show business, Winters developed a reputation—which made her most welcome on TV talk shows—as a garrulous eccentric who might (and usually did) say anything about anyone. She had the knack of what she termed "embellishing" and gladly gave gab program hosts and audiences what they wanted. As such, she appeared to be a self-absorbed kook with a love of food, culture, and telling nonstop (embarrassing) anecdotes involving a slew of celebrity names. As Winters reached senior citizen status, it was hard to distinguish her wacky persona from the real woman. Nevertheless, while her chatter could be exhausting, she was frequently entertaining. Obviously, ambitious and self-focused Shelley understood how to adapt divahood to carry her successfully through each stage of life.

She was born in East St. Louis, Illinois, in 1922, the second daughter of Johan Schrift, a cutter/designer for the men's clothing industry, and his wife, Rose Winter. Rose, who loved music, had once won a singing contest at the St. Louis Municipal Opera but abandoned her career dreams of studying abroad to remain near her parents until she wed. When Shirley was three, she began her show-business career by pushing her way onto the stage during an amateur talent contest and beginning to sing.

When Shirley was still very young, the family relocated to Brooklyn. However, her father got into business difficulties and wrongly ended up in prison for a year. In high school, the teenager participated in class dramatics and worked at a five-and-dime store after school to pay for acting lessons. Some months before graduation, shapely five-foot, four-inch Shirley quit high school to become a dress model in the garment district. At night, she studied acting at the New Theater School and decided on her professional name, Shelley Winter (the *s* was added in 1947 in Holly-wood). Persistent if not experienced, she hounded casting offices, worked in a club chorus line, and did summer stock. In 1942, she married Chicago textile salesman Paul Mack Mayer. He soon entered World War II military service; the marriage fell apart as her career prominence grew, and they divorced in 1948. Also in 1942, Shelley won a supporting role in the Broadway operetta *Rosalinda*. It led to a studio contract with Columbia Pictures, where she had bit parts in major pictures like *Cover Girl* (1944) or an occasional bigger role in B movies like *Sailor's Holiday* (1944). Because the newcomer did not fit any established mold, the studio dropped her contract at the end of 1944.

Determined to make good, Shelley undertook acting classes with film star Charles Laughton, studied dance and speech, and wore braces to help her pronounced overbite. Constantly networking, her chutzpah and perseverance paid off. She was cast in the small but showy role of the waitress killed by Ronald Colman in *A Double Life* (1947). This led to a contract with Universal Pictures, whose executives made her diet down to 118 pounds and promoted the voluptuous starlet and her impressive cleavage as a brassy blond siren (as in 1950's *Frenchie*). In this fledgling phase, she calculatedly planned her public life, but she insisted she let her spicy private life just happen. (Her spontaneous fraternizing included get-togethers with the likes of Burt Lancaster, Marlon Brando, William Holden, Howard Hughes, and John Ireland.)

Always latching on to intellectuals in the creative arts to inspire her, Shelley's career

John Payne and Shelley Winters in *Larceny* (1948). (Courtesy of JC Archives)

aspirations rose higher. She fought to win the part of the dowdy factory girl murdered in *A Place in the Sun* (1951). For her telling performance, she earned her first Academy Award nomination. Her acting in that film classic also received a qualified seal of approval from aging screen icon Joan Crawford, who noted tartly, "She gave a very moving performance, which surprised me, because Shelley is not a sensitive girl socially." But brash Winters didn't mind, because by early 1951 she was back in New York, studying acting at the Actors Studio. Universal put her on suspension when theater-minded Shelley did not return to the lot to make more schlocky movies for them. These conflicts ended when she returned to moviemaking, including *Meet Danny Wilson* (1952) with Frank Sinatra.

Shelley had a penchant for Italian men, which led her to marry Italian-born actor Vittorio Gassman in April 1952. Their daughter, Victoria, was born the following February.

(She later became a physician.) Vittorio hated Hollywood life and frequently returned home to Italy, where he was better appreciated. Shelley didn't want to lose the momentum of her Tinseltown career and stayed mostly in California. Their tempestuous union ended in divorce in 1954, the same year they appeared on-screen together in *Mambo*. On Broadway, Shelley teamed with Italian-American actor Anthony Franciosa in *Hatful of Rain* (1955). Although their ardent relationship already included clashing egos and career rivalry, they wed in May 1957. By November 1960, the highly emotional Winters and the equally volatile Franciosa had divorced.

An intuitive actress who knew how to make herself a woman for all seasons, thirty-seven-year-old Shelley played a fifty-something mother in 1959's *The Diary of Anne Frank*. It won her great acclaim and ushered in her era of zaftig character leads. By 1972's *The Poseidon Adventure* (for which she won her fourth Oscar bid), she'd grown into the weighty per-sona that became her new stock-in-trade. She was extremely busy in films, TV, and some stage work during the 1970s, including playing Elvis Presley's mother in the 1979 TV movie *Elvis*.

Winters inaugurated the 1980s with the first volume of her peppery autobiography (*Shelley: Also Known as Shirley*). The tell-all book encompassed her sexcapades with a wide range of Hollywood studs and renewed her celebrityhood. Part two of her saga appeared in 1989, covering her one-of-a-kind romp through life from 1954 to 1963. Slowing down her filmmaking a bit in the eighties, her roles ranged from her trademark Jewish-American yenta in *Over the Brooklyn Bridge* (1984) to playing, of all things, the dodo bird in the tele-feature *Alice in Wonderland* (1985). In the 1990s, Shelley gained a new audience when she took on the recurring role of Nana Mary, the title star's grandmother in the TV sitcom *Roseanne*. Winters taught acting classes, appeared in movie cameos such as *The Portrait*

*C*hoice remarks from the two-time Oscar winner during her blond sexpot phase were all geared to get her name in print. It worked! Here are some of the best:

*"I asked [poet] Dylan Thomas why he'd come to Hollywood and very solemnly he said, 'To touch a starlet's t***.' 'OK,' I said, 'but only one finger.'"*

"I did a picture in England one winter and it was so cold I almost got married."

"My face was always so made up, it looked as though it had the decorators in."

"My idea of a movie star is Joan Crawford, who can chew up two directors and three producers before lunch."

of a Lady (1996) and *Gideon* (1999). and was a gabby interviewee on documentaries about old Hollywood. Meanwhile, she suffered from ill health and a reported recurring addiction to pain pills, which she had started taking years ago for a work-related back problem.

A few years ago, an interviewer asked bombastic Shelley what motto had guided her best throughout her colorful life. The veteran performer said unhesitatingly, "I am the master of my fate; I am the captain of my soul."

Natalie Wood

[Natalia Nikolaevna Zakharenko Gurdin]

JULY 20, 1938–NOVEMBER 29, 1981

In several of her feature films as an adult—such as *Splendor in the Grass* (1961) and *Inside Daisy Clover* (1965)—not only was Wood's screen character emotionally desperate but one senses that the actress beneath was striving to keep a high-strung personality in check. In fact, Natalie had learned early in life, as a child performer, the art of burying her true feelings toward personal situations and always presenting a happy face to the public. Sometimes, in her teens, the veneer would crack and the emerging adult would lash out at her dominating stage mother, Maria, begging to be left alone. Other times, the teenaged actress would rebel by having love affairs. Occasionally, she attempted suicide. But

always, till the end, Natalie snapped into her movie star persona in public. She called this guise "The Badge."

Later in life, according to younger sister Lana Wood in *Natalie: A Memoir by Her Sister* (1984), the five-foot, one-and-a-half-inch movie star used her sibling as a dartboard. Lana suggested these venomous attacks were spurred on by a combination of Natalie's insecurity, jealousy over her sister invading the acting game, a constant drive to control, and a need to prove once again to someone close that she was actually a powerful star. According to Lana, Natalie had "what I came to think of as her Queen Victoria attitude: if you gave the slightest offense, Natalie made it clear she was not amused. There were no accusations, no verbal assaults, no sharp remarks, just a withering look and a back turned in your face. . . . You crossed Natalie at your own peril." Playwright (*The Boys in the Band*) and producer (TV's *Hart to Hart* series) Mart Crowley, who was at one time secretary to Natalie and her actor husband Robert Wagner and who stayed friendly with Wood till her untimely death, said, "You can take one step, just one, to either side of the line Natalie draws for you. But if you take two steps, you're in big trouble. . . . Natalie likes to be in control. Or else."

The future movie star was born in San Francisco in 1938, the daughter of Russian immigrants Nikolai and Maria (Zudilov) Zakharenko. (Maria had a daughter, Olga, by a prior marriage.) Little Natalia Nikolaevna got a new surname when Nikolai changed his family's name to Gurdin when he became an

Ralph Bellamy and Natalie Wood in *The Memory of Eva Ryker* (1980). (Courtesy of JC Archives)

American citizen. When Natasha (as she was nicknamed) was four, the family was living in Santa Rosa, California, and a movie company came to town to shoot location scenes for *Happy Land* (1943), a drama of Americana starring Don Ameche. Maria, always fanciful and ambitious, had already decided that her second child, the precocious and winsome Natasha, would somehow have a movie career and change the family's unpromising financial future. Maria maneuvered herself and the girl into bit parts in the film, having won the attention of the film's director, Irving Pichel.

By the time Pichel was preparing *Tomorrow Is Forever* (1945), Maria had moved the family to Los Angeles and made sure that the director tested little Natasha for a key assignment in the picture. The newcomer not only won the role but a new screen name—Natalie Wood. Pushing and prodding her compliant, talented daughter, Maria felt rewarded when Natalie scored so effectively as Maureen O'Hara's child in *Miracle on 34th Street* (1937). In her peak years as a child performer, Wood sometimes earned $1,000 a week, but she was not happy. When she was grown up, she admitted, "I spent practically all of my time in the company of adults. I was very withdrawn, very shy. I did what I was told and I tried not to disappoint anybody. I knew I had a duty to perform, and I was trained to follow orders." (In contrast, for fan magazine consumption, a seemingly chipper teenaged Natalie reported of her exciting childhood, "I worked steadily, had a ball, and can't even remember being miserable.")

One of the most traumatic experiences of Natalie's adolescence occurred while making *The Star* (1952), in which she played Bette Davis's daughter. The script called for the youngster to dive into deep water. Thanks to her superstitious mother, who had passed along forebodings of dangers lurking in Natalie's future from dark waters, the girl was inordinately terrified of doing the scene. The director insisted she, not a double, do the stunt. Natalie collapsed in hysterics. Only because of the intervention of Davis and others did a stunt double take over the diving task.

In the mid-1950s, Natalie was going through the awkward adolescent stage that makes it tough for a child actress to keep working. No longer always busy on films and having studio tutors, she attended Van Nuys High School. Suddenly she had to mingle with peers in a new setting that brought out her tremendous insecurities. On the other hand, it led her into new friendships, as well as allowed her to experience dating. The latter situation frightened stern Maria, who feared that the family's meal ticket might be swept off into a conventional romance and quit working.

Rebel Without a Cause (1955) was a big turning point in Natalie's life. It elevated her to professional prominence (she won an Oscar nomination as Best Supporting Actress). Moreover, she had an affair with the film's director, Nicholas Ray; came under the spell of the picture's rebellious star, Jimmy Dean; and made a new set of friends, including *Rebel* coplayers Nick Adams and Dennis Hopper. (Somewhere in this transition period, Wood was raped by a much-older, married film star; the trauma affected her for years to come.)

Although still living under Maria's stringent supervision, the "new" Natalie now sped around town in her own car, smoke, drank, and dated older men—including Frank Sinatra, Elvis Presley, and burly Raymond Burr. She had discovered the weapon of power and turned the tables on her one-time controller, Maria. Later, Natalie found a new diversion when she fell in love with young heartthrob

actor and playboy Robert Wagner. The couple wed in December 1957.

On-screen, Natalie appeared in such features as *Marjorie Morningstar* (1958) and teamed with Wagner in *All the Fine Young Cannibals* (1961). By 1962, Hollywood's dream marriage had fallen apart and the Wagners divorced. (In reaction to the breakup, Natalie took an overdose of sleeping pills, but she was discovered in time to have her stomach pumped.) Thereafter, Natalie had a series of high-profile romances, which included one with Warren Beatty. Unable to find a permanent romantic link, she nevertheless was at her career peak with *West Side Story* (1961), *Gypsy* (1962), and *Love with the Proper Stranger* (1963). However, by mid-decade, her box-office standing had crashed. In the summer of 1966, her esteem lowered because of her recent flops, Natalie again attempted suicide, but it was covered up. She made no movies between 1966 and 1968. In spring 1969, she wed British scriptwriter and agent Richard Gregson in a Russian Orthodox ceremony in Los Angeles. Their daughter, Natasha, was born in September 1970.

Natalie had a career resurgence when *Bob & Carol & Ted & Alice* (1969) was a sizeable hit. But thereafter, the first-time mother announced that she was retiring. Then her emotion-charged life took another turn. She and Gregson divorced in mid-1971 and the following year, she and Robert Wagner remarried aboard his yacht, *Rambling Rose*, as it lay anchored off Catalina Island. (In between being wed to Natalie, Robert had also married and had a child from that union.) In 1974,

Wood and Wagner became parents of Courtney Brooke.

Now in her thirties with her superstardom days gone, Natalie was at her acting best in the occasional TV projects she undertook, including *The Affair* (1973) and *The Cracker Factory* (1979). Meanwhile, Wagner had a career resurgence with the sophisticated adventure TV series *Hart to Hart* (1979–84) created by bestselling author Sidney Sheldon. Since the colead role of the wife on the show had been inspired by Natalie, many wondered why Stefanie Powers and not Wood played the key part. Some suggested that Wagner did not want to mix relatives with business (just as Natalie had pointedly not helped sister Lana with her acting career). However, the Wagners had frequently acted together, as in the TV movie *Cat on a Hot Tin Roof* (1976). This aside, the industry grapevine spoke of Natalie's great concern whenever a *Hart to Hart* episode script featured a love scene between Wagner and Powers. Reportedly, the offending sequence would often be toned down to pacify ever-vigilant Wood.

In November 1981, Natalie was costarring in the feature film *Brainstorm* and was going to make her stage debut in a forthcoming Los Angeles production of *Anastasia*. Then tragedy struck. On November 27, Wagner, Wood, and fellow actor Christopher Walken (Natalie's *Brainstorm* costar) boarded the Wagners' fifty-five-foot cabin cruiser, *The Splendour*, which was skippered by a one-man crew, Dennis Davern. On November 28, the trio went ashore for dinner. Reportedly, Wood drank heavily and flirted with Walken. The three returned to the vessel later in the evening. In events that may never be clarified fully, sometime very early Sunday morning, Natalie got into the dinghy, the *Valiant*, and disappeared in the dark. Later, Wagner requested the help of the harbor patrol to look for his missing wife. The coast guard and helicopters were added to the search party. At 7:44 that morning, her body was located—floating facedown beneath the water's surface—near Blue Cavern Point. The actress was buried in Los Angeles at Westwood (Village) Memorial Park on December 2, 1981. As to her last movie, *Brainstorm* was finally finished after several more months, with the picture edited to work around Natalie's undone scenes. Released in 1983, it received minimum audience response. It was a sad finale to Wood's lengthy screen career.

Loretta Young

[Gretchen Michaela Young]

JANUARY 6, 1913–AUGUST 12, 2000

In the seventy-two (!) years between 1917 (*The Primrose Ring*) and 1989 (*Lady in the Corner*), Loretta appeared in over one hundred feature films and two TV series. In the lengthy process, she won an Academy Award (for 1947's *The Farmer's Daughter*) and three Emmys (for 1953–61's *The Loretta Young Show*). For many show-business fans, the five-foot, six-inch Young, with her auburn hair and blue eyes, was a legendary symbol of beauty, glamour, and graciousness. For decades, she publicly radiated poise, piety, and purpose. She was dedicated to being a movie star, one who never dreamed of appearing in public—whether on a trip to the local grocery store or attending a major awards ceremony—without her hair and makeup in perfect order and her chic outfit more than appropriate for the occasion.

Her carefully crafted public image to one side, the real Loretta was surprisingly a lot like such tough peers as Bette Davis and Joan Crawford; she was calculating, shrewd, and manipulative in striving for show-business megasuccess. However, Loretta was far better than Davis and Crawford at hiding these unflattering traits from the attention of her legion of fans. As a shrewd businesswoman, she concluded early in her career in the "pretend" industry of moviemaking that box-office clout and a sizeable portfolio of assets were generally far more satisfying than dimensional screen roles. During her decades-long love affair with power and cash, she gathered many unflattering nicknames (such as "Gretch, the Wretch" and "The Chocolate-Covered Black Widow") from her movie and TV coworkers.

On-screen—with the exception of such entries as *Born to Be Bad* (1934)—Young generally played virtuous, sweet heroines. It was a movie type that could become cloying and saccharine, but shrewd filmgoers (especially men) sensed the unspoken high level of sexuality and flintiness beneath the actress's surface. In real life and glossed over to one degree or another by the movie press for decades, Loretta had the capacity to drive her leading men to romantic distraction. For example, in the early 1930s, she tantalized Spencer Tracy so much that the married actor was bewitched for many months after they teamed in *A Man's Castle* (1933). As for Clark Gable, their torrid love affair, which first sparked on the set of *The Call of the Wild* (1935), led to a studio-manipulated cover-up of her secretly having his baby and later adopting the little girl. (Hinted at for years by gossip columnists and others, the child in question confirmed the information in her 1994 memoir, *Uncommon Knowledge,* as did the star herself—very late in her life—in Joan Weston Anderson's 2000 biography, *Forever Young: The Life, Loves, and Enduring Faith of a Hollywood Legend.*)

Born Gretchen Michaela Young in 1913 in Salt Lake City, Utah, she was the third child of John Earl and Gladys (Royal) Young. (There were older siblings, Polly Ann and Elizabeth Jane, and brother John Royal was born in 1915.) Around 1916, John Earl, a traveling auditor for a railroad, disappeared from his family's life. By 1917, resolute Gladys had moved with her four children to Los Angeles, where a married sister lived. To support her offspring, she opened a boardinghouse. Through her brother-in-law, who worked at a film studio, she got pretty young Gretchen tiny roles in two 1917 silent features, as well as a part in *The Only Way* in 1919. Mrs. Young considered film acting a frivolous full-time occupation, insisting that her starstruck youngsters be properly educated. (Gretchen first attended the Romona Convent School in Alhambra, California, and then Immaculate Heart in Hollywood.) By 1923, Gladys had remarried. Her new husband was George U. Belzer, a Los Angeles businessman. The couple had one child, whom they named Georgiana.

As of the mid-1920s, Gretchen's two older sisters were working in movies. One day late in 1926, an assistant director at First National Pictures telephoned the Young home to ask if Polly Ann was available to do retakes on a Colleen Moore picture. A precocious, adolescent Gretchen answered the call and volunteered for the job herself, claiming that her sister was busy elsewhere and that she and Polly Ann bore a great resemblance. She was hired at $80 for the part. Before long, the youngster was under studio contract at $50 weekly and had been given a new first name—Loretta.

By 1929, Loretta was a seasoned screen ingénue, typically appearing in eight vehicles a year. During the making of *The Second Floor Mystery* (1930), she had great chemistry on and off camera with twenty-six-year-old Grant Withers. Loretta and the devil-may-care actor eloped to Yuma, Arizona. Young's shocked mother—along with the family priest—begged her to have the union annulled. Loretta insisted on remaining wed because she was "so much in love that I couldn't do my best work if we were not married." But, testing the waters, she shrewdly added, "If I had thought marriage would have harmed my career, I might have considered further!" She did eventually rethink the situation and, in September 1931, divorced Withers (whose career was not keeping pace with her popularity).

Her love life sparked again during the making of 1933's *A Man's Castle,* with sterling actor Spencer Tracy, then separated from his wife and children, as her new lover. The explosive love affair supposedly ended when she informed the media, "Since Spence and I are both Catholic and can never be married, we

Loretta Young and Warren William in *Employees' Entrance* (1932). (Courtesy of JC Archives)

have agreed not to see each other again." Nevertheless, the still-lovestruck Tracy continued to pursue her ardently for months to come. Finally they each went their own way.

When Darryl F. Zanuck, a bright young executive at Loretta's studio, left Warner Bros. to form Twentieth Century Production (later Twentieth Century-Fox), he lured her to join his fold. At $1,700 a week, she starred in *House of Rothschild* (1934) and *Clive of India*

(1935). By now the well-established actress could be snobbish when the cameras were not rolling. Victor Jory, one of her leading men of the period, noted that, when they worked together, she refused to talk with him on the set because he was a relative newcomer; in their on-screen love scenes, she made sure that not even their lips brushed when they kissed. However, with the hot box-office property Clark Gable, Young was passionate on and off the soundstage. Then she became pregnant. Her upcoming vehicle, *Ramona* (1936), had to be postponed while Loretta went into seclusion to have her baby. The media was fed hogwash about the overworked actress suffering from a mysterious ailment. In 1937, despite the fact that she was a single person seeking to adopt—which went against California law at the time—she adopted two children. One of them was reportedly reclaimed by its natural parents, while Loretta kept the other—her secret, real-life daughter Judy.

Self-proclaimed playboy William Buckner was one of Loretta's boyfriends whom she invited to stay at her guest house in the late 1930s. Later, he was arrested for mail fraud and sent to prison. At work, Young was initially attracted to handsome, charming Tyrone Power. But after several joint vehicles in which his role outmatched hers, she felt quite differently. She used all the tricks at her command to steal scenes from him, especially in *Suez* (1938), their last effort together. While making *The Story of Alexander Graham Bell* (1939), she openly rebelled at being pretty set dressing in pictures and ended her contract with Twentieth Century-Fox. Loretta counted on her great box-office appeal to win her a lucrative deal elsewhere. But she'd been blackballed by the men's club of moguls. Months of inactivity led her to dropping her per-film salary from $150,000 to $50,000 and signing with Columbia Pictures to make such fluff as *He Stayed for Breakfast* (1940) with Melvyn Douglas. That July, she wed radio/advertising executive Thomas H. A. Lewis, who had previously

dated actresses Bette Davis and Glenda Farrell. The thirty-eight-year-old Lewis had especially impressed the religious actress by being a far-more-conscientious Catholic than even she. After he returned from World War II duty, the couple had two sons (one born in 1944, the other in 1945) and Lewis adopted Loretta's daughter.

In the 1940s, it seemed that Loretta's screen career was again stagnating in decorative roles (including 1946's *The Stranger* opposite Orson Welles). Nonetheless, she won an Oscar for 1947's *The Farmer's Daughter*, playing an appealing Swedish American maid. Later, she won an Academy Award nomination for being a dauntless nun in *Come to the Stable* (1949). By 1953, the forty-year-old Loretta was considered old hat on the big screen. However, she engineered a terrific comeback by starring in an anthology series on TV that fall. *A Letter to Loretta* (also known as *The Loretta Young Show*) not only allowed her great versatility in her choice of weekly roles but provided a trademark entrance for each episode, with her sweeping on camera in a striking outfit that absolutely shouted glamour. As the Emmy nominations and awards piled up, a nasty power struggle evolved behind the camera between Young and her spouse. He was eased out of the series he had helped to create and produce, while Loretta became all things to all people on the show. (Loretta and Lewis were divorced in 1969.) When not controlling the program's content, she was monitoring the cast and crew's morality by insisting that anyone who swore on the set had to contribute to her charity box, with specified penalties for each level of cussword. By 1961, the TV series had ended; another one, *The New Loretta Young Show*, lasted but one season (1962–63).

If her acting career was suspended, controlling Loretta was very active with her (Catholic) charities, social engagements, and business enterprises. Anytime a deal went sour, her attorneys were quick to file a lawsuit on her behalf. By the 1980s, she had returned to Los Angeles after several years in Phoenix, where she was involved with the Loretta Young Youth Project. She turned up in two TV movies and, in September 1993, wed longtime pal Jean Louis, the famous costume designer. He died in April 1997, while Loretta passed away from ovarian cancer in 2000. Her ashes were placed in her mother's grave at Holy Cross Cemetery in Culver City, California.

When Loretta's estranged daughter, Judy, wrote a tell-all memoir in 1994, Young sought to pass off the shocking chronicle with "I cannot imagine why she wrote this book." All the veteran star needed to do was read the foreword to her daughter's tome, in which she stated, "It has taken me all this time to find the courage to write my story the way it must be written, without any lies or evasions. My life has been filled with hypocrisy and deception from the moment I was born." The chronicle reveals the icy and fabricated nature of the complicated lady known as Loretta Young.

BIBLIOGRAPHY

Books

Amende, Coral. *Hollywood Confidential: An Inside Look at the Public Careers and Private Lives of Hollywood's Rich and Famous.* New York: Plume, 1997.

Ammons, Kevin, with Nancy Bacon. *Good Girl, Bad Girl: An Insider's Biography of Whitney Houston.* New York: Birch Lane, 1996.

Andersen, Christopher P. *Madonna.* New York: Simon and Schuster, 1991.

———. *A Star, Is a Star, Is a Star!: The Lives and Loves of Susan Hayward.* New York: Doubleday, 1980.

Anderson, Joan Webster. *Forever Young: The Life, Loves, and Enduring Faith of a Hollywood Legend.* Allen, Tex.: Thomas More, 2001.

Andrews, Bart. *Out of the Madness: The Strictly Unauthorized Biography of Janet Jackson.* New York: HarperPaperback, 1994.

Arnold, Roseanne. *My Lives.* New York: Ballantine, 1994.

Aronson, Virginia. *Drew Barrymore.* Philadelphia, Pa.: Chelsea House, 2000.

Barr, Geraldine, with Ted Schwarz. *My Sister Roseanne: The True Story of Roseanne Barr Arnold.* New York: Birch Lane, 1994.

Barr, Roseanne. *Roseanne: My Life as a Woman.* New York: HarperPaperback, 1989.

Barrymore, Drew, with Todd Gold. *Little Girl Lost.* New York: Pocket, 1990.

Barrymore, Ethel. *Memories.* New York: Harper, 1955.

Basinger, Jeanine. *Silent Stars.* Hanover, N.H.: Wesleyan University Press, 2000.

Bego, Mark. *Cher: If You Believe.* New York: Cooper Square, 2001.

———. *Michael!* New York: Pinnacle, 1984.

Berlin, Joey (ed.). *Toxic Fame.* Detroit, Mich.: Visible Ink, 1996.

Birnbaum, Gail. *Dennis Quaid.* New York: St. Martin's, 1988.

Bodeen, DeWitt. *From Hollywood.* South Brunswick, N.J.: Barnes, 1976.

———. *More from Hollywood.* South Brunswick, N.J.: Barnes, 1977.

Bogle, Donald. *Dorothy Dandridge.* New York: Boulevard, 1998.

Bono, Sonny. *And the Beat Goes On.* New York: Pocket, 1991.

Bowman, Jeffrey. *Diva: The Totally Unauthorized Biography of Whitney Houston.* New York: HarperPaperback, 1995.

Bragg, Melvyn. *Richard Burton: A Life.* New York: Warner, 1988.

Britton, Ron. *Kim Basinger: Longer than Forever.* London, England: Blake, 1999.

Brodsky, Jack, and Nathan Weiss. *The Cleopatra Papers: A Private Correspondence.* New York: Simon and Schuster, 1963.

Brooks, Tim, and Earle Marsh. *The Complete Directory to Prime Time Network and Cable TV Shows: 1946–Present*, 7th ed. New York: Ballantine, 1999.

Brough, James. *The Fabulous Fondas.* New York: David McKay, 1973.

Brown, Peter Harry, and Patte B. Barham. *Marilyn: The Last Take.* New York: Dutton, 1992.

Butler, Brett. *Knee Deep in Paradise.* New York: Hyperion, 1996.

Carr, Larry. *Four Fabulous Faces.* New York: Penguin, 1970.

Carrier, Jeffrey L. *Tallulah Bankhead: A Bio-Bibliography.* Westport, Conn.: Greenwood, 1991.

Cawthorne, Nigel. *Sex Lives of the Hollywood Goddesses.* London, England: Prism, 1997.

Cher, as told to Jeff Coplon. *The First Time.* New York: Simon and Schuster, 1998.

Clarke, Gerald. *Get Happy: The Life of Judy Garland.* New York: Random House, 2000.

Collins, Joan. *Past Imperfect.* New York: Simon and Schuster, 1984.

———. *Second Act.* London, England: Boxtree, 1996.

Conner, Floyd. *Lupe Velez and Her Lovers.* New York: Barricade, 1993.

Considine, Shaun. *Bette & Joan: The Divine Feud.* New York: Dell, 1989.

Corliss, Richard. *Greta Garbo.* New York: Pyramid, 1974.

Crane, Cheryl, with Cliff Jahr. *Detour: A Hollywood Story.* New York: Avon, 1989.

Crawford, Christina. *Mommie Dearest*, 20th anniversary ed. Moscow, Idaho: Seven Springs, 1997.

Crawford, Joan. *My Way of Life.* New York: Simon and Schuster, 1971.

Crawford, Joan, with Jane Kesner Ardmore. *A Portrait of Joan.* New York: Paperback, 1964.

Crawley, Tony (ed.). *The Wordsworth Dictionary of Film Quotations.* Ware, England: Wordsworth Editions, 1991.

Cunningham, Ernest W. *The Ultimate Barbra.* Los Angeles: Renaissance, 1998.

———. *The Ultimate Marilyn.* Los Angeles: Renaissance, 1998.

Current Biography Yearbook: Vols. 1940–2002. New York: H. W. Wilson, 1941–2002.

D'Agostino, Annette. *From Soap Stars to Superstars: Celebrities Who Started Out in Daytime Drama.* Los Angeles: Renaissance, 1999.

Dandridge, Dorothy, and Earl Conrad. *Everything and Nothing: The Dorothy Dandridge Tragedy.* New York: Perennial/HarperCollins, 2000.

David, Lester, and Jhan Robbins. *Richard & Elizabeth.* New York: Ballantine, 1978.

Davidson, Bill. *Jane Fonda: An Intimate Biography.* New York: Signet, 1991.

———. *Spencer Tracy: Tragic Idol.* New York: Zebra, 1987.

Davis, Bette. *The Lonely Life*, updated ed. New York: Berkley, 1990.

Davis, Bette, with Michael Hershowitz. *This 'N That.* New York: Putnam, 1987.

Dietrich, Marlene. *Marlene*. New York: Grove, 1987.

DiOrio, Al Jr. *Little Girl Lost: The Life and Hard Times of Judy Garland*. New York: Manor, 1975.

Duke, Patty, and Gloria Hochman. *A Brilliant Madness: Living with Manic-Depressive Illness*. New York: Bantam, 1993.

Duke, Patty, and Kenneth Turan. *Call Me Anna: The Autobiography of Patty Duke*. New York: Bantam, 1988.

Dunaway, Faye, with Betsy Sharkey. *Looking for Gatsby: My Life*. New York: Simon and Schuster, 1995.

Duncan, Patricia J. *Jennifer Lopez*. New York: St. Martin's, 1999.

Durgnat, Raymond, and John Kobal. *Greta Garbo*. New York: Dutton Vista, 1967.

Dyson, Cindy. *Janet Jackson*. Philadelphia, Pa.: Chelsea House, 2000.

Eberly, Stephen L. *Patty Duke: A Bio-Bibliography*. Westport, Conn.: Greenwood, 1988.

Edgar, Kathleen J. (senior ed.). *Contemporary Theatre, Film and Television: Vols. 1–38*. Detroit, Mich.: Gale, 1992–2001.

Edwards, Anne. *Streisand*. Boston: Little, Brown, 1997.

Eells, George. *Ginger, Loretta and Irene Who?* New York: Putnam, 1976.

Eells, George, and Stanley Musgrove. *Mae West*. New York: Morrow, 1982.

Ewbank, Tim, and Stafford Hildred. *Russell Crowe*. London, England: Carlton, 2001.

Faris, Jocelyn. *Jayne Mansfield: A Bio-Bibliography*. Westport, Conn.: Greenwood, 1994.

Fidelman, Geoffrey Mark. *The Lucy Book: A Complete Guide to Her Five Decades on Television*. Los Angeles: Renaissance, 1999.

Finch, Christopher. *Rainbow: The Stormy Life of Judy Garland*. New York: Grosset and Dunlap, 1975.

Finstad, Suzanne. *Natasha: The Biography of Natalie Wood*. New York: Harmony, 2001.

Fleming, E. J. *Hollywood Death and Scandal Sites*. Jefferson, N.C.: McFarland, 2000.

Fox, Mary Virginia. *Ethel Barrymore: A Portrait*. Chicago: Reilly & Lee, 1970.

Frank, Gerold. *Judy*. New York: Dell, 1975.

French, Sean. *Jane Fonda*. London, England: Pavilion, 1997.

Fuller, Elizabeth. *Me and Jezebel: When Bette Davis Came for Dinner—and Stayed . . .* New York: Berkley Books, 1992.

Furman, Leah. *Jennifer Lopez*. Philadelphia, Pa.: Chelsea House, 2001.

Furman, Leah, and Elina Furman. *Happily Ever After: The Drew Barrymore Story*. New York: Ballantine, 2000.

Gabor, Zsa, Zsa, with Gerold Frank. *Zsa Zsa Gabor*. Cleveland, Ohio: World, 1960.

Gabor, Zsa, Zsa, with Wendy Leigh. *One Lifetime Is Not Enough*. New York: Delacorte, 1991.

Garraty, John A. (ed.). *Dictionary of American Biography: Supp. 5–10*. New York: Scribner's, 1977–1995.

Geist, Kenneth L. *Pictures Will Talk: The Life and Films of Joseph L. Mankiewicz*. New York: Scribner's, 1978.

Gerard, Jim. *Celebrity Skin Tattoos, Brands, and Body Adornments of the Stars*. New York: Thunder's Mouth, 2001.

Gilbert, Julie. *Opposite Attraction: The Lives of Erich Maria Remarque and Paulette Goddard*. New York: Pantheon, 1995.

Gill, Brendan. *Tallulah*. New York: Holt, Rinehart & Winston, 1972.

Golden, Eve. *Vamp: The Rise and Fall of Theda Bara*. Vestal, N.Y.: Emprise, 1996.

Guiles, Fred Lawrence. *Jane Fonda: The Actress in Her Time*. New York: Pinnacle, 1982.

Hack, Richard. *Hughes: The Private Diaries, Memos and Letters*. Beverly Hills, Calif.: New Millennium, 2001.

Hadleigh, Boze. *Celebrity Feuds! The Cattiest Rows, Spats, and Tiffs Ever Recorded*. Dallas, Tex.: 1999.

———. *Hollywood and Whine: The Snippy, Snotty, and Scandalous Things Stars Say About Each Other*. New York: Citadel, 2001.

———. *Hollywood Babble On: Stars Gossip About Other Stars*. New York: Perigee, 1994.

Hanut, Eryk. *I Wish You Love: Conversations with Marlene Dietrich*. Berkeley, Calif.: Frog, 1996.

Harris, Warren G. *Natalie & R.J.: Hollywood's Star-Crossed Lovers*. New York: Berkley, 1990.

Heymann, C. David. *Liz: An Intimate Biography of Elizabeth Taylor*. Secaucus, N.J.: Citadel Stars/Carol, 1996.

Higham, Charles. *Ava: A Life Story*. New York: Delacorte, 1974.

———. *Kate: The Life of Katharine Hepburn*. New York: Norton, 1975.

———. *The Life of Bette Davis*. New York: Macmillan, 1981.

Hill, James. *Rita Hayworth: A Memoir*. New York: Simon and Schuster, 1983.

Hine, Darlene Clark (ed.). *Black Women in America: An Historical Encyclopedia: Vols. 1–2*. Brooklyn, N.Y.: Carlson, 1993.

Hirsch, Foster. *Elizabeth Taylor*. New York: Galahad, 1975.

Houseman, Victoria. *Made in Heaven*. Chicago: Bonus, 1991.

Hunter, Allan. *Faye Dunaway*. New York: St. Martin's, 1986.

Hyman, B. D. *My Mother's Keeper*. New York: Morrow, 1985.

Israel, Lee. *Miss Tallulah Bankhead*. New York: Putnam, 1972.

Jackson, Katherine, with Richard Wiseman. *My Family, the Jacksons*. New York: St. Martin's, 1990.

Jackson, LaToya, with Patricia Romanowski. *LaToya*. New York: Signet, 1992.

Jacobs, Jack, and Myron Braum. *The Films of Norma Shearer*. Secaucus, N.J.: Citadel, 1977.

Johnes, Carl. *Crawford: The Last Years*. New York: Dell, 1979.

Johns, Michael-Anne. *Jennifer Lopez*. Kansas City, Mo.: Andrews & McMeel, 1999.

Kelley, Kitty. *Elizabeth Taylor: The Last Star*. New York: Dell, 1982.

Kiernan, Thomas. *Jane: An Intimate Biography of Jane Fonda*. New York: Putnam, 1973.

———. *Jane Fonda: Heroine for Our Time*. New York: Delilah, 1982.

Kimbrell, James. *Barbara: An Actress Who Sings — Vol. II*. Boston: Branden, 1992.

King, Norman. *Madonna: The Book*. New York: William Morrow, 1991.

Lacey, Robert. *Grace*. New York: Putnam, 1994.

Ladowsky, Ellen. *Julia Roberts*. New York: People Profiles, 1999.

Lamarr, Hedy. *Ecstasy and Me: My Life as a Woman*. New York: Fawcett Crest, 1966.

Lambert, Gavin. *Norma Shearer*. New York: Knopf, 1990.

LaSalle, Mick. *Complicated Women: Sex and Power in Pre-Code Hollywood*. New York: Thomas Dunne/St. Martin's, 2000.

Latham, Caroline, and Jeannie Sakol. *All About Elizabeth: Elizabeth Taylor, Public and Private*. New York: Onyx/Penguin, 1991.

Lavery, Byrony. *Tallulah Bankhead*. Bath, England: Absolute, 1999.

Leaming, Barbara. *Bette Davis*. New York: Simon and Schuster, 1992.

———. *If This Was Happiness: A Biography of Rita Hayworth*. New York: Viking, 1989.

———. *Katharine Hepburn*. New York: Limelight, 2000.

Lenburg, Jeff. *Peekaboo: The Story of Veronica Lake*. Lincoln, Nebr.: Backinprint.com, 2001.

Lewis, Judy. *Uncommon Knowledge*. New York: Pocket, 1994.

Linet, Beverly. *Susan Hayward: Portrait of a Survivor*. New York: Atheneum, 1980.

Love, Andrea. *The Ultimate Celebrity Love Secrets & Scandals Book*. Bristol, England: Siena/Carlton, 1988.

Luft, Lorna. *Me and My Shadows: A Family Memoir*. New York: Pocket, 1998.

Madsen, Axel. *Gloria and Joe: The Star-Crossed Love Affair of Gloria Swanson and Joe Kennedy*. New York: Arbor House/Morrow, 1988.

Mann, William J. *Behind the Screen: How Gays and Lesbians Shaped Hollywood: 1910–1969*. New York: Viking, 2001.

Martin, Mart. *Did He or Didn't He?: The Intimate Sex Lives of 201 Famous Men*. New York: Citadel, 2000.

Marx, Samuel, and Joyce Vanderveen. *Deadly Illusions: Jean Harlow and the Murder of Paul Bern*. New York: Random House, 1990.

McClelland, Doug. *The Complete Life of Susan Hayward . . . Immortal Screen Star*. New York: Pinnacle, 1975.

———. *Star Speak: Hollywood on Everything*. Boston: Faber and Faber, 1987.

McCoid, Sheridan (ed.). *Hollywood Lovers*. London, England: Orion, 1997.

McLellan, Diana. *The Girls: Sappho Goes to Hollywood*. New York: L.A. Weekly/St. Martin's, 2000.

Metz, Allan, and Carol Bensons (eds.). *Madonna: Two Decades of Commentary*. New York: Schirmer, 1999.

Mills, Earl. *Dorothy Dandridge*. Los Angeles: Holloway House, 1991.

Morella, Joe, and Edward Z. Epstein. *Lucy: The Bittersweet Life of Lucille Ball*. Secaucus, N.J.: Lyle Stuart, 1973.

———. *Paulette: The Adventurous Life of Paulette Goddard*. New York: St. Martin's, 1985.

———. *Rita: The Life of Rita Hayworth.* New York: Delacorte, 1983.

Morley, Sheridan. *Marlene Dietrich.* New York: McGraw-Hill, 1976.

Morton, Andrew. *Madonna.* New York: St. Martin's, 2001.

Morton, Danelle. *Meg Ryan.* New York: People Profiles, 2000.

Moser, Margaret, Michael Bertin, and Bill Crawford. *Movie Stars Do the Dumbest Things.* Los Angeles: Renaissance, 1999.

Nickson, Chris. *Mariah Carey Revisited.* New York: St. Martin's, 1998.

Oller, John. *Jean Arthur: The Actress Nobody Knew.* New York: Limelight, 1997.

Paris, Barry. *Louise Brooks.* New York: Knopf, 1989.

Parish, James Robert. *The Fox Girls.* New Rochelle, N.Y.: Arlington House, 1972.

———. *Hollywood Bad Boys.* Chicago: Contemporary Books, 2002.

———. *The Hollywood Book of Death.* Chicago: Contemporary Books, 2001.

———. *Hollywood's Great Love Teams.* New Rochelle, N.Y.: Arlington House, 1974.

———. *The Jeanette MacDonald Story.* New York: Mason Charter, 1976.

———. *Let's Talk! America's Favorite TV Talk Show Hosts.* Las Vegas, Nev.: Pioneer, 1993.

———. *The Paramount Pretties.* New Rochelle, N.Y.: Arlington House, 1972.

———. *The RKO Gals.* New Rochelle, N.Y.: Arlington House, 1973.

———. *Today's Black Hollywood.* New York: Pinnacle, 1995.

Parish, James Robert, and Don E. Stanke. *The Glamour Girls.* New Rochelle, N.Y.: Arlington House, 1975.

———. *Hollywood Baby Boomers.* New York: Garland, 1992.

———. *The Leading Ladies.* New Rochelle, N.Y.: Arlington House, 1977.

Parish, James Robert, and Lennard DeCarl. *Hollywood Players: The Forties.* New Rochelle, N.Y.: Arlington House, 1976.

Parish, James Robert, and Michael R. Pitts. *Hollywood Songsters.* New York: Garland, 1991.

Parish, James Robert, and Ronald L. Bowers. *The MGM Stock Company.* New Rochelle, N.Y.: Arlington House, 1973.

Parish, James Robert, William T. Leonard, et al. *The Funsters.* New Rochelle, N.Y.: Arlington House, 1979.

———. *Hollywood Players: The Thirties.* New Rochelle, N.Y.: Arlington House, 1976.

Parish, James Robert, with Gregory W. Mank and Don E. Stanke. *The Hollywood Beauties.* New Rochelle, N.Y.: Arlington House, 1978.

Pascal, John. *The Jean Harlow Story.* New York: Popular Library, 1964.

Peters, Beth. *True Brit: The Story of Singing Sensation Britney Spears.* New York: Ballantine, 1999.

Peters, Margot. *The House of Barrymore.* New York: Knopf, 1990.

Pierce, Arthur, and Douglas Swarthout. *Jean Arthur: A Bio-Bibliography.* Westport, Conn.: Greenwood, 1990.

Prideaux, James. *Knowing Hepburn and Other Curious Experiences*. Winchester, Mass.: Faber and Faber, 1996.

Quine, Judith Balaban. *The Bridesmaids: Grace Kelly and Six Intimate Friends*. New York: Pocket, 1990.

Quirk, Lawrence J. *Fasten Your Seat Belts: The Passionate Life of Bette Davis*. New York: Signet, 1990.

———. *Totally Uninhibited: The Life and Wild Times of Cher*. New York: William Morrow, 1991.

Rettenmund, Matthew. *Encyclopedia Madonnica*. New York: St. Martin's, 1995.

Riese, Randall. *Her Name Is Barbara: An Intimate Portrait of the Real Barbra Streisand*. New York: Birch Lane, 1993.

Riva, Maria. *Marlene Dietrich*. New York: Ballantine, 1992.

Robb, Jackie. *Britney Spears*. New York: HarperEntertainment/HarperCollins, 1999.

Sanders, Coyne Steven. *Rainbow's End: The Judy Garland Show*. New York: Zebra, 1990.

Sanello, Frank. *Julia Roberts*. Edinburgh, Scotland: Mainstream, 2000.

Saxton, Martha. *Jayne Mansfield and the American Fifties*. Boston: Houghton Mifflin, 1975.

Sealy, Shirley. *The Celebrity Sex Register*. New York: Fireside, 1982.

Shapiro, Marc. *Mariah Carey*. Toronto, Canada: ECW, 2001.

Sherman, Vincent. *Studio Affairs: My Life as a Film Director*. Lexington, Ky.: University Press of Kentucky, 1996.

Shipman, David. *The Great Movie Stars: The Golden Years*, revised ed. New York: Hill and Wang, 1979.

———. *The Great Movie Stars: The Independent Years*. London, England: Macdonald & Co., 1991.

———. *The Great Movie Stars: The International Years*, revised ed. New York: Hill and Wang, 1980.

———. *Judy Garland: The Secret Life of an American Legend*. New York: Hyperion, 1992.

———. *Movie Talk: Who Said What About Whom in the Movies*. New York: St. Martin's, 1988.

Silver, Charles. *Marlene Dietrich*. New York: Pyramid, 1974.

Slatzer, Robert F. *The Marilyn Files*. New York: Shapolsky, 1992.

Smith, Jessie Carney (ed.). *Notable Black Women*. Detroit, Mich.: Gale, 1992.

Souhami, Diana. *Greta & Cecil*. New York: HarperSanFrancisco/HarperCollins, 1994.

Spada, James. *Grace: The Secret Life of a Princess*. New York: Dell, 1988.

———. *Streisand: Her Life*. New York: Crown, 1992.

Spears, Britney, and Lynne Spears. *Britney Spears' Heart to Heart*. New York: Three Rivers, 2000.

Spoto, Donald. *Blue Angel: The Life of Marlene Dietrich*. New York: Doubleday, 1992.

———. *A Passion for Life: The Biography of Elizabeth Taylor*. New York: HarperCollins, 1995.

Stenn, David. *Bombshell: The Life and Death of Jean Harlow*. New York: Doubleday, 1993.

———. *Clara Bow: Runnin' Wild*. New York: Cooper Square, 2000.

Stine, Whitney, with commentary by Bette Davis. *Mother Goddam*. New York: Hawthorn, 1974.

Strait, Raymond, and Leif Henie. *Queen of Ice, Queen of Shadows: The Unsuspected Life of Sonja Henie*. New York: Stein and Day, 1985.

Summers, Anthony. *Goddess: The Secret Lives of Marilyn Monroe*. New York: Onyx/New American Library, 1986.

Swanson, Gloria. *Swanson on Swanson*. New York: Random House, 1980.

Taraborrelli, J. Randy. *Call Her Miss Ross*. New York: Birch Lane, 1989.

———. *Cher*. New York: St. Martin's, 1986.

———. *Michael Jackson: The Magic and the Madness*. New York: Ballantine, 1992.

Thomas, Bob. *Joan Crawford*. New York: Bantam, 1978.

Tracy, Kathleen. *Jennifer Lopez*. Toronto, Canada: ECW, 2000.

Troyan, Michael. *A Rose for Mrs. Miniver: The Life of Greer Garson*. Lexington, Ky.: University Press of Kentucky, 1999.

Tunney, Kieran. *Tallulah: Darling of the Gods*. New York: Dutton, 1973.

Turk, Edward Baron. *Hollywood Diva: A Biography of Jeanette MacDonald*. Berkeley, Calif.: University of California, 1998.

Turner, Lana. *Lana*. New York: Dutton, 1982.

Tuska, Jon. *The Films of Mae West*. Secaucus, N.J.: Citadel, 1973.

Vermilye, Jerry. *Bette Davis*. New York: Pyramid, 1973.

Victor, Barbara. *Goddess: Inside Madonna*. New York: Cliff Street/HarperCollins, 2001.

Wanger, Walter, and Joe Hyams. *My Life with Cleopatra*. New York: Bantam, 1963.

Watts, Jill. *Mae West: An Icon in Black and White*. New York: Oxford University, 2001.

Wayne, Jane Ellen. *Ava's Men*. New York: St. Martin's, 1990.

———. *Crawford's Men*. New York: St. Martin's, 1988.

———. *Gable's Women*. New York: St. Martin's, 1987.

———. *Grace Kelly's Men*. New York: St. Martin's, 1991.

———. *Marilyn's Men*. New York: St. Martin's, 1992.

Winnert, Derek. *Barbra Streisand: Quote Unquote*. New York: Crescent, 1996.

Winters, Shelley. *Shelley: Also Known as Shirley*. New York: Morrow, 1980.

———. *Shelley II: The Middle of My Century*. New York: Pocket, 1990.

Wood, Lana. *Natalie: A Memoir by Her Sister*. New York: Putnam, 1984.

Publications

Biography
Classic Film Collector
Classic Image
Current Biography
Daily Variety
Ebony

Empire
Entertainment Weekly
Film Threat
Filmfax
Films in Review
Films of the Golden Age
Globe
Hollywood Reporter
In Style
Jet
L.A. Weekly
Los Angeles Daily News
Los Angeles Times
Movie Collectors World
Movieline
National Enquirer
New Times—Los Angeles
New York Daily News
New York Observer
New York Post
New York Times
Newsweek
People
Playboy
Premiere
Sight & Sound
Star
Time

Total Film
Us Weekly
Vanity Fair

Television

A&E: *Biography*
E! Entertainment Television: *Celebrity Profiles*
E! Entertainment Television: *Mysteries & Scandals*
E! Entertainment Television: *Revealed*
E! Entertainment Television: *True Hollywood Story*
Lifetime: *Intimate Portraits*
MSNBC: *Headliners & Legends*

Internet Websites

All Movie Guide: www.allmovie.com
All Music Guide: www.allmusic.com
E! Entertainment TV Online: www.eonline.com
Find a Grave: www.findagrave.com/index.html
Internet Movie Database: www.pro.imdb.com

INDEX

Note: Numbers in bold refer to pages with photographs.

ABOUT THE AUTHOR

James Robert Parish, a former entertainment reporter, publicist, and book series editor, is the author of many published major biographies and reference books on the entertainment industry, including *Jet Li, Hollywood Bad Boys, The Encyclopedia of Ethnic Groups in Hollywood, The Hollywood Book of Death, Gus Van Sant, Jason Biggs, Whoopi Goldberg, Rosie O'Donnell's Story, The Unofficial "Murder, She Wrote" Casebook, Let's Talk! America's Favorite TV Talk Show Hosts, The Great Cop Pictures, Ghosts and Angels in Hollywood Films, Prison Pictures from Hollywood, Hollywood's Great Love Teams*, and *The RKO Gals*. Mr. Parish is a frequent on-camera interviewee on cable and network TV for documentaries on the performing arts. Mr. Parish resides in Studio City, California.

(Photo by Levon)